RATIONALIZING JUSTICE

SUNY Series in the Sociology of Work
Richard H. Hall, Editor

RATIONALIZING JUSTICE

The Political Economy of
Federal District Courts

Wolf Heydebrand
and
Carroll Seron

State University of New York Press

Published by
State University of New York Press, Albany

For information, address State University of New York
Press, State University Plaza, Albany, N.Y., 12246

Library of Congress Cataloging in Publication Data

Heydebrand, Wolf, 1930-
      Rationalizing justice: the political economy of federal district courts /
   Wolf Heydebrand and Carroll Seron.
         p.   cm. — (SUNY series in the sociology of work)
      Includes bibliographical references.
      ISBN 0-7914-0295-9. — ISBN 0-7914-0296-7 (pbk.)
      1. District Courts—United States—History.   2. Court
   administration—United States—History.   3. Courts—Economic
   aspects—United States—History.   I. Seron, Carroll.   II. Title.
   III. Series.
   KF8754.H45 1990
   347.73'2--dc20
   [347.3072]   89-19676
                                                                  CIP

10 9 8 7 6 5 4 3 2 1

Neither the life of an individual nor the history of a society can be understood without understanding both. Yet [people] do not usually define the troubles they endure in terms of historical change and institutional contradiction. ... They do not ... grasp the interplay of [individual] and society, of biography and history, of self and world. They cannot cope with their personal troubles in such ways as to control the structural transformations that usually lie behind them. ... What they need, and what they feel they need is a quality of mind that will help them to use information and to develop reason in order to achieve lucid summations of what is going on in the world and of what may be happening within themselves. It is this quality, I am going to contend, that journalists and scholars, artists and publics, scientists and editors are coming to expect of what may be called the sociological imagination. ... The sociological imagination enables us to grasp history and biography and the relations between the two within society. That is its task and its promise.

—C. Wright Mills
The Sociological Imagination

I will not cease from Mental Fight,
Nor shall my Sword sleep in my hand,
Till we have built Jerusalem
In England's green and pleasant Land.

—William Blake
And Did Those Feet

Contents

Figures

Tables

Foreword

If a Federal District Judge who had died in 1890 came back to his court in 1990, he would find much that was recognizable, but also much that was different. The first thing he would notice is that the mix of cases was vastly different. Where in 1890 he might have seen a large number of criminal filings and of diversity of citizenship cases, today he would see large numbers of prisoner's petitions and cases related to the expansion of public law—cases where the government was the plaintiff or the defendant. He would find that the nature of the solutions and processing of cases had changed. There are many more plea-bargains, pretrial conferences and dismissed cases today. Judge Van Winckle would be amused by the transformation of the court organization. There are now magistrates, court administrators, clerks, probation officers and other ancillary staff that share the duties of processing justice. The judge would find that he is a court administrator-executive as well as a judge. Finally, there is a system of oversight and training that did not exist at the turn of the century. Our judge would find himself more tightly integrated into a judicial system than he was in 1890.

Wolf Heydebrand and Carroll Seron have set out to describe, explain, and evaluate this transformation. In *Rationalizing Justice: The Political Economy of Federal District Courts*, they have shown how the transformation of society and of the state has impacted the case load and case mix of Federal District Courts. In turn, they show how the increased complexity of cases and increased demand has been coped with by the courts, in the face of the unwillingness of the Federal government to massively increase the resources of the courts. The movement from adjudication to negotiation, from case settlements at law to case dispositions in the shadow of the law, is part of the rationalization of justice.

They demonstrate the interconnection of changing demands on the courts and the transformation of the organization of the courts and methods of case disposal through a quantitative historical and cross-sectional analysis of district courts. They are able to present a detailed analysis of the causes of the variation of district courts' organization and case load since 1950, and they are able to analyze some time series data going back to the turn of the century.

It is quite an accomplishment. I believe that anyone seriously interested in the transformation of the judicial system will have to pay attention to their analysis.

Moreover, their analysis also has implications for understanding the transformation of the modern state: on the one hand, they show how the growth of the positive state changes the nature of disputes and of court adjudication of disputes; on the other hand, they show how the growth of the positive state has led to a diminished role for the courts, as other state agencies develop adjudicatory capabilities and quasi-judicial administrative apparatuses. Beyond the study of judicial administration, their analysis has relevance for students of state transformation.

I noted that Heydebrand and Seron intended to not only describe and analyze the transformation of the courts, they also wanted to evaluate that transformation. They believe that the rationalization of justice—possibly more accurately, the rationalization of the courts—has diminished justice. The development of technocratic solutions to the problem of case load management and the growth of non-adjudicatory solutions is something to be worried about. Moreover, they fear that the problems of the judicial system play into a legitimation crisis of modern capitalism.

I am less certain about these evaluative conclusions. Doesn't the evaluation of the transformation of adjudicatory justice require a broader set of considerations than they are able to provide? Surely poor defendants are better represented in the Federal courts today than they were in 1900. While it is true that pretrial conferences and plea bargaining diminish the pure application of impersonal law and the adjudicatory role of judges in the disposal of disputes, it is not clear that either the participants in the disputes or the wider public believe that justice is poorly served by these newer mechanisms.

Similarly, I believe that a presumed legitimation crisis of the judicial system and its relationship to the contradictions of capitalism requires more extensive consideration of alternative meanings and evidence of crisis. Heydebrand and Seron basically argue that the newer forms of dispute resolution (negotiation/administration) are in conflict or contradiction with the underlying normative principles of the law (formal legal rationality, due process, and the adversary system). What are the behavioral and systemic manifestations of contradiction and legitimation crisis? What are its normative manifestations? Does it result in more legal subterfuges? Or does the difference between the reality of judicial procedure and the normative premises of the system lead to more reversals on appeal, or more institutional hypocrisy? If one adopted a strong behavioral criterion, a legitimation crisis would be registered in large scale discontent of citizens and lawyers. Again, using a strong behavioral criterion, for there to be a legitimation crisis of the state in modern capitalism, there must be widespread withdrawal of support of the state or widespread demands for changes of fundamental institutions. I should note that Heydebrand and Seron do not make claims for these kinds of behavioral concomitants of contradiction. Their discussion opens up an important topic.

These ruminations do not detract from the central strengths of *Rationalizing Justice*. Heydebrand and Seron have done yeoman service in explaining the transformation of the Federal district courts and the administration of justice. They also have raised important questions about the relationship of that transformation to the quality of justice. They have made an important and lasting contribution.

—MAYER N. ZALD

Acknowledgments

This study began in 1972 with an invitation by a newly appointed circuit executive to do a systems analysis of changes taking place in the six federal district courts of the United States Court of Appeals for the Second Circuit. We are grateful to Robert Lipscher for this invitation and for opening up the fascinating world of federal courts to us. Through interviews and observations, we developed an appreciation for the concerns of judges and other court actors, particularly a sense of profound change, if not crisis, in their midst. We thank those individuals who shared their insights with us.

In undertaking this project we were equally affected by the intellectual crisis that existed among sociologists in the 1970s. These debates, particularly a rediscovery of a tradition of critical and reflexive sociology, played a central role in shaping the direction of this study. As we sought to understand the themes and patterns of change in the courts of New York, Vermont, and Connecticut, we realized that the issues they confronted—new cases, computerization, and accountability—raised deeper and broader questions about the role of federal courts in American society; that is, a concern to manage justice presented historical, organizational, and ideological issues that were ripe for study.

The evolution of this study has been marked by the tension between practical concerns to solve problems, and the intellectual curiosity to ask more questions. We were fortunate to receive financial support to explore these questions, and therefore are grateful to the Institute for Judicial Administration, and its then Director, Paul Nejelski, for providing initial funds, and to the Russell Sage Foundation, particularly Stanton Wheeler and George Vickers, for providing a larger grant. Along the way, many friends and colleagues participated in the dialogue that shaped this project. We are deeply grateful to Judith Blau, David Clark, Malcolm Feeley, Joel Handler, Christine Harrington, Louanne Kennedy, Richard Lempert, Craig McEwen, Frank Munger, Marie Provine, Edwin Schur, Alan Wolfe, and Mayer Zald for reading various portions of the manuscript and for their insightful comments, queries, and suggestions. Special thanks are due to David Greenberg and John Sutton for their expert advice and comments. It goes without saying that the remaining problems are our own responsibility.

Portions of this manuscript appeared in earlier articles: Wolf Heydebrand 1977, "The Context of Public Bureaucracies: An Organizational Analysis of Federal District Courts." 11 *Law and Society Review* 749; Wolf Heydebrand and Carroll Seron, "The Rising Demand for Court Services: A Structural Explanation of the Caseload of U.S. District Courts." 11 *Justice System Journal*, (Winter 1986); Wolf Heydebrand and Carroll Seron, "The Organizational Structure of American Federal Trial Courts: Professional Adjudication versus Technocratic Administration" 2 *International Review of Sociology*, (1987), 63; and, Wolf Heydebrand and Carroll Seron, "The Double Bind of the Capitalist Judicial System." 9 *International Journal of the Sociology of Law* (1981) 207.

Introduction

There is a quiet revolution taking place in American courts. We are witnessing a slow, but cumulative, process of change in the organization of this American political institution. Traditionally, when a dispute was filed it was assumed that it would go to trial; if a trial was not appropriate, the dispute would, in all likelihood, be dismissed—or settled, but without intervention of the courts. Today, however, the menu and use of options for dispute resolution has grown inordinately; cases may be resolved through a variety of informal procedures such as pretrial conferences, alternative dispute resolution, plea bargaining, or minitrials.

Changes in the forms of case disposition are, however, only one part of a much larger and deeper transformation in the form of adjudication in American trial courts. Of equal importance, there has been a growth in the range, variability, and complexity of demands on federal district courts as well as the addition of a host of new organizational actors, including court managers, computer experts, parajudges, and support staff. In short, there has been an increase in the demands placed on this institution coupled with a growing reliance on new forms of administration, which has consequences for the process and role of this branch of government.

In this book, we present the results of an investigation of the changing forms of law and judicial administration in federal district courts. This study represents the first empirical attempt to relate the dynamics of the modern political economy to the historical and institutional transformation of courts as organizations. Based on quantitative, qualitative, and historical data we show how environmental forces—the political economy and demography—generate civil litigation and criminal filings, how the volume and complexity of cases affect the organization of courts, and how caseload and organization, in turn, impinge on judicial decision-making.

The relatively wide scope of this analysis is, we believe, justified and, indeed, demanded by the complex historical connection between the state, the economy, and the form of law in American society. A brief comment on

1

the term political economy seems appropriate in view of the fact that it has been used both as a technical term and as a codeword. Technically, political economy refers to the interaction of political and economic forces operating in a given sociohistorical context, be it an organization, a network of organizations, or a whole society (Zald 1970; Wamsley and Zald 1973; Benson 1975; Fainstein and Fainstein 1980). As a codeword, political economy refers to a tradition of neo-Marxist analysis that assumes the dominance of private corporate interests over those of the government and law in a capitalist society. In this study, we are interested in treating the nature of the interaction between state, law, and economy not as an assumption, but as a hypothesis to be investigated. Thus, measures of corporate and governmental activity in relation to courts and the legal form are an important part of our analysis, but we treat the effects of state and economy as an empirical question, not as a foregone conclusion. As it turns out, our findings tend to disconfirm the hypothesis of a direct corporate effect on litigation and court organization, and instead show the emergence of a strong governmental effect on litigation and the form of law.

In light of these broad developments we ask: What are the historical forces affecting the institutional structure and dynamics of federal district courts? How have the volume and composition of the district court caseload changed during this century? What is the nature of the ecological environment of federal courts, that is, what impact do the political economy and urbanization have on civil litigation and criminal filings? How does the court system respond to the double-bind of rising demand and lagging resources? How do the environment, the demand for adjudicatory services, and the organizational structure of courts affect judicial decision-making? What is the role of the federal government in litigation and in the nature of civil and criminal dispositions? In short, why has the organization of the federal district courts changed so dramatically over the course of the twentieth century?

In this book we seek to answer these questions. The questions posed require an analysis of the practical as well as the theoretical dilemmas confronting American courts of law. At a practical, empirical level we focus on the caseload, organization, and performance of U.S. district courts, the trial courts of the federal judicial system. By investigating changes in the concrete organization and operation of the legal system, as seen through the history and structure of courts, we emphasize changes in the *form of law*, as compared to its *content* or *substance*. Thus, we are *not* concerned with doctrinal legal issues and changes in the nature and content of judicial decisions or in the substance of laws and judicial opinions. Rather, we seek to understand the way in which the particular circumstances of litigation and prosecution (what cases are filed in courts) and of adjudication and administration (how they are disposed of) are changing.

Under the double impact of increasing demand for services and limited fiscal and organizational resources, the administration of justice is rationalized. Courts are changing from professionally and collegially controlled, semifeudal domains of judges, to modern businesslike, administrative agencies concerned with speed, efficiency, productivity, simplification, and cost-effectiveness in the delivery of judicial services. Adjudication, under the aegis of due process and adversary procedure, is moving toward case-management, plea bargaining, and informal negotiation within an organizationally integrated system based on technical-managerial expertise and computerized information technology.

To accomplish this inquiry, we begin by analyzing the demand for services emanating from the economic, demographic, and political characteristics of the courts' jurisdictions. Jurisdiction here refers not only to the power (of a judge) to hear and determine a case in a particular subject matter (say, federal question jurisdiction), but in a particular territory and with respect to legal actors residing within that territory. At this level of analysis, then, we will illuminate the transformation of the federal courts of law under the impact of environmental forces and demands.

At a more theoretical, abstract level, we will show that changes in the forms of law reflect tensions within liberal legalism between substantive and procedural due process, dispute resolution and policy-making, or law and order. This analysis reveals a contradiction in the roles or functions of the court to insure and extend social harmony, to guarantee and preserve social order, and to conserve and maintain its institutional integrity (see, e.g., Balbus 1973). These divergent institutional roles convey different sets of social expectations. For example, when a court acts to suppress workers' strikes, it is being repressive; yet, when a court enforces the civil rights of minorities, it enfranchises and empowers a group. Carried to its logical conclusion, however, its repressive role may undermine or transform its democratic promise, and vice versa. Furthermore, the form of these roles is shaped by historical conditions. Thus, we may speak of the historically embedded contradictory roles of courts. This definition, then, should be distinguished from a conflict model where it is assumed that various institutional roles are inevitably in opposition throughout history.

The demands posed by this balancing act are, moreover, not limited to the Third Branch of government, but rather resonate with the problems and contradictions confronting the state in American society. For some time, now, scholars have begun to document the government's attempt to preserve social harmony, or legitimacy, while simultaneously ensuring economic growth or accumulation. Economically, this contradiction is said to create a "structural gap" between the state's resources and expenditures, thus producing a "fiscal crisis" (O'Connor 1973). Politically, this contradiction suggests that there are historical limitations on the state's ability to balance economic growth and social legitimation (Wolfe 1977; see also Alford and Friedland 1985). Like the notions of political economy and contradiction, the terms legitimation and crisis also engender great debate. Thus, it may be useful to pause briefly and clarify the use of our terms. Building on the notion of historical contradiction, we assume that there is a potential for crisis that is driven by a structural mismatch between democratic demands and economic resources. When courts deal with this problem, they introduce short-term strategies that may undermine their own normative premises, the rule of law. In our view, this is not just a problem of credibility, but a problem of legitimacy. Our notion of crisis should be distinguished from the social construction of, e.g., a litigation crisis which emphasizes definitions of participants, but ignores constraints imposed by organizational structure. Similarly, our notion of legitimacy emphasizes the fundamental normative integrity and justification of a social order, not its behavioral or political acceptance by citizens as a result of habit or rational choice (but see Hyde 1983).

In sum, this study addresses a series of organizational questions about federal district courts in the twentieth century that begins with the premise that organizational structures and processes "matter" because they "affect political culture, encourage some kinds of group formation and collective political actions (but not others), and make possible the raising of some political issues (but not others)" (Skocpol 1985, 21).[1] Whether one begins with a neo-Marxist or a neo-Weberian perspective, a classical theme of social and political theory is to sort out the ways in which organizational forms structure, shape, and empower political actors. Furthermore, in keeping with an appreciation for the contradictory pulls placed on courts of law, we also begin with the premise that organizational structures and processes must be studied with a sensitivity to the historical contingencies facing them during specific periods in time.[2]

The American Judicial System: In "Crisis" or Merely Strained?

Since the late 1960s, research and debate concerning the nature of courts and adjudication have been preoccupied with the question of whether or not the American judicial system and its framework of legitimation, the rule of law, are faced with a crisis. From a variety of viewpoints, observers, students, and participants of the judicial system talked about a "crisis in the courts" (James 1971), or that "justice is the crime" (Katz, Litwin, and Bamberger 1972). These commentators went on to speak of "justice denied" (Downie 1971), the "administration of injustice" (Sykes 1975), and the "twilight of the adversary system" (Blumberg 1967). Officials in the legal community spoke about the "crisis in law enforcement" (1971, 33), the criminal justice system's "anachronistic delays and its failure to respond to the needs of society" (1971, 36) and a "sense of crisis," that is, "the recurring theme of most discussions on the administration of justice in the United States in the third quarter of the twentieth century" (1971, 45).

While many of these observers and critics referred to the criminal justice system, it was clear that the civil justice system was not exempt. As John P. Frank (1969, 182) put it, ". . . American civil practice has broken down; the legal system fails to perform the tasks that may be expected of it . . . the collapse is now . . . the curve is down: the situation is getting worse . . . we have no generally accepted remedy. We do not even have a generally accepted program for discussion."

A decade later, the results of a public opinion survey on the courts conducted by Yankelovich, Skelly, and White, Inc. (1978) confirmed the continued and widespread dissatisfaction of the American public with the performance of courts and judges. Moreover, while it is true that since 1977 informal alternatives to formal justice have been promoted as possible remedies for the ills of the justice system (Nader 1980; Tomasic and Feeley 1982), critics of informal justice have argued "that it is unnecessary, that it has failed, that it is sinister, and that it is impossible" (Cain 1985, 336). Indeed, prominent and concerned voices in law and social science speak of the "crisis of the federal courts" (Posner 1985), the "contradictions of informal justice" (Abel 1982, I:267), the "dialectics of formal and informal control" (Spitzer 1982, 167), and the need to go "beyond informal justice" (Cain 1985), and invoke against informal practices such as "managerial" judging (Resnik 1982) and settlement strategies (Fiss 1984; see also Alschuler 1983).

Dissenting from this chorus of concerned voices are others who view the increasing demand on federal courts since 1960 as part of a series of normal, local, or self-limiting changes in an otherwise relatively peaceful landscape (Galanter 1985, 1986). They feel that the introduction of case-management techniques into the arsenal of judicial decision-making does not detract from its conventional and legitimate character (Flanders 1984). They argue that courts tend to be like arenas in which cases are settled by negotiation (Galanter 1985) and that this fact does not necessarily imply the lowering of quality since there is "justice in many rooms" (Galanter 1981).

But in spite of these generally optimistic assessments, there is a lingering sense that the capacity of federal courts to deliver on their promise is seriously strained. This sense was expressed by Chief Justice Warren Burger throughout his tenure and it is shared to this day by top leaders of the federal judiciary (e.g., Posner 1985; see also the remarks by Associate Justice Scalia and U.S. Appeals Court Judges Edwards, Feinberg, and Friedman, New York University Symposium on Federal Courts, 14-15 Nov. 1987).

In short, whether the "dissatisfaction with the administration of justice" (Pound 1906) is popular, official, or professional, there seems to be continued concern, eighty-five years after Roscoe Pound's pronouncement, that the federal judicial system is strained, if not in crisis.

Writing in the late 1960s, Herbert L. Packer both deepened and transformed our understanding of the problems of courts. Packer's seminal work focused, of course, on the tensions between due process and social control in the criminal justice system. According to Packer, the "crime control model" places

> a premium on speed and finality. Speed, in turn, depends on informality and on uniformity; finality depends on minimizing the occasions for challenge. ... It follows that extra-judicial processes should be preferred to judicial processes, informal operations to formal ones. But informality is not enough: there must also be uniformity. Routine, stereotyped procedures are essential if large numbers are being handled. The model that will operate successfully on these presuppositions must be an administrative, almost a managerial, model. (1968, 159)

Packer goes on to argue that ". . . if the Crime Control Model resembles an assembly line, the Due Process Model looks very much like an obstacle course" (ibid., 163). In its emphasis on quality control, the due process model tends to cut down on quantitative output. The proponents of the due process model, Packer asserts, "would accept . . . a substantial diminution in the efficiency with which the criminal process operates in the interest of preventing official oppression of the individual" (p. 166).

Clearly, Packer's typology is tailored to the criminal process. But the impulse behind the crime control model applies also to civil procedure where corporate interest in conflict control complements the state's interest in crime control (Ford Foundation 1978). In civil procedure, efficiency and speed, informality and uniformity, and simplification and finality are increasingly preferred over the "obstacle course" of due process (see also Feeley 1979). The normative antinomy and practical contradiction between these two models, then, is a measure of the depth of the crisis of the judicial system and a force in the process that pushes toward the rationalization of civil and criminal justice.

Rationalization—the process of systematization, simplification, standardization, and routinization in a quest for efficiency, productivity, and cost effectiveness—has, we will show, left its imprint on the federal judiciary in the twentieth century through a distinctly observable transformation in the structure of courts. A new emphasis on speed and efficiency is changing the organization of dispute resolution and, in so doing, exposes the limitations of the due process model. Yet, the politics of rationalizing organizational practices are not limited to the federal district courts. Indeed, forms of rationalization capture the state's task to mediate structural contradictions in advanced capitalist societies (Alford and Friedland 1985, 178-181, 362-367).

The analytically most powerful work on the state begins with a straightforward observation. The state's role in a capitalist economy is to fulfill at least two opposing tasks. On the one hand, the state must insure the development of an environment suitable for expansion of a private market economy; this role evolves out of a liberal, or Lockeian, tradition. On the other hand, the state must insure the legitimacy of an egalitarian polity composed of enfranchised and empowered citizens; this role evolves out of a democratic-communitarian, or Rousseauian, tradition. Liberal and democratic politics shape state activities and organization. Furthermore, as liberal and democratic tensions become more pronounced in response to changing social expectations, contradictory pulls are exacerbated. Yet, it is the state's task to balance these problems, to legitimate the social, economic, and political demands generated by contending forces. Of course, carried to its logical extension, each tradition has the potential to undermine or expose the limitations of the other and thereby reveal, in turn, the limits of the state's legitimacy (Wolfe 1977; Wolin 1960). For example, Alan Wolfe (1977) has documented the unfolding role of the state from that of a relatively passive observer of early market relations to a proactive, though often disguised mediator of conflicting liberal and democratic demands. As Wolfe goes on to show, forms of state organization have changed dramatically over the course of American history in response to social, political, and economic demands, but each permutation shares a common core that can be traced to the inherent tension between accumulation and legitimation.

Related to this theme, James O'Connor (1973) presents a framework for analyzing the state's budget, again suggesting the inherent tensions as reflected in fiscal allocations to preserve, on the one hand, social harmony or demands for democratization and, on the other, to expand capital accumulation or demands for liberalization of economic relations. While O'Connor's (1973) concept of the "fiscal crisis of the state" emerged from a perhaps overly mechanistic and reified notion of inherent capitalist crisis tendencies, the well-known tensions between budget deficits, productivity drives in government, and widespread backlash against taxation and welfare spending are all too obvious to be ignored. Taken together, they suggest a crisis of the welfare state that began to take shape in the 1960s.

In the last decade, partially in response to a resurgence of interest in neo-Weberian and neo-Marxist questions, there has been a growing body of research on the organization of the state (Block 1977; Wright 1978; Skocpol 1980, 1985; Skowronek 1987; Lehman 1988). Whereas a Weberian tradition asks us to take seriously the autonomy of state action, a Marxist tradition pushes us to explore the realms of the contradictory interests of polity and economy. While the scope and implications of this difference in approach cannot be underestimated, there is a general consensus that, for the United States, the Progressive Era marks a "watershed" in American political history. The federal government became an active regulator of the economy (see, e.g., Commager 1950; Wiebe 1967; Kolko 1976; Wolfe 1977), while state and local governments became active policy-makers and managers of social programs (see, e.g., Weinstein 1968; Skowronek 1982). During the New Deal period, the reach and activity of the state was expanded, as the federal government also became a more active participant in domestic policy making. The discovery of rational bureaucracies to carry out these tasks provides the glue that binds this era together. Debate between neo-Weberians and neo-Marxists turns on the implications, meanings, successes, and failures of this social invention: Are bureaucracies, and their more recent organizational permutations, part of the problem or the solution? How can we unravel the meaning, implications, and dimensions of modern rationalization? Do these rationalized strategies of organizational change solve the problems of contemporary political economies and their institutions, or are they symptoms of a continuing underlying contradiction?

A motivating question of our project has been to analyze the role of the Third Branch, focusing on the federal district courts, in the context of an understanding of the role of the state in a modern political economy. Specifically, we investigate the forms and processes of the rationalization of justice in the twentieth century. It is our contention, moreover, that analysis of the Third Branch is a fruitful arena for enriching the theory of the state precisely because the courts predate the bureaucratic invention of the turn of the century and, therefore, provide an especially useful setting for understanding modern modes of rationalization.

We begin this endeavor with an appreciation of C. Wright Mills's observation about social research. He wrote:

> The formulation of problems . . . should include explicit attention to a range of public issues and of personal troubles; and they should open up for inquiry the causal connections between milieux and social structure. In our formulation of problems, we must make clear the values that are really threatened in the troubles and issues involved; who accepts them as values, and by whom or by what they are threatened. (1959, 130)

The values threatened by the rationalization of justice are those held by the advocates of the formal equality of law, formal justice, and formal-legal rationality. These values include the commitment to impartiality and judicial independence embodied in adversary procedures, procedural rights and guarantees, and the notion of due process. They constitute the essence of the formal autonomy of law so central to nineteenth century conceptions of the role of law in a democratic society. This did not make the form of law democratic, but it served the purposes of a political democracy intent on preserving individual liberties while protecting property rights against the alleged evils of economic democracy. Ironically, positivist work in the social sciences has tended to eschew the analysis of contradictions between values and institutional realities. Many political theorists working in the tradition of legal realism tend to construct, for example, legal values from a hands-on, law-in-action perspective, claiming that they are merely looking at the world from the pragmatic viewpoint of realpolitik. Yet, this claim begs the critical question raised by Mills that one must begin by making explicit the values and contradictions of the institutions being studied. We believe this is not a naive, romantic, or utopian stance, but simply good social science.

Today, however, it is not economic democracy that is threatening the formal autonomy of the legal system, but the contradictions of governmental policies bent on achieving technical efficiency and ideological control over what government should do in the face of budget deficits and growing demands on governmental services, including legal and judicial services.

A Framework for Study

Because this is a study of the rationalization of justice in American federal district courts in the twentieth century, we use the organization of the court, including its jurisdictional-territorial environment, as the unit of analysis. Building on the observations of students of the contemporary state, the "milieu" of federal district courts includes economic, governmental, and demographic variables—indicators of processes and relations between economic, governmental, and demographic developments. These courts' "social structure" includes the demands for its services, that is, the range, variability and complexity of cases filed, as well as its personnel and resources—judges, parajudges, support staff, and fiscal resources—to handle these demands. Our research question is: Do these factors explain changes in the nature and distribution of dispositions (e.g., dismissals, pretrials, and trials) in federal district courts? Equally important, do these changes point toward the rationalization of the organizational processes of federal district courts?

Operationally, we constructed a data set where the U.S. district and its environment is the unit of analysis. Figure 1 provides a schematic overview of our model. Each of the four main dimensions—environmental profile, task structure, resources, and output—consists of a set of specific analytic elements. The general causal assumption represented by this diagram is that environmental characteristics of courts are independent variables, and that

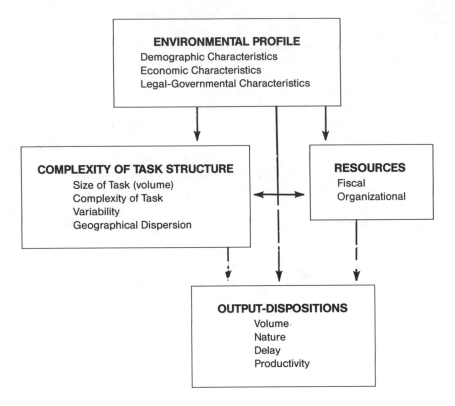

Figure 1. Descriptive Model of Four Basic Dimensions of Analysis of Federal District Courts.

the output characteristics are dependent variables, with task structure, resources, and organization of courts as intervening variables. Because we are especially concerned to examine the impact of environmental factors at different points in time, data were collected to analyze these sets of relations in 1950, 1960, and 1970—the post-World War II period. The restriction of our ecological-statistical analysis to these three points in time is a function of the vagaries of funded academic research, the availability of data, and the limitation of resources. On the one hand, statistical data of the kind required for our analysis were only available at that time for certain years. We made every effort to match them with the appropriate census data that were aggregated from the county level to that of the jurisdiction of each of the U.S. district courts.

On the other hand, we view our statistical analysis as support of, but not the sole basis of, our argument. In the absence of a time series analysis based on annual data, we were limited to a cross-sectional analysis at three points in time. While such an approach could be extended to correspond to new census data, it is not meant to represent a longitudinal, dynamic analysis of change.

Our time frame, however, did enable us to compare the effects of the turbulent, expansive 1960s with the quiescent, stable 1950s. Such a comparison is particularly meaningful in the context of the federal judiciary because federal civil litigation began to grow dramatically after 1960 and major reform initiatives began to be instituted by the end of that decade. Indeed, we will show that the current structure and practices of the federal trial courts had their origin in the institutional reforms of the late 1960s and early 1970s (see chaps. 1 and 6).

To supplement and enrich our work, we also examined historical trends in the courts' caseload, resources, and output from the turn of the century to 1985 and, in some cases, to 1988. Furthermore, we analyzed systematically the debates over reform and modernization of the courts beginning in 1789 to contextualize and to specify the meaning and definition of our quantitative variables. At the beginning of this project we did open-ended interviews with judges and other court personnel in the federal district courts that constitute the Second Circuit of the United States. These interviews were designed to give us a better understanding of the courts from the standpoint of informed insiders. Finally, one of the researchers did work on the emergence and role of U.S. magistrates (see Seron 1983, 1985, 1986, 1987, 1988), which included participant observation and extensive open-ended interviews with judges, magistrates, nonjudicial personnel, and lawyers across different district courts. Thus, following the methodological concept of triangulation (Denzin 1978) we have relied upon multivariate analysis, content analysis of historical documents, and participant observation of court practices to check, and balance, the shortcomings inherent in each of these methodologies.[3]

Returning to Mills' observation, however, we take seriously our task to relate these findings, themes, and patterns, to "public issues," and to a critical and reflexive interpretation of data and results. This means that we do not simply describe, for example, the caseload crisis of the courts in order to chime in with the currently fashionable policy proposals for managerial and judicial reform. On the contrary, we feel strongly that description and explanation in social research are not enough and must be transcended by critical interpretation.

Thus, the notion of "rationalizing justice" can also be given a second meaning. It refers to the frequently observable attempts by judicial policy makers and managers to establish or preserve continuity in the meaning of justice and to insist that justice is being served even though the procedures of adjudication have changed. Plea bargaining, informal negotiations, and

settlements deviate significantly from the conventional notion of adjudication and of using adversary procedures in the resolution of civil disputes and
the disposition of criminal cases. But the putative speed of informal procedures is often praised by reference to the old adage "justice delayed is justice
denied." The greater efficiency of modern courts is seen as providing better
access to justice to a larger number of people. The higher cost-effectiveness
of the modern system is presented as an advantage for poor defendants and
possibly as a sign of good government.

It may very well be true that greater speed, efficiency, productivity, and
cost-effectiveness of courts have improved the administration of justice from
the perspective of managerial categories of performance. Simplified procedures of informal justice may also generate greater satisfaction among those
who have to endure the process. What we do not know, however, is the extent
to which the new justice is good justice or justice at all since, in a democratic
polity, it is precisely the procedural rights of citizens that guarantees a constitutional baseline for defining and providing justice. Does a change in procedure change the substance and quality of justice?

There is no easy answer to this question and our study does not address
it directly since it is mainly concerned with the forms and extent of change,
not with the quality of justice. But the *a priori* insistence that the new forms
still serve the old values, that there is justice in many rooms no matter what
the decor, that justice is being delivered as long as people believe that they
are getting justice: these affirmative, optimistic evaluations can be seen as
attempts at rationalizing justice in the sense of explaining away the possible
negative consequences of change or even denying its occurrence.

In that sense, then, rationalization is equivalent to an ideological production of reasons, grounds, explanations, and judgments that have the
concealed purpose of justifying a given state of affairs. It is not the "absolute
truth" or the "true value" of justice, then, that is at stake here, but the hidden
intent, indeed, the unacknowledged compulsion to insist that there is no real
change or that whatever change there is does not threaten the institutional
order of society. It is a deeply conservative impulse that may be born of fear of
change as much as it is animated by a denial of change.

A primary goal of our approach is to contribute to an understanding of
the impersonal, structural forces faced by judges and other actors in the court
system. Hence, it is important to interpret the historical trends and structural
patterns from a reflexive perspective that takes the definitions of problems
and the reform impulses responding to problems themselves as data to be
analyzed. For example, some of the managerial reforms that are put in place
to expedite case disposition and improve judicial productivity may seriously
undermine the very normative foundations of the judicial system itself and
pose a danger to the constitutional balance of powers. Judges, the targets of

much reform activity today, may find themselves in the position of an embattled profession defending the rule of law against inroads made by technocrats who advocate systematization, routinization, and simplification, that is, rationalization. Rather than serving as guardians of cherished values and as interpreters of legal principles, judges may be called upon to make common cause with the expediency of managerial innovations and the simplification and routinization of procedures.

While not defending a particular model of justice or advocating particular reform policies, we nevertheless take a position with respect to the way in which the rationalization of justice tends to undermine and threaten the rule of law. It is in this sense that we seek to preserve an essential distance from our data and explanations in order to retain the role of critical observer and interpreter.

Dimensions of the Technocratic Rationalization of Justice

By way of providing an overview and preview, it may be helpful to describe some of the more salient dimensions that capture the rationalization of justice. Concretely, the rationalization of justice can be described in terms of several dimensions and consequences, all of which have in common the decline of the adversary system of formal justice and the rise of informal and alternative forms of dispute resolution and case disposition. Specifically, the rationalization of justice includes:

Respect for a "Business" Orientation. Beginning with the Taylorist panacea of scientific management, there has been a trend toward the introduction of business methods of management and improvement of cost-effectiveness and productivity into courts as service organizations.

Decline of a "Service" Orientation. There has been a transformation of courts as service organizations dominated by a professional elite—judges—into an administrative agency in which a new technical-instrumental rationality designed to achieve results (effective case disposition) undermines or replaces the formal rationality of law and due process characteristic of traditional forms of law (autonomous law) and adjudication (judicial application of law to fact: "law-finding").

Legitimation of Court Administration. One may trace a spillover effect from judicial administration to judicial procedure such that attempts to streamline, rationalize, and simplify administrative procedures in courts have begun to affect judicial outcomes. This spill-over effect is visible not only in the various forms and revisions of the federal rules of civil procedure and the recent (1983) amendment to Rule 16(b), the encouragement of "judge-hosted" settlement, or the increase in court-annexed arbitration, but also in the actual practices known as "managerial judging" and similar forms of activist judicial intervention in case processing and case management. Adjudicative procedures and services reveal the constitutional promise in the process of adjudication itself. If the process is changed, by rules or by ad hoc practices, so is the promise as well as the product of adjudication. Whereas adjudication dovetails with a professional model of justice, procedural changes that increase the flexibility, informalism, and efficiency of this process can be said to complement a technocratic model of justice.

Diminution of Independence. There has been a gradual incorporation of courts into a broader system, that is, into a "justice system." This trend has been especially apparent on the criminal side where police, prosecution, probation, jails, parole, and other agencies work in close concert. But, these developments are not limited to criminal justice. While many have suggested that these changes point toward the bureaucratization of justice under the impact of increasing demand and declining resources, we believe that it is more accurate to speak of a movement toward a technocratic form of judicial administration. This new mode of administration is neither "professional" (with autonomous or dominant judges upholding the adversary system and the rule of law) nor "bureaucratic" (with hierarchical lines of authority, a strict division of labor, and formal organizational procedures and rules). Rather, it seeks to maximize systemic flexibility, informalism, decentralization, "results" in terms of case disposition and termination, efficiency, reduction of delay, productivity, speed, and cost-effectiveness, as well as the overall viability of the system as a whole; indeed, under the impact of technocratization courts and judges are seen as only one part of a larger, interdependent network.

Decline of Autonomy of Judicial Branch. A trend toward the incorporation of courts, judges, and the third branch of government into the executive branch, including administrative and regulatory agencies, is, perhaps, the most far reaching dimension of judicial rationalization. This development may be documented through the types of cases and disputes terminated, where public law litigation has become the mainstay of federal court tasks. In addition, the procedures and techniques used to deal with the ever-increasing case load reaching the federal courts show a relaxation of the "obstacle course" of adjudication. This amounts to a shift in the traditional separation of powers between judicial, legislative, and executive branches toward the dominance of, or the contest between, two. In other words, the incorporation of the justice system into the agenda of the executive branch results in the blurring of lines between the branches.

An Overview of the Chapters

In order to spell out these developments in greater detail, we will pursue the following strategy of exposition. Chapter 1 considers the structural and historical aspects of the American federal judicial system, focusing on the organization of district courts and their jurisdictions and on the rationalization of federal judicial administration since the Progressive Era. In this context, we present what amounts to a novel periodization of the administrative history of the federal judiciary.

In chapter 2 we examine the rising demand for court services, documenting the changing dimensions of this process since the turn of the century. In chapter 3 using census data and administrative and judicial statistics, we provide an analysis of the factors that help to explain the rising demand for court services since World War II. This is the first time that such statistics have been used to construct environmental profiles of the federal district courts' jurisdictions. Such profiles constitute a particularly useful instrument for gauging the impact of economic, demographic, and governmental changes on the caseloads confronting courts.

The combined purpose of chapters 2 and 3 is to document the historical patterns of change in federal court caseloads and to explain the notable rise of civil litigation since 1960. While this analysis is important in its own right, it doubles here as an empirical premise for our further argument that the federal courts are confronted with an unprecedented dilemma of rising demand and limited resources.

Chapter 4, then, presents our second premise: the dimensions of the fiscal constraints facing the courts. Here, we provide a budgetary analysis of the courts and focus on the contradiction between the rising demand for services at a time when there is a relative decline of resources due to the fiscal constraints on government. This double-bind of the American judicial system has been particularly acute since the 1960s, although—as we demonstrate—its roots go back to the early history of the republic.

Chapters 5 and 6 address the consequences of this double bind for the activities, organization, and output of courts. Beginning in chapter 5, we explore the extent to which the demand for services shapes the forms that dispute resolution may take. Of particular interest to us here is the way in which increases in demand affect the procedures of formal justice such as plea bargaining, dismissals, trials, and the use of juries. Chapter 6 is devoted to an analysis of the organizational functioning of the district courts. Here we show how the courts have grown in size and complexity, how various new categories of personnel have emerged, and how these changes affect the decisions of judges and the productivity of courts as a whole.

Chapter 7 provides an especially detailed analysis of the role of governmental litigation and the effect of the executive branch on the judiciary. Here, we show that the heavy agenda of adjudication generated by governmental policies and regulations reveals in particular detail the contradictions of a system that requires the continuous legitimation of its actions while being progressively unable to allocate adequate resources to this task.

Finally, chapter 8 returns to a consideration of the theoretical underpinnings and historical dimensions for understanding the crisis of the rule of law as well as the policy implications that may be drawn from this study. In this context, we present a typology of six models of justice that co-exist in one form or another as possible options for contemporary legal and judicial policymaking. In particular, we focus on the conflict between the two models that occupy center-stage in current policy debates, the professional model of adjudication and the technocratic model of judicial administration and rationalization. It is, in our view, the technocratic rationalization of justice that today threatens to undermine if not eliminate the conventional procedures of formal justice in American courts of law.

These considerations signify, once again, our intention not to retreat from the normative implications that inevitably inform empirical work in the social sciences. This means, above all, that we intend to reveal critically, wherever possible, not only the tension between formal justice and actual practice in the operation of courts, but also the contradictory tendencies that characterize the pressures to abandon the conventional model of adjudication, as well as the mobilization of resistance and opposition against the new forms of judicial administration. If, at times, our analysis or conclusions are critical of court managers, the judiciary, or other actors, we hope they will understand that our critique is not of a personal but rather a structural nature. This means that we are attempting to describe, explain, and interpret critically the operation of social and political forces, not to blame particular individuals for the actions they are taking in the context of those forces.

By the same token, however, we do not intend to defend, or advocate a return to, the conventional due process model of adjudication—even though that model is closely identified with the professional values of the legal-judicial community and with the normative standards of formal justice. Nor do we speak as advocates of managerial or technocratic reform, even though we feel that this model may well be the wave of the future and is likely to continue to inform the quest for efficiency, productivity, cost-effectiveness as well as flexibility, informalism, and conflict control. Rather, we want to illuminate the changing nature of adjudication, its transformation into new forms of administering justice, and the problems and conflicts this transformation expresses and generates. We want to undertake this task in the spirit of a critical theory that is committed to both a positive understanding and explanation of the social forces affecting the judicial system and to a reflexive and critical examination of the presuppositions and theoretical methods that guide this inquiry.

CHAPTER 1

*

The Organization and Rationalization
of the Judiciary

The central thesis of this study is that the gradual erosion of the conduct of judicial affairs from adjudication to administration has consequences for the legitimacy and role of the third branch of government. We propose to investigate this shift historically and empirically as it is occurring in American federal courts and in the context of the changing political economy of their jurisdictions. In contrast to state and local courts, the federal courts are one forum where nationally relevant economic and social legislation is tested and contested and where the historic confrontation between the U.S. government and the American corporate economy is taking shape. Within that system, the U.S. district courts—the trial courts of the federal judiciary— constitute the first line operating level. It is for these reasons that we feel justified in choosing the U.S. district courts as a *locus operandi* of the larger trends occurring in the third branch of government.

In this chapter, we shall specify concretely the organizational units and processes we propose to analyze. What kinds of organizations are the federal district courts? What are the economic, legal, governmental, and demographic characteristics of the environment of these courts? What kinds of fiscal and organizational resources do these courts have available in order to deal with the demand for their services? What is the nature of the courts' output, that is, the product or service that is so important in a society governed by a rule of law? How did the federal court system become what it is today, and what are the concrete historical forces combining to transform it?

In responding to these questions, let us first identify the functional and organizational characteristics of federal district courts, and then address the historical process of rationalization and transformation.

The "Functions" of Courts

From the traditional perspective of the adequacy or effectiveness of organizations, it may be instructive first to examine the tasks, goals, or "functions" of courts before raising the question of how they are organized to perform these tasks and achieve their goals. Of course, apart from the organizational rationality assumption hidden in this perspective, it is notoriously difficult to define precisely what tasks or functions public and professional service organizations perform. Historicist wisdom has it that "every generation has to decide for itself what it believes to be a realistic jurisprudence" (Hurst 1950, 184). Nevertheless, we assume there are some rough indicators or general benchmarks that one may use for comparative purposes.

The most interesting method of determining functions is offered by James Willard Hurst (1950, 1981-82) who provides historical and empirical descriptions of what courts and judges do, derived from statistical and other sources. Thus, for Hurst, functions become variables that assume different values in different historical periods depending on the relative presence, salience, or dominance of particular judicial activities. The potential drawback of this method is the "realist" or behaviorist baseline that is created by such a description. As a result, the researcher may give up any criterion or independent vantage point for evaluating whether what judges do has anything to do with legality or justice. Still, it is a way of determining where the system is moving relative to its own assumptions, origins, and norms. Hurst himself, for example, does not hesitate to evaluate or criticize courts, noting that they have not been able to check the social consequences of corporate power and economic concentration. Let us take a closer look at these "social functions of courts."

The dominant judicial functions emerging from the analysis of various observers are norm enforcement, that is, deciding civil disputes, criminal cases, and appeals as well as providing a check on legislative, executive, and investigative activities by means of judicial review; legitimation of government and the social order; judicial administration, including rulemaking; and policy-making and policy administration (Hurst 1950, 1981-82; Peltason 1955; Mayers 1964; Jacob 1972; Horwitz 1977) This list of functions comprises the whole spectrum of governmental activities, although not all of them were fully represented in the early stages.

For the federal district courts, these functions can be narrowed and specified. The jurisdiction of civil cases includes litigation between citizens of different states when more than fifty thousand dollars is in controversy (diversity jurisdiction), and three categories of public law litigation: federal questions arising from the Constitution, U.S. laws, and treaties; litigation where the U.S. government is the plaintiff and cases where it is the defendant. Moreover, federal district courts have exclusive jurisdiction over admiralty and maritime cases, bankruptcy proceedings, cases arising under the patent and copyright laws, and a number of other minor categories. In addition, district courts deal with criminal cases involving federal criminal statutes.

The administrative functions of judges are, to some extent, linked to those of adjudication. For example, judges have a uniform rulemaking power that allows them to determine the procedures under which cases are to be decided. These procedures are rules about rules that set the terms and conditions of adjudication (Grau 1978). In addition to the Federal Rules of Civil Procedure adopted in 1938, each district court has its own local rules. Judicial administration also includes the coordination and direction of court activities under a chief judge, an administrative judge, or a regular judge. Furthermore, judges may function as "trial directors" (Frankel 1975, 21) and may, in the management of their cases, exercise "judicial supervision over litigation" in the context of an expanded view of the "adversary judicial system" (Kaufman 1962). The degree to which this active participation or intervention of the judge is advocated reveals the continued "realist" critique of the adversary system voiced most forcefully by Roscoe Pound some eighty years ago. It also indicates a movement toward a more interventionist, inquisitorial model typical of continental European code law.

Finally, there is still another sense in which judges perform administrative functions, namely, in the disposition of routine legal matters and routinizable mass cases such as judicial certification of legal status (for example, uncontested wills or divorces) and the processing of already negotiated guilty-pleas (Blumberg 1967; Friedman and Percival 1976). This routinization may be less common in federal district courts than in state, county, and municipal courts. Yet, the very existence and vitality of delegalization reform movements as well as other attempts to shift the burden of minor litigation from the courts to informal methods of dispute resolution attest to the continued urgency and ubiquity of this type of demand on judicial time (Harrington 1982; Spitzer 1982).

A third set of functions, in addition to law-finding and administration, is lawmaking or policy-making and the corollary activity of policy administration. While most political scientists feel that this function has always been part of judicial activity (e.g., Shapiro 1980) there is some evidence to suggest that judicial policy-making can be suddenly activated. The power of judicial review of the constitutionality of legislation and of executive and administrative action was present from the time of the Judiciary Act of 1789 (Hurst 1950, 193; Mayers 1964, chaps. 8, 10, 11; Horwitz 1977, 266). Especially under the common law, the procedure of law-finding or "declaring law," in contrast to interpreting the statutes framed by legislators under a code system, gave judges ample opportunity for legislative creativity and policy-making. This activity was not confined to the appeals courts, although it might appear to be more obvious there. As Hurst argues, a "large share of the working policy shaped by judges was made in the unappealed cases. The largest body of reported trial court decisions—those of the federal district courts—offered evidence to support this inference" (Hurst 1950, 189).

But even though policy-making is integral to judicial activity, two relatively recent trends have sharply activated the latent redistributive and regulatory political functions of courts. On the one hand, there was a significant increase in the extent of policy-making and policy administration of courts after World War II (Chayes 1976; Levi 1976; Berger 1977; Horowitz 1977) On the other hand, there has been a shift from judicial administration to executive or administrative adjudication, a trend toward policy-making by executive and administrative authority (Hurst 1950, 387-90; 1981-82, 470). This "steady loss of ground to other policy-makers" (Hurst 1950, 436) occurred in the wake of the New Deal legislation and the new trend in regulation. It endowed the executive branch and its administrative agencies with expanded powers to make and enact public policy (Jaffe 1965; Stewart 1975; Freeman 1978; Handler 1978; Rabin 1979, 1986; Breyer and Stewart 1979; Hurst 1981-82). But insofar as courts are still called upon to review the decisions of administrative agencies, and insofar as there exists a measure of "deference of courts to the administrative construction of statutes" (Hurst 1950, 404), one may observe an increasingly close cooperation and functional partnership between the judicial and executive branches (Lorch 1969).

Finally, the most "profound social function" of courts is their contribution to the legitimacy of government (Hurst 1950, 194). However, this is not only a question of popular confidence in law, but of the reproduction of the socio-economic order by mediating the contradictions of an advanced capitalist society. Courts and judges continuously seek to affirm and reproduce the rule of law even though they "failed in coping with issues presented by the concentration of economic power," as Hurst (1950, 195) noted forty years ago. We will show in this book that the courts' capacity for legitimation is undermined by the very institution they are to legitimate: the interventionist and regulatory state.

In sum, courts can be said to perform broadly defined functions such as norm enforcement and dispute resolution, administration, policy-making, and legitimation. Without entering into the question as to whether these functions are truly "functional" for the adaptation or survival of modern society, whether they are effectively performed, and whether they are compatible or incompatible with each other, let us now turn to an examination of the organizational and structural characteristics of courts.

The Organization of Federal District Courts

The jurisdictional pyramid of the federal judicial system consists of ninety-four district courts from which cases can be appealed to twelve U.S. Circuit Courts of Appeal, and ultimately to the U.S. Supreme Court. The Judicial Conference, chaired by the chief justice, represents the administrative arm of the federal courts, together with the judicial council and judicial conference of each of the eleven circuits, as well as the Administrative Office of the U.S. Courts and the Federal Judicial Center.

There is at least one district court in each of the fifty states, with some states having as many as four districts. Districts never cross state boundaries, whereas circuits always combine several states. The number of judges in each district ranges from at least two in less populated districts to as many as twenty-seven in the metropolitan districts. Most cases are heard by one judge, although a very small proportion of cases require a panel of three.

It is important to note two aspects often overlooked in the study of courts. First, notwithstanding the popular image of courts, there is much more to courts than courtrooms and judges' chambers. District courts, especially the larger ones, are fairly complex organizational units that are structurally different from courtrooms as the public workplaces of particular judges. There is, for example, a degree of segmentation into different subunits depending on the number of judges in a given court. But in addition, there is a more or less differentiated and stratified judicial, administrative, and auxiliary staff that operates in the court on a continuous basis.

Second, a great deal of earlier research on judicial process was concerned with appellate courts and the Supreme Court (see, for example, Baum, et. al. 1981-82; Jahnige and Goldman 1968; Howard 1981). By contrast, the organization of district courts, the courts of first instance of the federal judicial system, have not received as much empirical attention, although this situation has been changing (Dolbeare 1969; Richardson and Vines 1970; Chase 1972; Fish 1973; Grossman and Sarat 1975; Flanders 1977; Heydebrand 1977; *Law and Society Review* 1980-1981; Heydebrand and Seron 1981, 1986, 1987; Clark 1981).

The district courts, then, can be defined as public, heteronomous (Scott 1965), professional service organizations that receive requests for decisions from individual and corporate actors residing in a jurisdictional and interorganizational environment with fixed boundaries but variable complexity, and that provide dispositions under conditions of labor-intensive service and relatively low levels of bureaucratic formalization and centralization. Let us spell out the analytic dimensions of this definition.

1. The degree of environmental complexity, stability, and boundedness
An essential part of a court's organization is the scope and nature of its

jurisdiction. A jurisdiction is both a set of rules under which cases can be filed with the court (certain types of civil disputes and criminal cases) and for which it has authority and competence (the issue of "standing"), as well as a defined geographical district in which these cases arise. Thus, the court's environment is clearly bounded, in contrast to the unbounded markets of corporations or the relatively open-ended service areas of hospitals and other public organizations. There is some similarity between courts and public schools that also serve legally defined districts and have a segmented organizational structure in that each subunit (courtroom, schoolroom) is a separate workplace.

In federal districts, this jurisdictional area is a geographical unit composed of a number of counties that make up either one of the fifty states or, in highly urbanized areas, part of a state. Hence, such factors as caseload, casemix, judicial composition of the court, local history, rules, and practices as well as the nature and speed of dispositions both reflect and feed back into the jurisdictional environment (Frankfurter and Landis 1928; Peltason 1955; Hart and Wechsler 1953; Richardson and Vines 1970; Goldman and Jahnige 1985; Jacob 1972).

The advantage of studying the effects of the environment on *federal* courts is, of course, that substantive rules are uniform throughout the federal system (excluding diversity jurisdiction). Hence, federal statutes and case law are differentially activated in federal jurisdictions by the economic, legal-governmental, and the demographic dynamics of the district. An early study of federal courts describes the characteristics of jurisdictional districts that affect the "initiation" (in contrast to the "conduct") of litigation. Among those viewed as relevant are "attitudes and policies of local administrative and judicial officials, the trends of business, the customs of the bar, the comparative efficiency, cost and speed of state and federal courts and the differences in rules of law which they follow, and other non-statistical factors" (American Law Institute 1934; Part 2, 50). In order to be able to measure systematically the degree of environmental complexity, we will take into account a series of economic, demographic, and governmental indicators for each district that are derived from census data and other statistical sources.

In addition, the degree of stability of a jurisdiction can be gauged from a comparison of different time periods (e.g., 1950-60-70-80) and by observing the rates of change in various environmental characteristics. The environmental profiles constructed from these measures will be an important basis for assessing the nature and complexity of the political economy surrounding each particular district court.

2. The degree of task complexity

Most trial courts are nonspecialized or "generalist" organizations in that they are competent to hear all types of cases filed. However, there are often separate subdivisions for civil and criminal cases, and some courts are completely specialized, for example, family and juvenile court, small claims, housing, traffic, narcotics as well as misdemeanor versus felony, probate, or customs.

Apart from the issue of general versus limited jurisdiction, one may observe other patterns of specialization and division of labor among courts that have a bearing on specialization within certain types of courts. For example, federal trial courts are "specialized" in that almost three-fourths of their dockets consist of civil cases of which three-fourths, in turn, involve federal statutes ("federal question") or the federal government. By contrast, state and local trial courts deal mainly with criminal cases and with civil actions that tend to be fairly routine. Hence, the American judicial system can be said to be characterized by a de facto division of labor between state and federal courts, the latter dealing, generally, with civil cases including corporate, civil rights, government and labor litigation.

3. The degree of autonomy

Courts are by definition heteronomous rather than autonomous organizations (Weber 1968). This means that resources (budgets, positions, and major appointments), organizational structure and boundaries, and jurisdiction (domain) are externally defined and controlled by legislatures or executives. Indeed, legislation specifies the organization, boundaries, personnel structure and jurisdiction of federal courts (28 U.S.C.). Similarly, the federal courts are financed by annual appropriations resulting from congressional authorization and review in consultation with the Judicial Conference and the Administrative Office of the U.S. Courts. In addition, courts are, of course, often politically responsive to their local environment and thus tend to be constrained by aspects of local political culture (Peltason 1961; Dolbeare 1969; Cook 1970; Richardson and Vines 1970; Chase 1972).

It may be useful to distinguish legal and political autonomy from functional and economic autonomy. Insofar as courts are an arm of government, they share the *de jure* (legal) autonomy of the third branch in the American federal system. Courts are therefore quintessentially public sector organizations. They constitute an integral part of the state's capacity to enforce norms through the interpretation of legislative and constitutional provisions.

Among these different functions of courts, judicial dispositions (judgments, sentences, decrees, acquittals, convictions, etc.) are relatively easy to measure. Questions of legitimation, judicial policy-making, judicial quality, and effectiveness are, by contrast, difficult to specify and require broad historical and political yardsticks (Black 1973a, 52; Nonet 1976, 532).

The difficulty of determining the public accountability of federal district courts derives in part also from the fact that they are functionally relatively independent units within the largely decentralized structure of the federal judiciary. To be sure, district courts are at the low end of the professional-judicial hierarchy because their decisions can be reviewed and overturned by higher courts. But, there is no administrative authority that subordinates district court judges to direct bureaucratic control, although the power of the circuit councils has occasionally attempted to move in that direction [*Chandler v. Judicial Council*, 398 U.S. 74 (1969)]. Hence, the low level of economic and political autonomy does not necessarily imply operational or functional dependence. For example, the annual allocation of a budget and the virtual monopoly of courts over the service they provide (authoritative decision-making) also render them functionally and, in the short run, economically less dependent on their immediate environment than business corporations are on their markets and suppliers. This relative functional autonomy is a well-known characteristic that courts share with government agencies and other budgeted organizations (Niskanen 1971).

4. The degree of initiative as to the task domain

Courts are relatively passive organizations within a demanding environment or, one might say, "reluctant organizations in an aggressive environment" (Maniha and Perrow 1965; see also Black 1973b; Friedman 1975, 191). Trial courts initiate few activities themselves but rather respond to the demands for service that emanate from their jurisdictional environment, mediated by lawyers and prosecutors. Judicial passivity should not, however, be overstated. One can observe historical shifts between different degrees of restraint and activism, related to changes in emphasis between judicial policy-making as against lawfinding and norm-enforcement.

Nevertheless, a given court cannot create a market for itself in a way a business organization can. It is for this reason that caseloads, while historically fluctuating, tend to be relatively stable from year to year, their increase or decrease being largely a function of environmental change and new legislation.

5. The degree of technological intensity and complexity

Courts are labor-intensive service organizations rather than capital-intensive, high-tech structures. This means that an essential service, for example, dispute resolution, is provided to clients (litigants) by a trained labor force (the judicial service) under the direction of professionals (judges). Thus, even though the formal organizational functions are externally defined in terms of jurisdictional authority and domain, judges, as the central professional-technical core, specify the functions and the task structure, and they direct and carry out decisions and services on the basis of special knowledge of substantive and procedural rules.[1]

In general, the work organization of small courts is on the whole still characterized by pre-bureaucratic forms of service delivery and coordination. Professional autonomy is relatively high and is jealously guarded by a collegial status group. A sharp distinction is maintained between doctrinal "judicial" matters and nondoctrinal "administrative" issues (Wright 1970, 49; American Bar Association 1974, 86). Machine technology is still largely absent, although there is a trend toward the gradual adoption of information and data-processing equipment as well as video technology.

6. The degree of formalization and centralization

The elements of formalization and centralization include the dichotomies of formal structure versus loosely coupled network, administrative versus professional dominance, and centralization versus decentralization. First, courts are networks of organized activities rather than bureaucratically integrated formal organizations. Obviously, the absence of a formal organizational structure does not say anything about the degree of legal formalization that may or may not characterize judicial proceedings. In trial courts, the more or less informally organized network that makes up the organization includes the activities of judges, courtroom deputies, law clerks, magistrates, judicial secretaries, court reporters, clerks, public defenders, probation officers, and court-appointed counsel. It also includes two categories of personnel from the executive branch (the Department of Justice in federal courts), *viz.* prosecutors and court-based law enforcement officers. This operational definition of the court's organizational boundaries includes positions that are permanent and integrated into the daily work process of the court, that is, it *excludes* private attorneys and their clients, witnesses, jurors, news reporters, and bail bondsmen.

The total work process of courts as organizational units is in many ways similar to the teamwork approach of multiservice organizations (for example, hospitals) since there is little formal or external coordination, but much reliance on self-direction, functional interdependence, discretion, and self-coordination. However, work routines involving recurrent types of decision-making, such as those found in courts, are probably more permanent, patterned, established, and stable than those of teams or task forces insofar as the latter tend to be more activist, "ad hoc," target-oriented, and nonroutinized.

There are three theoretical advantages of looking at courts as networks of organized activities rather than as unitary systems or integrated formal organizations. First, particular sets of activities may vary independently in terms of different organizational characteristics, for example, types of authority (Weber 1966), centralization (Leibenstein 1960), or bureaucratization (Hall 1963). For example, the internal governance of courts is based on the *collegial authority* of judges. Matters of judicial administration are handled by a chief judge, a *primus inter pares* who—in larger courts—is assisted by a committee of judicial colleagues in the formulation of policy and court rules, as well as procedural matters such as hiring and firing of nonjudicial personnel. Furthermore, a collegial-professional network of lawyers—attorneys, prosecutors, and judges—dominates the respective chains of decision-making which—while not without conflicts—are nevertheless highly interdependent.

By contrast, the organization of the clerk's office is probably closest to the notion of *bureaucratic authority.* That is, the structure of this office grows out of a hierarchical, formalized, rule-bound, and impersonal structure much as Max Weber described. Of course, it is important to note that the bureaucratic contours of the clerk's office may develop next to a quite collegial organization among judicial personnel, a theme we will return to in later chapters.

Second, a loosely connected network of activities such as a court of law leaves much room for internal *political processes* such as the formation of coalitions, co-optation, conflict, negotiation, bargaining, exchange, and compromise between the various groups and actors (Cyert and March 1963; Thompson and Tuden 1959; Thompson 1967; Cole 1973). While these processes are designed to minimize losses, maximize gains, and reduce uncertainty, the outcomes are not wholly predictable. An additional element of instability and uncertainty derives from the fact that private attorneys, defense counsel, and U.S. Attorneys tend to rotate relatively frequently and thus play a somewhat episodic role, whereas judges are the more permanent fixtures of courts, especially federal judges who have tenure appointments for life.

Third, the role, salience, and differential access to power of various actors may be seen to *change historically* in different and uneven ways. For example, the ascendancy of the "treatment model" of criminal justice has given rise to large, professionalized probation departments with considerable input into the judicial decision-making process (American Friends Service Committee 1971; Kittrie 1971; Schur 1973; Greenberg 1975). The emphasis on law enforcement and crime control in the 1960s has accentuated the gatekeeping function of prosecutors and U.S. Attorneys (Cole 1970; Goldman and Jahnige 1985; Eisenstein 1973; Hartje 1975). Most interestingly, court administrators, the most recent arrivals on the court scene, are beginning to deal with the same kinds of organizational problems and role definitions that hospital and school administrators encountered fifty years ago (Saari 1970; Friesen, et al, 1971; Perrow 1965). Court administrators are both creating, and responding to, the increasing rationalization of court procedures.

Finally, courts vary in the extent to which they are vertically and horizontally decentralized (Mintzberg 1979, 181-86). Small, prebureaucratic courts may well be centralized in the sense that all decision-making power rests with a single judge and is neither shared horizontally with other actors or delegated vertically to lower levels. This form of professional centralization or dominance must be distinguished from the various forms of administrative centralization or decentralization. In some forms of professional decentralization decision-making authority may be shared, for example, with probation officers or with the other lawyers in the courtroom work group (Eisenstein and Jacob 1977; but see Sheskin 1981), but there may be vertical administrative centralization with respect to court clerks and clerical personnel.

Modern courts may also move in the direction of simultaneous centralization and decentralization: though budgetary processes and some procedures are centrally controlled, much of the actual work process is functionally decentralized. Traditionally, the federal court system has been characterized by a considerable degree of internal decentralization. Today courts tend to move away from professional or bureaucratic models and toward an open systems model of work organization. Thus, we can expect the co-existence of various elements of centralization and flexible, informal decentralization (Baar 1975; Gallas 1976; Saari 1976).

7. The degree of interorganizational integration

Although they have strict boundaries as organizations, courts exhibit varying degrees of integration with interorganizational networks. Again, one must distinguish between vertical integration and horizontal unification with other segmented units of a larger court system on the one hand, and horizontal integration with differentiated units of an encompassing "justice system" on the other. For example, trial courts are vertically tied into higher levels of the judicial-professional hierarchy and authority structure such as appeals courts, judicial councils and conferences, and congressional committees.

Horizontally, the type and degree of integration, segregation, or even isolation depend on the extent to which courts have moved away from their traditional position of centrality as the "fulcrum of the justice system" (Rubin 1980) toward becoming either a bureaucratic subunit of a larger court system, or one specialized unit among others in a comprehensive justice system. For example, the court unification movement has succeeded in many states in consolidating trial courts and establishing centralized management, rule-making, budgeting, and state financing (Berkson and Carbon 1978). Similarly, there are widespread efforts at work to integrate criminal courts with police and prosecution, on the one hand, and probation, parole, and jails, on the other (Skoler 1977). Proposals for the training of lawyers in adequate courtroom practice seek to achieve a greater degree of articulation of common interests between the bar and the courts. Newly appointed judges are being invited to participate in training seminars to develop and upgrade their managerial skills, to sensitize them to the "systemic impact of their actions," and to learn "to organize and cooperate with one another or experiment with new methods of handling judicial business" (Institute of Judicial Administration 1965; Cook 1971; Bird 1975; Berkson and Carbon 1978, 75).

8. The nature of the product or output

We have already indicated that one may treat the authoritative decisions resulting from adjudication as an operational measure of the product or output of courts. Here, any "termination" of a case—whether by discontinuance or decree, dismissal or trial—must be examined from the point of view of judicial involvement. For example, what is the probability of a given case coming to trial, or to what extent is this probability influenced by heavy case-loads or the pressure for speedy justice?

Regardless of the nature and probability of dispositions, it bears repeating that courts do not produce commodities, but services in the form of decisions. Hence, attempts to increase the productivity and speed of court performance must be evaluated in the light of the capacity of services to be rationalized and still function as services rather than mass-produced commodities. Of course, as Lawrence M. Friedman put it, "If the social interest in rapid, efficient processing is superior to the social interest in carefully individuated justice, it is certainly possible to devise mass production legal methods" (Friedman 1967, 810 as quoted by Lazerson 1981, 119). But the consequences of such a shift in social interest and in the methods of case disposition tend to move adjudication closer to the model of administration, especially the technocratic administration of justice.

Let us therefore take a brief look at the movement toward rationalization from a historical perspective. To what extent has the judiciary become more and more rationalized? How do the attempts at improving the administration of justice today differ from those of fifty and seventy-five years ago? And how have the organizational characteristics of federal courts changed as a result of the rationalization movement?

The Historical Development of Court Rationalization

Like most organizations and interorganizational networks, the federal judicial system is not a stationary or unchanging entity. The federal judiciary finds itself in the midst of quantitative expansion, internal differentiation, and qualitative transformation. New judgeships are being added, districts and circuits are being integrated or subdivided, and the administrative structure and work organization of the courts are constantly being rationalized. As a first approximation to a working definition, we are defining the term *rationalization* as a combination of different processes such as systematization, codification of procedures, simplification, and routinization of work. These processes are governed by the principles of efficiency, productivity, cost-effectiveness, and the optimization of resources such as time, space, energy, organization, and human services. The result of rationalization is assumed to be the production of cheaper goods and the delivery of cheaper and more efficient services to a larger number of consumers and clients at selected time points, locations, and levels of choice and quality.

When we speak of the rationalization of the federal judicial system, it is not assumed that the original judiciary was not rational. Nor do we claim that the whole history of the judiciary is a process of progressive rationalization in the sense just defined. Rather, we will show that the judicial system was organized in terms of a certain logic (Alford and Friedland 1985), but that this logic is being transformed into something quite different from what the federalist founding fathers had in mind. To trace this process, let us first examine the rise of rational administration within the framework of a developmental history (Schluchter 1981) and spell out the major details of this two-hundred year process. Restricting ourselves largely to the events that have occurred in the federal judicial system since the Judiciary Act of 1789, we are confronted with a historical period of two centuries. This period can be divided into three major phases, or five phases if we further subdivide the last eighty years when most of the significant development took place.

1. 1787-1865: The political origins of the court system.

The U.S. Constitution of 1787 vested judicial power in "one Supreme Court and such inferior courts as the Congress may from time to time ordain and establish" (Art. III; Richardson and Vines 1970, 18). The Judiciary Act of 24 September 1789 served to carry out this mandate and to establish the federal courts: a Supreme Court consisting of a chief justice and five associate justices; thirteen district courts, with eleven of the original thirteen states each made into a federal judicial district, all grouped into three circuits. The circuit courts were to meet periodically and were composed of two Supreme Court justices and the district judge.

The political struggle between the federalist government and Jeffersonian antifederalists led to reform proposals with the result that President John Adams reorganized the lower courts in the Judiciary Act of 1801. This act "eliminated circuit riding, created sixteen circuit judgeships, and greatly extended the jurisdiction of the lower courts" (Richardson and Vines 1970, 25). However, the act was repealed in 1802 after the defeat of the federalists, although certain changes of 1801 were retained. It was not until 1875 that the federal courts were once again given the full range of federal jurisdiction. One other event close to the middle of the nineteenth century needs to be mentioned: the adoption of the New York Field Code in 1848. While the Field Code marks a more general procedural reform by merging law and equity, it did become a model for later procedural innovation, including the Federal Rules of Civil Procedure to be established ninety years later. Thus, it can be viewed as "the 'rationalization' of procedure" or as the "final and complete emasculation of equity as an independent source of legal standards" (Horwitz 1977, 265).

This first phase, then, can be seen as the "formative period of American law" (Aumann 1940), although the term *formative* begs the question of why the transformation took place. This question is answered by Horwitz (1977) with reference to the link between formal law and the growth of capitalism in the sense that common law was used as an instrument of social and economic change. Judicial decision-making became intertwined with policy-making, which went beyond the confines of particular disputes. The rise of legal formalism was an integral element of this change. "This transformation of American law," Horwitz argues, "both aided and ratified a major shift in power in an increasingly market-oriented society" (1977, 253).

2. 1865-1905: The rise of professionalism

The second period in the development of the federal judiciary is still marked by legal, procedural, and jurisdictional changes rather than by organizational ones. The dominant development was a movement away from the colonial and antebellum system of justice "which in some instances was administered by laymen who were unable to give full service to the rule of law" and toward a system "administered according to law by a trained judiciary" (Aumann 1940, 68; see also, Provine 1986). Thus, "a scientific, objective, professional, and apolitical conception of law ... now comes to extend its domain and to infiltrate into the everyday categories of adjudication" (Horwitz 1977, 266).

The emergence of legal-professional dominance was given expression by the founding of the American Bar Association in 1878. The legal system of the period was "centered around and typified by courts, whose function is to announce, apply, interpret (and sometimes change) rules on the basis of or in accordance with other elements of ... normative learning," and "the basic, typical, decisive mode of legal action is adjudication, that is, the application of rules to particular controversies by courts or court-like institutions in adversarial proceedings" (Galanter 1977, 19).

Organizational reform of the judiciary, during this period, was essentially confined to four congressional actions: an act in 1869 in which Congress provided a circuit judge for each of the nine circuits; two acts in 1875 shifting federal business from the Supreme Court to the circuits, and extending federal jurisdiction (the Removal Act making it possible to "remove" federal question cases from the state courts to the federal district courts); and an act of 3 March 1891 creating the U.S. Circuit Courts of Appeal as we know them today (Richardson and Vines 1970, 29-31). In general, it can be said that "the late nineteenth century was not a period of radical innovation in judicial organization" (Friedman 1973, 336).

3. 1906-1937: The rise of rational administration

With the onset of the Progressive Era at the turn of the century, we enter into a period of momentous changes for the administration of justice, which have had repercussions to this day. In one sense, one could treat the last eighty years as a period of progressive rationalization of the judiciary. But there are also some subtle undercurrents and countercurrents that suggest the wisdom of sorting out the contradictory forces that affected the course of development. Accordingly, we will distinguish an initial period of change (1906-37) from two subsequent ones: the bureaucratization of professionals (1938-66), and the technocratic administration of justice (1967-present).

The general trend emerging at the turn of the century was a reaction to legal formalism, a dissatisfaction with the formal legal order dominated by a legal elite, and the emergence of sociological jurisprudence, legal realism, and a "movement for socialization of law" (Aumann 1940, 215). These tendencies signified a fundamental

> shift from some variant of formal rationality to some mode of purposive rationality. . . . [Previously] legislation expressed and clarified values annunciated by previous judges; . . . the contemporary rationalization . . . is less concerned with the expression of values than with the realization of practical goals conceived in utilitarian terms and pursued according to canons of scientific reasoning (Abel 1977, 222-23).

The political context of this attack on legal formalism and judicial dominance was represented in part by the populist impulses of the Progressive Era, in part by the ascendancy of the executive branch due to American entry into a new period of economic development, and a shift from national capital accumulation to international competition, expansion, and imperialism.

For the judiciary, the event signaling the turn from formalism and professionalism to a new administrative ethos was Pound's 1906 speech on "The Causes of Popular Dissatisfaction with the Administration of Justice." While Justice Oliver Wendell Holmes had already sounded a note of "realism" in his legal opinions, it was Pound (1906, 1940) who articulated the need for administrative and procedural reforms to influence and direct the course of adjudication through a more rational ("realistic") administration of justice. In his endeavor to promote sociological jurisprudence and administrative rationality, Pound would later be joined by the realist scholar Karl Llewellyn and by a number of illustrious judges, among them Jerome Frank, Benjamin Cardozo, and Louis Brandeis.

The contradiction in sociological jurisprudence was that Pound was a conservative reformer who wanted to "ward off governmental control" and limit the "capabilities of law" (Friedman and Macaulay 1977, 9). Accordingly, Pound "attacked the independence and authority of the courts" (Aumann 1940, 214), no doubt in part because of the widely shared distrust of the power of nonelected professionals and officials. While Pound's 1906 speech encountered strong opposition at the beginning, his approach was incorporated into the court reform movement and was widely adopted in the 1960s (Berkson and Carbon 1978, 2). There was possibly another influence that made itself felt in Pound's overall program: the scientific management of Frederick Taylor (1911). Thus, some students of courts have ascribed the rise of rational-bureaucratic administration in courts to the influence of Taylorism (Berkson et al., 1976, 130; see also Harrington 1985).

But besides bureaucratization which, after all, appears as an organizational extension of legal formalism, the new administrative ethos also sought to introduce a degree of flexibility in order to loosen the hold of formal procedures. Thus, Taylorism and bureaucratization are not necessarily of one piece and one can discern, in the multiple tensions between legal formalism, professionalism, Taylorism, and the new administrative ethos the outlines of future conflicts that would develop in the later phases of judicial administration in the twentieth century.

During the period from 1906 to 1937, the groundwork was laid for some of the "major advances" of the federal judicial system (Chandler 1963). In the act of 3 March 1911, a revised judicial code succeeded in abolishing "the anachronism of two courts of first instance" (district and circuit) and establishing the district courts as courts of first instance of the federal judicial system (Hurst 1950, 112; see also Richardson and Vines 1970, 32). This reorganization of the lower courts completed the previous reforms of 1875 and 1891.

In the wake of the new zeal for efficiency, various reform organizations sprang up, one of the most influential and enduring of which was the American Judicature Society in 1913, whose founders included Pound and Brandeis. In 1914, Pound, Brandeis, and others wrote a "Preliminary Report on Efficiency in the Administration of Justice," addressed to the National Economic League (Wheeler and Whitcomb 1977, 47-55). Perhaps it is also relevant to note that a few years later, in 1916 and 1919, there is evidence of the first significant jump in the rate of plea bargaining. This was due, among other things, to the pressures of selective service cases surrounding America's entry into World War I (1917) and of liquor cases after the onset of Prohibition (1919). Thus, in federal district courts, the annual percentage of guilty-pleas rose from 34 percent of all criminal cases terminated in 1908 to 74 percent in 1930, with the year 1916 marking the first major jump in the guilty-plea rate (American Law Institute 1934, 56). During the same period, guilty-pleas as a percentage of all convictions rose from 52 percent in 1908, to 90 percent in 1930. Thus, while "plea-bargaining emerged as a significant practice only after the American Civil War" (Alshuler 1979, 211), it did not reach the epidemic proportions of today until the emergence of the mass-proceedings and growing caseloads produced by World War I draft cases and the Prohibition period of 1919 to 1933 (see also Haller 1979, 273).

However, the most important "advance" in judicial administration during this phase was the establishment of the Judicial Conference in 1922, which followed former President Taft's appointment as Chief Justice in 1921. Initially set up as a Conference of senior Circuit Judges, with the Chief Justice an *ex officio* member, the Judicial Conference became an organ of professional-judicial self-administration. While widely regarded as establishing "central, planned control of the administration of the federal court business" (Hurst 1950, 113), the Judicial Conference represented the thrust of strengthening the professional control by the judicial elite through an extension of administrative control. This double impulse was to mark the subsequent development of federal judicial administration (Fish 1973).

Besides establishing a governing structure for the federal courts, the 1922 act "gave the Chief Justice authority to assign district judges to service anywhere in the country" (Hurst 1950, 114). A vivid description of the political preliminaries and consequences of the 1922 act was provided by Henry Chandler who was later to become the first director of the Administrative Office of the U.S. Courts. Chandler believes that the real history of judicial administration starts after 1922, because up until 1922 "administration in the federal courts was pretty much as it had been from the beginning of the government in 1789" (1963, 313).

The viability and effectiveness of the Judicial Conference after 1922 owes much to Taft's chief justiceship from 1921 to 1929 and his zeal as a "leading conservative reformer" (Fish 1973, 24). In 1925, the so-called Judges Bill led to the codification of federal appellate jurisdiction, greatly strengthening the power of the circuit courts of appeal (Richardson and Vines 1970, 32). In 1929, a National Commission on Law Observance and Enforcement was established under the leadership of George Wickersham who had been Attorney General under President Taft almost twenty years earlier (Fish 1973, 25). Besides various reports, the Wickersham Commission produced "A Study of Business of Federal Courts" which was published in 1934 under the auspices of the American Law Institute with support from the Rockefeller Foundation. Although limited to selected federal courts, this study was one of the first to provide systematic evidence about the flow of cases in federal courts.

This period of increased bureaucratic strength of the professional judiciary ends with the defeat of President Roosevelt's court-packing bill in 1937. Seeking to reverse the trend of negative reviews of some of his programs by the Supreme Court, Roosevelt unsuccessfully proposed to "remake the Federal Judiciary" and expand the Supreme Court by six additional associate justices. However, this defeat of the executive notwithstanding, the administrative and bureaucratic inroads into the judiciary were wide-ranging and deepening. In a forthright review of contemporary trends in law administration covering roughly the same period (1900-1935), Aumann (1940, 226-235) details some of the "remarkable changes which have taken place . . . from the standpoint of organization and procedure."

First, there was an emerging awareness of the growing demand for speedy settlement of cases and a reappraisal of legal precedent (*stare decisis*). Thus, there was a tendency to modify the traditional judicial method of settling conflicts. The American Judicature Society began advocating unified and specialized courts, the American Arbitration Society, founded in 1926, favored less formal methods of settling disputes, and the American Law Institute pushed for a restatement and clarification of law, that is, for codification, simplification, and systematization.

The New Deal, in particular, was instrumental in establishing regulatory boards and commissions. Because the "delay, expense, and technicality" of formal justice provided a negative incentive to move toward "speedy settlement, finality, and freedom from procedural contentions" (Aumann 1940 227), New Dealers advocated a more efficient administrative alternative (Lowi 1969). In general, one could begin to observe a movement toward administrative adjudication and "executive justice" (Aumann 1940; Pound 1940). Certain classes of cases were withdrawn from the conventional methods of procedure and assigned to small claims courts, conciliation, and arbitration. Juvenile and domestic courts were described as "more an administrative than a judicial agency" (Aumann 1940, 233; see also Harrington 1982; Auerbach 1983). In sum, a new attitude had emerged toward the legal order and its traditional values such as separation of powers, supremacy of an independent judiciary, rules of evidence, jury trial, and appeal.

4. 1938-66: The Bureaucratization of Professionals

The next thirty years can best be described as a consolidation of professional judicial power by means of bureaucratization. But at the same time, administrative rationalization—the demon that had been called to facilitate this process and produce efficiency—was not about to remain an acquiescent little helper, but turned into a powerful force in its own right, threatening to transform its original master.

The initial signposts were the formulation of *Standards Relating to Court Organization* by a committee of the American Bar Association, the establishment of Federal Rules of Civil Procedure (Burbank 1982) and the delegation of bankruptcy proceedings from judges to referees in 1938 (Parness 1973; Seron 1978). But the main event was the establishment, in 1939, of the Administrative Office of the U.S. Courts, an agency by means of which the Judicial Conference extended its power through administrative machinery.

The 1939 act establishing the Administrative Office had been in the making since a Judicial Conference meeting in 1926 with a broad bill having been drawn up by the then Attorney General in 1936 and "cooperation between him and Arthur Vanderbilt, then President of the American Bar Association, in 1937-38" (Chandler 1963, 367-95; see also Vanderbilt's 1949 *Minimum Standards of Judicial Administration*). The act of 1939 provided that the Administrative Office would take over the preparation of the total judicial budget from the Department of Justice and systematically collect statistics as to the work of the courts (another function that had up to then been performed by the Attorney General). Moreover, the act established a Judicial Council in each circuit charged with the supervision of the efficiency of all business, including the work of district judges. Finally, an annual conference of all district and circuit judges was to devote itself to the business of the courts and the improvement of judicial administration. The general effect of the 1939 act was to foster efficiency in courts, reporting on delay, more flexibility in the temporary assignment of judges among different circuits, increased attention to judicial statistics, and promotion of pretrial procedures (Chandler 1963, 446-52).

A variety of other organizational changes followed. In 1940, the bankruptcy referee system was reorganized and a Bankruptcy Division of the Administrative Office was established. Court reorganization began in the state courts, although it gained momentum only in the 1950s and 1960s (Mayers 1964, 368; Berkson and Carbon 1978, 19). The U.S. commissioner system was reformed in 1946, providing for the first time regular salaries instead of fees.

In 1946, the Administrative Procedure Act was passed, which established a more uniform set of procedures for regulation. This act was relevant to the courts only insofar as it clarified the importance of judicial review of administrative procedures. Over the long term, the act had the effect of drawing judges into the administrative process, especially at the appellate level (see chap. 7).

In 1948, the Judicial Code was revised, once again, with a view toward providing stronger, more specific administrative language. The circuit councils were given explicit jurisdiction over "the administration of the business of the courts within the circuit," that is, over the district courts (Fish 1973, 389). Still, this strengthened provision would not encounter its real test until the *Chandler* case in 1969, to be discussed later in this chapter. In 1954 Earl Warren was appointed Chief Justice, inaugurating what was later to be perceived as a period of judicial activism and the expansion of the legislative powers of the judiciary. New procedures for adopting Federal Rules of Civil Procedure were introduced in 1958. The provision authorized the Judicial Conference to establish a committee of judges, lawyers, and law professors. The Conference would then receive the committee's recommendations and, if acceptable, refer them to the Supreme Court for action. The procedures would become effective in ninety days unless they were specifically disapproved by Congress within that period. The Judicial Conference was also instrumental in the development of the Criminal Justice Act of 1964, which resulted from the 1963 Supreme Court decision of *Gideon v. Wain-*

wright (372 U.S. 336; Sup. Ct. 792). This decision led to a request by the conference for federal funds for the defense of indigents in federal courts and helped to establish the Public Defender System.

From the perspective of organizational change, the 1950s and early 1960s were a relatively quiescent period for the federal courts. Caseloads were relatively stable throughout the 1950s and the courts seemed to have achieved a certain inner balance. But the historical events and the social movements of the 1960s were to change that appearance and would plunge the federal court system, together with other institutions, into a new period of crisis to which it began to respond in altogether new ways.

5. 1967-present: The technocratic administration of justice

Our account and interpretation so far suggest that the rise of bureaucratic administration after the turn of the century represented a reaction to nineteenth-century formalism and professionalism, but that the nature of the reaction also began to strengthen judicial power as symbolized by the Judicial Conference after 1922 (see also Fish 1973). Similarly, the establishment of the Administrative Office in 1939 meant the organizational consolidation of the judiciary, but it assumed a new form that we called the "bureaucratization of professionals." Thus, while the rise of administrative structures increased the external power of judges and the judiciary as a whole, the bureaucratic changes after 1938 also represent a period of reformalization (i.e., the use of rules, reporting to the Administrative Office, and standardization of administrative procedures) and a gradual transformation of the internal structure of the judiciary.

We are not assuming here a theory of cyclical change, that is, the operation of a cyclical fluctuation between formalism and realism and back to formalism, or between formal and purposive rationality. Rather, our interpretation of the historical shifts observed leads us to posit a dialectical movement whereby external elements threatening to change a given structure may become internalized and lead to a self-transformation of that structure at a later point. More concretely, the new administrative rationality, that at first threatened professional power structures after the turn of the century, was subsequently incorporated into these very power structures, but also began to transform them in the process. Moreover, the process of transformation did not stop arbitrarily. Professional structures were changed by bureaucratization, but so was the bureaucratizing element. Thus, both professional and bureaucratic structures can be said to transform each other in the process of interpenetration. And while the conflict between the two is not over and continues to surface at different times and places, a new synthesis of bureaucratic and professional elements is beginning to emerge that has incorporated features of both yet cannot be said to be either. We are calling this emerging synthesis technocratic administration.

The historical event symbolizing this new approach to administration was the establishment of the Federal Judicial Center in 1967. Significantly, as Peter G. Fish (1973, 371) notes, "The new agency ... was virtually autonomous, its activities supervised by a specially constituted board, rather than by the Judicial Conference or by the Administrative Office director," although the Chief Justice and the Administrative Office director are members of the board, together with two federal appellate and three trial court judges elected for staggered terms by the Judicial Conference.

The Federal Judicial Center had been advocated by Chief Justice Warren and was designed, in President Johnson's words, to "enable the courts to begin the kind of self-analysis, research, and planning necessary for a more effective judicial system" (Fish 1973, 370). The two major functions of the Center were to be training and research. The training function included not only continuing education and in-service training for judges and support personnel, but also information exchange and improving the effectiveness of "the network of regional and national conferences, institutes, and seminars which had been established by the Judicial Conference or by statute" (Fish 1973, 371). The research function is best summarized by Senator Tydings (as quoted by Fish)

> Research into the administrative problems of the Federal courts and development of recommended solutions are the primary functions of the Center. ... It will collect data, conduct research, depict the contours of each problem. Practitioners of the arts and services of administration will then formulate recommendations for solution to the problems. Management experts, systems analysts, data interpreters, personnel experts, as well as judges, academicians, and practicing attorneys, will bring the skill and experience of their disciplines to the Center. (1973; 374)

This is as clear a blueprint for a technocratic mission as can be imagined. As it operates today, the Federal Judicial Center is neither a bureaucratic extension of the Administrative Office nor an instrument of traditional professional control. It has become the symbol of a new approach to administration that seems to have superceded the old dichotomy of professional versus bureaucratic, or judicial versus administrative control. The new approach, like the new Center, works with the concept of total systems in which the particularity of sectional interests is subordinated to the universal interest of the system as a whole. However, this does not mean that sectional interests do not persist. As Fish put it: "... Congress sought to infuse the judiciary's highly decentralized administrative apparatus with a healthy dose of centralized direction—this time in the realm of research and education. But significantly neither judges nor legislators contemplated any fundamental changes in that apparatus" (1973, 378).

This point contains an important insight that was to become painfully visible two years later in the 1969 Supreme Court case of *Chandler v. Judicial Council* [398 U.S. 74, 86 (1969)]. The case, resulting from an attempt of the Judicial Council of the Tenth Circuit to discipline one of the district judges within its jurisdiction, might have become the first real test of the administrative and supervisory powers granted to the judicial councils in 1939 and explicitly reaffirmed in 1948. However, both the council and the Supreme Court backed away from an outright confrontation between administrative and judicial power—the council by modifying its initial attempt to relieve Judge Chandler of all of his duties, the Supreme Court by refusing to review the underlying issue, declining jurisdiction over the case, and denying Chandler's petition on the technical grounds that his petition did not address the council's modified order.

While the Court's majority opinion was written by the then newly appointed Chief Justice Burger, the really important (partially concurring, partially dissenting) opinion was that of Justice Harlan, with Justices Douglas and Black dissenting from the Court's decision on the grounds that Judge Chandler had been deprived of his constitutional rights. Harlan's opinion reaffirms the separation of administrative and judicial functions. The technocratic approach to administration seeks to fuse or subordinate judicial functions to an administrative-systemic rationality. For Harlan, by contrast, the judicial administration of the judicial councils is first and foremost judicial. In his view, the council acted—and could only act—as a (circuit) court, not as an administrative council. Hence, Harlan did not view the powers of the Judicial Council as anything other than *judicial* powers. Therefore, these powers could also not be seen as an incursion on the independence of the judiciary, as Black and Douglas had argued. Consequently, Harlan argued that the actions of the council were, indeed, reviewable by the Supreme Court since it would merely be acting as a higher tribunal that naturally had jurisdiction over the cases of lower tribunals.

The upshot of the *Chandler* case is that judicial councils retain their "administrative" power over the district courts, but that "obscurity continues to veil both the enforcement and review of council sanctions" (Fish 1973, 426). In his discussion of this issue, Fish concludes that the "formal powers ... are at variance with the actual practice of most councils. Informality, negotiations, bargaining, and compromise are the hallmarks of council strategy" (1973, 426). What this means, of course, is that at this level of the judicial system, collegial norms continue to hold sway over bureaucratic actions and that judicial administration continues to be perceived as a juridical, that is, professional, prerogative.

Reflecting the initiative of the federal system, research and development bodies were organized to serve the needs of state courts as well. In 1970 the

Institute of Court Management was established, dedicated to the training of court administrators of state courts. This was followed by the establishment of the National Center for State Courts in 1972, which serves as a research center and clearinghouse for state court administration. In 1974, a committee of the American Bar Association revised the 1938 Standards Relating to Court Administration (see also McGowan 1969, 64-69).[2]

With the establishment of these organizations to rethink, study, and educate the judiciary, a new agenda for reform emerged in state and federal courts. The most notable features of these developments have been a push toward informalism in dispute resolution, a growing awareness of the importance of education of all court personnel, and an ongoing concern to manage judicial administration.

In the federal courts, one of the first steps to implement this more modern notion of management was the creation of the position of circuit court executive in 1971 to "exercise such administrative powers and perform such duties as may be delegated ... by the Circuit Council" (84 Stat. 1907). The tasks delegated to the circuit executive introduced a qualitatively new concept into the agenda of federal court administration; that is, this manager was charged with the complex, and frustrating, task of overseeing and coordinating the work of appellate and trial judges and support staff within a circuit. In an organizational setting marked by judicial autonomy and independence, the task of coordinating work has posed quite a challenge and met with some resistance. For example, about ten years after the adoption of the position of circuit executive, a survey of district court judges and clerks of courts found that there was "little reported need" for an additional court administrator or executive (Dubois 1984). Nevertheless, district court executives were introduced into larger, metropolitan courts on an experimental basis in the early 1980s and, reflecting the research and development mind-set of technocratic administration, were monitored to describe, and share across courts, the duties performed by these new executives (Eldridge 1984).

With a view toward streamlining and simplifying the appellate process in 1973, the Freund Commission (Federal Judicial Center 1973) recommended, among other things, the abolition of three-judge tribunals and the establishment of a National Court of Appeals. It was the recommendation of this commission that there was a need for a new appellate court situated between the courts of appeal and the U.S. Supreme Court. This new court was to be charged with the task of screening out certain appeals and helping to reduce the workload of the Supreme Court. The proposal became a point of debate within the judicial community (Klein and Witzum 1973, 717). Indeed, an intermediate appellate court has not, to date, been established. In 1982, the Chief Justice put forward a proposal to establish an Intercircuit Tribunal to be composed of sitting appellate judges who are to be charged with the task of hearing cases on reference from the Supreme Court. Though there has been some support, the proposal has not moved forward, no doubt because it raises many complicated political questions (also see Posner 1985).

At the district court level, the accent on dispute resolution has also been one of simplification, diagnosis, and informality. Clearly, the most commonly discussed change has been the expansion and conscious use of plea bargaining to resolve criminal cases. Underscoring the acceptance of this less formal route to disposition, the Supreme Court held in 1973 that plea bargaining is "an essential component of the administration of justice" (*Santobello v. New York*, 404 U.S. 257).

Changes in the civil arena have been equally notable, if somewhat less discussed. Building on the creativity permitted through pretrial conferences, in the late 1970s selected federal district courts introduced court-annexed, nonbinding arbitration programs to resolve smaller diversity cases. While the details of these programs vary from district to district, the general thrust of the initiative is to call upon lawyers in the community to volunteer their time to sit and hear cases and to then issue a "ruling"; these programs are non-binding in the sense that decisions of arbitrators may be appealed to the court (for a further discussion, see Lind and Shapard 1981; Provine 1986, 43-67). Initially, this program was introduced into four district courts and subsequently expanded to ten more; again, the Federal Judicial Center has been an active participant in this program as it has been called upon to monitor the impact of arbitration.

Underscoring this push to find creative solutions to resolve civil disputes, Rule 16 of the Federal Rules of Civil Procedures (FRCP) was amended in 1983. In the original 1938 version of Rule 16 the discussion of the kinds of activities to take place during pretrial were somewhat vague, but contemplated preparation for trial. In the 1983 amendments to the Rule, two new elements of pretrial are now spelled out: procedurally, cases must be scheduled; substantively, settlement should be included among the topics for discussion during pretrial. Furthermore, the amendment instructs districts to work out their own procedures to be clarified through local rule.[3] The 1983 amendments to the rule suggest an agenda for pretrial that may, or may not, be preparation for trial and contemplate that courts will take early and assertive control of pretrial preparation. The amendment, then, formally decentralizes decision-making about procedure to judges in respective courts, while also encouraging a stronger managerial twist to pretrial oversight.

Decentralization, scheduling of the case, and settlement discussions in light of the scope of the dispute suggest a procedural reform built on the notion that processing a civil case should fit specific demands. Whereas the older model of adjudication was built on the assumption that all disputes seemed to require, more or less, the same mode of treatment, this amendment suggests that dispute resolution must "fit" the issues posed, that is, that there is no one procedure that is appropriate in all instances. Assessment, analysis, and appropriate treatment to be worked out on a case by case basis carry decentralization one step further—from the court to the case itself. Illustrative of this change, Judith Resnik argues that the recent amendments have "undermined" the "trans-substantive" premises of the 1938 project (1986, 526). Another commentator has written that "advocates of managerial judging are making a fundamental critique of the existing procedural regime" (Elliott 1986, 310). There has, indeed, been an evolving disenchantment with standardized civil procedures that is quite clearly articulated in the amendments to Rule 16 of the FRCP.

The accent of this organizational environment is on change, creativity, and experimentation. In response to the expectation of unpredictability, court managers have also expanded techniques for ongoing education and dissemination of materials through seminars, video cassettes, and newsletters as a way to reassert and rearticulate the common culture of judicial administration. Judges who have developed innovative strategies for resolving civil disputes are called upon to share their ideas with others (Provine 1986). Thus, the education of federal judges has revolved around an effort to help them develop techniques for managing and organizing their office and staff and to inform them of the innovative ideas of their peers.

This, too, is a notable departure from more traditional practices. Historically, judges, much like doctors, have had a great deal of control over the form and substance of their work. Thus, more self-conscious efforts at education and training are an interesting and important departure from an earlier model where a judge simply came on the bench and learned by trial and error. Today, it is assumed that there are benefits to be gained from sharing a body of evolving wisdom concerning techniques for record keeping, scheduling, using law clerks effectively, drafting opinions, or managing a docket (Miner, 1987).

Conclusion

In this recounting and interpretation of the history of rationalization of the federal judicial system, enough has been said to indicate the forces at work, the nature of the trends, and the issues involved. But lest one thinks that rationalization represents an inevitable, unidirectional development of a technocratic system, one should be aware of the opposition, resistance, and occasional throwbacks, which sometimes reassert the ethos of earlier periods and other value positions, for example, professional or bureaucratic ones. We believe that the rationalization of the judiciary is closely linked to the larger movements of the economy and to the state in the twentieth century. The rationalization of the judicial system can, therefore, be seen as both cause and consequence of the crisis of the judiciary and of the rule of law as we will show in the course of this book.

CHAPTER 2

*

The Rising Demand for Court Services: A Historical View

Since the New Deal and post-World War II period, U.S. federal district courts have experienced a sharply rising demand for services. In this chapter, we begin by documenting the scope of the increase in the caseload confronting courts. Consideration will turn on the question: What are the dimensions of the increase in the workload of the federal district courts? In the following chapter we will then be able to consider two additional questions: What factors explain the rise in litigation in a forum that may not be quantitatively large, but that adjudicates disputes and policy conflicts of national social and economic importance?[1] And, to what extent do forces other than population growth—for example, the structure of the American political economy—help to account for the unprecedented changes confronting the courts? While the next chapter will be devoted to the problem of explanation of these processes of change, the present chapter provides a description (see also Clark 1981).

Thus, we report changes in the demands on U.S. district courts from 1904 to 1985. Our focus will be on the change in the incidence of court filings over time as well as on the total demand for court services in terms of volume and variability of cases. This focus necessarily requires a historical overview of the courts' task structure[2] that have occurred during this century, the variability of these changes, and their components.

Because this issue has become the center of a hotly contested debate in the academic and popular press, it is essential to clarify our approach. In response to former chief justice Burger's many claims that the United States is on the verge of a litigation crisis, legal scholars and political scientists have undertaken an examination of this proposition. Indeed, this work (see, e.g., Lieberman 1981, 1984; Galanter 1983; Daniels 1984) has shown that on balance state court filings, controlling for population growth, have probably declined (Krislov 1986, 362). While this may be accurate for state courts, the federal picture is different. Furthermore, exclusive focus on changes in the size of an organization's task structure can be quite misleading. Extensive comparative research on organizations has demonstrated that the variability and complexity of the task structure are equally, if not more, important indicators of demand (Anderson and Warkov 1961; Perrow 1967; Child 1973; Heydebrand 1973); in keeping with this tradition, we will consider changes in the size and variability of the district courts' task structure. As we demonstrate, the task confronting the federal district courts has become absolutely larger, more variable, and—albeit indirectly—more complex over the course of the twentieth century and especially since 1960.

The Rising Volume of Demand: 1904-1985

Like all administrative statistics collected for in-house consumption, these data—especially for the early decades—are probably not completely accurate due to problems of definition and classification as well as to general problems of reporting and collection reflecting the state of the art in the early part of the century. The data are, however, the best approximation available and probably represent a fairly close estimate of the trends in the volume and nature of the tasks confronting the federal courts.[3]

From these data it is evident that, during the first eight decades of this century, the total volume of cases filed in federal courts has grown almost tenfold, from 33,376 (1904) to 326,354 (1985; see table 2.1).

Table 2.1
Changes in the Task Structure of the Courts, 1904-1985

| | Filings | | | Filings per 100,000 Adults (18 years +) | | |
Year	Civil	Criminal	Total	Civil	Criminal	Total
1904	14,888	18,488	33,376	29.9	37.1	67.0
1910	13,788	14,864	28,652	24.0	25.9	50.0
1920	22,109	55,587	77,696	33.1	83.9	116.2
1930	48,325	87,305	135,630	60.4	109.0	169.4
1940	32,779	32,958	65,737	35.7	35.9	71.6
1950	52,501	37,165	89,666	50.2	35.5	85.7
1960	56,842	29,257	86,099	48.9	25.2	74.1
1970	87,321	39,959	127,280	64.6	29.6	94.2
1980	168,789	27,968	196,757	103.7	17.2	120.9
1985	273,670	52,684	326,354	—	—	—

Sources: 1904-1930 Annual Report of the U.S. Attorney General; 1904-1930 American Law Institute; 1940-1985 Report of the Proceedings of the U.S. Judicial Conference; 1904-1980 Historical Statistics of the U.S.

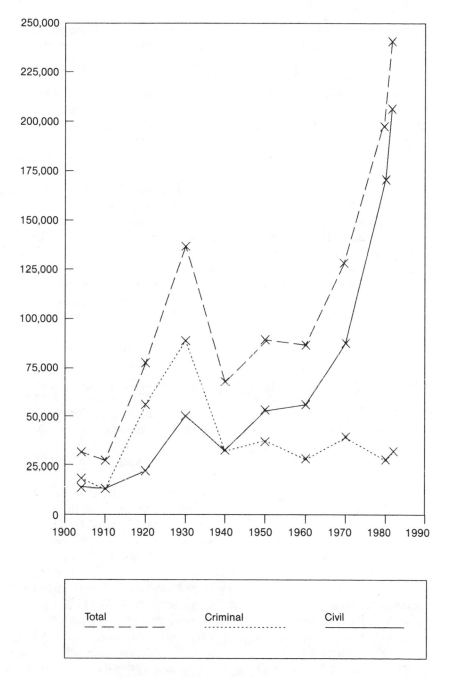

Figure 2.1 Filings

Court filings include two types of formal legal action: civil cases filed by the attorney of a complaining private party or by the U.S. government, and criminal cases filed and prosecuted by the U.S. Attorneys whose offices are attached to each federal district court. On the civil side, this includes corporate cases (e.g., patents, trademarks, and contracts), labor cases (e.g., employer-employee disputes), prisoner petitions, civil rights cases, and personal injury cases to name but a few. On the criminal side, federal district courts hear cases involving violent crimes, burglary, larceny, embezzlement, auto theft, forgery, narcotics, liquor tax, corporate federal crimes, and selective service violations.

As is apparent from table 2.1, civil cases have grown more than criminal ones, from a mere 14,888 in 1904 (less than the corresponding number of criminal cases) to over five times the number of criminal cases in 1985. Part of the increase in civil cases is due to the expansion of categories of case types during the twentieth century. For example, all types of civil rights cases as well as prisoner petitions and labor cases today constitute a notable portion of the district courts' docket; in 1904, these types of cases were nonexistent. That is, the number of case categories entering the federal district courts has grown since the turn of the century. One indicator of task structure—the number of subtasks—has grown over the course of the twentieth century. Organizationally, as the number of subtasks increases, problems of coordination are complicated (Child 1973; Heydebrand 1973). We will have occasion to return to this problem in later chapters.

Because the American population also grew during this period, one needs to relate the growth of cases to the growth of the population. For this purpose, we have calculated the number of filings as a proportion of the legally competent adult population of 18 years and over, divided by 100,000 to obtain a rate.[4] Table 2.1 shows the civil, criminal, and total filings per 100,000 adult population from 1904 to 1980 (see also fig. 2.1).

The number of per capita civil filings (the so-called litigation rate) behaves differently from the rate of criminal filings, as they did in the raw filings. As table 2.1 shows, the civil litigation rate has an overall tendency to increase during this century, though there are some ebbs and flows from decade to decade. By contrast, in 1904 the criminal rate is higher than the civil rate, peaks in 1930, and then tends to decline to its current low point of 17.2 percent in 1980. The increases up to 1920 and from 1920 to 1930 are due, in part, to selective service cases during and following World War I, but especially to liquor law violations resulting from the Eighteenth Amendment, which ushered in the Prohibition era and that was not repealed until 1933.

Clearly, the number of civil filings has not only grown in absolute terms, but it has also increased relative to the population. Does this mean that American society has become more litigious? An examination of the variability of filings over time sheds further light on this question. Using the percent change in filings for each decade as an indicator of the variability (i.e., growth or decline), the answer is not so obvious.

Table 2.2 reports the percent change in total filings for each decade.

Table 2.2
Variability of Filings by Decade, 1904-1985

Intervals	Percent of Changes in Total Filings	Percent of Changes in Civil Filings	Percent of Changes in Civil Filings per 100,000 Adults (18 years +)
1904-1910	−16.5	−8.0	−24.6
1910-1920	+171.2	+60.3	+37.9
1920-1930	+74.6	+118.6	+82.5
1930-1940	−106.3	47.4	−69.2
1940-1950	+36.4	+60.2	+40.6
1950-1960	−4.1	+8.3	−2.7
1960-1970	+47.8	+53.6	132.1
1970-1980	+54.6	+93.3	+60.5
1980-1985	+65.8	+62.1	−

Here we see that there are fairly sizable changes (increases and decreases) at some periods (e.g., 1910-40), but almost no change (−4.1) in 1950-60. These total percentage changes are influenced by the rather erratic behavior of criminal filings in federal courts (see table 2.1). When we look at the percent changes in civil filings, the picture is a bit more steady, showing a general tendency of growth though at uneven rates. The crucial test, however, is the variability of the litigation rate, which reached a high point during the 1920s, decreased during the 1930s with the end of Prohibition, and reached a virtual standstill in the 1950s, lending credence to the proverbial "slowness" of that decade. During the 1960s and 1970s, however, we witness again an increase in the litigation rate due to the social and political protest movements of these decades as well as to the "due process revolution" spawned by the social and procedural legislation of the 1960s.[5]

While the litigation rate has been increasing in the last thirty years, reaching its highest point of 104 in 1980 (table 2.1), there is no way of telling whether this trend will continue. Moreover, the figures in table 2.2 show considerable variability from decade to decade, reflecting both historical and legislative events (see, e.g., Friendly 1973; Chayes 1976).

From the point of view of the work of the courts and judges, the variability of filings—the sudden increases and decreases in the volume of the task—poses an organizational challenge. In contrast to commodity-producing corporations, public service organizations, such as courts, must always be ready to provide their services, whether or not they are actually demanded. Furthermore, public service organizations, including courts, do not control the range of services to be processed. Whereas a commodity-producing organization may determine the opportune time to develop new products, most tasks in a public service organization are decided by acts of Congress or as a result of political contingencies. Consequently, a high degree of variability in the existing demand for services coupled with variability in the emergence of new types of demands or tasks creates special problems. It becomes especially difficult to calculate accurately future demands for services and, hence, personnel needs. We will return to a consideration of the consequences of this problem in later chapters. But with this in mind, let us examine some additional aspects of variability.

The Changing Caseload of Civil Cases: 1904-1985

In order to get a rough handle on trends in the federal district courts' civil caseload we have developed two measures: the proportion of civil filings of total filings and the proportion of U.S. civil filings (where the U.S. government is either a plaintiff or a defendant) of all civil filings.[6]

Table 2.3 reports these developments in the federal district courts from 1904 to 1985, as measured by the percent of civil filings of total filings, and the percent of U.S. filings of civil filings. The proportion of civil filings has increased dramatically from 44.6 percent in 1904, to 83.9 percent in 1985. Thus, as we already noted, at the beginning of the century American federal courts processed more criminal than civil cases. Since 1940, however, the balance has shifted toward civil cases; after 1970 it is safe to say that the typical federal district court is a civil court. Indeed, by 1985 only a little over 16 percent of the court's filings were criminal cases. While not every case involves large corporate issues or sophisticated remedies following demanding civil rights cases, there have been new categories of civil litigation, leading to newer and narrower areas of specialization which, in turn, pose unpredictable challenges for courts (see Chayes 1976; Flanders 1977, 73). We interpret these changes as indicative of an increase in the complexity of the federal civil caseload.

Historical changes in the scope of cases involving the federal government are also important. In 1904, U.S. cases constituted only 12.1 percent of all civil filings. By 1985, the proportion had grown to 42.9 percent, with high

Table 2.3
Changes in Task Complexity, 1904-1985

Year	Number of Civil Filings	Percent of Civil Filings	Number of U.S. Civil Filings	Percent of U.S. Civil Filings
1904	14,888	44.6	1,803	12.1
1910	13,788	48.1	3,170	23.0
1920	22,109	28.5	5,726	25.9
1930	48,325	35.6	24,934	51.6
1940	32,779	49.9	13,001	39.7
1950	52,501	58.6	22,404	42.7
1960	56,842	66.0	20,766	36.5
1970	87,321	68.6	24,965	28.6
1980	168,789	85.8	63,628	37.7
1985	273,670	83.9	117,488	42.9

points characterizing the Prohibition and Roosevelt eras from 1920 to the 1940s. Clearly, the federal government is now demanding a much larger share of the services of its courts than was the situation at the beginning of this century. This is not the whole story; the shift in the basis of jurisdiction of federal courts' civil docket also poses a qualitatively new set of demands.[7] With time, many areas of government litigation may become quite routine and predictable (e.g., social security, VA cases, and student loans); at the same time, however, there has been a constant expansion in the agenda of government questions as Congress has taken steps to alter or to clarify its policies (see e.g., Lowi 1969; Friendly 1973; Freedman 1978).

As the composition of civil filings has shifted over the course of the twentieth century, it is also instructive to look at changes in backlog since 1904, using the number of cases pending at the end of the respective year as an indicator. Table 2.4 shows changes in the backlog and total demand of courts from 1904 to 1985.

As we have noted earlier (see table 2.1), here too we observe that the number of civil cases pending shows a tendency to increase, especially since 1950, whereas the number of pending criminal cases, again, shows a more erratic pattern. Usually, there is greater pressure in criminal matters to achieve swift disposition of the case. This pressure, typically emanating from the government's interest in maintaining civil order and exercising social control (Balbus 1973; Quinney 1974), was given voice in the speedy trial standards promulgated by the American Bar Association and may have con-

Table 2.4
Changes in Backlog and Demand, 1904-1985

| Year | Number of Pending Cases | | | Total Filings | Total Demand (filings & pendings) |
	Civil	Criminal	Total		
1904	46,093	12,084	58,177	33,376	91,553
1910	48,608	9,222	57,830	28,652	86,482
1920	39,042	49,979	89,016	77,696	166,712
1930	58,471	35,849	94,320	135,630	229,950
1940	28,705	9,488	38,193	65,737	103,930
1950	54,229	8,011	62,240	89,666	151,906
1960	60,436	7,616	68,052	86,099	154,151
1970	93,207	20,910	114,117	127,280	241,397
1980	186,113	14,759	200,872	196,757	397,629
1985	250,292	28,951	279,243	326,354	605,597

tributed to the lower number of pending criminal cases reported after 1970. Clearly, though, the number of pending cases is staggering and corresponds in magnitude to the number of filings (see table 2.1), even though the parallel increase of filings and pending cases can be expected on technical grounds, that is, "the number of pending cases increases as the system expands" (Flanders 1977, 74).[8] By combining filings and pending cases, it is possible to measure the total demand confronting courts during a given year. This figure was 91,553 in 1904, but reached over 600,000 in 1985 (see table 2.4; see also fig. 2.2).[9] We will have occasion to examine the environmental determinants of total demand in the next chapter.

Let us look at the number of pending cases in relation to terminations. As a matter of course, one may expect a portion of the number of pending cases to increase with the number of filings. It is therefore necessary to relate the number of pending cases to total demand and, of even greater relevance, to the number of terminations. Table 2.5 presents the results of these analyses (see also fig. 2.3). First, it is apparent that while the absolute number of pending cases has increased from 1904 to 1985, the percentage of pending cases of total demand shows a slight tendency to decrease. Thus, while 63.5 percent of the total demand consisted of unfinished business in 1904, that figure was only 46.1 percent in 1985, with a low point of only 36.7 percent in 1940. A similar observation can be made about the percent of pending cases, suggesting, as we will detail in later chapters, the increased effectiveness of administrative techniques to expedite disposition and to reduce backlog.[10]

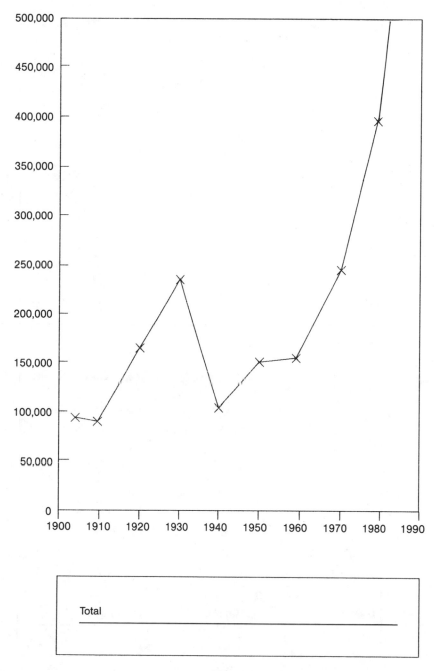

Figure 2.2 Total Demand

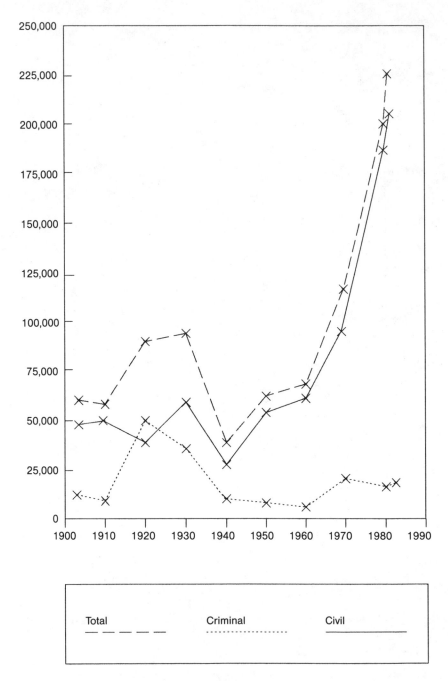

Figure 2.3 Pending Cases

Table 2.5
Selected Aspects of Complexity and Demand, 1904-1985

Year	Percent of Total Pending Cases	Percent of Pending Civil Cases	Percent of U.S. Pending Cases
1904	63.5	75.6	59.8
1910	66.9	77.9	56.1
1920	53.4	63.8	52.4
1930	41.0	54.8	46.1
1940	36.7	46.7	41.3
1950	41.0	51.0	48.1
1960	44.1	51.5	43.4
1970	47.3	52.4	45.0
1980	50.5	50.0	48.0
1985	46.1	47.8	41.0

The findings reported in table 2.5 underscore two important points. First, with the exception of 1980, the pending rate for civil cases is always hiqher than the corresponding rate for all cases. This difference, we feel, may be taken as another indicator of the relatively greater complexity of civil cases than criminal ones. In the aggregate, civil cases tend to be more complicated and contribute disproportionately to the backlog of courts.

Second, the pending rate for government cases is consistently lower than the pending rate of all civil cases. What factors might account for this pattern? We believe that the lower government pending rate helps to explain the pressure—both inside and outside the judiciary—to dispose of government cases expeditiously. This pressure, backed up by the tremendous resources of the Department of Justice, has gradually increased over time. Furthermore, some government cases raise enforcement issues that require speedier intervention to be effective. By contrast, the civil pending rate has been relatively stable since 1950, indicating that the rate of unfinished civil business has been on a par with new civil filings.

Additional light can be thrown on the question of relative backlog, and specifically of government pressure to move cases expeditiously, by examining the ratio of pending cases to terminations, a procedure suggested by Flanders (1976, 65).

The findings reported in table 2.6 again show a downward trend in unfinished business for both civil and U.S. cases. But, we also see more clearly now that since 1930 the ratio of U.S. pending cases to U.S. civil terminations has been notably lower. This does not say anything about possible fluctuations

Table 2.6
Relative Backlog of Civil and U.S. Cases, 1904-1985

Year	Number of Civil Terminations	Ratio of Civil Pendings to Civil Terminations	Number of U.S. Civil Terminations	Ratio of U.S. Civil Pendings to U.S. Civil Terminations
1904	13,052	3.53	2,066	1.30
1910	12,909	3.77	3,464	1.17
1920	18,883	2.07	5,526	1.14
1930	48,465	1.21	24,722	0.86
1940	35,597	0.81	13,420	0.68
1950	51,200	1.06	22,731	0.91
1960	56,715	1.07	20,897	0.76
1970	80,435	1.16	23,767	0.86
1980	160,481	1.16	61,065	0.96
1985	269,848	0.92	121,425	0.67

during the decades examined, but the downward trend is apparent and suggests that the federal courts are becoming more efficient in disposing of cases and reducing the burden of unfinished business, especially where the government is concerned.

Conclusion

We may sum up this overview by concluding that there is an overall increase in the volume and variability of civil cases in federal district courts. If variability in the volume of cases results in sudden overload, the addition of new categories of civil filings adds its own share to the problem of unpredictability and backlog in courts.

Furthermore, these findings suggest that the government has increasingly made its presence felt in courts. Quantitatively, the proportion of civil cases involving the government has grown; qualitatively, the government appears to be able to obtain court services on a priority basis. We will return to this issue in more detail in chapter 7.

It is our contention that the two most proximate causes of strain of the federal judicial system are the increasing demand for services that tend to put pressure on courts and the relative decline in the court's resources that is fueled by the larger budgetary problems of the state. In this chapter, we have documented one leg of the problem—the increasing demand for services. Before turning to an analysis of the fiscal and personnel resources of the courts, however, we must examine the sociopolitical and economic factors that explain this rising demand.

Lest we leave the wrong impression, taken alone these data do not document a "crisis." Rather, we must examine the implications of caseload trends in the context of the district court's organizational procedures, capacity, resources, and practices—the subject of the following chapters.

CHAPTER 3

*

The Ecological Environment of Courts: Political Economy and Demography

We now turn to an explanation of the changes in the incidence of filings and the prevalence of demand in federal district courts by examining the effect of the aggregate ecological environment on the task structure since 1950. Our central focus will be an analysis of the demographic, economic, and governmental factors—in short, the structure of the external environment—that has given rise to civil litigation. By way of comparison, we will also examine briefly the effect of ecological variables on criminal filings in federal courts.

Our focus in this chapter will specify our discussion in chapter 1 of the degree of environmental complexity as an aspect of courts as organizations. That is, the discussion in this chapter documents the fact that environmental variables explain a notable share of the variance in civil litigation in federal courts. To this end, we will consider a number of related questions: Which aspects of the environment have the strongest effect? How do environmental factors shape the filings of specific types of cases (civil rights, corporate, labor, etc.)?

Clearly, legislative developments are an important factor for understanding changing patterns of civil litigation. Because we are looking at the entire court system, however, this variable may be treated implicitly as it manifests itself in the types of cases litigated before federal courts. For purposes of this analysis, therefore, legislation will be treated as an indirect response to the ongoing changes in the larger society.

A second consideration to be addressed is the mobilization of law. In order to explain the filing of a case in a given court, it is not only necessary to consider the environmental conditions for litigation and the availability of statutes under which a case may be filed, but also the activation of a particular statute by a particular plaintiff. This activation of legal rules and statutes by litigants is known as the mobilization of law (Black 1973; Sarat and Grossman 1975).

We have no direct measure of how law is mobilized for litigation. All we know is the actual number of court filings which, in the absence of other information, must serve as a proxy for both the availability and the mobilization of law. It is conceivable that there is, for example, a civil rights statute on the books that is not activated to the fullest extent possible, even though there may be much actual conflict over civil rights in a given community. This question cannot be addressed with our data. For our purposes, the actual filing of a civil rights case in a district court must, therefore, serve as an indicator that (a) a civil rights statute exists and (b) that it has been mobilized. We believe a focus on statutes and their mobilization is perhaps important for studying the transformation of disputes into lawsuits, but less important for studying the structural effects of the environment on actual litigation in court, as we are proposing to do here.

The issue of the relation between the demand for court services and the larger social structure has received considerable attention, but from different theoretical perspectives and at different analytic levels.

At the most general theoretical level, much of the sociology of law provides a conceptual framework for the proposition that structural changes in a given society will affect not only the nature of law and legal institutions, but the nature and frequency of disputes (Abel 1973; Felstiner 1974; Black 1976; Hunt 1978). Emile Durkheim (1964) expected societies with a complex division of labor and with organic solidarity to develop restitutive civil law and to experience a rise of administrative regulation, leading to increased public law litigation (see also Schwartz and Miller 1964).

This functionalist view of the correlation between societal and legal complexity needs, however, to be supplemented, if not modified, by the observation that law may be created and imposed by the state and by other "legitimate" power holders for the purpose of domination and repression, rather than for mere functional regulation. Thus, in echoing Bakunin's view of the state as the historical cause of violence, Stanley Diamond (1974, 255) shows that the "rule of law" imposed by the modern state tends to displace and to destroy the indigenous "order of custom" by which societies regulate themselves. The active role of government in shaping legal outcomes must, therefore, be considered as an explicit hypothesis in addition to the effects of mere societal complexity (see also Black 1976).

In line with this expanded view of environmental forces having political significance, Weber (1966) argued that the development of industrial capitalism had led to an increase not only in the law of coordination (private and civil law) and the law of subordination (public law), but also in the rationalization of the law itself. Thus, formal-legal rationality would come to characterize both law and legal institutions, among others (see also Trubek 1972a,

1972b; Unger 1976; Tigar and Levy 1977; Nonet and Selznick 1978). Clearly, Weber was aware of the potentially coercive and repressive aspects of law, even though the categories of his sociology of law did not permit an explicit treatment of law as a form of domination (see also Hunt 1978, 148). Outside the boundaries of legality and formal-legal legitimacy, domination could not be grasped as "legal." Within these boundaries, power and domination were legitimate and, therefore, were seen as taking the form of rational authority. Despite this double constraint, much of the current scholarship on modern dispute institutions, including courts, emphasizes the pervasive influence of the political environment on litigation for both theoretical (Wechsler 1953; Peltason 1955; Goldman and Jahnige 1985) and historical reasons (Hurst 1950; 1980-81; Friedman, 1975).

At the level of empirical analysis, the proposition of environmental influence on the caseload of courts has received somewhat less, although still considerable, attention as well as some confirmation. An early study of the business of the U.S. Supreme Court (Frankfurter and Landis 1928) was clearly informed by the assumption that there was a causal link—however complex—between social structure and court business (but see Casper and Posner 1974 who assign greater causal importance to the expansion of legal rights and changes in court policy, a perspective that has some validity especially in view of the massive legislative changes of the 1960s).

In a pioneering study of federal courts, Richard J. Richardson and Kenneth Vines (1970, 45 ff.) argue that "judicial constituencies usually reflect the distinctive characteristics of state political and social systems" and conclude that the local legal and political culture has an influence on the business and operations of the courts (p. 174). An analysis of state supreme court decisions by Burton M. Atkins and Henry R. Glick (1976) shows that environmental characteristics of the courts' jurisdictions are important predictors of the types of issues and cases resolved by these courts. Atkins and Glick focused particularly on political factors such as political participation and party competition, characteristics of the legislative, judicial, and executive branches of the states, and intergovernmental fiscal structures; socio-economic characteristics such as levels of industrialization, education, and income; and public policy profiles in the areas of education, welfare, highways, and natural resources.

Two well-known empirical-historical studies of litigation in California (Friedman and Percival 1976; see also Lempert 1978) and Spain (Toharia 1976) suggest that litigation and subsequent formal dispute settlement may be at relatively high levels at the beginning of industrialization in a given social structure, but tend to remain stable or taper off with further advances in economic development due to the social and economic costs of litigation. Frank Munger (1988), in a longitudinal study of litigation in the courts of three West Virginia coal-mining counties from 1870 to 1925, shows that litigation is not a functional or automatic response to industrialization or rapid social change, but a conflict strategy of corporate and individual actors in particular socioeconomic and historical circumstances. Finally, based on an analysis of litigation (1902-1972) in the federal courts, Joel Grossman and Austin Sarat come to a surprising conclusion that asserts "the relative unimportance of external, environmental factors" (1975, 344). These authors found negative or weak correlations between the litigation rate (number of civil filings per 100,000 population) and such socioeconomic factors as the percent employed in manufacturing, population density and urbanization, farm value, and industrialization.[1]

Moreover, in an attempt to explain the absence of findings, Grossman and Sarat suggest that changes in federal law "uniformly applied in all federal courts may help to account for the relative unimportance of external, environmental factors" (1975, 344). But it is necessary to realize that it is precisely the uniformity of federal law and the relative passivity of federal courts that permit the social scientist to study the differential effects of environmental factors on civil and criminal court filings. Consequently, when uniform federal statutes are mobilized in different districts, the specific environmental characteristics of their jurisdictions affect this process in different ways and degrees, resulting in different outcomes.

Thus, we may indeed study the effect of environmental differences and variation precisely because we can hold the existence and nature of the law constant, as it were. This logic of research also holds, of course, where federal law changes over time, since the change is introduced into the federal judicial system as a whole, whereas the districts vary in terms of environmental dimensions (see also Goldman, et al. 1976, 216).[2]

Following the theoretical and methodological leads of organizational ecology and sociology of law, our statistical analysis is designed to relate various indicators of the task structure of the courts, some of them familiar from the previous chapter, to an environmental profile of the courts' jurisdictions aggregated from U.S. census data for 1950, 1960, and 1970. The guiding working hypothesis for the overall analysis may be stated simply: the jurisdictional environment, including the relative presence of the state apparatus in the form of government agencies, affects the volume and range of demand for judicial services. As one judge put it in commenting on the "crisis" of the courts: "What has caused such an avalanche in the caseloads of the federal courts? Obviously the growth and increasing complexity of our society and evolving notions of the role of federal courts in mediating problems traditionally handled on state and local levels. . . ." (*The Third Branch: Bulletin of the Federal Courts*, May 1977).

Explaining the Volume of Litigation

The external environment of the federal courts is shaped by at least three related processes. First, the processes of economic growth and decline generate social conflicts and, hence, legal disputes that are apt to affect the caseloads of courts. Given the American capitalist economy's need to grow, to produce surplus value, to realize profits, and to accumulate capital, conflicts about the distribution of social wealth and the continued inequality among social groups may provide a steady flow of business for federal courts. Insofar as courts provide a forum where these conflicts may be resolved, they may contribute to the stability and legitimacy of dominant social and economic relations. To gauge the overall influence of economic factors on the courts' task structure, we have selected the number of corporations with at least one hundred employees as an indicator of these factors.

Second, the state has become increasingly involved in the allocation, distribution, and redistribution of wealth, in the attempted stabilization of the private economy's gyrations (inflation, recessions, stagnation, and stagflation), and in the production of social services that the private sector cannot or is not willing to provide. To be sure, the state's role in this process is supported by a liberal tradition that has "been responsible for the accumulation of capital and for the protection of agencies doing the accumulating" (Wolfe 1977, 198). This includes a vast network of regulatory agencies whose long-term goal is to help insure economic stability and growth. It also includes the emergence of a neocorporatist "industrial policy" in which labor unions are being asked to cooperate with corporations and the government under the umbrella of a new consensus or "social contract" (Thurow 1980; Magaziner and Reich 1982; Reich 1983; Rohatyn 1983). But at the same time, the American political arena supports a democratic tradition that must respond to the popular demand from below for equality of opportunity and for a semblance of fairness. The history of the transformation of the state has been documented by others and need not be recounted here. As we have argued, the crisis of the judiciary reflects the contradiction between these opposing policies—accumulation versus legitimation—which the state is called upon to pursue.

Supporting this theme, today, the public sector (i.e., federal, state, and local governments) is of course the largest single employer in the United States (see, e.g., Kolko 1976). In 1965, the National Bureau of Economic Research found that the United States is the first nation to have "more than half of the employed population ... not involved in the production of food, clothing, houses, automobiles and other tangible goods" (as quoted in Miller 1968, 5), not a surprising trend for an increasingly capital-intensive and service-oriented economy. Hence, the presence of government agencies in a district court's jurisdiction, be it at the federal, state, or local level, should, we suggest, affect the business of that court in a variety of ways, not the least of which are suits by and against the federal government.

Finally, the tensions between state and economy unfold in urban settings. Industrialization has driven urbanization and, conversely, been driven by urbanization, especially in view of the need to concentrate large working populations in urban manufacturing centers, the creation of new white-collar strata by the growing service economy, and the concentration of minorities and immigrants in urban labor markets. Urbanization and structural differentiation of an environment are concepts that imply large, concentrated, heterogeneous populations as well as the existence of specialized services and an expanded division of labor. The distinction between "town" and "country" captures the symbolic importance of this modern way of life. Whereas "country" life evokes images of people held together by familial and communal ties, small industries, "natural" instruments of production, and the use value of products, city life is characterized by the dominance of impersonal role relations, mass production, exchange value, and money. As Marx and Engels observed in 1845, "the greatest division of material and intellectual labor is the separation of town and country" (Marx 1967, 443). The modern American urban setting is more than the natural evolution of traditional rural communities. Rather, it is one outcome of the historical transformation of capital. It is for this reason that urbanization and industrialization are closely related and must be seen as separate aspects of a common process of social change (Harvey 1976). Consequently, population density, an indicator of urbanization, should have an impact on court caseloads. Indeed, it was the size of a district's population that was traditionally taken as an indicator of the need for additional judgeships, similar in significance to the correlation between population and political representation for federal expenditures in congressional districts. As we shall see, however, population variables are not necessarily or always the most important determinants of court business.

Thus to summarize, we have selected population density, the number of corporations, and the number of government employees[3] as roughly representative indicators of three key environmental dimensions of federal district courts: demography, economy, and government. Table 3.1 reports the results of the simple correlation and a multiple and partial regression analysis, that is, the standardized partial regression coefficient (b or beta), the unstandardized partial regression coefficient (b), and the joint effect (R^2) of population density, corporations and government on demand. All variables, except population density, are divided by population size of the district. Demand represents the overall volume of cases in a district court and combines pending civil and criminal cases with civil and criminal filings for the years 1950, 1960, and 1970.

Table 3.1

Effects of the Environment on Per Capita Demand, 1950-1970[a]

Demand/Population

	1950			1960			1970		
	r	*b*	*b**	*r*	*b*	*b**	*r*	*b*	*b**
Population Density	.66	7.50-07[b]	.71****[c]	.57	2.50-07	.29**	.43	1.20-07	.25**
Number of Corporations/ Population	−.03	−.12	−.17	.04	−3.70-04	−.01	−.03	3.00-04	0
Number of Government Employees/ Population	—	—	—	.73	.08	.57****	.73	172.60	.09
1/Population[d]	.07	427.70	.16*	.11	214.50	.09	.30	.02	.58****
R^2			.49			.59			.58

a The number of district courts is N = 84 for 1960 and 1970; N = 83 for 1950.

b The unstandardized regression coefficient for population density in 1950 is b = 7.50-07 = .00000075. We are using the scientific notation to simplify the presentation and to facilitate comparisons across years.

c Significance levels are given even though we are analyzing the total population, not a sample. The following levels are used: * = .05; ** = .01; *** = .001; **** = .0001.

d Please note that all the variables are divided by the population size of the district, except population density. The term *1/Population* or *1/P*, is included in this and other analyses to eliminate any possible spurious contributions to the regression from ratio variables that have common terms in the denominators.

e The points made in footnotes a, b, c, & d refer, as well, to the other tables in this book that have a similar format.

The results of the multiple and partial regression analysis show that in 1950, population density (b* = .71) contributes the main share to the explained variance in total demand. In 1960 and 1970, population density (b* = .29 and .25) remains significant, though relatively less so. The findings reported for 1960 suggest that it is the combination of demographic and governmental activity that contributes to a notable explanation (R^2 = .59) of the court's demand. Finally, examination of the unstandardized coefficients from 1950 to 1970 discloses a real decline in the influence of population density on demand.

Rationalizing Justice

These findings may be further illuminated by looking at the effect of these three independent variables on total and civil filings (see table 3.2). The results presented in table 3.2 underline and clarify the findings reported in table 3.1. Again, these findings suggest that the presence of corporations does not have an effect on total filings in 1960 and 1970, except for a negative effect in 1950. The number of corporations, however, emerges as a significant factor in an explanation of civil filings in 1950 ($b^* = .38$). Population density has an effect on total filings in 1950 and 1960, but on civil filings only in 1960. By 1970, the effect of density disappears.

Table 3.2
The Environment and the Filings and Litigation Rates, 1950-1970

| | | Total Filings/Population | | | Civil Filings/Population | | |
		1950	1960	1970	1950	1960	1970
Population	r	.58	.45	.46	.22	.63	.46
Density	b	4.10-07	1.30-07	2.70-08	1.10-08	1.30-07	2.60-08
	b*	.63****	.21*	.09	.16	.29****	.12
Number of	r	−.10	0	−.07	.41	.05	.06
Corporations/	b	−.09	−.03	−.01	.02	2.80-03	−.01
Population	b*	−.22*	−.05	−.05	.38***	.01	.04
Number of	r	−	.64	.78	−	.84	.73
Government	b	−	.06	.02	−	.05	.01
Employees/	b*	−	.52****	.70****	−	.69****	.64****
Population							
1/Population	r	.07	.13	.21	.06	.10	.20
	b	254.30	262.00	176.57	13.10	88.50	125.94
	b*	.15	.12	.15	.08	.06	.15
R^2		.40	.45	.62	.20	.77	.55

The relative size of the governmental sector shows a strong effect on both total and civil filings in 1960 and 1970. On balance, these findings suggest that the presence of government activity is a central factor in an explanation of court filings in federal district courts.

In sum, we may begin to explain rising demand for federal court services as the result of environmental complexity, where governmental presence appears to have a particularly powerful effect on filing rates. By the same token, the demographic factor tends to have a relatively declining effect on the number of cases. Together, the findings suggest that by 1970 the activities of the government are more central in an explanation of the activities of district courts. While urbanization is a part of capital accumulation and state intervention, it appears that more purely urban-rural differences have become relatively less important in an explanation of federal district court case filings.

The Court's Civil Docket: A Closer Look at the Range of Civil Litigation

It is clear from the previous findings that environmental effects explain a notable share of the variance in the incidence of filings and the total demand for court services. Let us now turn to a closer examination of the nature of these demands and their implications for understanding task complexity.

In service organizations such as courts of law, the problem of task complexity deserves special consideration. It is particularly difficult to categorize specific types of cases as intrinsically more or less complex. As many lawyers will argue, court cases are not by definition complicated. Rather, the social, political, and economic issues embedded in a dispute are what tend to make legal challenges more or less complicated than another dispute of the same type—a point noted by Tocqueville (1969) when he commented on Americans' proclivity to turn social disputes into legal problems. This issue is, moreover, especially problematic for court managers in their attempts to rationalize, through the system of weighted caseloads and forecasting, the work of judges and to gauge and improve judicial productivity. It is not surprising to read that "the weakness of current forecasts is their inability to adequately incorporate the impact of future events" (*The Third Branch: Bulletin of the Federal Courts*, November 1975), including, of course, the impact of future changes in social, political, and economic relations.

We have already seen that by 1970 the overall demand for court services was interwoven with governmental activities. Furthermore, if lawyers are correct in their observation that cases become complicated as they raise more demanding social, political, or economic issues then it follows that various types of civil cases will be associated with, and explained by, different constellations of environmental variables. That is, labor or corporate cases, for example, become more complex legal procedures as the social relations of production present ever new problems and demands.

By way of developing an initial and overall picture of the relationship between environmental and task complexity it may be informative to examine the effect of environmental variables on complex civil and criminal cases in 1970. The dependent variables reported in table 3.3 represent those cate-

Rationalizing Justice

gories of civil and criminal cases which, in the aggregate experience of courts and judges, are time-consuming, legally complicated or challenging, protracted, or otherwise "complex" (having many diverse elements), based on a weighting system developed by the Federal Judicial Center (Flanders 1976). On the civil side, corporate and civil rights cases are typically included. The complex criminal caseload is similarly defined, that is, it constitutes a selection of typically complicated cases and excludes routine matters.

Table 3.3
Environment and Task Complexity in 1970

	Complex Civil Filings/ Population			Complex Criminal Filings/ Population		
	r	b	b^*	r	b	b^*
Population Density	.55	1.10-09	.03	.35	1.30-09	.01
Corporations/ Population	−.13	−5.20-04	−.01	.05	1.70-03	.01
Mergers/ Population	.41	4.3	.36****	.02	−.17	0
Government Employees/ Population	.68	1.60-03	.39****	.72	9.90-03	.74****
Blacks/ Population	.64	3.30-04	.41****	.27	−2.60-04	−.10
Net Migration	.00	1.70	.03	−.10	−4.50	−.03
1/Population	.11	29.8	.17*	.33	130.70	.22**
R^2			.72			.58

Before turning to the findings shown in table 3.3, some of the environmental variables require comment. In order to represent the scope of the dimensions of the jurisdictional environment, we have added a number of independent variables to the equation. Thus, in addition to the independent variables used in tables 3.1 and 3.2, population density, number of corporations, and number of government employees, we have added variables that measure corporate merger activity, the presence of the black population, and net migration.[4]

Table 3.3 shows clearly that, overall, environmental variables are more strongly associated with complex civil litigation ($R^2 = .72$) than with complex criminal filings ($R^2 = .58$). Turning to a consideration of the key factors in these equations, the findings show that mergers ($b^* = .36$), government ($b^* = .39$), and the black population ($b^* = .41$) are the significant factors in an explanation of complex civil filings in federal district courts. In this regard it is interesting to compare the impact of corporations and mergers: supporting the patterns reported in tables 3.1 and 3.2, the presence of corporations is an insignificant factor in an explanation of these civil filings. As noted, this is not the case with mergers. To the extent that mergers capture an aspect of monopolistic economic transactions, this finding suggests that federal court business is more responsive to this concentrated sector of the economy than to the more traditional, competitive sector (O'Connor 1973).

By contrast, economic and demographic variables are insignificant in explaining complex criminal cases. The primary factor in an explanation of these cases is the presence of the government ($b^* = .74$). But this is not surprising because federal criminal cases either involve governmental personnel and activities, or are prosecuted by the Department of Justice (or U.S. Attorneys) involving such matters as organized crime, narcotics, immigration, embezzlement, forgery, and interstate theft.

In general, however, the influence of the environment on criminal prosecution is more indirect and mediated than is the case for complex civil litigation. The criminal docket reflects a host of influences, ranging from environmental pressures and opportunities to the availability of government surveillance, the probability of detection and apprehension, the decision to prosecute selectively according to internal policies and priorities (e.g., narcotics versus interstate auto theft), the willingness to invest resources in the information-gathering apparatus necessary for successful prosecution, the resources of the defendants and their relative capacity to mount an effective legal defense, and the risks and stakes involved in conviction. While some of these elements also operate in civil litigation (e.g., risk-benefit evaluation and resources), there is less organizational or governmental interference in the decision to file a civil suit and, hence, a greater likelihood for litigation to be activated directly by dispute-generating conditions in the larger society.

In sum, the findings reported in table 3.3 suggest that complex civil cases are more responsive to environmental factors than complex criminal ones, that is, that the range of civil litigation is more tightly interwoven with the shape of the court's surrounding political economy and with ethnic heterogenity. To clarify the relationship between environmental and task variables further, it may be helpful to disaggregate civil filings into subcategories. To this end, we will focus on corporate, civil rights, and labor cases as well as prisoners' petitions and personal injury cases. The sociolegal history surrounding each of these case categories itself tells an important and complicated story about the role of courts in mediating social relations and tensions between blacks and whites, men and women, or labor and management.

Our question here is somewhat different and turns on a concern to understand the scope of the organizational problem posed by variable environmental and task structure relations. If combinations of environmental variables explain a notable share of civil case categories then these findings would lend strong support to the claim that shifting socio-political relations and tensions are an inescapable part of the *organizational* context of courts as service organizations, that is, that complex social conflicts are a part of the court's task structure. For our purposes, and for the history being discussed here, this is an especially important question. A complex and varied task structure poses a difficult managerial problem. Keeping in mind our larger concern to understand the organizational dilemma confronting federal district courts we may ask: Do court managers confront a task structure that is not easily amenable to routine administration? Let us consider, then, the factors that explain selected, but important, categories of civil litigation for 1970.

Corporate Cases. To quote Calvin Coolidge's famous aphorism, "The business of America is business." Starting with small businesses, entrepreneurs tapped new technologies, reorganized work and the relations between people, and invented the corporate entity, thus transforming the nature of industrial capitalism (Polanyi 1957; Chandler 1977). The success of this endeavor is, of course, the centerpiece of American history and complements, as we have noted earlier, a liberal political tradition.

Ironically though, liberal claims to the contrary not withstanding, "capitalists generally detest competitive capitalism and are the first to undermine it" (Wolfe 1977, 162; also see McConnell 1966; Kolko 1967, 1976; Miller 1968; O'Connor 1973). In various guises and permutations, we may trace a long history of government effort to stabilize market forces. In this regard, the courts played a central role in developing legal protections for corporate "individuals." The power of the court, beginning with Marshall, in protecting the nationalization of corporate forms through private litigation is an important aspect of early American history and continues, in fact, to play an important, though less crucial, role to the present.

The findings of table 3.4 substantiate this claim. Cases include contracts, patents, real estate, interstate commerce, antitrust, and bankruptcy and tax suits, that is, those civil matters that arise between and within business units.[5] Thus, the dependent variable shown in table 3.4, corporate cases, encompasses both private economic-legal questions (e.g., contracts,) as well as public economic-legal questions (e.g., the Economic Stabilization Act of 1970 and review of enforcement). The independent variables shown in table 3.4

are different from those reported earlier and require some explanation. The demographic variables include population density, the black population, and the total population. Economic and governmental variables are measured in a slightly different way. In order to represent the scope of the economic dimension of the jurisdictional environment, we have constructed an index of industrialization that is a composite of the number of corporations and mergers, the volume of retail and wholesale trade, and the number of white-collar workers. The second leg of the political economy, the legal-governmental sector, is represented by another composite index comprising government employees and lawyers. The socio-economic level refers to a composite of median education and median income.[6]

Table 3.4
Environment and Corporate Litigation in 1970

Environmental Variables	Corporate Cases	
	r	b^*
Industrialization[a]	.60	.98
Legal-Governmental Sector[a]	.55	.42
Net Migration	.28	−.24
Black Population	.41	−.20
Socioeconomic Level[a]	.33	−.08
Population Density	.38	.10
Total Population	.37	−.55
R^2		.49

[a] For an explanation of these composite indicators see n. 6.

From table 3.4 it is clear that these conflicts that appear at the district court level emerge from the twin effects of the modern political economy. The index of industrialization has a strong partial ($b^* = .98$) effect on corporate cases. But the legal-governmental sector also has a sizable effect, although it is lower ($b^* = .42$) Population variables (net migration, the black population, density, and population size) have only moderate or negative effects.

Given the nature of the structural units involved in corporate litigation, these results are not surprising. They suggest that it is the *structural* aspects of corporate-government interaction of the jurisdictional environment that shape corporate litigation. This point is further supported by the weak effect of socio-economic level on the corporate caseload.

Yet, the combined effect of these environmental variables on corporate caseloads ($R^2 = .49$) is not as great as one would expect.[7] There are a number of reasons for this. First, despite the economic and political dominance of the Fortune 500 companies, the size and complexity of corporations remains extremely varied—from small, competitive units to large, oligopolistic firms. Hence, many corporate cases raise questions that are unaffected by the contemporary thrust of economic concentration and government regulation.

Second, while corporate work is an important part of legal practice in general (Auerbach 1976; Heinz and Laumann 1982; Nelson 1988), both the plaintiffs and the defendant's attorneys are essentially gate-keepers. This means that attorneys have input into determining if a case should proceed to the court for litigation or, once in the court, should proceed to trial. Thus, an out-of-court settlement or a pre-pretrial settlement is a function of a set of complex interactions and negotiations. Corporate cases are, given the enormous financial sums that are often at stake, quite likely to be resolved through precourt settlements. This is not to say that there are fewer corporate disputes in total but rather, corporate issues may raise such challenging and expensive questions to the respective parties that there is pressure to settle out-of-court where the decision-making process need not be left to an unknown third party—a judge or a jury.

Corporate cases, on the whole, may be the most demanding work of lawyers; they nevertheless do not today place as dramatic a demand upon courts as compared to other types of cases. This remains true as such cases meander through the judicial hierarchy of the federal court system. "The power of the Supreme Court, at its peak in the early years of the twentieth century, has diminished since then to a position of relative insignificance in economic-policy matters. This is not to suggest that the Court is wholly without power, simply that its eminence has vanished" (Miller 1968, 63).

Civil rights cases. The second aspect of the civil caseload to be examined is civil rights litigation. Unlike corporate cases, however, civil rights cases are a relatively recent category of federal litigation. Yet, the political forces giving rise to civil rights litigation are deeply ingrained in American politics. The democratic tradition takes as its starting point the claim to equality and participation. In its earliest form, however, America's gentlemanly statesmen permitted a rather narrow construction of democratic participation (see e.g. Krislov 1968, 57-58; Skowronek 1982). Indicative of this point, only property holders were granted the right to vote—the most basic ingredient for democratic participation among equals.

Yet, the success of the American project, coupled with the pressures of industrialization, urbanization, migration, and immigration left an imprint on those at the bottom, including a populist demand for democratic participation. In the end, this process helped to transform America into an urban society of employed workers who posed all the potential demands of an alienated and exploited working class (Wolfe 1977). The political response to this process of economic transformation and political struggle was the extension of basic democratic rights, creating a new variation on the theme of political equality.[8]

This extension of democratic rights, animated by the hopes of minimizing the potential for social upheaval, eventually, though belatedly, had its effect on the federal courts (Krislov 1968, 3). The first and most clear-cut turn in this direction occurred right after the Civil War with the passage of the Civil War Amendments granting the abolition of slavery (Thirteenth), due process of law to all citizens (Fourteenth) and the extension of the franchise (Fifteenth).

The passage of these amendments along with other civil rights legislation would eventually provide the bedrock upon which civil rights and public interest lawyers would chip away with some success, and many setbacks, at the inequalities left by a liberal tradition (Piven and Cloward 1977; Handler 1979; Kinoy 1983). The common approach of public interest lawyers is to use the courts as an arena to test, to engineer, and to extend rights of this nation's racial, ethnic, and political minorities (Kluger 1976; Freeman 1978; Handler 1979; Sparer 1984).

The findings presented in table 3.5 clearly substantiate the operation of these forces for the early 1970s. That is, legal questions involving such issues as one's voting rights, access to public accommodations, and employment discrimination are associated with governmental activity ($b^* = .28$) and with the black population ($b^* = .55$). This analysis suggests that the majority of civil rights cases is initiated from within the political economy, activated by the demands of a large black population in a given district.[9]

Labor cases. Today, as civil rights lawyers continue the battle for equal protection under the law, labor litigation, by contrast, often appears calmer, somewhat more amiable, if not friendly. But in the not too distant past the fight for employees' rights and union protection was one of the bloodiest and most explosive areas of social confrontation. If during the post-Civil War period "liberty of contract" was used in support of monopolistic expansion, this logic carried over into the arena of early labor questions. That is, freedom of contract was also the grounds upon which the court denied unions the right to organize ([*Adair v. United States* 208 U.S. 208 161 (1908) and *Coppage v. Kansas* 236 U.S. 1 (1915)], as cited in Klare 1978). Recall that the law recognizes individuals qua individuals, but takes a myopic view of groups

Rationalizing Justice

Table 3.5
Environment and Civil Rights Litigation in 1970

Civil Rights Cases/Population

	r	b	b*
Population Density	.36	−1.30-09	−.05
Corporations/Population	−.20	−9.70-04	−.04
Mergers/Population	.15	1.20	.16
Government Employees/Population	.57	6.80-04	.28**
Blacks/Population	.69	2.70-04	.55****
Net Migration	−.06	1.00-10	0
1/Population	.18	22.50	.21*
R^2			.59

or organizations; hence, employee and employer were approached as equals by the courts, "even though that employer was a collectivity, a corporation, and a person in law only by application of a transparent legal fiction" (Miller 1968, 57). With the passage of the Sherman Anti-Trust Act, the Court had more ammunition in its arsenal to squelch unionization. To add to our growing list of legal ironies, the Supreme Court, on the same day in 1895, ruled that income tax legislation was class-based, that the Sherman Anti-Trust law did not apply to manufacturers but that it did apply to unions (Wolfe 1977, 54).

Whereas civil rights litigation is the product of extended democratic principles, the transformation of labor law from criminal to civil practice illustrates the effects of a more complex division of labor, a society held together by organic, rather than mechanical modes of solidarity and hence a greater emphasis upon restitutive, rather than repressive, sanctions (Durkheim 1964; see also Wolfe 1977). While the legal transformation of employer-employee relations echoes the Durkheimian thesis, it did not transpire in a smooth, evolutionary manner. Business fought unionization, only gave in when there were few remaining options, and then negotiated with the more conservative unions (Klare 1978; Kinoy 1983). The legislative outcome of this conflict, the

National Labor Relations Board, was a lawyer's creation that mediated, at least temporarily, the most obvious points of conflict between labor and management.

Since World War II, the paradigm of labor law has changed in the direction of industrial pluralism and a new conception of "shared authority" or "joint sovereignty" of management and labor (Stone 1981). Today, when labor questions are posed before the district courts, it is assumed that both labor and management are equal parties to the dispute and that they generally come seeking legal enforcement of an administrative guideline. That is, an underlying social tension has been transformed into legal questions that pose essentially technical enforcement issues raised by various pieces of labor legislation (e.g., the Fair Labor Standards Act, the Labor Management Relations Act, and the Labor Management Reporting and Disclosure Act), thus leaving the larger questions untouched and, in the process, subverting the development of a strong, radical labor movement (Weinstein 1968; Piven and Cloward 1971; Kolko 1976).

The significance of labor cases being an "internal" issue of the industrial sector is underlined by the findings, or rather by the absence of findings, reported in table 3.6. Our analysis shows that environmental factors do not explain the enforcement issues in labor relations that come before federal

Table 3.6
Environment and Labor Law Litigation in 1970

	Labor Cases/Population		
	r	*b*	*b**
Population Density	.29	7.40-10	.05
Corporations/Population	−.17	−2.20-03	−.18
Mergers/Population	.21	.77	.19
Government Employees/Population	.37	3.50-04	.27
Blacks/Population	.26	6.40-06	.02
Net Migration	.02	1.40	.01
1/Population	.03	6.70	.12
R^2			.20

district courts. But it underscores the varied roles that federal courts are called upon to play in a regulatory state: in this context, the district court acts as an enforcer of regulatory matters, rather than as a dispute resolver or law-maker.[10]

Prisoner's petitions. The steps leading up to a "civil rights revolution behind bars" (Goldfarb 1975, 369) has generated a change in the court's docket and in the proliferation of prisoner petitions (see e.g., Marquant and Crouch 1985). The Eighth Amendment prohibits "cruel and unusual punishment" for those awaiting trial in jail or convicted of crimes in prisons.

Beginning in the early sixties there was an unexpected demand to reconsider the conditions of American prisons as riots within these institutions echoed the words of their compatriots on the streets. The grievances coming from these prisons were consistent, the clearest being a demand to be treated with some dignity.[11]

Despite the Eighth-Amendment provisions and the claims of modern penology and science, conditions in American prisons can only be described as usually cruel punishment.[12] Implicitly supporting these conditions, the courts at that time took little responsibility, arguing that "separation of powers demanded this" (Goldfarb 1975, 373).

But a number of Supreme Court decisions gave reform lawyers means to demand reconsideration of this judicial posture. The 1966 *Miranda* decision coupled with the 1964 *Escobedo* and *Mapp*[13] decisions gave reformers their first important wedge. The Court recognized that the normal practices and procedures of police and prosecution might prejudice defendants' chance to a fair trial.

From another angle the Court ruled in *Monroe v. Pape* that federal courts, under the 1964 Civil Rights Act, were to hear cases in which individuals claimed interference with federally protected rights, even if all state remedies had not been exhausted. Then, in 1964 the Supreme Court ruled that the Civil Rights Act of 1964 did protect the rights of convicts in state prisons.[14] Taken together, the Court gave movement lawyers grounds on which to argue that, by modern "scientific" standards, prisons are unfit for human development or rehabilitation. In one of those "fascinating examples of social engineering" (Goldfarb 1975, 438), using lawyers, experts, and courts, grounds were established to test the meaning of the words contained in the Eighth Amendment. The "jail-house lawyer" was the product of these events. Beginning with a trickle of cases in 1964 (6,240) prisoner's petitions soon presented yet another crisis in the courts as 16,266 such cases were filed by 1971, an increase of 160 percent in a six-year period (*Administrative Office of the U.S. Courts Annual Report of the Director,* 1964, 1971).

As table 3.7 suggests, these cases are directly associated with and explained by the presence of the government ($b^* = .49$) and black population (b* = .45) The strong effect of the governmental sector in 1970 is noteworthy. (Interestingly, these findings parallel those for civil rights cases reported earlier.) The record of the Burger court in protecting the rights of prisoners was, in fact, a more liberal one than that of the Warren court (Goldfarb 1975; Fiss 1979, 4; McNeil-Lehrer Report 9 July 1979). But, of equal note, Chief Justice Burger was especially concerned with court administration, i.e., with "bringing the courts into the twentieth century" as advocates of court modernization usually put it. Because prisoner petitions are complaints of America's unwanted who file, as one judge has called them, "repetitive and frivolous actions" (*The Third Branch, Bulletin of the Federal Courts*, July 1977), it should come as no surprise that reform strategies were quickly proposed that seek to administer this caseload. The Bureau of Prisons and the Parole Commission have "work[ed] together to reduce these prisoner cases" (*The Third Branch, Bulletin of the Federal Courts*, April 1977) by holding preliminary hearings within prisons. In the interim, most prisoner petitions are initially heard by magistrates (Seron 1983) with the expectation that the burden on judges will be reduced. It appears, in fact, that the number of such cases have begun to decline to only 3,713 cases in 1979-80 (*Annual Report of the Director of the Administrative Office of the U.S. Courts*, 1980, tables C-3, A-18). However, it remains to be seen if this filtering method improves the conditions of prisons or temporarily placates the prisoners.

Table 3.7
Environment and Prisoner Petitions in 1970

Prisoner Petitions/Population

	r	b	b*
Population Density	.41	5.80-10	−.01
Corporations/Population	−.08	8.80-03	.13
Mergers/Population	.06	−.54	−.03
Government Employees/ Population	.70	3.40-03	.49****
Blacks/Population	.64	6.10-04	.45****
Net Migration	−.02	2.20-09	.03
1/Population	.13	12.10	.04
R²			.62

Personal injury cases. While prisoner petitions are one of the newest areas on the civil agenda, personal injury cases, like aspects of corporate work, are one of the oldest. Generally, personal injury cases are filed in federal court because of diversity of jurisdiction, that is, cases in which the plaintiff and defendant are citizens of two different states with at least ten thousand dollars in controversy.[15] While a large share of the caseload, these matters are often viewed as straightforward, simpler disputes.

Indeed, it was one of former Chief Justice Burger's main initiatives—though unsuccessful—to return the diversity docket to states. In his efforts to introduce this reform, Burger often had the support of the corporate "hemisphere" of the profession (Heinz and Laumann 1982) as well as their more prestigious legal organs such as the Association of the Bar of the City of New York. For example, this organization has advocated "no fault" systems for many types of personal injury cases even though members of this association "never touch" such cases. Of course, such steps are "vigorously opposed by personal injury plaintiffs' lawyers" (Heinz and Laumann 1982, 327) To date, personal injury lawyers have successfully marshalled their political clout and populist appeal—often through the American Trial Lawyers Association—to keep the diversity docket in the federal courts. As the legal profession becomes further specialized and bifurcated, it will be interesting to follow whether the personal client "hemisphere" of the legal profession will continue to exert its influence in this arena of reform debate.

Table 3.8
Environment and Personal Injury Litigation in 1970

Environmental Variables	*Personal Injury Cases*	
	r	b^*
Industrialization[a]	.50	.40
Legal-Governmental Sector[a]	.52	.15
Net Migration	.07	−.65
Black Population	.56	.18
Socioeconomic Level[a]	.24	.03
Population Density	.51	.25
Population Size	.38	.32
R^2		.60

[a] For an explanation of these composite indicators, see n. 7.

For now, however, these cases remain a burden on the federal district courts, as table 3.8 reveals.[16] Personal injury cases are the results of the unfortunate accidents of an industrialized society ($b^* = .40$) whose victims live in urban areas (population density $b^* = .25$; population size $b^* = .32$; black population $b^* = .18$; net migration $b^* = -.65$). All things considered, industrialization and demographic factors combine to explain 60 percent of the variance in personal injury cases.

Though Chief Justice Burger was unsuccessful in his efforts to return diversity cases (and hence most personal injury matters) to state courts, intermediate alternatives to adjudication are in place. Currently, for example, ten federal districts are experimenting with court annexed, nonbinding arbitration where a panel of between one to three volunteer attorneys hear and recommend their estimate of the value of the dispute; parties can, of course, request a *de novo* hearing, though many courts view arbitration as a substitute for trial. Thus, a pretrial alternative is being developed to siphon these cases off the adjudicatory track.

Conclusion

In this chapter, we have documented the influence of the aggregate ecological environment on the task structure of courts. To explain the rising demand for court services we analyzed the partial and joint effects of economic, governmental, and demographic variables on the court's caseload in 1950, 1960, and 1970. Characteristics of the jurisdictional environment's political economy predict and explain those of the court's docket. These environmental influences were present in 1950 (and probably before), but they are especially clear in 1960 and 1970. More specifically, it is the effect of governmental presence that is notably significant for understanding the growth of the civil docket and has the most important impact on the courts.

This set of findings should be of special interest to many court administrators who use population size as the principal basis for determining the need for additional judicial slots. Caseload developments are not the result of simply more people in an area producing more work for the courts, the implicit assumption of this perspective. Though one tends to forget, people move to locales to find work or retire, not the other way around (see also Harvey 1976). The primary impact of these locales is their ensemble of structural characteristics, i.e., large-scale organizations, corporations, and government agencies.

In addition, we examined specific categories of the district court's civil docket in 1970, including corporate, civil rights, labor, prisoner, and personal injury cases. These analyses disclose two important sets of findings for under-

standing the organizational structure of federal district courts. The environmental profile of a district is more strongly associated with complex civil than
with complex criminal cases. Furthermore, our findings show that most of
the specific categories of civil cases are associated with, and explained by,
dimensions of the court's environmental profile.

What do these findings suggest about the organization of federal district
courts? First, we may trace an interdependence between the district courts
and the surrounding political economy. Second, the civil caseload of district
courts is affected by structural developments in the surrounding political
economy. Indeed, together these findings suggest that environmental relations are an intrinsic part of the court, that these relations shape the contours of the federal district courts' tasks.

The history of these structural relations—tensions between economic and
political forces—discloses the formation and transformation of social relations between, for example, blacks and whites, employees and employers,
men and women, rich and poor. Because this history has hardly been static, it
is reasonable to speculate that a central feature of its future will be change.
For federal district courts, this means that its tasks will, in turn, vary as new
problems of American society unfold. While it would be foolhardy to predict
the content of change, it would be equally naive to suggest that the court can
close itself off from socioeconomic transformations.

For court managers this poses a dilemma. There is very little, if any,
evidence to suggest that the task structure of the federal district courts will,
on balance, fit a predictable mold. Rather, these findings suggest that court
managers must cope with a variable and changing task structure generated
by the structural tensions of American society. This is, we would submit, a
complex demand. The multiple ways in which the judicial community is artic-
ulating and addressing these organizational developments is the subject of
the following chapters.

CHAPTER 4

*

Rising Demand and Declining Resources: A Double Bind

Echoing Schumpeter's (1954) insight, government budgets provide a useful barometer for gaging political and social priorities. In the post-New Deal period, debate has often focused on the tension between military and social welfare expenditures—underscoring larger political themes in American society. These and other social expenditures, (e.g., health, education, and welfare; urban renewal; the War on Poverty in the 1960s; and criminal justice in the 1970s) document recent demands and cleavages (Bachrach and Baratz 1962; Wolff 1968; Connolly 1969; Lowi 1969; Rogin 1970; Balbus 1971, 1972; O'Connor 1973; Giddens 1973; Wolfe 1977; Cohen and Rogers 1983). But, what of governmental tasks, such as those performed by the judiciary, which took form prior to the expansion of the welfare state at the turn of the century? Has the changed structure of American government and the expansion of the presidency, with the centralization of power within the executive branch, altered the role of the courts?

In order to get a handle on these questions and on their impact on the courts, we turn to some budgetary considerations. The first section presents an analysis of the fiscal budget of the third branch from 1910 to 1984, focusing on a comparison between the federal courts and other social expenses. We begin by mapping the historical parameters of the courts' task, followed by a consideration of some institutional responses to new demands. Section 2 presents an organizational analysis that links the increase in demand (documented in chaps. 3 and 4) to the personnel and organizational resources of trial courts.

The Relative Share of the Budget of the Third Branch: 1910-1984

In a society of local markets, or as Tom Bottomore (1964) has put it, a "property owning democracy," what was the role of the judiciary? The Founding

81

Fathers argued that "among the advantages promised by a well-constructed Union, none deserves to be more accurately developed than its tendency to break and control the violence of faction" (*Federalist Papers*, No. 10, 77). The structure of the judiciary itself is debated in *Federalist Papers* Nos. 78-81; the jurisdiction of courts, the length of office of judges, and other details are discussed. The place of the judicial branch within a government of "limited" powers is, however, the crucial issue to understand; as Sheldon Wolin (1960) suggests, the *Papers* are in fact a discussion of how to "constitutionalize" Hobbes's *Leviathan*. Thus, the courts are to "mitigate" the severity and "confine" the operation of laws that are implicitly "unjust and partial" (No. 78, 470). Building on a Lockean liberal tradition, it is assumed that there will be economic inequalities and hence there will be laws with unequal effects. While not as strong a voice as liberalism, the democratic ideal of equality before the law is also among the earliest cornerstones of justice. Yet,

> it was only with tremendous upheaval wrought by the Civil War . . . that the principle of equal protection of laws, with all that it could be held to require in making sure that the laws themselves were genuinely equal, was written into the Constitution and converted from a general and insubstantial ideal into a positive obligation of government. (Pole 1978, 2)

It is the task of the courts to control the severity of such laws, in a word, to legitimate the "various and unequal distribution of property." These governmental tasks are to be accomplished by the courts taking a passive, merely responsive, posture to the affairs of society. In other words, in the tradition of common law, judges are seen to be independent arbiters of conflicts of interest between individuals (Chayes 1976).

The American court system has been called upon to guarantee equally the substantive and procedural rights of all citizens. Foreshadowing the tension inherit in this role, Alexander Hamilton argued that if the courts are to be "a bulwark of a limited constitution" (*Federalist Papers* No. 78, 469), then they must be granted independence to act without reprisals. The guarantees of "formal rationality" will be preserved if the courts can preside autonomously over conflicting claims of polity, law, and economy, a set of tasks that naturally followed from the English common law tradition (Hay 1975; Klare 1978, 1979). Indeed, in its earliest form the courts could claim hegemonic control over formal rationality, even in the face of "reckless material exploitation" (Hartz 1955, 56), precisely because a comprehensive understanding of democratic equality—political, social, and economic—had not yet been raised in the political arena. In this context the principles of legal rationality, with an emphasis upon rules, procedures, and the logic of legal reasoning, took root and shaped a professional-judicial form of organization.

The nineteenth century witnessed a challenge to the Lockean creed (Commager 1950; Hofstadter 1955; Wiebe 1967; Kolko 1976) and, in its wake, the role and posture of the judiciary. In the face of massive immigration, universal franchise, urbanization, and overwhelming industrialization democratic "pluralism" became an important cornerstone of legitimation, giving rise to multiple reforms of the political fabric, including popular elections, professional party workers, systematic campaigns (Kolko 1976; Wolfe 1977, 64) and new public services (Katz 1978). These turns in the democratic road encompass an emergent ideology of democratic pluralism.

> Such reforms were responsive to the democratic, not the liberal, element within the state. For that very reason, passage of them was neither smooth nor complete; yet they were victories for popular rule that fundamentally altered the beneficiaries of state action. (Wolfe 1977, 76)

As the possibility for working-class consciousness—the other side of pluralism—emerged in the United States, a governmental posture of limited power was less feasible or viable. "Representative" democracy became "mass" democracy and a "tolerance for diversity" (Wolff 1968) was proclaimed through various Progressive Era reforms beginning in the 1890s.

Placed in this context, the judiciary is an older political organizational form of legitimation, that is, a traditional form tied to a professional-judicial base. Because part of its task has been to mitigate the conflicted development of political factions and to preserve social harmony (Krislov 1968), the courts have also shared in the process of equalizing access to political institutions. But, the courts participate in the preservation of social harmony within the limitations described by a special and historically specific tradition. Thus, the courts are only granted the power to respond to "conflicts of interest;" they are passive organizations with little, if any, real power to initiate activities (Black 1973; Friedman 1975). That is, the courts may only respond, rather reluctantly, to the demands that are generated by the larger political economy. Historically, courts are not granted a mandate to intervene actively in the social, political, and economic conflicts of interests that permeate the social fabric (Choper 1980; but see also Miller 1968). And, as these conflicts are exacerbated, the passive pose of the courts becomes cumbersome.

Yet, we have seen that the courts face new demands for service—as well as new fiscal constraints. Examination of budgetary allocations concretizes this point and provides an enlightening entry point for discussion.

Table 4.1 shows comparative budgetary allocations for the judicial branch, the legislature, and the Department of Justice from 1910 to 1984. These figures document that from 1950 to 1970 the judiciary was allocated .06 percent of the total federal budget—even less than the amount earmarked for the

Table 4.1
The Budget of the Judiciary, Legislature, and Department of Justice, 1910-1984
(millions of dollars)

	1910	1921 [a]	1930	1940	1950	1960	1970	1980	1984
1. Judiciary (total)	8.0	13.3	18.1	11.0	24.00	49.40	124.80	564.000	907.000
2. Judiciary (% increase)	—	66.0	36.0	−65.0	118.00	106.00	153.00	351.000	61.000
3. Judiciary (% of total)	—	0.2	0.5	0.1	0.06	0.06	0.06	0.097	0.107
4. Dept. of Justice (total)	1.0	4.0	41.4	53.0	136.00	267.00	743.00	2,632.000	3,262.000
5. Dept. of Justice (% increase)	—	256.0	935.0	28.0	157.00	96.00	178.00	254.000	24.000
6. Dept. of Justice (% of total)	—	0.7	1.0	0.6	0.30	0.30	0.40	0.454	0.384
7. Legislature (total)	14.0	19.0	20.0	23.0	67.00	112.00	341.10	1,218.000	1,583.000
8. Legislature (% increase)	—	39.0	3.0	18.0	188.00	68.00	205.00	257.000	30.000
9. Legislature (% of total)	—	0.4	0.6	0.2	0.20	0.10	0.17	0.210	0.187
10. Total U.S. Budget	—	5,116.0	3,440.0	9,297.0	40,312.00	79,574.00	197,885.000	579,613.000	848,483.000
11. Percent Increase of Total, U.S. Budget	—	—	−49.0	170.0	334.00	97.00	149.00	193.000	46.000

Source: *The Budget of the United States Government*, fiscal years ending 1984, 1972, 1962, 1952, 1942, 1932, 1922 (summary Table 3); *Congressional Record 94* (II) 80th Cong., 2d sess., pp. 2576-77.
[a] 1920 actual outlays not available.

legislative branch. The outlays for 1980 and 1984 do show a slight increase in the relative share of the total budget to the third branch, .10 and .11 percent, respectively, but an increase that is offset by comparable changes in the other sections of the budget under examination. Since 1930, however, the Justice Department, one agency of the executive branch, has received a larger share of the budget than either the legislative or judicial branches. While there is a marked increase from 1921 to 1930 in the budgets of all three agencies under examination, the most notable change is the allocation for the Justice Department.[1]

The Justice Department includes the U.S. Attorney's Office, the FBI, the Federal Prisons, Immigration and Naturalization, and more recently the National Institute of Justice (NIJ, formerly LEAA) and the Bureau of Narcotics and Dangerous Drugs. The tasks of these agencies include law enforcement (FBI), prosecution (U.S. Attorney's Office), and "applied" research and development (NIJ). The Justice Department received its biggest increase in the decade from 1921 to 1930 (935 percent); moreover, its budget has continued to increase at varying rates ever since. More specifically, during the depression years (1930-1940) Department of Justice allocations increased by 28 percent; whereas judicial allocations decreased by 65 percent. Furthermore, while the judiciary has received a significant increase in its budget in the post World War II period (see table 4.1), the absolute and relative share remains markedly less than that of the other governmental units under examination.

The relative allocation of the budget to each of these agencies during the 1930-1940 period suggests a shift in government priorities. The courts are the fulcrum of a traditional, adversarial form of dispute resolution. The Department of Justice is one important gate-keeper to that arena. As we have seen, dispute resolution is a passive form of political legitimation. By contrast, gate-keeping—deciding criminal caseload priorities and U.S. plaintiff cases to be filed—is a proactive process that may shape, define, or clarify political agendas of presidential administrations. In the face of exacerbated economic demands brought on by the depression, the shift in allocation, with an increase to the Department of Justice, captures a larger trend in American political institutions, particularly the role granted the executive to shape political debate and implement policies.

The courts confront a dilemma. They receive a small share of the budget to perform dispute resolution and, furthermore, they operate within a set of basic organizational constraints. As we showed in chapter 2, the judiciary may be described as a collegial, traditional, and professional organization that is pivotal to its political role. In the face of contemporary demands, however, this eighteenth century solution has become part of the problem.

In a rather prophetic comment, Saint-Simon wrote, "The philosophy of the 18th century was critical and revolutionary; that of the 19th century will

be inventive and organizational" (as quoted in Wolin 1960, 376). Or, as former Chief Justice Burger has stated in more colorful language, "In the supermarket age we are trying to operate the courts with cracker-barrel corner
methods and equipment; vintage 1900" (1971, iv). Today the judicial branch
is called upon to adjudicate cases generated by a growing pluralist spectrum,
yet is under pressure to participate in a modern organizational revolution.
While the collegial organization of the courts has been crucial for preserving
adjudicatory procedures, due process, and the rule of law, the concrete budgetary constraints coupled with a modernist demand for efficiency and accountability go a long way toward explaining why the courts have been forced to
introduce organizational planning, or in Karl Mannheim's words, "the rational
mastery of the irrational" (1940, 149). But the courts are not alone as "the
measurement of productivity in the formerly exempt soft services, the slogan
of accountability, the introduction of management-by-objectives and zero-
base budgeting, all accompanied by shortages of certain kinds of fiscal
resources, become a steady trend. . . ." (Oppenheimer and Canning 1978-79,
20). Seen against the backdrop of ever-increasing budgetary constraints it
becomes apparent why the courts are under pressure to introduce more efficient management, i.e., administrative solutions to the problem of adjudication. Interestingly, if one compares increases in the allocation of funds to the
judiciary with the growth in caseload (see table 2.1), one might conclude that
funds have been at least adequate to demand, especially for recent decades.
But before drawing such a conclusion, it is necessary to examine more closely
where these funds have been allocated within the judicial system itself. Let us
turn, therefore, to an examination of the judiciary's intraorganizational budget.

The judicial-nonjudicial division within courts represents, in simplified
form, the difference between the professional and bureaucratic strategies of
organizational coordination. Table 4.2 shows the total budget and certain
subcategories of the judicial and nonjudicial budget of the third branch from
1950 to 1984.

We have taken judges' salaries and jury expenses to represent judicial
expenses and salaries of support staff and the Administrative Office of the
Courts and the Federal Judicial Center to represent nonjudicial allocations
and administrative support services. Do the intraorganizational priorities of
the courts suggest a more expanded role for support and administrative functions in the late twentieth century?

An examination of table 4.2 discloses that the nonjudicial side of the
court's allocations has received a larger share, both in absolute and relative
terms, of the resources available than the judicial side since 1950. Moreover, while both categories of judicial expenses have increased absolutely, the
relative allocation to each subcategory of judicial expenses has tended to
decrease.[2]

Table 4.2
Budgetary Outlays and Percentage Increase for the Total Judiciary, Judicial, and Non-Judicial Allocations, 1950-1984
(Thousands of Dollars)

	1950	1960	1970	1980	1984
1. Total Judiciary Budget	23,967.0	49,363.0	124,842.00	564,145.0	907,411.0
2. Percent Increase over Previous Point		106.0	156.00	351.0	61.0
3. Appeals and District Courts	21,764.0	45,703.0	120,715.00	520,075.0	844,734.0
4. Percent Increase		110.0	164.00	331.0	62.0
5. Salary of Judges	4,828.0	9,097.0	22,725.00	45,768.0	69,880.0
6. Percent of Total (Row 3)	22.2	19.9	18.20	8.8	8.3
7. Percent Increase		88.0	150.00	101.0	53.0
8. Fees of Jurors and Commissioners	3,304.0	4,735.0	14,794.00	36,471.0	44,355.0
9. Percent of Total (Row 3)	15.0	10.0	12.00	7.0	5.3
10. Percent Increase		43.0	212.00	147.0	22.0
11. Salaries of Support Personnel	9,859.0	21,485.0	52,405.00	196,971.0	329,742.0
12. Percent of Total (Row 3)	45.0	47.0	42.00	37.9	39.0
13. Percent Increase		118.0	149.00	276.0	67.0
14. Administrative Office of the U.S. Courts	510.0	1,170.0	2,618.00	14,282.0	27,092.0
15. Percent of Total Judiciary (Row 1)	2.0	3.0	2.00	2.5	3.0
16. Percent Increase		129.0	124.00	446.0	90.0
17. Federal Judicial Center			576.00	8,113.0	8,913.0
18. Percent of Total Judiciary (Row 1)			0.50	1.4	1.0
19. Percent Increase				1,309.0	10.0
20. All Other Categories of Judiciary	1,693.0	2,490.0	933.00	21,675.0	26,672.0
21. Percent of Total Judiciary (Row 1)	7.1	5.0	.75	3.8	2.9
22. Percent Increase		47.0	167.00	2,223.0	23.0

Source: *The Budget of the United States Government,* Analysis of Budget Outlays by Agency, 1984, 1972, 1962, and 1952.

It must be noted here that the positions of judges and support staff are linked in the sense that, as a rule, each federal judge, once appointed, is provided a courtroom deputy (now referred to as a caseload manager), a secretary, and one or two law clerks. For example, the number of authorized judgeships more than doubled between 1950 and 1980, from 215 to 516. It can be assumed that there was a corresponding increase in the number of courtroom deputy clerks, secretaries, and law clerks during this period. Nevertheless, the correspondence between judicial and nonjudicial positions is not perfect, nor can it account for the relative decline of judicial compared to nonjudicial resources.

Moreover, the growth of the Administrative Office and the Federal Judicial Center has been significant in its own right, indicating the increased importance of these agencies to the operation of the courts, especially after 1970. As we indicated in chapter 1, the Administrative Office was established in 1938 and is responsible to the Judicial Conference, the governing body of the federal judiciary. Among its functions are the overall administration of the federal court system, the collection of statistical data, and the publication of annual statistical reports, including *Annual Management Statistics*.

By contrast, the Federal Judicial Center, established in 1968 with a relatively small initial budget, as table 4.2 shows, was mandated to be the research and development arm of the third branch. The personnel of the Federal Judicial Center includes lawyers, political scientists, and sociologists, as well as systems analysts and other technical experts. For example, one of the more important research projects undertaken by the Federal Judicial Center was the development of COURTRAN, the court's first computerized data processing system (*The Third Branch, Bulletin of the Federal Courts* May 1976, January 1977, December 1979; Wheeler and Nihan 1982).[3]

Whereas the Administrative Office is a bureaucratic agency with a fixed hierarchy and division of labor, the Federal Judicial Center is a professional-technical service organization characterized by shifting assignments to various project teams. The Center's work focuses on researching new policy strategies for courts, with a markedly larger budget in 1980 as compared to its beginnings. In fact, the Federal Judicial Center received the largest increase of any individual budgetary category under consideration between 1970 and 1980 (1,309 percent). From 1980 to 1984 the Center's budget has, however, increased by only 10 percent, after a 14 percent decline to a little over seven million dollars in 1982.

An additional point of evidence of changes in priorities is revealed by the relative allocation of resources for the operation of juries (table 4.2, rows 8-10). The jury is less and less evident in the courtroom. We will document the actual fate of jury trials in federal courts in Chapter 5. Suffice it to say here that although the expenditures for juries increased especially during the 1960s, the relative share of these expenses as a percentage of the total court budget has decreased from 15 percent in 1950, to 4.3 percent in 1984. While it is true that the total base has changed considerably, we believe this decline in jury expenditures to be indicative of a shift in the priorities of judicial policymakers.

Despite these changes in the expansion of the courts' support services and the range of activities now included under this umbrella, the role of judges should not be ignored. They are still the authoritative center of courts and are perceived as representing a crucial bastion in the defense of a democratic tradition (see Hodge, Siegel, and Rossi 1964; Sennett and Cobb 1972). During the post-World War II period, the number of judges has grown in absolute terms. As table 4.3 shows, there was a small increase in the total number of authorized judgeships from 1950 to 1960 (14 percent), and a larger one from 1960 to 1970 (64 percent), with another smaller increase occurring between 1970 and 1980 (29 percent). After many years of lobbying and nego-

Table 4.3
Total and Percentage Increase in the Number of Authorized Judgeships,
1950-1988

Year	Total Number	Percent Increase
1950	215	—
1960	245	14
1970	401	64
1980	516	29
1988	575	8

tiating, Congress passed a bill in 1978 granting 115 new district court and 35 new appeals court judicial slots (see *The Third Branch, Bulletin of the Federal Courts*, January, April, December 1977; February, October 1978; February 1979). Up until the Judgeship Bill of 1982, this was the largest single increase in judicial personnel in the history of the third branch, with many of these slots allotted to courts located in the Sunbelt (e.g., Arizona, Texas, and Florida). But while this addition of judgeships is dramatic, it is not, as Chief Justice Burger quickly pointed out, at all clear that it will be sufficient to the task (*The Third Branch, Bulletin of the Federal Courts*, April 1977). During the Reagan administration, of course, almost 60 judges were added to the district courts.

In sum, the problems arising out of urbanization, industrialization, and the growth of the state sector have left their mark upon the resources and organizational form of the third branch. This development is concretized in the budgetary constraints that the courts face and that will, one may assume, be exacerbated in the years ahead. One may endlessly debate the mystique or reality of judicial autonomy in yesteryear's so-called "simple" society (see, e.g., Alschuler 1979; Friedman 1979; Haller 1979; Langbein 1979). But today it is apparent that the pressures of a modern political economy are altering the organizational resources and structure of the third branch. With this in mind, let us take a closer look at these processes from the perspective of the courts' political, economic, and demographic environment.

Jurisdictional Environment, Resources, and Personnel: 1950-1970

In this section, we explore the question of the effect of the surrounding political economy of the jurisdictional environment on one of the central resources of the court, the number of judges. The conventional wisdom of court organization has it that the number of judges will tend to reflect the incidence of new filings and, consequently, the population size of a district. In order to sort out empirically the accuracy of this commonly held notion, all variables are divided by the population size of the district for each of the three time points under examination. Furthermore, in order to obtain a reasonably comprehensive estimate of the environmental and task demands, net of population, we include the following independent variables in the analysis of the factors that might explain the number of judges in 1950, 1960, and 1970: population density, number of corporations, government employees, and civil filings. In light of the findings reported in chapter 3 we expect to find a greater interdependence—or symbiosis—between the courts and their environmental setting when looked at over time.

Table 4.4 shows the unstandardized, standardized, and joint effects of environmental demands on the number of district court judges in 1950, 1960 and 1970. The findings reported in this table crystallize a number of important themes shaping federal district courts in the post-World War II period. In 1950, the benchmark for this phase of the analysis, the number of judges is not associated with or explained by environmental factors of the court's jurisdictional profile; rather, the number of judges was only moderately associated with civil filings in a district ($b^* = .31$) which was, in turn, the main variable in an explanation of this organizational resource. In many respects, the findings reported for 1950 support the conventional wisdom just noted, that the number of judges is a function of task demand. Thus, it appears that in 1950 there was a relatively clear boundary between the organization of the court and the environment.

Table 4.4
Effects of the Environment and Litigation Rate on Judge/Population Ratio, 1950-1970

Judges/Population

	1950			1960			1970		
	r	*b*	*b**	*r*	*b*	*b**	*r*	*b*	*b**
Population Density	.05	3.40-11	.06	−.03	9.5-11	.23*	.56	1.30-10	.13**
Number of Corporations/ Population	.12	−1.90-05	−.04	.38	7.1-05	.21*	−.02	1.70-06	00
Number of Government Employees/ Population	—	—	—	−.08	−6.4-07	−.01	.88	4.70-05	.53****
1/Population	.71	.92	.69****	.62	9.2	.64****	.31	.73	.19****
Civil Filings/ Population	.37	2.60-03	.31****	.10	2.9-04	−.32	.83	1.60-03	.25****
R^2			.62			.50			.88

But, the findings reported in table 4.4 for 1960 begin to challenge this commonly held view about courts and sources of growth. First, environmental variables (i.e., population density and corporations) constitute significant, even if only weak-to-moderate, factors in an explanation of the number of judges. Supporting the emergence of these factors in shaping the push to expand judicial resources, the findings reported in table 4.4 also show an increase in the unstandardized coefficients for population density and corporations from 1950 to 1970, thus revealing a growing interdependence between environment and organization. Finally, the absence of a significant relationship between civil filings and judges in 1960 may be a function of a notable imbalance, or lag, between task demands and organizational capacity —a point that is supported by the pattern shown for the unstandardized coefficients from 1950 to 1960 to 1970.

But, in 1970 the number of government employees emerges as the significant environmental factor in an explanation of judges ($b^* = .53$).[4] By

1970, judicial capacity is a response to the demands posed by the governmental sector, population density, and new civil filings, where government is the strongest factor. Echoing the findings reported in chapter 3, here too we see that the presence of a larger governmental sector acts as a key force in the organization of the courts. Where the findings in Chapter 3 showed that the government is pivotal to an explanation of caseload demands, these findings suggest that this political force also emerges as a factor in determining the size of a district's judicial labor force by 1970.

While we will return to a more detailed discussion of the impact of the governmental sector on the federal courts in chapter 7, these findings foreshadow a key theme of this study. A traditional notion of separation of powers among the branches of government is seen as a foundation of the legitimacy of the courts and the state as a whole; the findings reported here suggest that in practice there is a great deal of interdependence among the branches so that the courts, for example, are structurally less independent than is claimed politically. There is an obvious dissonance between the theory and practice of governmental relations. Thus, the environmental profile, and specifically the size of the governmental sector of a district, is a critical, if hidden, factor in the decision to add judges.

It should be kept in mind, however, that the bolstering of judicial personnel in these more diverse judicial environments is likely to have the serendipitous effect of also introducing a support apparatus to complement a judge's work. In essence, the expansion of administrative supports may be an intrinsic by-product of a demanding court-environment relationship. Let us consider this theme in light of additional empirical evidence.

Environmental and Organizational Effects on Nonjudicial Personnel

Courts remain labor-intensive organizations in which modern technology is only gradually and reluctantly being introduced. The court's political economy has had an historically increasing effect upon the number of judges, the center of this labor-intensive organization, from 1950 to 1970. How, then, does the modern political economy affect the court's nonjudicial personnel?

Table 4.5 shows the standardized, unstandardized, and joint effects of environmental indicators on the court's other personnel in 1970.[5] The dependent variable, i.e., court personnel, is broken down as follows: total personnel, magistrates, law clerks, nonjudicial support staff, (secretaries and deputy court clerks), clerk's office, and the number of positions in the court as a whole. Following our general methodological strategy, all variables are analyzed net of population size in a district.

Table 4.5
Effects of the Environment and Litigation Rate on the Size and Structure of District Courts, 1970

	Total Personnel/ Population			Magistrates/ Population			Law Clerks/ Population		
	r	b	b^*	r	b	b^*	r	b	b^*
Population Density	.55	1.50-09	.08	.40	—	.03	.35	—	.07
Number of Corporations/ Population	.02	9.60-04	.05	−.15	—	−.08	−.05	—	.19
Number of Government Employees/ Population	.92	1.30-03	.69****	.64	—	.31*	.51	—	.35*
1/Population	.31	13.29	.17****	.07	−.03	−.03	.14	−.04	.00
Civil Filings/ Population	.80	.02	.23****	.67	.00	.43	.47	.00	.20
R^2			.92			.50			.33

	Support Staff/ Population			Clerks' Office/ Population			Number of Positions/ Population		
	r	b	b^*	r	b	b^*	r	b	b^*
Population Density	.55	—	.11	.56		.08	.18	—	.02
Number of Corporations/ Population	−.03	—	−.02	−.01	—	.04	.16	—	−.06
Number of Government Employees/ Population	.90	—	.67****	.92	—	.63****	.55	—	.27****
1/Population	.32	2.24	.21****	.26	2.29	.11**	.85	9.86	.80****
Civil Filings/ Population	.77	0	.18**	.84	.01	.32****	.59	0	.22****
R^2			.88			.92			.95

The findings shown for the court's total personnel essentially confirm the findings of table 4.4. That is, the size of the court's total personnel resources is explained, in large part, by the combined effect of the governmental sector ($b^* = .69$) and civil filings ($b^* = .23$). When other personnel categories of the court family are considered, moreover, the governmental sector remains a strong factor in an explanation of court resources.

Let us now look specifically at the magistrates, law clerks, secretaries, and docket clerks that form a network to prepare, or even partially to take over, the tasks of judges. Historically, the courts have, as we argued earlier, been characterized by a clear distinction between judicial and nonjudicial personnel reflecting the professional prerogative in the process of adjudication.

Among parajudicial personnel, magistrates are the newest rung on the judicial hierarchy. When the magistrate system was introduced in 1968 they automatically took over the existing criminal case responsibilities of the older commissioner system. Technically, magistrates are parajudges, i.e., they are lawyers and share many responsibilities with judges but they are not Article III officers and cannot speak for the court (Parness 1973; McCabe 1980; Seron 1983). Today, however, they often do, in fact, perform many tasks traditionally reserved for judges. The point of controversy in the use of magistrates has revolved around the scope of responsibility they should be granted in civil matters. That is, to what extent may they independently decide pretrial questions in civil cases? While magistrates have been able to "hear and recommend" actions to judges since the inception of the program there have been strong pressures, especially from magistrates themselves, to grant additional authority, resulting in the 1976 and 1979 amendments to the magistrate's act (McCabe 1980).[6] There remains a vocal opposition among judges who have refused, or only very reluctantly agreed, to incorporate magistrates into the process of judicial decision-making by turning over pretrial hearings and other pre-courtroom negotiations (Flanders 1976).[7] This judicial opposition is, in the context of present developments, a lingering voice of professional conservatism. But given the court's backlog, and the growing role of magistrates in the adjudication process, it is not surprising that their presence is explained by the twin factors of the governmental sector ($b^* = .31$) and the litigation rate ($b^* = .43$), although the latter is not significant. That is, in the earliest stages of the magistrate system these court actors were added when pressures from the larger political economy were most acute.

While many features of court procedure convey the image of having been conducted in the same way since the beginning of time, the use of law clerks was not authorized until 1886. It was a practice begun by Justice Gray in 1882 when he paid young lawyers out of his own pocket to work for him (Abraham 1986, 253). It is the personal, if not patrimonial, aspect of this organizational relationship which is perhaps most noteworthy and enduring

(Weber 1968; Kanter 1976). Law clerks are selected by judges and are under their direct supervision for a period of one or two years. Hence, they work at a judge's discretion and their tasks vary considerably from chamber to chamber within a district. Each federal district judge is assigned two law clerks, although there are some judges who also use law students in a clerk-like fashion. The jurisdictional environment explains 33 percent of the variance in the number of law clerks which is smaller than that shown for other categories of personnel. This finding suggests that their presence is, more than that of any other personnel group, the product of traditional expectations, rather than rational planning in response to demand. That is, once a new judge's slot has been approved, two law clerk slots are also automatically added to the personnel of the court—regardless of need or use.

There are, however, drifts in the air to modify the personal accent and temporary nature of this relationship. Proposals are being suggested, and in some state courts and federal courts are in place, to introduce a centralized permanent "career legal staff" composed of young lawyers who commit themselves to work for a specific district or circuit for a designated period of time. Rather than working for a specific judge, staff law clerks are on call for any professional member of the court as the need may arise. Certainly from the point of view of a court manager, augmenting the temporary law clerks by permanent legal staff makes a great deal of sense since it would "border on the bizarre to propose the annual rotation of the entire professional staff in any other major institution of American life" (Cannon 1975, 111). It is important to note that the career legal staff is proposed as an addition to the personnel of the court and not as a substitute for law clerks. Given judges' reluctance to modernize, especially at the federal level, a proposal to eliminate law clerks might raise the specter of bureaucratic encroachment.

Other support services for judges include a courtroom deputy clerk and a secretary, but in practice there is some variation in the allocation of these resources (also see chap. 6). The findings shown in table 4.5 suggest that such variations are, essentially, a response to the governmental sector ($b^* = .67$) and to the litigation rate ($b^* = .18$), thus adding more support to the theme we have sounded throughout this chapter.

Finally, the clerk's office is responsible for overall docketing of the court's caseload. The organizational structure of the clerk's office is shaped by the traditions of a district, thus creating the basis for wide variation in its activities and procedures. Augmenting the overall findings reported in table 4.5, the size of the clerk's office is explained by the governmental sector ($b^* = .63$) and new civil filings ($b^* = .32$).

The expansion of the court's management needs has had a notable effect on the personnel of the clerk's office as well as the selection of clerks of court. Beginning in 1938 with the formation of the Administrative Office, the gen-

eral push of this effort has been to systematize operations. Here too, moreover, this theme remains as reforms center around efforts to standardize
nationally the organization of this office (*The Third Branch, Bulletin of the
Federal Courts*, August 1975). Traditionally a position of political patronage,
clerks are increasingly selected for their managerial skills for the clerk's office
comes closest to our image of a classical bureaucratic, governmental operation. Mirroring the executive branch civil service, the personnel of the clerk's
office work within a system of grades and steps. The final panel in table 4.5
shows the number of different positions within the court, although it reflects
mainly the differentiation of the clerk's office. In a summary fashion, this
panel reports the relative bureaucratization—or division of labor—of the functions of the court. And, in keeping with the theme of this chapter, this dimension of support is associated with the governmental sector ($b^* = .27$) and with
the litigation rate ($b^* = .22$).

More recently, of course, the division of labor within the clerk's office has
moved from a labor-intensive operation to a combination of computer and
labor power. Indeed, with the recent introduction of micro-computers a new
problem lurks on the horizon. It is now quite feasible to decentralize court
administration in new ways and to exert much more control at the local level
thereby undermining the very attempts to standardize nationally and, ironically, giving a renewed scope to an accent on local control. As this process
unfolds, and as computer literacy becomes increasingly important for effective management of court operations, one may also begin to detect a fascinating turf battle unfolding over appropriate credentialing to be a clerk.

Together, these findings and considerations lend support to the claim
that both the jurisdictional environment and the task structure generate an
emergent organizational division of labor that goes beyond the traditional
collegial structure dominated by a single judge. If we consider the organization of work itself as a type of resource that courts have available—over and
above fiscal resources—then this evidence points not only to the *expansion* of
the nonjudicial sector, but also toward the *transformation* of the traditional
organization of work and its elaboration in the direction of a more complex
structure. That this new organizational structure generates different modes
of managerial coordination and control can only be surmised at this point.
But other evidence is noteworthy, particularly the appointment of circuit executives in the early 1970s and, more recently, the experimental appointment
of district court executives in selected metropolitan districts (Eldridge 1984).
The role of these court executives is, precisely, to coordinate the work of the
different specialized personnel categories in the nonjudicial sector, to facilitate increased cost-effectiveness, speed, and productivity, and to conduct the
administration of justice according to the principles of managerial efficiency
and technical rationality. While it is quite likely that many smaller courts are

still rather antiquated organizations, constrained by the traditions of adjudication and professional-collegial control, larger, more urban courts are changing dramatically—on both the judicial and support side of the fence. One may even argue that judges are working within a new professional paradigm in that they have relatively less control over their work, a question that we will return to in chapter 6 (on the issue of de-professionalization, see Haug 1973, 1977; Oppenheimer 1973; Miller 1976, 111; Ehrenreich and Ehrenreich 1977; Larson 1980; Heydebrand 1985).

Conclusion

In this chapter, we have examined the fiscal and organizational resources of district courts and certain managerial strategies the judicial branch has introduced in order to meet the demand for its services. Drawing upon a crucial question raised by recent work on the theory of the state, we have sketched the effects of the state's budgetary priorities upon the judicial branch. Analysis of the judicial system presents a unique entry into this problematic because it is an institutional sphere that predates the government's fiscal troubles, yet has played a crucial role in mediating its contradictory task to legitimate unequal social relations. Historically, the ideological or normative pillar of the court's mediative role has been "formal rationality," i.e., the professional, traditional, independent, apolitical passivity of law summed up in the notion of due process and the rule of law.

Yet, with the expansion of larger state activities and demands to mediate actively, the courts face an organizational dilemma that has wider political implications. Thus, the technical rationalization of the courts, under the impact of budget constraints and shifting political agendas, must be understood both as a threat to the traditional form of law and judicial administration, and as a powerful force transforming the organization of work and the authority relations of courts themselves. At the same time, this process must be seen as occurring over the lingering and intermittent opposition of the "traditional intellectuals" of the system—judges, legal scholars, and legal practitioners.

At its core, administrative and adjudicatory processes are antithetical: the former demands technical rationality and cost effectiveness; the latter emphasize judicial autonomy, quality, and formal rationality. But adjudication is expensive and inefficient because it must rely upon a labor-intensive staff of highly trained generalists (Flanders 1977). In this light, and in the face of a larger twentieth century organizational and managerial revolution, shifting allocations to administer court services have begun to leave their mark. This shift in allocation is, we have suggested, more than a line item on a budget and suggests an emergent set of more managerial, rational, and administrative calculations. This push, in part, emanates from the demands of districts' political economy; yet, the implications of these developments go much deeper and will be explored in the conclusion.

CHAPTER 5

*

The Effect of Environment and Demand
on Judicial Decision-Making

At bottom, traditional models for disposing of court cases—especially jury and non-jury trials—contradict the organizational guidelines of modern management. Nevertheless, from various quarters, we have explored the push to introduce more rational practices and procedures into federal courts. Under pressure generated by more caseload demands coupled with constrained resources, the federal courts have begun to adopt more integrated models for disposing of civil and criminal cases—the subject of this chapter.

Thus, we may ask: Does the demand for service generated by the dynamics of the court's environmental profile or court resources shape the volume and nature of judicial outputs? Specifically, we distinguish between the effects of environment and demand on the *quantity of output*, i.e., the sheer number of terminations, on the one hand, and *qualitative outcomes*, i.e., the use of trials and other modes of judicial dispositions.

We will begin by documenting the changing output of courts from 1890 to 1988. This descriptive analysis will be followed by an explanation of variations in the number of terminations in light of environmental and organizational variables. We will then turn to a similar analysis of jury trials. Finally, we will inquire into the changing nature of judicial dispositions by examining the balance (or imbalance) between no-action dispositions, pretrial actions, and trials in civil cases and between dismissals, guilty pleas, and trials in criminal cases, as well as on the effects of environment, task structure and judicial resources on these judicial dispositions.

The Changing Output of District Courts, 1890-1988

If one indicator of work in the courts is simply the volume of cases that are terminated, then one must conclude quickly that work is certainly being done. Table 5.1 shows the total number of terminations, criminal termina-

99

tions, civil terminations, and percent civil cases of the total terminated from 1890 to 1988. Total terminations increased almost ten-fold from 26,244 in 1890 to 279,739 in 1988. Most of this was due, however, to an increase in the proportion of civil terminations, from 39 percent in 1890, to over 85 percent in 1988. Thus, there was not simply a quantitative increase in the work of the courts, but also a qualitative change as well (see chaps. 3 and 4). The unusually large number of total terminations in 1930 (131,074) reflects the work produced by prohibition cases that disappeared after 1933 with the repeal of the Eighteenth Amendment.

Table 5.1
The Changing Output of Courts, 1890-1988

Number of Terminations

Year	Total Cases	Criminal Cases	Civil Cases	Percent of Civil Cases
1890	26,244	16,016	10,228	39.0
1900	29,094	17,033	12,061	41.5
1910	28,280	15,371	12,909	45.6
1920	53,113	34,230	18,883	35.6
1930	131,074	82,609	48,465	37.0
1940	69,023	33,426	35,597	51.6
1950	88,124	36,924	51,200	58.1
1960	85,748	29,033	56,715	66.1
1970	117,253	36,819	80,435	68.6
1980	195,712	35,231	160,481	82.0
1988	279,739	40,986	238,753	85.3

Sources: 1890-1930 Annual Report of the U.S. Attorney General; 1940-1988 Report of the Proceedings of the U.S. Judicial Conference.

In general, the rise in terminations reflects the increasing number of filings and, more indirectly, the impact of demography and government, as we have shown earlier. But the question arises, did terminations keep pace with filings? Table 5.2 shows the ratio of total terminations to total filings, of civil terminations to civil filings, and criminal terminations to criminal filings from 1904 to 1988.

Since a figure below 1.0 means that terminations lagged behind filings and a figure above 1.0 means that more cases were terminated than filed, we can conclude that, by and large, total terminations kept pace with total filings

Table 5.2
Ratios of Total Terminations to Total Filings and Criminal and Civil Terminations to Respective Filings, 1904-1988

Years	*Termination Ratios*		
	Total	*Civil*	*Criminal*
1904[a]	.91	.88	.94
1910	.99	.94	1.03
1920	.68	.85	.62
1930	.97	1.00	.95
1940	1.05	1.09	1.01
1950	.98	.98	.99[b]
1960	1.00	1.00	.99[b]
1970	.92	.92	.92
1980	.99	.95	1.26
1988	.99	1.00	.94

[a] Data not available before 1904.
[b] Differences in the ratios are due to rounding errors.

because most of the figures hover around 1.0. An exception occurred in 1920 when the lagging disposition of criminal cases reduced the ratio of total terminations. It appears to be a small miracle that the onslaught of cases in 1920 and 1930 did not lead to a significantly lower termination ratio (.62 for criminal and .68 for all terminations). However, it may also indicate a modification in prosecutorial and judicial procedures in dealing with the flood of cases; for example, the percentage of guilty pleas jumped significantly in 1920 and 1930, as we will show later.

Table 5.2 shows that civil terminations occasionally lag behind criminal terminations, a lag that is due, we believe, to the relatively more complex demands of civil cases in federal courts. After 1970, however, another development occurred that helps to explain the change in ratios for those years. The proportion of civil terminations reached over 85 percent of the total in federal courts (see table 5.1, last col.). As table 5.2 shows, the civil termination ratio after 1960 dropped to pre-1930 levels although it increased again to 1.0 in 1988.

Let us now turn to an analysis of the effect of environmental and organizational variables on total, civil, and criminal terminations. Certainly, the outcome of a given case is dependent upon the decisions of judges, lawyers, and other special factors, such as press coverage, financial resources, and jury selection. Nevertheless, the activities of legal and judicial decision-making are also delineated by larger structural constraints, including the court's environmental profile, task demands, and resources. These factors circumscribe the parameters of activity within which judges may act. The interface between structural and particularistic factors is distinctly salient when considering the court's output. To substantiate this point, table 5.3 shows the standardized, unstandardized, and joint effects of selected environmental and organizational variables on total, civil, and criminal terminations for 1950, 1960, and 1970. (Note that all variables are analyzed as ratios where the denominator is the population of the district.)

Per capita demand and the relative size of the governmental sector are the primary environmental variables in an explanation of court activities.[1] Population density has declined over time as a significant influence on terminations: as these findings show, total and civil terminations were associated with population density in 1960 but not in 1970. The effect of density on criminal terminations was negative in 1950, but disappears in subsequent decades. It is likely that the strong and persistent effect of per capita demand on terminations mediates most of the demographic influences emanating from the environment.

Overall, the number of corporations has no effect on terminations, except for a negative effect on criminal terminations in 1960. The presence of government agencies, on the other hand, generates a pervasive effect, from caseload to termination.

Overall, these findings suggest that simply focusing on judicial resources of the court is inadequate in an explanation of terminations. While the full implications of this conclusion will be explored in chapter 6, these findings begin to suggest that judicial capacity by itself is not sufficient to explain caseload termination. With this in mind, let us now turn to an analysis of a hallowed but endangered institution: the jury trial.

The Historical Context of Jury Trials

Trial by jury is one of the central elements of the Anglo-American legal tradition. Likened to notions of due process, equal protection, and rule of law, jury trials signify that minimal aspect of the democratic process that is embedded in the work of the third branch. As Ann Strick (1977, 167) put it, "Juries tend to be invested with the import of democracy itself." Yet when all is said and done, the civil and criminal cases that demand the judicial services of our courts rarely come to trial. By and large, cases are terminated through other channels. The reasons for the peculiarity of this system are part of a debate among those who study courts. There are, on the one hand, the

Table 5.3
Effects of the Environment, Demand, and Judges on Terminations, 1950-1970

		Total Terminations/Population			Civil Terminations/Population			Criminal Terminations/Population		
		1950	1960	1970	1950	1960	1970	1950	1960	1970
Population Density	r	.61	.52	.46	.67	.64	.26	.32	.43	.54
	b	-1.60-08	7.20-08	-3.90-09	2.80-08	6.50-08	1.20-08	-4.40-03	7.50-09	-3.30
	b*	-.03	.14***	.02	.06	.16**	.05	-.22*	.07	-.01
Corporations/ Population	r	-.05	.01	.01	-.01	.05	.11	-.13	-.15	-.11
	b	0	-.01	.01	0	.01	.02	-.01	.02	-7.70-03
	b*	-.01	.01	.02	.01	.04	.08	-.07	-.22***	-.04
Government Employees/ Population	r	—	.55	.77	—	.85	.41	—	.69	.91
	b	—	.03	.02	—	.03	.01	—	3.10-03	.01
	b*	—	.38****	.62****	—	.41****	.47*	—	.19*	.59****
1/Population	r	.10	.13	.25	.05	.10	.25	.20	.27	.17
	b	90.80	167.50	294.50	54.60	73.50	266.70	36.20	94.10	28.10
	b*	.06	.10	.19*	.04	.05	.28*	.07	.27**	.03
Demand/ Population	r	.97	.59	.66	.97	.87	.36	.71	.79	.77
	b	.58	.29	.44	.42	.22	.29	.16	.07	.15
	b*	.99****	.51****	.51***	.93****	.47****	.54**	.84****	.59****	.31***
Judges/ Population	r	.07	-.09	.76	.02	-.11	.41	.15	-.03	.89
	b	-45.30	-84.90	-1.60	-67.70	-63.30	-143.80	22.40	-11.10	22.30
	b*	-.04	-.07	-.30	-.07	-.07	-.58	.06	-.05	.10
R²		.94	.88	.69	.94	.87	.29	.56	.73	.89

"rationalizers," pragmatists who take the position that we may as well accept things as they are and work with the resources we have. Then there are, on the other hand, the "professionalizers," romantics and moralists who assume that it is possible to make the system work (see Alford 1975 for this distinction and its implications). In the pages that follow we will touch upon various facets of this dialogue.

Before turning to this, one point is in order. Whether one takes a pragmatic, romantic, or some other view of these matters at the core is a common factual point of departure. At the federal level less than 10 percent of all cases filed actually come to trial; at the state and local level it is commonly an even smaller percentage. For observers of the court this is old news. But what is remarkable, and what is all too often dismissed, takes us far beyond percentages or numbers. Put most simply, the courts, given our collective democratic myths, tend to dispose of most of their caseload removed from the judge's courtroom while, at the same time, preserving the drama and mystique of trials as the important business of courts.

Analytically, what is the *organizational* role of judge or jury in the adversary process? Under adversary procedures, the process of inquiry into fact and law is not integrated within one structure, but is *structurally bifurcated*. This means that both sides of a dispute use processes of fact finding, reasoning, and proof for the purpose of establishing the validity of their own theory and winning their case. The logic of liberal legal dispute resolution in which judge or jury delivers the ultimate verdict assumes not one but at least two processes of decision-making. It is only at the point of ultimate resolution or final appraisal that the process is reunified under the authority of the judge or jury.

The process of structural bifurcation in the adversary system is a dualistic decision-making procedure where compromise or zero-sum gain are the only outcomes, except if the whole conflict is denied the benefit of impartial adjudication. In that latter case, the dispute is forced back into an indeterminate situation, i.e., into the arena of conflicting economic and political forces that had generated the dispute in the first place. Such a denial of adjudication without benefit of an impartial, public problem-solving process negates the legal safeguards protecting the "public interest." Moreover, such denial jeopardizes the individual parties' constitutional rights. The dualist character of the adversary process is underlined by the fact that only one outcome is valid, viz. the court's decision (Galanter 1974). The judge or jury, representing the state, guarantees or legitimates the victory of one side and, short of appeal or renewed litigation, enforces the acceptance of defeat by the other side.

The structural bifurcation of the adversary model contradicts modern paradigms of decision-making in which the process is *integrated* within one person, one office, or one decision-making structure. What is it, then, about this process of decision-making that makes it such a problem in contemporary society?

The history of professions shows a tendency for service to be rendered by one person—be it the doctor or the lawyer—who has the authority of expertise to make certain decisions regarding a particular case. Similarly, the history of bureaucracy, so vividly documented by Max Weber, reveals the consolidation of decision-making on the basis of written rules and the exercise of formal legal authority vested in an "office" and its "incumbent." In both cases, integration of decision-making in the hands of a person or an office describes the overarching theme of modern society, that is, the tendency toward rationality. While the value rationality of professional judgment is more "rational" than mere guesswork, tradition, or charismatic vision, it is not as formally rational as the decision-making of a routine bureaucratic administrator. And, neither the professional nor the bureaucratic decision-making processes are as technically rational as the output of a computer in which the technical process provides solutions to the substantive problem at hand. If, to repeat an earlier theme, bureaucratic conservatism tends to "turn problems of politics into problems of administration" (Mannheim 1936) and if "professionals tend to turn every problem of decision-making into a question of expertise" (Bendix and Roth 1971, 148), then a new technocratic strategy can be said to turn problems of politics, experts, and administrators into problems of cybernetic systems control or the ultimate "administration of things."

By now it should be absolutely clear that the traditional adversarial process contradicts all notions of modern, integrated decision-making, which is one reason why Max Weber (1966) described the Anglo-American legal process as a nonrational, if not irrational, anachronism.

As the proponents of reform, or integration and rationalization, emerged in education or social welfare and sought to codify or formalize the knowledge-base of these fields so legal reformers began to carve out a similar task.[2] During the early nineteenth century the courts were increasingly asked to decide the commercial questions of a fledgling mercantilist American economy. Traditional practices dictated that such delicate questions be determined by a jury. Morton Horwitz (1977) shows, however, that procedural changes laid the groundwork for restriction of the scope and discretion of the jury. First, towards the end of the eighteenth century lawyers more commonly relied upon the precedent of a "'special case,' or 'case reserved,' a device designed to submit points of law to the judges while avoiding the effective intervention of the jury" (p. 142). Second, by the turn of the century "the award of a new trial for verdicts 'contrary to the weight of evidence'" (p. 142) became commonplace. And third, "[B]y 1810, it was clear that the institutions of the court, originally advisory, had become mandatory and therefore juries no longer possessed the power to determine the law'" (Nelson, as quoted in

Horwitz 1977, 143). Taken together, these procedural modifications contributed to a diminished reliance on the jury.

Then, beginning in the mid-nineteenth century a debate ensued concerning the viability of writing down the common law without destroying its texture. The first attempt was the Field Code, a written civil code, which was adopted by many states (Friedman 1973; Tigar and Levy 1977, 240). This theme is today seen in the work of the American Bar Association's Commission on Uniform State Laws. Echoing the modern world's concern with rationalization, there was a clear agenda in the work of these reformers: the legal system that works best is one that most conforms to legal rationality, a "system which is most clear, orderly, systematic (in its formal parts), which has the most structural beauty, which most appeals to the modern, well-educated jurist" (Friedman 1973, 354). The formation of the American Bar Association in 1887 gave further impetus to this development as it took on the task of reorganizing and reforming the legal profession (Halliday 1987).

This move toward codification had significant implications for the relationship between judge and jury: what had been an "informal chat" arising out of a community conflict was transformed into a rather clearly-defined division of labor in which the judge was seen to be the master of law and the jury was to be the instrument of fact finding. By the early nineteenth century, with the pressures of an emerging capitalist economy, the courts became arbiters of commercial questions in which a jury's discretion quickly proved to be all too irrational. One sees a reduction in the use of juries and when juries are used the judge's prerogative to reverse their verdicts is often exercised. The movement, then, for codification of the common law and the restrictions of juries captures a form of rationalization, reflects an attempt to fit a traditional body of procedure to the demands of a modern world, and foreshadows the central concerns of court reformers today. Even so, the assumptions behind a bifurcated adversarial framework of dispute resolution were not challenged.

Because adversarial decision-making is organizationally outmoded, there is a powerful push toward a decision-making process that has a more rational, integrated base, including pretrials and settlements. Like most organizational practices, however, there are interesting reform efforts that express a different voice: one hears contradictory calls to reform the jury. There are those, including former Chief Justice Burger, who advocate the further restriction of jury usage and rest their case on the grounds that the institution is costly, inefficient, and unpredictable. Yet, there are others who advocate the introduction of modifications to help insure better performance. For example, twenty-eight district judges in the Second Circuit recently volunteered to participate in an experiment to determine if various aids improve the decision-making capabilities of juries. These aids ranged from changes in the instructional charges to the jury to permitting jurors to take notes to providing the jury with a written copy of the judge's charge. Though these experiments were not developed in a controlled context, the findings suggest, the authors conclude, that "individual judges should feel free to use them in particular cases" (Sand and Reiss 1985, 459). Clearly, the major change pushes toward the further restriction of juries; yet, it is equally important to document, as these experiments with juries highlight, that change is never unidirectional. Thus, a fundamental question remains, can the formal legal paradigm be adapted to the exigencies of a rational, technocratic world? In our concluding chapter we will contribute a few thoughts to this question, but for now let us turn to a more detailed analysis of district court trials.

First, table 5.4 shows the number and percentage of criminal trials from 1890 to 1988 and of civil trials from 1940 to 1988. It is all too obvious that in criminal cases since 1930 there has been a dramatic shift away from the use

Table 5.4
Number and Percentage of Criminal and Civil Trials, 1890-1988

Year	Number of Criminal Trials	Percent of Criminal Terminations	Number of Civil Trials	Percent of Civil Terminations
1890	12,769	79.7	—[a]	—
1900	12,299	72.2	—	—
1910	10,946	71.2	—	—
1920	25,678	75.0	—	—
1930	20,320	85.1	—	—
1940	6,331	19.0	6,692	18.8
1950	2,311	5.4	4,979	9.7
1960	3,515	12.1	6,488	11.4
1970	6,583	17.9	9,449	11.7
1980	6,634	18.8	12,951	8.0
1988	7,365	18.0	12,536	5.3

[a] Data not available before 1940

of trials as a dominant mode of termination. While about three-quarters of all criminal cases were disposed of by means of a trial from 1890 on, climbing as high as 85 percent in 1930, the percentage dropped to less than one-fifth after 1940.[3] Nevertheless, even then, the percentage of criminal trials was slightly higher than that of civil trials which, from 1950 to 1970, hovered around 10 percent, only to decline further after 1980.

The significant shift in court practices after 1930-40 is also visible when we consider the use of jury trials separately from all trials. Table 5.5 shows that jury trials constituted between 10 and 17 percent of all terminations from 1910 to 1940, but dropped thereafter to between 6.5 and 3.4 percent.

Table 5.5
Number and Percentage of All Trials and Jury Trials, 1910-1988

Year	All Trials	Percentage of All Terminations	Jury Trials	Percentage of All Terminations	Percentage of Jury Trials of All Trials
1910	10,946[a]	71.2	2,210[a]	14.4	20.2
1920	25,678[a]	75.0	5,936[a]	17.3	23.1
1930	20,320[a]	85.1	9,352[a]	11.3	46.0
1940	13,023	18.9	7,012	10.2	53.8
1950	7,290	8.3	3,252	3.7	44.6
1960	10,003	11.7	5,549	6.5	55.5
1970	16,032	13.7	7,597	6.5	47.4
1980	19,585	10.0	7,338	3.7	37.5
1988	19,901	7.1	9,598	3.4	48.2

[a] Criminal trials only

However, court (judge) trials did not completely replace jury trials. As the last column of table 5.5 shows, the proportion of jury trials of all trials tended to increase from 1910 to 1960 and has only thereafter exhibited a slight downward trend. Still, as table 5.6 shows, the majority of those jury trials took place on the criminal side of the federal court docket.

A comparison between criminal and civil jury trials clearly shows that juries are still predominantly used in criminal cases, and that the real decline has been experienced on the civil side, from an already low 5.8 percent in 1940 to 2.3 percent in 1988. Table 5.6 also shows that juries are used in one-half to three-quarters of criminal trials, whereas this is true only for about one third to two fifths of civil trials (table 5.6, last col.).

Our analysis of the fate of trials under the impact of the rationalization of court procedures also throws light on the big shift after 1930, which we observed in tables 5.4 and 5.5. We can see now that it was mainly judge trials in criminal cases as well as all civil trials that decreased drastically after 1930. The proportion of jury trials of all trials (See table 5.5, last col.) and the corresponding proportions of criminal and civil jury trials (see table 5.6, col's 3 and 6) are comparatively stable and do not show the kind of downward shift from 1930 to 1940 observed in tables 5.4 and 5.5. Thus, while the jury as an institution is in decline when we consider it in relation to all terminations, it has clearly not disappeared as an ultimate weapon of legal defense, especially in criminal cases.

Table 5.6
Number and Percentage of Criminal and Civil Jury Trials, 1910-1988

| | | Criminal Jury Trials | | | Civil Jury Trials | |
Year	Number	As percent of Criminal Terminations	As percent of Criminal Trials	Number	As percent of Civil Terminations	As percent of Civil Trials
1910	2,210	14.4	20.2	—[a]	—	—
1920	5,936	17.3	23.1	—	—	—
1930	9,352	11.3	46.0	—	—	—
1940	4,941	14.8	78.0	2,071	5.8	30.9
1950	1,487	4.0	64.3	1,765	3.4	35.4
1960	2,509	8.6	71.4	3,040	5.4	46.9
1970	4,226	11.5	64.2	3,371	4.2	35.7
1980	3,418	9.7	51.5	3,920	2.4	30.3
1988	4,150	10.1	56.3	5,448	2.3	43.5

[a] Data not available before 1940

In short, jury trials are the exception and not the rule, though more cases are actually tried in American courts than in any other country (Abraham 1986; Moore 1973) Today, the further restriction of the jury process is advocated by court reformers who argue that it is highly inefficient and, as we are all told repeatedly, inefficiency is bad for everyone.

It is in this sense, then, that the jury trial is the court's Achilles's heel because, at bottom, it contradicts the integrated processes of decision-making on which modern administrative and technocratic strategies are based. The fate of juries can be put into larger perspective when considered together with other types of dispositions that contribute to the overall termination of cases. We will, therefore, turn to an analysis of the major types of dispositions.

The Reality of American Justice: Disposing of the Court's Caseload

There are three possibilities for disposing of civil and criminal cases, each one capturing different modes of involvement on the part of the court's personnel (see fig. 5.1).

	Criminal	**Civil**
Stage I	Dismissal	No Action
Stage II	Guilty Plea	Pretrial
Stage III	Trial	Trial

Figure 5.1 Types of Civil and Criminal Dispositions

While a case may be filed with the court, it is possible that it will never-theless require very few, or no, court services. In the case of criminal questions, a case may be *dismissed* for lack of evidence whereas in a civil case the parties may withdraw or settle out of court, hence requiring *"no action"* by the court. The history, constitutionality, and ethics of plea bargaining criminal cases opens a Pandora's box for members of the criminal justice community; yet nearly all agree that the process generally tends to guarantee a conviction on a *guilty plea* by the offender and thereby eliminates the need for a formal trial. A somewhat analogous (Rosenberg, 1964; Glaser 1968) development has occurred on the civil side; that is, disposition before, during, or after *pretrial conference* gives the court the options to negotiate, to settle, to mediate a resolution of a dispute short of trial; here, the demarcation between umpire and manager as dispute resolver begins to get muddled. Finally, a civil or criminal case may proceed to a full *trial*, with or without a jury. As we have seen, jury trials are very few in number; in the pages that follow we will compare all trials to the other forms of civil and criminal dispositions.

From Professional to Technocratic Justice: Disposing of the Court's
Criminal Docket: 1890-1988

The development of a more rationalized process of disposition of the court's criminal caseload cannot be understood apart from the history of the professionalization of police, prosecution, and defense.

If the jury trial, in general, is the central myth of the adversary system, the specific notions of "innocent-until-proven-guilty" plays a comparable role in criminal procedure. Organizationally, the traditional goal of criminal justice assumes that errors are both possible and to be expected; therefore, the structure must provide for cautious decision-making, a process of "disjointed incrementalism" or "muddling through" in which it is assumed that there is no one "right" answer that can be *a priori* dictated (Lindblom 1965). It is an organizational strategy that is workable but hardly optimal by today's standards of efficiency and objectivity. "Muddling through," however, might very well describe the traditional adversarial process. And in the area of criminal justice, in its earliest form, this meant a system run by "amateurs"; a police force that worked part time (Friedman 1979; Haller 1979); a defense attorney selected by the accused; and, at the federal level, prosecution by the United States Attorney, who also worked part time. In fact, until 1814 the Attorney General's office did not receive appropriations to maintain offices in Washington, D.C. That is, the government's legal counsel worked at home, "sending his opinions to the President by mail and appearing in person only when it was necessary to present a case before the Supreme Court" (Crenson 1975, 69). All of this worked rather well, if awkwardly, before America felt the effects of industrialization, urbanization, and then immigration. As Lawrence Friedman has said:

> Perhaps there never *was* a time when full-scale trial by jury was the norm. In any event, the rise of professional police and full-time prosecutors would have put an end to any such golden age. In a system run by amateurs (or part time officials), without technology or police science—no fingerprints, blood tests, ballistics reports—the classical trial might be as good a way as any to filter out the innocent from the guilty. In the course of the nineteenth century, the center of gravity shifted away from amateurs and part-timers to professionals. As this change took place, society no longer *presumed* that trial was the normal way to deal with people accused of crime. After all, the defendant had already been 'tried' by police and prosecutors long before the trial stage. Part of the public might have thought that trials were a waste of time and money. Nor was trial by jury the right way to deal with the criminal class. . . . (1979, 257 258)

Indeed, the institutionalization of plea bargaining seems to coincide with the professionalization and bureaucratization of police, prosecution and defense.[4] Rather than a system of "muddling through," "[t]he reality of American [criminal justice] . . . is more akin to modern supermarkets, in which prices for various commodities have been clearly established and labelled in advance. . . . In a supermarket customers may complain about prices, but they rarely 'bargain' to get them reduced" (Feeley 1979, 262).

As police, prosecution and defense became more professionalized,[5] so the trial process itself was transformed into a very formalized set of practices. The formalization of the adversarial process coupled with the development of new rules of evidence "has caused the common law jury trial to undergo a profound transformation" (Langbein 1979, 262; also see Friedman 1973).

In addition, the accused has been given counsel; there is *voir dire* [formal selection] of jurors; the accused is protected against self-incrimination; and, there is now a complex appeals process. What Langbein has so perceptively suggested is that in the name of reform we have rendered the trial itself "unworkable as an ordinary or routine dispositive procedure for cases of serious crime" (1979, 265).

Surely it is more than a coincidence, then, that Friedman (1979) can document different phases in the development of plea bargaining in his sample of cases from Alameda County, California. From 1880 to 1900 he finds a "mixed system" of trials and "explicit" bargaining; from 1900 to 1950 evidence suggests that it is "plainly worthwhile to plead guilty" (p. 265) and that there are fewer trials and fewer dismissals; finally, from 1950 to the present, plea bargaining has taken "center stage" so that the "normal" practice is "outright negotiation" prefaced by overcharging (also see Sudnow 1965).

Turning to federal court data, it is also clear from the historical record that convictions on a plea of guilty—the product of bargaining between prosecutor, defendant, defense counsel, and judge—have long been the common practice for criminal dispositions. These practices predate the court's caseload growth (see, e.g., Heumann 1977) though most would agree that caseload pressures contribute to their continued popularity and open acceptance.

Table 5.7
Types of Criminal Dispositions, 1890-1988

Year	Dismissals Number	Dismissals Percent	Convictions Total Number	Convictions On Guilty Pleas	Convictions Percent on Plea	All Trials Number	All Trials Percent[a]
1890	—	—	9,913	—	—	12,769	79.7
1900	—	—	10,390	—	—	12,299	72.2
1910	4,425	28.8	9,453	4,550	48.1	10,946	71.2
1920	951	2.8	23,653	19,648	83.1	25,678	75.0
1930	3,890	4.7	67,748	60,938	89.9	20,320	24.6
1940	2,098	6.3	42,089	37,080	88.1	6,331	18.9
1950	3,237	8.8	33,502	31,739	94.7	2,311	6.3
1960	2,596	8.9	26,728	24,245	90.7	3,515	12.1
1970	6,608	17.9	28,178	24,111	85.6	6,583	17.9
1980	6,633	18.8	28,598	23,111	80.8	6,634	18.8
1988	8,368	20.4	42,902	36,917	86.0	7,365	18.0

[a] Based on criminal terminations

However, a significant turning point occurred as early as 1920 when 83.1 percent of all convictions were obtained this way (see table 5.7). Table 5.7 shows the number and percentage of dismissals, convictions (total number and those obtained on a guilty-plea), the percentage of guilty-pleas, and all trials from 1890 to 1988. Interestingly, with this transformation, fewer cases were dismissed for lack of evidence between 1920 and 1960 (see table 5.7).

Environmental and organizational effects on criminal dispositions: 1960-1970. Following our previous strategy of analysis, we examine the unstandardized, standardized, and joint effects of environmental and organizational variables on two types of criminal dispositions: convictions and trials. We do not separate convictions from guilty pleas here since between 85 to 90 percent of convictions in 1960 and 1970 were based on guilty-pleas. Table 5.8 reports this set of findings for the ratio of criminal trials to the population of a district for 1960 and 1970.[6]

Table 5.8
Effects of the Environment, Demand, and Judges on
Criminal Trials, 1960-1970

| | | *Criminal Trials/Population* | | | | |
| | | *1960* | | | *1970* | |
	r	b	b^*	r	b	b^*
Density	.54	3.20-09	.12	.18	−4.80	.05
Corporations/ Population	−.09	−2.30-03	−.11	−.02	7.30-05	.01
Government Employees/ Population	.82	1.70-03	.29****	.49	5.50-04	.61****
1/Population	.13	12.40	.14*	.32	1.30	.03
Demand/Population	.83	.01	.45****	.95	4.60-03	.21*
Judges/Population	−.14	−7.60	−.12	.42	1.20	.12
R^2			.80			.86

Corroborating the impact of these variables on criminal terminations reported earlier (see table 5.3), these findings show that it is the effects of the governmental sector as well as demand that are key to pushing criminal cases to trial. Based on these findings, we may suggest that the changing caseload,

especially the immediacy of new filings does affect the number of criminal
trials. Speculating, we suggest that the presence of government agencies in a
district exerts what one might call a "law and order" influence.

Table 5.9 reports the effect of our model on the ratio of criminal convictions to the population of a district in 1960 and 1970. The results reported
here parallel those shown in table 5.3 for all criminal terminations. Demand

Table 5.9

Effects of the Environment, Demand, and Judges on Criminal
Convictions, 1960-1970

| | | *Criminal Convictions/Population* | | | | |
| | | 1960 | | | 1970 | |
	r	b	b^*	r	b	b^*
Density	.40	5.20-09	.06	.55	−8.40-10	−.03
Corporations/ Population	−.17	−1.60-02	−.24***	−.13	1.30-03	−.05
Government Employees/ Population	.66	2.10-03	.15	.91	1.60-03	.57****
1/Population	.28	82.40	.29***	.13	.49	.00
Demand/Population	.76	.05	.59****	.75	.03	.45****
Judges/Population	−.02	−9.50	−.05	.89	.52	.02
R^2			.70			.91

exerts the strongest influence on convictions in both 1960 and 1970. The
effect of government agencies is particularly visible in 1970, contributing
significantly to the explanatory power of the model ($R^2 = .91$). Echoing earlier findings, the number of corporations in a district shows a negative effect in
1960.

As we consider the rate of dismissals and guilty-pleas (in contrast to trials
and convictions) a significant, new factor emerges: the effect of judges. The
findings reported in table 5.10 show that while demand remains an important factor in explaining dismissals and guilty-pleas, it is also apparent that
judges are associated with, and contribute to, an explanation of these modes

of disposition. Furthermore, the significant government effect on guilty-pleas produces an especially strong model for explaining this variable ($R^2 = .87$). As more qualitative studies have suggested, guilty pleas are often the result of efforts in the corridors of justice (see, e.g., Sudnow 1965; Blumberg 1967; Lazerson 1981).These findings lend support to the theme that the government plays a heavy role in obtaining these outcomes.

While evidence suggests that plea bargaining predates the increase in the court's caseload (see, e.g., Heumann 1977), it is equally apparent that such pressures cannot be ignored. Thus, when all is said and done, a great deal of criminal justice activity revolves around obtaining a guilty plea, as the findings in table 5.10 makes clear. As plea bargaining to obtain a guilty plea has moved from an "implicit" to an "explicit" procedure (Newman 1970), our findings suggest that the governmental sector influences this outcome.

Table 5.10
Effects of the Environment, Demand, and Judges on Dismissals and
Guilty Pleas in 1970

	Dismissals/Population			Guilty Pleas/Population		
	r	*b*	*b**	*r*	*b*	*b**
Density	.50	4.80-09	.02	.53	5.20-09	−.01
Corporations/Population	−.10	−2.40-03	−.05	−.10	−2.80-03	−.02
Government Employees/Population	.80	2.40-03	.23	.91	9.30-03	.54****
1/Population	.18	−7.00	−.04	.16	−20.00	−.04
Demand/Population	.73	.01	.21*	.76	.02	.15*
Judges/Population	.82	23.70	.46**	.88	44.00	.31**
R^2			.73			.87

From another perspective, the explicitness of plea bargaining is revealed in discussions of criminal justice reform; here, one may detect an open acceptance and acknowledgement of plea bargaining as a legitimate, even necessary, method and that all we need is to fine-tune the existing process, rather than take steps to use the trial process more effectively (Church 1976).

Interestingly, this change more or less coincides with Supreme Court decisions. That is, the Court's clear position of support has, it seems, given reformers of criminal justice a legitimate basis upon which to build a more rational, practical system. For example, Milton Heumann concludes in his study that "[o]ne reform strategy, then, is to work within the criminal justice system to make plea bargaining as palatable as possible" (1977, 167). Or in a Note in the *Harvard Law Review* (1977) a writer suggested the introduction of an active "magistrate" whose job would be to orchestrate procedure and coordinate various facets of plea bargaining, thereby making criminal justice into a qualitatively new—one might say, technocratic process. While there remain a few "abolitionists" (Kipnis 1979) they are, by and large, a small minority with, basically, a myth in their arsenal.

Historical, Environmental, and Organizational Effects on Civil Dispositions

The rationalization of the civil process, while apparent, is far less advanced than that of the criminal process. Basically, civil procedure is more complicated to control organizationally. Private attorneys are the gate-keepers and they may exercise the prerogative to determine when and if a case shall be litigated. Thus, an out-of-court settlement may be very complex and yet entered as a "no action" by the court, though with the prompting and approval of magistrates and judges (see Ross 1970; Sarat 1976). Gate-keeping strategies of civil lawyers are used for very different reasons and may, in specific cases, have very different effects. Ironically, a case recorded as no action by the court may have raised such technical legal questions that the gate-keepers settled out-of-court, with the result that the disposition process may tend to be less complicated and time consuming from the point of view of the court's personnel. By contrast, cases that come to trial, for example contract cases, may be relatively less complex from the point of view of the lawyers involved, but require the greatest input from judicial personnel and hence constitute a drain on resources. In general, then, the entire civil process is subject to far more idiosyncratic pressures, thus making it much more difficult to rationalize by managerial experts.

The most dramatic change in the disposition of civil cases was the adoption of the pretrial conference by the Judicial Conference in 1938. It is noteworthy that this is the same year that the Administrative Office for the U.S. Courts was established and one year after the court-packing fight in which Roosevelt rested his case on the need for greater efficiency within the judiciary. In the same spirit of administrative efficiency, formalization of pretrial conferences represents a move toward direct, active, and rational control of civil matters by judges. In a pretrial conference, the court may call a meeting of lawyers with or without the presence of clients; the purpose of this meeting is to clarify the issues, the scope of the controversy, and to articulate alternative solutions for the dispute.

This represents a departure from a traditional, structurally bifurcated adversarial procedure. Simply put, the court, rather than the lawyers, attempts to intervene in the final settlement (Rosenberg 1964). In so doing, the traditionally passive, arbiter role of the judge, in particular, is transformed into that of a more active initiator or manager (Resnik 1985).

Yet, in the face of exacerbated social conflicts the traditionally passive, wait-and-see posture of the judge translates into a fairly ineffective social expense of the larger budget of the judiciary. Intraorganizationally, the pretrial conference shifts the adversarial procedure toward an administrative process by providing the judge with the option to intervene actively in a case by issuing orders and preparing work prior to trial. It must be emphasized, however, that this is an ongoing process. For example, more recent incarnations of the pretrial conference can be found in the establishment of local court rules that expedite early disclosure of facts and other matters and, in effect, attempt to "rule out delay" (Flanders 1977; Grau and Sheskin 1982).

Historical changes in the nature of civil dispositions: 1890-1987. Prior to 1938 the disposition of cases followed basically one of two options: no

Table 5.11
The Changing Nature of Civil Dispositions
1890-1987

Year	No Action		Pretrial		All Trials	
	Number	*Percent[a]*	*Number*	*Percent*	*Number*	*Percent*
1890	4,990	48.9	—	—	—	—
1900	6,165	51.1	—	—	—	—
1910	6,616	51.3	—	—	—	—
1920	9,756	51.7	—	—	—	—
1930	18,968	39.1	—	—	—	—
1940	12,639	35.5	6,189[b]	17.4	6,692	18.8
1950	18,891	36.9	16,806	32.8	4,979	9.7
1960	25,111	44.3	16,730	29.5	6,488	11.4
1970	31,056	38.6	40,435	50.2	9,449	11.7
1980	68,747	42.8	76,147	47.4	12,951	8.0
1987	97,804	41.2	127,765	53.8	11,913	5.0

[a]Based on civil terminations (237,482 in 1987).
[b]Pretrial conference adopted in 1938

action or trial. Table 5.11 shows that from 1890 to 1920 about 50 percent of all civil cases received no action by the judiciary and were either withdrawn or settled out of court, with the remainder going to some type of trial disposition. This means that about 50 percent of civil cases were terminated by trials, although there were no official figures available. From 1930 on, the proportion of no action dispositions hovered around 40 percent. The adoption of pretrial conferences after 1938 was at first relatively slow (17.4 percent in 1940). But the procedural innovation began to take a larger share of civil dispositions in the ensuing decades and stands at about the 50-percent level since 1970. One of the main effects of the pretrial conference as a new mode of disposition was to reduce the proportion of trials, from approximately 40 to 50 percent prior to 1930, to 18.8 percent or less after 1940. Although the absolute number of trials has grown between 1970 and 1980, the proportion of trials to all civil terminations has shown a downward trend and stood at 5.0 percent in 1988.

Insofar as the pretrial conference maps out the issues in dispute it also rationalizes and organizes an actual trial should a case move to such a conclusion. As one judge has said, it "prepares the trial judge and counsel 'for the best possible trial' and assures that 'neither surprise nor technicalities win the battle'" (Rosenberg 1964, 8). Yet, pretrial procedures —often a whole series of conferences—may take as much time as a trial and therefore do not necessarily produce the efficiencies and economies they were originally expected to provide (Rosenberg 1964; Glaser 1968). Nevertheless, the pretrial conference, coupled with other modifications to further rationalize adjudication, legitimates negotiation prior to the actual trial process; thus, judges know the script before the trial and are thereby able to organize their time more efficiently.

But the question then arises: Does the pretrial conference also affect the substance—i.e., due process—of adjudication? To what extent can the preparation, procedure, and process of adjudication be separated from its substance? The introduction of plea bargaining has certainly rationalized criminal procedure and in the end challenged, if not undermined, the substance of due process (see esp. Packer 1968). While it can be persuasively argued that the pretrial conference has a similar net effect, there are a number of important differences between these two forms of disposition. Moreover, these differences emphasize the uneven and contradictory forms and an uneven transformation of dispute resolution. Plea bargaining is an informal procedure where the desired guilty plea to a lesser charge concludes the case: The pretrial conference, by contrast, is a more formal procedure that may produce a written record and order by the court. While it is hoped that this conference concludes the case, it may actually be used as preparation for trial. The pretrial conference still incorporates many aspects of a bifurcated organizational model; it is an example of a reform that complements the assumptions of adjudication, though it does give the judge a stronger, more assertive option.

In spite of important differences between criminal and civil dispositions both plea bargaining and pretrial conferences are, nevertheless, the common, or usual, form of legal resolution. That is, both types of conferences must be understood as a more or less incomplete organizational response to greater demands and constrained resources. Moreover, both pay homage, albeit in different ways, to the form and substance of the court's organizational tradition. The origin of these changes is rooted in the rationalization of the state sector, resulting in the court's increasing burden and decreasing judicial resources.

Yet the output of courts is, in one sense, quite removed from the environmental demands of a district since both the caseload and particularly the personnel and resources of this organization theoretically buffer this more external effect. However, legal-governmental factors are essential for explaining the demand on the organization of district courts. Thus, the question arises: Can the court maintain its relatively precarious autonomy and thus account for the delivery of its service? Or, do environmental factors remain important variables for explaining the court's increasing reliance upon more rationalized forms of dispositions? We might also conceive of this question in a slightly different way. Clearly the pressure toward the rationalization of services has its origins in the changing political economy of the district court's environment. But once the court adopts these more rational techniques is it then able to reassert its quasi-independent role? Let us attempt to throw some empirical light on these questions on the basis of an analysis of civil dispositions for 1960 and 1970.

Environmental and organizational effects on civil dispositions: 1960-1970. Table 5.12 shows the simple, unstandardized, standardized, and joint effect of environmental and organizational variables on the ratio of no action dispositions to the population of a district for 1960 and 1970. The striking result of this analysis is that both population density and demand significantly influence the probability that civil cases will be disposed of through no actions. The pressure of an urban environment thus clearly asserts itself in both 1960 and 1970. In 1960, in addition, government presence adds to the explanatory power of the model ($R^2 = .85$). In 1970, we find a small corporate effect, and the total variance explained is relatively small as well.

The rate of pretrial dispositions is influenced by demand and government presence, as table 5.13 shows. For 1960, there is an additional effect of population density, which disappears by 1970. Indeed, we find a significant negative effect of the number of judges on pretrial dispositions ($b^* = -.56$), although the total explained variance ($R^2 = .43$) is only half of that for 1960 ($R^2 = .86$)

Table 5.12
Effects of the Environment, Demand, and Judges on No Actions, 1960-1970

| | No Actions/Population | | | | | |
| | 1960 | | | 1970 | | |
	r	b	b^*	r	b	b^*
Density	.70	2.80-08	.23***	.30	2.80-08	.26*
Corporations/ Population	.15	.01	.08	.24	.02	.22*
Government Employees/ Population	.78	5.40-03	.27****	.15	−1.20-04	−.01
1/Population	.07	−15.50	−.04	.10	46.20	.11
Demand/Population	.87	.07	.54****	.22	.11	.50*
Judges/Population	−.02	13.00	.04	.21	−42.10	−.39
R^2			.85			.22

Table 5.13
Effects of the Environment, Demand, and Judges on Pretrials, 1960-1970

| | Pretrials/Population | | | | | |
| | 1960 | | | 1970 | | |
	r	b	b^*	r	b	b^*
Density	.61	1.40-08	.12*	.23	−1.3	−.09
Corporations/ Population	.02	2.10-03	.02	−.01	−3.80-03	−.03
Government Employees/ Population	.86	.01	.47****	.57	9.60-03	.72***
1/Population	.08	15.50	.04	.28	174.20	.30**
Demand/Population	.85	.05	.43****	.42	.15	.48**
Judges/Population	−.13	−22.20	−.08	.53	−84.70	−.56*
R^2			.86			.43

Finally, the civil trial rate is successfully explained by our model for 1960 where density, demand, and government combine to explain 85 percent of the variance (see table 5.14). But, in 1970 the picture is quite different: the effect of these variables is not significant in an explanation of the civil trial rate. Because demand has, generally, the most persistent influence on civil dispositions, we can only speculate that the government's law-and-order policy had its intended effect to push the court to move criminal cases in a more timely fashion. But, the picture becomes somewhat more complicated and subtle as the findings of chapter 6 reveal.

Table 5.14
Effects of the Environment, Demand, and Judges on Civil Trials, 1960-1970

| | *Civil Trials/Population* | | | | | |
| | *1960* | | | *1970* | | |
	r	b	b^*	r	b	b^*
Density	.57	6.00-09	.12*	−.13	−2.60-09	−.11
Corporations/ Population	.00	−1.20-03	−.03	.11	−1.30-04	−.01
Government Employees/ Population	.84	3.40-03	.42****	.06	8.80-04	.39
1/Population	.20	29.20	.17**	.38	46.40	.48***
Demand/Population	.85	.02	.45****	.09	.02	.35
Judges/Population	−.06	−9.90	−.08	.06	17.00	−.68
R^2			.85			.20

Conclusion

A distinct organizational feature of American forms of dispute resolution used to be a structurally bifurcated decision-making model that was exemplified most clearly in a trial. Indeed, the techniques and procedures of the trial itself became more formalized and majestic, complementing its traditional, inefficient underpinnings.

As the institution confronted growing demands, the upshot of this predicament created the conditions for a manager's nightmare that became especially clear during the New Deal and post-World War II years. Thus, until quite recently the federal courts have remained unusually impervious to managed or self-initiated organizational change, though the current picture is changing.

During the Great Depression, with the benefits of plea bargaining established, if little discussed (but see The American Law Institute, *A Study of the Business of the Federal Courts*, 1934), and the expanded role of the state leaving its mark on the civil docket, the tendency toward experimentation in the disposition of civil cases began to unfold. The adoption of the pretrial conference, giving the court, through the judge, a more active, interventionist role was an organizational response to this dilemma. But, unlike plea bargaining, the scope of control that the government might exert is subject to many countervailing checks and balances, if not contradictions. Therefore, even as procedural techniques have been refined they continue to prove costly since adjudicatory trappings and formal procedures are nearly unavoidable in the civil arena.

Not surprisingly, then, one hears of other alternatives being suggested. If the problem lies in the fact that once a civil case is before the court, in whatever form, it requires costly techniques, then the obvious solution is to push for diversion and informal dispute resolution outside the court where such exigencies can be put to rest. Hence, there are proposals to establish strategies for "semi-automatic relief," coercive arbitration, ombudsmen, and mediation, in addition to delegalization and no-fault laws (Johnson, et al 1977; Harrington 1982). That is, reforms in the disposition of civil cases are moving in the direction of informal pre-pretrial and extra-judicial alternatives (also see NIDR).

The more rationalized and—we would say—technocratic procedures, be it permutations on plea bargaining or pretrial conferences, find their way into the courts through means that complement the unique features of this institution's history and political role. Max Weber (1968) suggested that modern organizations must inevitably become bureaucratically structured in order to survive the demands of a rationalized world. The organizational history of the judiciary is a dramatic challenge to that assumption. That is, bureaucratic coordination, as such, is only one among many strategies of social and organizational control (Edwards 1979; Heydebrand 1983). In the case of courts, both plea bargaining and pretrial conferences rationalize the irrational; that is, they systematize and simplify the dispensation of justice. Yet, to date, they have not incorporated or demanded a bureaucratic hierarchy or division of labor typical of, for example, the civil service.

Translated into practice, however, it is clear that such strategies yield to some pressures more than to others. While the language of efficiency and productivity tends to be universalistic (i.e., efficiency is defined as a gain for all, for the whole society), it clearly has differential consequences for various groups and classes since it generates priorities and unequal treatment. It determines who gets to use the courts and who does not, who gets to see a judge, who can insist on a trial, and who can use the courts to produce a favorable legal change.

In sum, it is abundantly clear that the ambiguous outcome of the activity of courts is circumscribed by environmental and caseload demands which, in turn, generate managerial strategies of rationalization. Judicial action—indirect or direct, passive or active—is the end product of complex and powerful structural constraints on the organization of the court. While legal theory assumes that judges must be above constraints to be effective because they are trained to be professionally objective umpires, such a notion is, it seems, an artifact of a liberal tradition. Yet the persistence of that peculiarly American tenet is eloquent evidence of the resilience of long-held ideologies.

But it is also true that those who promise efficient delivery are winning the ear of judges and the findings from this chapter may certainly begin to explain why. Whether they deliver what they promise, and at what price, depends upon numerous factors, and is the subject of the next chapter.

CHAPTER 6

*

The Organizational Structure of Courts
and Judicial Decision-Making

Professionally, judges lay claim to legitimacy because of their monopoly over skill and knowledge in decision-making (Larson 1977). We have seen that the forms of civil and criminal dispute resolution have moved in a more integrated, flexible, and simplified direction in which judges have assumed a more proactive role. Yet, a shift from trial to pretrial may still be orchestrated by judges themselves without undermining their professional judicial control.

By contrast, managers of professionals lay claim to legitimacy by improving the nature of decisions measured in terms of cost-effectiveness and productivity (Freidson 1986). Because a manager's task is to insure productivity, we now turn to a consideration of this important issue. To this end, in the first section we trace the productivity of courts from 1910 to 1988 and relate output to judicial as well as to nonjudicial personnel in order to weigh the impact of management concerns.

While analysis of the numbers is essential, it is only part of the story of managerial influence. Indeed, reading insiders' commentaries—especially judges and some legal academics—suggests that courts have become revolving door bureaucracies. Thus, in section two we turn to this insiders' discussion of bureaucracy and consider how this development is described. Because *bureaucracy* is such a loaded term, it is especially important to analyze precisely the changes in courts to which it refers.

But, to move this discussion further, we then turn to an analysis of the intraorganizational structure of courts and its impact on forms of dispute resolution by selected categories of cases. This detailed analysis again demonstrates the importance of weighing the effect of the whole organization on modes of output. Of more analytic importance, these findings document a trend toward a technocratic mode of coordinating work, one where we may trace elements of bureaucratic and professional coordination but combined in qualitatively new ways. In this chapter, we present the last link in the over-

Table 6.1
The Growth in the Number of Judges in U.S. District Courts, 1882-1988

Year	Judges	Year	Judges	Year	Judges	Year	Judges	Year	Judges	Year	Judges
1882	54	1900	65	1918	95	1936	151	1954	245*	1972	400
1883	57	1901	71	1919	98	1937	168	1955	244	1973	400
1884	55	1902	74	1920	99	1938	175	1956	244	1974	400
1885	56	1903	70	1921	96	1939	183a	1957	242	1975	400
1886	57	1904	74	1922	100	1940	190	1958	243	1976	399
1887	–	1905	74	1923	110*	1941	191	1959	245	1977	398
1888	58	1906	78	1924	119	1942	193	1960	245	1978	399
1889	58	1907	81	1925	128	1943	192	1961	307*	1979	516*
1890	58	1908	84	1926	125	1944	192	1962	307	1980	516
1891	64	1909	85	1927	125	1945	193	1963	307	1981	516
1892	64	1910	88	1928	130	1946	195	1964	307	1982	516
1893	65	1911	91	1929	140*	1947	194	1965	307	1983	515
1894	66	1912	88	1930	146	1948	193	1966	336*	1984	515
1895	65	1913	92	1931	147	1949	193	1967	342	1985	575*
1896	65	1914	93	1932	149	1950	215*	1968	342	1986	575
1897	66	1915	93	1933	148	1951	218	1969	341	1987	575
1898	67	1916	94	1934	148	1952	218	1970	401*	1988	575
1899	66	1917	93	1935	134	1953	218	1971	400		

* An increase of ten or more judges over the previous figure.　　Underlined figures indicate figures for decades.
aFigures from 1939 on refer to authorized district judgeships rather than actual judges.

Sources: 1882-1938: *Federal Reporter*, as compiled by Michael Luttig and Anthony Marks for the U.S. Supreme Court; 1939-1988 *Administrative Office of the U.S. Courts*.

all chain of causation: the impact of organizational structure and resources on the outcomes of judicial decision-making.

Judicial Productivity in Historical Perspective

The American federal judicial system has undergone such dramatic organizational changes that it is difficult to speak of it as one system. In chapter 1 we documented some of the major administrative changes and reorganizations that marked the growth of the federal judiciary, suggesting at the same time a new periodization for its administrative development. These largely qualitative changes in the organizational evolution of the third branch are also described by quantitative changes, namely, the growth in the number of judges. We are not suggesting the existence of a perfect correlation between qualitative administrative change and numerical increase in the judicial labor force. While both types of changes depended largely on congressional action, the growth in the number of judges shows some characteristic discontinuities that are due both to presidential initiatives and to the intermittent political (congressional) resistance to administrative requests by the judiciary for increased judicial labor power. It is this phenomenon that explains the uneven pattern of growth of the past 100 years, a period in which the number of district judges increased over tenfold, from 54 in 1882 to 575 in 1988 (see table 6.1).

In examining this pattern of growth, we can detect certain breaks where, after a period of no or slow growth, the number of judges suddenly jumped by ten or more slots, often in response to surveys and pressures by the judiciary. After 1922 these pressures were somewhat more formalized and exerted by the Judicial Conference. These breaks occurred between 1922 and 1923, 1928 and 1929, and 1935 and 1938, and in the years 1950, 1954, 1961, 1966, 1970, 1979, and 1985. David Clark (1981, 100) suggests that the major changes in the number of district court judges can be related to specific presidential terms. Thus, it was during the presidential terms of Harding (1921-23), Roosevelt (1937-40), Kennedy (1961-63), Nixon (1968-72), Carter (1977-80), and Reagan (1980-84) that particularly large increases in the number of judges occurred.

While the growth of the U.S. population and the litigation rate had, of course, something to do with this growth of the federal judiciary, as we documented in chapter 3, other social and political factors also had an influence [also see Clark's (1981) analysis]. Moreover, the Judicial Conference conducted periodic surveys to determine the need for judgeships in federal courts (Cunningham 1980). As a result of the 1972 survey, the Senate's Judiciary Committee developed certain standards for determining the need for additional judgeships:

1. Annual filings in excess of 400 cases per judge

2. Annual terminations in excess of the national average of 358 per judge

3. Judicial work time (bench time) averaging more than 110 days per year per judge

4. Efficient use by the district court of existing judges, supporting personnel, and procedural devices in order to cope with its existing workload.

Some of these standards were relaxed in later deliberations, due to the recognition of the complexity of cases in larger metropolitan courts and due to the variations in judicial styles of decision-making (e.g., traditional adjudication vs. judicial case management).

Let us look at the empirical patterns of growth. Table 6.2 shows the growth, in 10-year intervals from 1910 to 1980, of the adult U.S. population 18 years or older, the number of total filings in federal district courts, the number of district court judges, the ratio of the number of judges per one million adult population, and the number of judges per 1000 filings (civil

Table 6.2
Dimensions of Case Filings, 1910-1980

Year	Adult Population 18 yrs. + (in thousands)	Total Filings	Number of Judges	Judges Per Adult Population (in millions)	Judges per Filings (in thousands)	Number of Filings per Judge
1910	57,346	28,652	88	1.53	3.07	326
1920	66,839	77,696	99	1.48	1.27	785
1930	80,069	135,630	146	1.82	1.08	929
1940	91,763	65,737	190	2.07	2.89	346
1950	104,624	89,666	215	2.05	2.40	417
1960	116,146	86,099	245	2.11	2.85	351
1970	135,177	127,280	401	2.97	3.15	317
1980	162,761	196,757	516	3.17	2.62	381

and criminal). Table 6.2 discloses that there is a gradual increase from 1.53 judges per one million adults in 1910, to 3.17 judges in 1980, with slight deviations from the pattern in 1920 and 1950, possibly due to postwar delays in litigation and prosecution. In contrast to the ratio of judges per one million adults the ratio of judges per 1000 filings in district courts suggests a more erratic pattern as it moves from 3.07 judges per 1000 filings in 1910, to 2.62 judges in 1980, with a low of 1.08 judges in 1930 and a high of 3.15 judges per 1000 filings in 1970.

Similarly, as table 6.3 shows, the total caseload demand (filings and pending cases) per judge follows a relatively erratic pattern. Thus, the demand

Table 6.3
Total Demand (total filings and pending cases), Number of Judges,
Demand per Judge, and Percent Change in Demand per Judge for
U.S. District Courts, 1910-1988

Year	Total Demand	Number of Judges	Demand per Judge	Percent of Change in Demand per Judge
1910	86,482	88	983	—
1920	166,712	99	1,684	+ 71
1930	229,950	146	1,575	− 7
1940	103,930	190	547	−188
1950	151,906	215	707	+ 29
1960	154,151	245	629	− 12
1970	241,397	401	602	− 4
1980	397,629	516	771	+ 28
1988	552,642	575	961	+ 25

of 983 cases per judge in 1910 was only slightly higher than the 961 cases per judge in 1988, with 1920 and 1930 again constituting the high points (mainly due to prohibition cases) and 1940 the low point of only 547 cases per judge. Together, the figures reported in tables 6.2 and 6.3 reveal considerable variation in the workload of judges from 1910 to 1988.

The real question of productivity of judges, however, can best be approached by looking at the number of terminations per judge (see also Landes 1971; Gillespie 1976). Moreover, we need to take into account the number of nonjudicial personnel who provide organizational "support" for judges. Tables 6.4 and 6.5 as well as figure 6.1 give the results of this analysis.

Table 6.4
Total Number of Terminations, Terminations per Judge,
Percent Terminations per Judge of Demand per Judge,
Total Civil Terminations, Civil Terminations per Judge,
Total Civil Trials, and Civil Trials per Judge for
U.S. District Courts, 1910-1988

Year	Number of Terminations	Terminations per Judge	As Percent of Demand per Judge	Number of Civil Terminations	Civil Terminations per Judge	Number of Civil Trials	Civil Trials per Judge
1910	28,280	321	32.7	12,909	147	—	—
1920	53,113	536	31.8	18,883	191	—	—
1930	131,074	898	57.0	48,465	332	—	—
1940	69,023	363	66.4	35,597	187	6,692	35
1950	88,124	410	58.0	51,200	238	4,979	23
1960	85,748	350	55.6	56,715	231	6,488	26
1970	117,253	292	48.5	80,435	201	9,449	24
1980	195,712	379	49.2	160,481	311	12,951	25
1988	279,739	487	50.7	238,753	415	12,536	22

Table 6.4 shows that the productivity of judges has not increased markedly over time. Indeed, the variation in the number of terminations per judge (from a high of 898 in 1930, to a low of 292 in 1970) roughly mirrors that of the demand (total workload) confronting judges (see table 6.3). Productivity was highest in 1920 and 1930 when the demand suddenly increased. But the same was not true for the increase in terminations from 1960 to 1980. Productivity declined from 350 terminations per judge in 1960 to 292 in 1970, but rose again to 487 in 1988 (note that the average for 1972 was pegged at 358).

On the whole, however, judges appear to have coped valiantly with the workload confronting them. Calculating the number of terminations per judge as a percentage of the demand per judge shows an increase in demand-related productivity from 32.7 percent in 1910 to a high of 66.4 percent in 1940 (see table 6.3). After 1940, the figures decline somewhat and appear to stabilize around 50 percent from 1970 to 1980. These figures suggest that judges have generally kept pace with the balance between the backlog of pending cases and new filings.

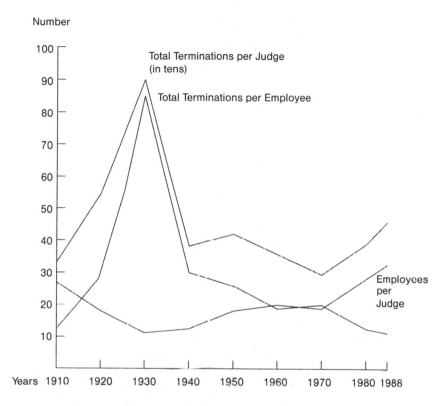

Number

Figure 6.1 Number of Total Terminations, 1910-1988

Civil terminations per judge show a pattern similar to that of total terminations per judge, although at a somewhat lower level of variability. The rise of the civil caseload in federal courts (see chapter 2) does not only imply a numerical increase in volume, but an increase in the complexity of cases (see chapter 3). Thus, increasing complexity of the civil caseload may in itself be a factor in the relatively low number of civil terminations per judge. Nevertheless, judges seem to rise to the occasion when the demand increases, although the intermittent increase in the number of judges may cause the average productivity figures to decline. Still, in 1988 the number of civil terminations per judge stood at its highest level ever (415). The number of civil trials per judge was highest in 1940, but seems to be relatively stable from 1950 to the present, that is, about 20 to 25 trials per judge.

Table 6.5
Productivity of Court Personnel, 1910-1988

Year	Number of Judges	Percent Increase of Judges	Number of Employees	Percent Increase of Employees	Employees per Judge	Termi-nations per Judge	Termi-nations per Employee
1910	88	—	2,252	—	26	321	13
1920	99	13	1,827	−23	18	536	29
1930	146	47	1,547	−18	11	898	85
1940	190	30	2,221	44	12	363	31
1950	215	13	3,492	57	16	410	25
1960	245	14	4,679	34	19	350	18
1970	401	64	6,389	37	16	292	18
1980	516	29	13,903	118	27	379	14
1988	575	11	20,743*	49	36	487	13

Source: Adapted from David Clark, "Adjudication to Administration: A Statistical Analysis of Federal District Courts in the Twentieth Century," 55 *Southern California Law Revisions* (1981), (table 2, p. 86). The figures exclude federal judges at the district and circuit levels as well as those serving at certain special courts between 1910 and 1930.

Annual Report of the Director,, Administrative Office of the U.S. Courts, 1988.

The question arises: generally, would judicial productivity be lower were it not for the enormous growth in the organizational support staff of courts, especially after 1970? Table 6.5 represents an attempt to throw some initial light on this question although it cannot provide a complete answer.[1] Obviously, the organizational support system of the courts, as measured by the number of nonjudicial employees, grew tremendously after 1940, that is, after an initial decline from 2,252 in 1910, to 1,547 in 1930. The major increases occurred from 1940 to 1950 (57 percent), and especially from 1970 to 1980 (118 percent). The ratio of nonjudicial employees per judge grew in a similar way, with the greatest increase occurring from 1970 (16) to 1988 (36).[2]

The productivity of nonjudicial employees by and large parallels that of judges (see table 6.5 and fig. 6.1). Both curves increased dramatically during the prohibition period, then tended to decline up to 1970. From 1970 to 1988, however, there is a curious divergence in that the productivity of judges goes up as that of the nonjudicial sector declined.

Superimposing the curve for the ratio of employees per judge on these two productivity curves in figure 6.1 shows that during this last decade, the ratio of employees per judge rises parallel to that of the productivity of judges. One might speculate that up to 1960, the growth of the organizational support system represented a bureaucratic drag on the federal judiciary. As nonjudicial employees were added to the system, productivity tended to decline because there were now more employees per termination. But from 1960 on, and especially from 1970 to 1988, we can observe an increase in both the ratio of employees per judge and in judicial productivity, suggesting a qualitative change in the way the organizational support system affected the output and productivity of the federal judiciary as a whole. This change, then, might also explain why the number of terminations per employee tended to decrease from 1970 to 1988 while both the ratio of employees per judge and judicial productivity increased. These findings suggest that this change was the first time in the judiciary's history that organizational innovations, rather than generating a drag, contributed positively to judicial and court productivity.[3]

Indeed, the increased productivity of the court coincides with the formation of the Federal Judicial Center, and a more self-conscious effort to think through policy options for administering courts. This emergence of a technocratic approach to judicial administration must be distinguished from the effect of earlier approaches to case management (also see chapter 1.) During the 1960s and 1970s, with the introduction of new organizational and administrative approaches to the district courts, the growth of nonjudicial personnel began to affect positively judicial productivity. During this period, the courts did not merely add personnel to their otherwise unchanged authority relations and methods of disposition, but rather began to modify relations and methods themselves. As Clark puts it, "The doubling of support personnel (between 1970 and 1980) is likely to facilitate case processing, but at the same time to increase the administrative responsibilities of federal judges" (1981,88).

Traditionally, administrative responsibility was discharged by the chief judge and the chief clerk in small courts, and by a committee of judges and the clerk's office in larger courts. Predictably, however, the growth of the support staff led to pressures to appoint district court executives. Between 1981 and 1984, the Judicial Conference and the Congressional Appropriations Committee authorized a pilot program involving the experimental appointment of district court executives in six metropolitan courts (Eldridge 1984, 9). The difficulties in implementing such an experiment are underscored by the fact that it took over three years to install six district court executives and that, despite the availability of a comprehensive description of their duties, there was considerable variation in the roles and functions the district court executives were actually assigned or permitted to perform within the traditional administrative structure of the participating district courts (Eldridge 1984, 17-21).

Let us now turn to a brief look at the nature and internal structure of this organizational support system of district courts.

The Organizational Control of Courts: Professional or Bureaucratic Control?

We have defined courts as public, professional, labor-intensive service organizations and as loosely coupled networks of activities, rather than bureaucratically integrated formal organizations (see chap. 1). This definition does not prejudge the degree to which courts may be actually professionalized or bureaucratized. Clearly, small district courts are more likely to have a traditional structure than large metropolitan ones (see chap. 4). They are also more likely to be preprofessional and prebureaucratic where judges or chief judges have the option to run their district courts more like a personal feudal fiefdom or patrimonial principality than a modern rationalized organization with an elaborate staff and a bureaucratic clerk's office which, in turn, has a hierarchical division of labor, formal rules, well-defined career lines, and impersonal relations among officials and between them and clients (Weber 1968).

But, to emphasize again, we are not suggesting that large modern district courts are bureaucracies or that the federal judiciary finds itself in a process of bureaucratization. The discussion of this issue in the relevant literature is often complicated by differences in the use of the term *bureaucracy* and by uncertainty as to the process or unit of analysis to which the term *bureaucracy* might or might not apply.

There are at least four separate ways in which the notions of bureaucracy and, less frequently, routine administration are used in discussions of the organizational aspects of courts. First, the routinization of work due to simple, repetitive cases and stable caseloads is sometimes seen as leading to an administrative mentality in decision-making that is distinguished from the more demanding, reflective, deliberative and reasoned adjudication of complex disputes in the light of formal rules and legal doctrine (Friedman and Percival 1976; Fuller 1981). Here, routinization of the task is seen as leading to the kind of low-level administrative rationality sometimes associated with bureaucracy. These authors, however, have little to say about the actual organization of courts, the notion of case management by "managerial judges," or the bureaucratization of the judiciary as a whole.

Second, there is the recent literature on the activist, interventionist role of the judge in pretrial proceedings and post-trial implementation of decisions (Chayes 1976), in case management (Flanders 1977; Peckham 1981), in the "twilight of the adversary system" (Blumberg 1967), in the emergence of the "managerial judge" (Resnik 1982; Flanders 1984), and in various forms of legal negotiations such as plea bargaining (Feeley 1979), and the mandatory settlement conference (Menkel-Meadow 1984, 1985). Together, this literature points to a change in the methods of case dispositions. Here, we find intermittent references to modern organization theory, but generally only very selective treatment of the rationalization of judicial procedures in terms of "management" rather than "bureaucracy." Steven Flanders (1976, 1977, 1984) points out that in district courts the clerk's office may have certain "bureaucratic" characteristics, but he generally emphasizes the professional-collegial character of courts and the complexity of judicial decision-making.

Third, a number of authors, many of them active judges at higher levels of the federal judiciary, speak about bureaucracy and the bureaucratization of the judiciary in a more global sense. For example, Judge Patrick E. Higginbotham (1980) decries bureaucracy as the "carcinoma of the federal judiciary," referring to a number of different factors such as the introduction of efficiency procedures and scientific method into courts, the rise of managerialism and judicial activism, and the delegation of judicial functions and powers to magistrates and bankruptcy referees.

Judge Alvin B. Rubin (1980), emphasizing—like many others—the increasing volume and complexity of cases, speaks of the need to curb bureaucratization, to clearly separate judicial functions (adjudication) from managerial ones (administration), and to subordinate administrative staff and support functions to the guidance of judicial-collegial authority. Like many judges, he advocates the reduction of federal jurisdiction and an increase in resources as solutions to case overload without, however, changing the traditional authority structure of the courts. Similar proposals are voiced and discussed by David Clark (1981, 148-52), Harry Edwards (1983), Richard Hoffman (1982), Wade McCree (1981), and Joseph Vining (1981). An exception is Judge Richard Posner's (1985) proposal to eliminate "bureaucracy" together with the federal court crisis by means of introducing a market model of justice. Owen Fiss (1981, 26), taking a somewhat more academic approach, defines a bureaucratized judiciary as "a highly complex organization characterized by a number of hierarchical relationships and which tends to insulate judges from critical educational experiences and to diffuse responsibility." Unfortunately, no clear distinction is made between *judicial hierarchies*, which resemble traditional professional hierarchies based on degrees of expertise, status and jurisdiction, and *bureaucratic hierarchies* where there is formal super- and subordination of offices based on rank authority. Needless to say, the power of supervision and judicial review of lower courts by higher ones is professional rather than bureaucratic in nature and has little to do with the potential bureaucratization of courts, a point well grasped and discussed by Judge Patricia Wald (1983).

Fourth, the bureaucratization of courts is often discussed in the context of the changing role of the third branch vis-à-vis the executive and legislative branches of government. This is the problem of the "imperial judiciary"(Glazer 1975) on the one hand and, on the other, the fear that through unfettered judicial activism (i.e., the intervention of the courts in legislation and social policy-making) the third branch will replace Congress or else become an adjunct of the executive branch (Wald 1983, 773). Notwithstanding the mild contradiction in this position (courts as dominant political institutions, yet adjuncts of the modern state), the possible constitutional shift in the role of the judiciary has evoked much commentary (Bickel 1962; Cox 1976; Berger 1977; Horowitz 1977). And while much of this debate focuses on the role and decisions of the Supreme Court, the trial courts of the federal judicial system are equally involved since they are the courts of first instance with a wide range of original jurisdiction. Curiously, there is little discussion in this literature of the fiscal dependency of federal courts on Congress and of their relative political disadvantage vis-à-vis the power of the federal bureaucracy (see chap. 4 for a description of the "double bind" of the judiciary's budget).

The four constructs of "bureaucratization" of the courts just outlined—routinization of cases, the rise of case management and the managerial judge, the development of bureaucratic support staffs under the guidance of court executives, and the notion of judicial activism and "government by judiciary"—represent, of course, important perspectives on the transformation of modern courts and judicial behavior under the impact of changes in the environment and task structure of the judiciary. But it is difficult to discern in what sense the term *bureaucratization* appropriately captures what is described or what is going on in federal courts. First, the routinization of cases and of the task structure may be a real phenomenon in certain trial courts at the county or municipal level. However, in federal courts the civil caseload is, if anything, becoming both more routine (e.g., social security, prisoner petitions, and some types of diversity cases) and more complex (e.g., civil rights, patents, antitrust) and requires greater expertise; therefore, the managerial dilemma of federal courts is that routine administration and case processing of tasks are simply not adequate for the full array and unpredictable filings of federal cases.

Second, judicial case management may be on the rise in federal courts, but it is questionable whether it has the rule-bound, public characteristics of bureaucracy or complements the contours of the adversary process. If anything, judicial case management—just like plea bargaining—has accentuated informal procedures, early involvement of the court, fashioning a resolution to fit the dispute and the efficiency of quick results (guilty pleas or settlements) over the values of due process. No doubt, when pressed, all members of the judicial family point out that some cases require adjudication, including trial; there is, however, a tendency to reduce this requirement to a minimum—to try as few cases as possible. Conceptually and practically, good case management translates into good pretrial preparation and termination prior to trial.

Third, the judiciary may be "imperial" with respect to policies and decisions that have augmented the active involvement of judges in administrative agency litigation and in the daily life of many social institutions. But it is precisely by virtue of that involvement that the judiciary is also carrying out the work of the legislative and executive branches. We will return to this issue in the next chapter.

Finally, there are some definite changes occurring in the organizational structure of courts, commonly referred to as bureaucratization. Few of the observers concerned with this issue, however, raise the question as to what extent modern courts experience organizational changes other than bureaucratization or, alternatively, shoring up the traditional professional model of organizational control. That is, rationalization is not distinguished from bureaucratization. It is as if Max Weber's pessimistic vision of the "iron cage" —the increasing and inevitable bureaucratization of modern life—is accepted as axiomatic, with the only alternative being the return to, or the "modernization" of, the professional model of judicial administration in which adjudication and adversary procedure still play a dominant role. Even Owen Fiss (1981, 8) who rightly rejects Weber's model of bureaucracy for courts, nevertheless believes "the bureaucratization of the judiciary, like the bureaucratization of the world, cannot be avoided."

What is the justification for such pessimism? Is judges' power being usurped by bureaucratic officials? Is there any empirical evidence for the bureaucratization of the organizational structure of the courts? Or, do the data point toward a rationality of a different sort?

The Internal Structure of the District Courts

An empirical examination of the internal relations of U.S. district courts suggests that the traditional professional core of court structure—the district judges—co-exists quite comfortably with a number of so-called "bureaucratic" elements, such as the judicial support staff, the clerk's office, and various other measures of vertical (grade-step level) and horizontal differentiation (number of positions). Even magistrates, a recent administrative innovation in district courts (Seron 1983, 1985), fit in with this structure.

Table 6.6 shows the simple correlations between nine "internal" (Variables 1-9) as well as four more "external" (Variables 10-13) aspects of the organizational structure of all district courts in 1973. Internal dimensions of the courts' structure include the personnel and resources within this organization, such as law clerks, magistrates, personnel in the clerk's office. External dimensions of the courts' structure include personnel directly tied to the institution of the court, but who are either privately employed (e.g., lawyers) or who work for other agencies of the government (e.g., Department of Justice employees).

Table 6.6
Simple Correlations among Thirteen Organizational Variables for
U.S. District Courts in 1973 (N = 84)

	1	2	3	4	5	6	7	8	9	10	11	12
1. District Judges	—											
2. Support Staff	.94	—										
3. Clerk's Office	.93	.90	—									
4. Nonjudicial Personnel	.94	.94	.95	—								
5. Total Personnel	.95	.95	.95	.99	—							
6. Total Resources	.95	.95	.94	.97	.97	—						
7. Number of Positions	.83	.82	.80	.83	.83	.82	—					
8. Grade-step	.49	.44	.36	.51	.50	.45	.59	—				
9. Magistrates	.85	.80	.83	.90	.87	.83	.81	.57	—			
10. Lawyers	.72	.67	.66	.75	.79	.73	.79	.84	.79	—		
11. U.S. Attorneys	.89	.87	.92	.94	.94	.94	.73	.43	.82	.67	—	
12. Dept. of Justice Personnel	.78	.76	.75	.84	.83	.83	.80	.71	.85	.89	.76	—
13. Total Federal Judicial Personnel	.82	.79	.76	.86	.85	.83	.85	.81	.85	.95	.76	.93

Let us first look at the triadic constellation of judges, support staff, and personnel in the clerk's office. The correlations between these three traditional elements of court structure range between .90 and .94. This is not surprising since the size of the support staff of a judge is mandated and fixed (2 law clerks, 1 secretary). The size of the clerk's office is also closely related to the number of judges (see also Eldridge 1984, table 1, p. 5; and Dubois 1984, both of whom describe the administrative structure of the largest metropolitan district courts). The size of the court (nonjudicial personnel, total personnel) is highly correlated with the number of district judges (.94 and .95). In other words, the relationships hold in both large and small courts. The only other variable that is highly correlated with these basic elements of district court structure is the amount of financial resources, measured here by the total salaries for judicial and nonjudicial personnel as well as financial resources available to the chief judge of the court as a whole (jury expenses, Criminal Justice Act services, and expenses for court-appointed counsel). Resources are correlated with size and nonjudicial personnel (.97), the number of district judges (.95), and the clerk's office (.94).

Three elements in the structure of district courts may be construed as "bureaucratic"; they are the number of positions (horizontal differentiation or division of labor), average grade-step level of nonjudicial personnel (skill level), and the number of magistrates, the newest arrival on the court scene. The number of positions and average grade-step level describe patterns of differentiation, or hierarchy, within the support structure of the courts. For example, the grade-step scheme is the judicial service counterpart to the civil service levels in the federal bureaucracy.[4] The number of magistrates describes differentiation of professional-judicial personnel, i.e., the emergence of two tiers of judicial officers.

Both dimensions of the court's "bureaucracy" are related to the traditional structure of the district courts, but, as the findings in table 6.6 show, at a lower level of statistical association. Obviously, size and resources of judicial and nonjudicial labor will be highly correlated. But, it is equally apparent from the findings in table 6.6 that the size of the judicial labor force is only weakly related to a *differentiated* nonjudicial support system. Thus, the average grade-step level is only moderately correlated with the number of judges (.49), the judicial support staff (.44), and the clerk's office (.36), as well as with resources (.45). On the other hand, grade-step level shows slightly higher correlations with the size of the nonjudicial labor force [nonjudicial personnel = (.51), total personnel (.50), and number of positions (.59)] while the correlations between number of positions and clerks office (r = .80) and nonjudicial personnel (r = .83) are each stronger.

These findings suggest that larger courts are able to achieve economies of scale of a specific type. As courts get larger so, too, do the number of different types of nonjudicial workers (.99); however, such workers tend to be drawn from a less skilled labor pool. Although the size of the nonjudicial sector does not decrease with the increasing total size of the court, the level of training (grade-step) for these positions does not keep pace (.51). This is even more striking for the clerk's office (.36).

Conventionally, "economies of scale" means that larger organizations may reduce their "administrative overhead" or "support staff." Consider the problem from the following point of view. Smaller and structurally simpler courts may have certain inherent inefficiencies from the point of view of administrative overhead and optimal budgeting because an organizational minimum must be met. But, smaller courts are also more labor-intensive and are able to achieve a more unrestricted, hence efficient, utilization of labor power. By contrast, larger courts may develop complexities of communication and coordination that offset the gains from scale (Blau, Heydebrand, and Stauffer 1966). Larger courts may, therefore, require either an increase in the administrative overhead proportional to the increase in structural complexity, or an altogether different form of organization and administration capable of dealing with structural complexity. The practice of assuming that larger units are, by definition, more cost-effective reflects the managerial ideology of business administration that is influencing courts, just as it did hospitals some fifty years ago, even though courts are still much less thoroughly rationalized. In sum, large courts seem to achieve economies of scale not through an absolute reduction of administrative overhead (clerk's office, .95), but rather through a reduced cost of those employed (grade-step .50).

In contrast to the relationship of skill level to the traditional "internal" structure of courts, the correlations between grade-step level and the "external" variables (Variables 10-13, ranging from .71 to .84) are relatively high, with the exception of U.S. Attorneys (.43). This suggests that the presence of external agencies and forces in the immediate environment of district courts generates demands for special and more highly skilled services. Certainly the presence of Department of Justice agencies (Variable 12, .71) and other federal courts and judicial services (Variable 13, .81) would fall into this category, as do lawyers, especially in view of the heavy civil caseload of district courts.

Early experimentation with the use of magistrates revolved around the delegation of pretrial motions and case preparation as some judges began to see the advantages of sharing tasks with these new players. The findings reported in table 6.6 for 1973 show that the number of magistrates is correlated with the size of courts (.87), support staff (.80), but that each of these correlations is weaker than the respective associations shown for judges (row 1, cols. 1-6). The correlation shown between resources and magistrates (.83) is also less than that shown for judges (.95). By contrast, the correlation between magistrates and grade-step (.57) is greater than for judges (.49).

Together, these findings suggest that magistrates were first used in courts with access to fewer resources, i.e., fewer judges.

In the early 1970s, the courts experienced a notable increase in filings (see chap. 3) without a concomitant increase in judicial labor force (after 1969) in part due to Democratic party resistance to give President Nixon the opportunity to appoint federal judges in light of political controversies surrounding Watergate. The districts that were especially affected by this problem included the then rapidly expanding areas of the Southwest and West—the Sunbelt. Indeed, when Congress finally acted to expand the judicial labor force in 1978, many of these districts doubled in size. During this early period of no-growth coupled with increased work pressures, delegation of duties to magistrates—sometimes of duties that were not clearly within their power at the time—was one of very few options available for coping with the organizational dilemma of system overload.

Though district judges have been, generally, reluctant to accept innovations, including the use of magistrates, the confluence of these forces during the early seventies necessitated a change in practice—especially in some of the smaller and medium-size courts that were also experiencing rapid increases in their caseload. Thus, it was the midsize range of the court system which, generally, turned to the use of magistrates when faced with the alternative and more complex process of attaining additional judges. To the extent that magistrates may substitute for judges in some instances (Resnik 1985; Seron 1985) the literature also suggests that such practices were more common in the smaller- and middle-sized courts of the federal judicial system.

The delegation of pretrial responsibilities to magistrates remains a controversial point of debate because it challenges the traditional boundaries of professional responsibility of Article III judges. Nevertheless, the expanded use of magistrates coupled with the development of newer judge-magistrate work relations does foreshadow an important development. In some districts a teamwork approach between judge and magistrate has begun to emerge (Seron 1985, 1986). That is, some judges participate in an organizational model whereby magistrates hear all pretrial matters and determine when or if the assigned judge's assistance is necessary. Here, the initial burden for getting the case ready for trial is with the magistrate, and the judge intervenes only if some additional authority or clout is required. In practice, the magistrate becomes a judicial officer with responsibility for the gamut of issues that may arise during pretrial and with discretion to decide when the trial judge is needed during this phase of case processing.

This approach evidences an important change in case management procedures: where formerly all decisions were in the hands of the judge, in the teamwork model the tasks associated with case management are shared between two individuals who have discretion to make decisions, albeit at different stages in the process. The development of a division of labor unfolds around the actual processing of the case. While it would be naive to under-estimate the scope of Article III authority, in this approach the judge does become organizationally dependent upon magistrates for the day-to-day completion of tasks. Thus, the teamwork model combines professional and bureaucratic roles for judge and magistrate. The magistrate and judge are professionals to the extent that each has discretion. The magistrate and judge are bureaucrats to the extent that responsibilities are demarcated. Yet a new work relationship emerges: judge and magistrate share responsibility for the management of cases and, consequently, develop a dependence whereby neither is able to work without the other to complete the task.

There are, of course, still the resistant judges who do not accept these changes. But, the expanded use of magistrates is in place in some courts and introduces a new step in civil procedure: the magistrate screens the caseload by preparing a package to be completed by a judge. Whether these strategies will in fact reduce delay and increase productivity remains to be seen (for some positive evidence, see table 6.11 *infra*); what is clear, however, is that these practices further blur the distinct and well-defined boundaries of the role of Article III judges in the formal judicial process (also see Higgin-botham 1980).

In sum, court procedures and roles are not clearly divided between judi-cial and all other court personnel. Rather, our discussion suggests that cases are "screened" in response to external and structural factors of the larger American political economy, as apparent, for example, in the Northern Dis-trict of Georgia (Seron 1985). The expense and inefficiency of adjudication has made it nearly impossible for courts to process cases in a manner that complements the traditional, structurally bifurcated form of decision-making. And, as a result, more and more cases are being decided at earlier and earlier stages under the supervision of an expanded team of court players. This development has been especially apparent for criminal cases for quite some time. But, a similar pattern is emerging for civil cases as the pretrial confer-ence is seen to be inadequate to the task at hand, the authority of magis-trates is incrementally expanded, and alternative dispute resolution strate-gies are developed.

Finally, let us turn to the role of the more "external" organizational variables (Variables 10-13) in the structure of courts. Table 6.6 (Variables 10-11) shows the relationship of lawyers and U.S. Attorneys, respectively, to the inner core of the district court structure. A comparison between these two sets of relationships underscores the well-known fact that although lawyers are important to courts and are probably attracted by the presence of courts, they are not really part of the organization. The correlations between the number of lawyers and the first six variables range from .66 for the clerk's office to .79 for overall size. By contrast, U.S. Attorneys have an office the size of which is roughly commensurate with the size of the court (.94) and other size and resource variables. The correlations between U.S. Attorneys and judges as well as support staff are somewhat lower (.89 and .87, respectively) since the main function of local U.S. Attorneys is prosecutorial and varies with the volume of criminal cases.

The relationships of U.S. Attorneys to the "bureaucratic" variables (Variables 7-9) are reversed (i.e., lower) compared to those of lawyers, especially the relationship to grade-step or skill level (.43). An obvious exception is the correlation between magistrates and U.S. Attorneys (.82), a function of the increasing criminal pretrial caseload handled by magistrates (Seron 1985).

We have used Department of Justice personnel to indicate the presence of other justice-related agencies of the federal government. Obviously, the presence of these agencies is important for the internal structure of the district courts, but not as much as one might expect. Still, the correlations between U.S. Attorneys and Department of Justice employees, on the one hand, and internal measures of the court range from .71 to .86, indicating a notable level of association. By contrast, the correlations among these more "external" factors (disregarding U.S. Attorneys and considering only Variables 10, 12, and 13) range from .89 to .95. The three correlations for U.S. Attorneys and these "external" variables are lower (from .67 to .76) than those for the "internal" variables (from .87 to .94), suggesting again the closer historic tie between the U.S. Attorney's office and the federal district court, even though the former is part of a different branch of government and concerned mainly with criminal matters.

The preceding analysis of the internal organizational structure of the district courts suggests that there is no overwhelming evidence for the global bureaucratization of courts. Moreover, bureaucratic and professional (judicial) elements not only coexist, but they seem to be interdependent, suggesting that courts may be described as "professional bureaucracies." A problem remains, however, inasmuch as the actual roles of the participants are neither strictly bureaucratic (in the sense of formal-rational hierarchies) nor strictly professional (in the sense of autonomy of skill, knowledge, and the ability to develop policies and evaluate performance). A further conceptual refinement is necessary. Given the mixture of elements and the far-reaching interpenetration of professional and bureaucratic elements, it is more accurate to speak of a new form of organizational control that characterizes courts of law. This new form has been described elsewhere in terms of the "technocratic administration of justice" (Heydebrand 1979). The systemic integration of judges, law clerks, the clerk's office, and magistrates, among others, into a new, integrated team approach combines professional and bureaucratic elements, yet transcends both (see also Seron 1985). It transcends the bureaucratic mode of organizing work, and it transforms the remaining professional and bureaucratic elements into "systemic" functions whereby teams and work groups take the place of the formerly neatly separated administrative and judicial functions (see, e.g., Eisenstein and Jacob 1977; Seron 1985). It is the integration of managerial-bureaucratic and judicial-professional roles that characterizes the technocratic administration of justice as a qualitatively new and different form. In the extreme, technocratic administration in courts tends to deprofessionalize the judicial system, although not without vigorous opposition from judges (see, e.g., Berkson et al. 1977; Sheskin and Grau 1981; Seron 1985).

The excessive emphasis on the potential bureaucratization of courts is misplaced and simplifies the scope of the organizational transformation under way. Rather than being bureaucratized, the courts may be in a process of incipient technocratization, with consequences not only for the organization of work and authority, but also for the nature of decision-making and judicial outcomes. In this context, the danger to the nature of the judiciary may not so much lie in bureaucratization, but in the potential shift in the role of the judiciary from a relatively autonomous branch of government to an adjunct of the federal government, i.e., the executive branch. As Judge Wald suggests, "Those who decry the creeping bureaucratization of the judiciary through the addition of more staff or clerks may be missing the main event" (1983, 773).

Let us examine, then, the effect of the judicial contingent and of other organizational components on the various decisional outcomes of district courts.

The Impact of Organizational Structure on Decisions

The final portion of this chapter is devoted to an analysis of the effect of organizational variables on terminations. In this analysis, we will first examine the overall effects of structural components on civil and criminal terminations (see table 6.7). We will then analyze these structural effects on specific types of civil dispositions, from no-action and pretrial dispositions to trials (see table 6.8) and on these three types of dispositions within selected categories of cases such as prisoner petitions, civil rights, and labor and corporate cases (see tables 6.9a and 6.9b). We will also look at the impact of district court structure on four categories of criminal dispositions: dismissals, guilty-pleas, and trials with two outcomes: acquittals and convictions (see table 6.10). Finally, we will analyze the role of time interval or time pressure (number of days from filing to disposition) in decision-making (see tables 6.11-6.13). These analyses are designed to throw light on the way and the extent to which organizational characteristics influence the output of courts, and the extent to which they complement and are interdependent with the work of judges.

The Effects of Organizational Variables on Terminations. As we have shown in chap. 5, the jurisdictional environment and the task structure have sizeable effects on the terminations and dispositions of district courts. From this analysis we learned that the courts' task structure mediates the effects of environmental forces, but that the legal-governmental profile of a district remains an important factor in the disposition of cases. These findings can now be specified and elaborated.

We focus first on civil and criminal terminations as a whole (see table 6.7) To measure the relevant organizational characteristics of district courts, we use three crucial groups of actors: judges, magistrates, and U.S. Attorneys.

Table 6.7

Effects of Demand and Organization on Terminations in 1970[a]

	Civil Terminations/ Population			Criminal Terminations/ Population		
	r	*b*	*b**	*r*	*b*	*b**
Judges/ Population	.41	−35.00	−.14	.89	−29.60	−.13
Number of Positions/ Population	.38	−39.60	.51	.58	− .02	0
Magistrates/ Population	.27	−36.50	−.04	.72	58.20	.07
U.S. Attorneys/ Population	.40	16.80	.33	.94	40.70	.87****
Demand/ Population	.36	.28	.53**	.77	.08	.17
1/Population	.25	593.40	.61	.17	56.90	.06
R²			.26			.90

[a] Findings in this table should be interpreted with caution due to possible problems of multi-collinearity. This is true for Tables 6.8-6.10.

The "bureaucratic" element of courts is measured by the number of positions and the task structure is measured by total demand. As before, all components are divided by the population of a district and the inverse (1/population) is added to the models.

When all factors are entered into the equation, civil terminations are influenced significantly by demand ($b^* = .53$) though the explained variance is relatively small ($R^2 = .26$). Criminal terminations, by contrast, are significantly associated with the number of U.S. Attorneys in a district ($b^* = .87$) which, in turn, explains most of the variance ($R^2 = .90$). While this finding is hardly surprising, it does suggest that U.S. Attorneys appear to upstage the role of judges in the criminal disposition process. Do the broad contours of this pattern hold for various modes of civil and criminal disposition?

Organizational Structure and the Civil Disposition Process. When we decompose civil terminations, it is clear that the influence of demand on terminations is associated with no-action dispositions (see table 6.8). That is, the greater the combined pressure of pending cases and new filings, the more likely it is that cases will be settled or disposed of prior to a full adjudi-

Table 6.8
Effects of Demand and Organization on Civil Dispositions in 1970

	No Actions/ Population			Pretrials/ Population			Civil Trials/ Population		
	r	b	b^*	r	b	b^*	r	b	b^*
Judges/ Population	.21	11.20	.10	.53	26.80	.18	.06	−.94	−.04
Number of Positions/ Population	.15	−30.00	−.89	.47	−.96	−.02	.27	−4.50	−.58
Magistrates/ Population	.08	−58.50	−.15	.40	49.70	.09	−.03	−.32	0
Demand/ Population	.22	.16	.71**	.42	.09	.29	.09	.02	.31
Geographical Dispersion/ Population	.04	−15.10	−.12	.20	20.10	.12	.33	2.40	.08
1/Population	.10	342.60	.82	.28	70.50	.12	.38	76.20	.78
R^2			.17			.33			.18

cation. While the overall explanatory power of the model is small ($R^2 = .17$), and organizational variables are not significant, caseload pressure is clearly a factor in pushing toward disposition where no court action is taken. We may speculate that because criminal dispositions tend to require more immediate attention, which itself exerts a pressure on the court, civil demands are pushed toward no actions. But is this true for all types of civil cases? Let us turn to a consideration of this question.

Differences Among Case-specific Dispositions. Civil rights cases may raise complex and subtle issues of law. Yet, the findings in table 6.9a suggest that demand remains a significant factor in an explanation of civil rights no actions, pretrials as well as trials. It is also of interest to note that the more bureaucratic dimension of court sturcture (number of positions) begins to emerge as an influence on civil rights cases that are terminated at pretrial (where it contributes to a sizable joint effect $R^2 = .79$).

Table 6.9a
Effects of Demand and Organization on Civil Rights Cases in 1970

	No Actions/ Population			Pretrials/ Population			Trials/ Population		
	r	b	b^*	r	b	b^*	r	b	b^*
Judges/ Population	.38	−.89	−.24	.80	−.81	−.08	.12	−1.76	.64*
Number of Positions/ Population	.22	−.72	−.63	.57	1.80	.59*	.16	−1.30	−.15
Magistrates/ Population	.22	−2.90	−.22	.61	−1.00	−.03	.15	1.16	.12
Demand/ Population	.43	.01	1.24****	.68	.01	.70****	.21	0	.83***
Geographical Dispersion/ Population	.05	−.07	−.02	.21	1.20	.11	.25	.88	.28*
1/Population	.05	7.40	.52	.20	−17.30	.45*	.13	1.60	.15
R^2			.49			.79			.26

Geographical dispersion measures the number of places at which court is held in a given district. Thus, a federal district in a more urban setting, with a more concentrated population, may have only one or two locations for holding court. By contrast, in more rural settings districts are required to have multiple locations which, in turn, means that judges must ride the district to hold court. In this sense, geographical dispersion is an especially sensitive measure of the relationship between demographic density and court structure. Turning to the findings reported in table 6.9a, these findings reveal that civil rights trials are associated with geographical dispersion ($b^* = .28$) suggesting that trials are more likely in rural settings. Corroborating this theme, table 6.9a also shows a strong inverse, and significant, partial relationship between judges and civil rights trials ($b^* = -.64$), suggesting that the larger the court (i.e., the more judges there are in a district), the less likely is the case to come to trial. Speculating from this pattern of findings, we may suggest that geographically dispersed courts—that is, more rural courts where

Table 6.9b
Effects of Demand and Organization on Prisoner Cases in 1970

	No Actions/ Population			Pretrials/ Population			Trials/ Population		
	r	b	b^*	r	b	b^*	r	b	b^*
Judges/ Population	.84	1.04	.95****	.65	− 8.20	−.14	−.02	−2.00	−.71*
Number of Positions/ Population	.55	.08	.23	.45	4.70	.26	.18	.52	.58
Magistrates/ Population	.54	−.51	−.13	.57	26.70	.13	.23	5.70	.56***
Demand/ Population	.63	0	−.14	.61	.08	.68****	−.02	0	−.05
Geographical Dispersion/ Population	−.09	−.26	−.20**	.10	11.20	.17	.26	1.20	.33
1/Population	.18	−.61	−.14	.13	−57.60	−.25	.21	−3.60	−.32
R^2			.74			.59			.27

the demands of caseload pressure tend to be less—are more likely to dispose of civil rights cases through trials, the more traditional pattern of resolving civil disputes.

The findings for prisoner petitions reported in table 6.9b underscore this pattern. These findings show that geographical dispersion is inversely and significantly associated with no actions ($b^* = -.20$) and positively associated with trials ($b^* = .33$). In addition, we see that judges are positively associated with no action dispositions ($b^* = .95$) and inversely associated with trials ($b^* = -.71$), suggesting that pressures are placed on settling these disputes through less formal channels in metropolitan courts. Since the inception of the magistrates' program in 1968, one of their key roles has been to handle the prisoner petition docket; the findings reported in table 6.9b reflect this policy decision as they are the main factor in an explanation of the trials of these types of civil disputes ($b^* = .56$). Taken together, these findings suggest that the effect of demand and organizational factors push toward no action ($R^2 = .74$) rather than pretrial ($R^2 = .59$) or trials ($R^2 = .27$).

Table 6.9c
Effects of Demand and Organization on Corporate Cases in 1970

	No Actions/ Population			Pretrials/ Population			Trials/ Population		
	r	b	b^*	r	b	b^*	r	b	b^*
Judges/ Population	.62	−.52	.01	.89	14.80	.26*	.62	−1.20	−.19
Number of Positions/ Population	.33	−11.50	−.72*	.60	8.70	.49*	.60	.10	.05
Magistrates/ Population	.49	−11.30	−.06	.73	22.20	.11	.54	4.60	.21
Demand/ Population	.56	.13	1.19****	.73	.04	.37****	.58	01	.64****
Geographical Dispersion/ Population	−.09	−9.90	−.17	.03	4.50	.07	.25	.85	.12
1/Population	.03	118.30	.60*	.17	−95.10	−.44	.38	5.00	.21
R^2			.73			.86			.57

Turning to the findings reported for corporate cases in table 6.9c a slightly different pattern emerges. Here, judges, in combination with administrative support and demand, remain significant factors in an explanation of pretrial dispositions. Reflecting the decline in efforts devoted to trials, our model is a better "fit" (i.e., more of the variance is explained) for corporate no actions and pretrials.

Finally, table 6.9d reports the impact of task variables on labor cases, controlling for type of disposition. There is a notable difference between the findings reported for corporate and labor cases: first, magistrates remain an important and significant variable in an explanation of labor no actions (b^* = .32) and pretrials (b^* = .26). But, no actions are more likely in urban courts where, as one might expect, demand also exerts an influence (b^* = .42) [note the significant inverse correlation between geographical dispersion and no actions (b^* = −.35)]. Second, there is a strong inverse partial relationship between judges and labor trials (b^* = −.77), suggesting that as courts get larger in terms of the size of the judicial labor force, these types of cases are

Table 6.9d

Effects of Demand and Organization on Labor Cases in 1970

	No Actions/ Population			Pretrials/ Population			Trials/ Population		
	r	b	b*	r	b	b*	r	b	b*
Judges/ Population	.39	1.40	.37	.68	.03	.01	.11	−.80	−.77*
Number of Positions/ Population	.18	−1.40	−.12*	.41	.15	.13	.19	.31	.95
Magistrates/ Population	.45	4.20	.32*	.66	3.40	.26*	.18	.31	.09
Demand/ Population	.25	0	.42*	.56	0	.51***	.23	0	.34
Geographical Dispersion/ Population	−.22	−1.50	−.35**	−.07	−.12	−.03	.03	−.03	−.02
1/Population	.00	15.30	1.00**	.06	−1.80	−.12	.12	−1.90	−.49
R^2			.33			.61			.12

Table 6.10
Effects of Demand and Organization on Criminal Dispositions in 1970

	Dismissals/Population			Guilty Pleas/Population		
	r	b	b*	r	b	b*
Judges/ Population	.82	1.30	.02	.88	−29.00	−.21
Magistrates/ Population	.71	25.10	.14	.69	−.35	0
U.S. Attorneys/ Population	.85	3.60	.34	.94	20.40	.71****
Probation/ Population	.84	3.80	.26	.93	12.90	32*
Demand/ Population	.73	.01	.17	.76	.05	.15*
Geographical Dispersion/ Population	.01	−.38	−.01	.04	12.20	.08
1/Population	.18	7.50	.04	.16	−6.30	−.01
R²			.76			.91

	Acquittals/Population			Convictions/Population		
	r	b	b*	r	b	b*
Judges/ Population	.83	−13.60	−.22	.89	−6.00	−.19
Magistrates/ Population	.66	−4.90	−.02	.73	−.09	0
U.S. Attorneys/ Population	.91	8.90	.71***	.94	2.50	.39**
Probation/ Population	.89	6.20	.35*	.94	4.40	.49****
Demand/ Population	.76	.02	.12	.75	.02	.38****
Geographical Dispersion/ Population	−.01	5.00	.07	0	1.10	.03
1/Population	.09	−18.10	−.08	.13	−5.20	−.04
R²			.85			.94

less likely to be tried; this set of findings is, in fact, yet another way of documenting the pattern that urban courts are more likely to report no-action and pretrial dispositions in the face of caseload demands.

Organization, Demand, and Criminal Dispositions. To analyze the effect of organizational variables on criminal dispositions, we have added some variables to our model, including the number of probation officers and U.S. attorneys. This analysis considers four types of criminal disposition: dismissals, guilty-pleas, acquittals, and convictions. The findings are reported in table 6.10.

A quick glance at the findings reveals that the crucial organizational actors in the criminal justice process are U.S. Attorneys and probation officers. U.S. Attorneys are the obvious gate-keepers of the system in that they negotiate the charges brought against criminal offenders and have a stake in both the plea as well as the outcome—acquittal or conviction. The findings reported here also underscore the important, if slightly more behind-the-scenes role, of probation. As many studies show, the recommendations of probation officers, based on previous information as well as *de novo* investigation of the case, are usually accepted by the court and influence judicial decision making (Davis 1979). The empirical evidence reported in table 6.10 corroborates this theme.

Interestingly, the overall influence of demand is less pronounced in criminal than in civil cases, though we note that demand remains important in an explanation of convictions and guilty-pleas. Finally, the findings reported in table 6.10 suggest that the role and influence of judges and magistrates is mediated significantly by law enforcement and probation personnel.

Delay, Demand, Organization, and Disposition

One of the most protracted debates in the management of the judicial process surrounds the causes and consequences of delay (for an early discussion of the issue, see Zeisel, et al. 1959). To this point, it is quite clear that demand measures an indirect and important element of delay to the extent that it includes pending cases which, in the view of court actors, constitute one form of backlog. But, the average number of elapsed days from filing to disposition provides a more direct way of looking at the delay in resolving civil and criminal cases.

First, we may consider: What factors explain this time interval? Table 6.11 shows the impact of task (demand) and organizational variables (judges, magistrates, geographical dispersion, and U.S. Attorneys) on elapsed time-delay for civil and criminal cases. Not surprisingly, demand is a major factor $(b^* = .50)$ in an explanation of the time interval for civil cases. In other words the greater the number of pending cases and new filings, the longer the average time from filing to disposition for civil cases.

Table 6.11
Stepwise Regression* of Demand and Organization on Interval from Filing to Disposition in 1970

	Civil: Number of Days-Filing-Dispositon		*Criminal: Number of Days-Filing-Dispositon*	
	r	*b**	*r*	*b**
Demand/Population	.21	.50***	.14	.14
Judges/Population	.08	NS	.10	NS
Magistrates/Population	−.04	−.39**	.02	−.33*
Geographical Dispersion/ Population	−.20	−.17	−.43	−.46****
1/Population	−.21	−.14	−.30	NS
U.S. Attorneys/ Population	—	—	.19	.28
R²		.19		.27

* Variables above .50 probability level are not entered

In criminal cases, however, demand does not show a partial effect, though the interval for both civil and criminal cases is affected by magistrates. As the number of these officers increases in a district, the elapsed time decreases (i.e., note the inverse and significant relationship for both measures). Interval in criminal cases is also inversely related to geographical dispersion. This suggests that delay is, in part, related to court location and structure and that where more innovative steps have been taken to expand support and to modernize, delay may indeed be reduced.

Finally, U.S. Attorneys show a very slight positive effect on criminal time to disposition, but it is not significant. Speculation suggests that U.S. Attorneys generate work—and delay—and that it is the task of court support, particularly magistrates, to deal with the problem (also see Balbus 1973; Dixon 1988).

Let us now consider the influence of delay, in conjunction with other organizational variables, on civil and criminal terminations, controlling for

Table 6.12
Effects of Demand, Organization and Interval on Civil Dispositions in 1970

| | Civil Dispositions/Population | | | | | |
| | No Actions | | Pretrials | | Trials | |
	r	b*	r	b*	r	b*
Demand/ Population	.31	.47	.52	.38	.06	NS
Judges/ Population	.21	−.26	.58	.20	.06	NS
Interval	.24	.19	−.11	−.18	−.13	NS
Geographical Dispersion/ Population	.04	NS	.20	.14	.33	.14
1/Population	.10	.15	.28	NS	.28	.28*
R^2		.15		.35		.15

Table 6.13
Effects of Criminal Filings, Organization and Interval on Criminal Dispositions in 1970

| | Criminal Dispositions/Population | | | | | | | |
| | Dismissals | | Guilty Pleas | | Acquittals | | Convictions | |
	r	b*	r	b*	r	b*	r	b*
Criminal Filings/ Population	.94	.81****	.94	49****	.93	.60****	.88	.31****
Judges/ Population	.82	.18*	.88	−.06	.83	.09	.89	.13
Interval	.09	.11	.07	NS	.09	.03	.10	.02
U.S. Attorneys/ Population	.85	NS	.94	.49****	.91	.40**	.94	.24
Probation/ Population	.84	NS	.93	.10	.89	.10	.94	.35**
1/Population	.18	NS	.16	NS	.09	−.07*	.13	−.08*
R^2		.92		.97		.94		.94

type of disposition. On the civil side, the findings reported in table 6.12 show that delay has a very slight positive effect on no actions (b* = .19), but a negative relation (b* = −.18) to pretrials, though neither are significant. One might argue that pretrial dispositions themselves contribute to a slight reduction in delay, as was originally intended.

The parallel findings for criminal dispositions, reported in table 6.13, show a quite different picture. The incidence of filings has a strong, positive, and significant effect on all types of dispositions. As the number of judges increases, so does the number of dismissals (b* = .18); that is, as courts become larger in metropolitan areas, criminal cases are slightly more likely to be dismissed. This finding, in light of the influence of delay on dismissals, corroborates findings from more qualitative studies of the criminal justice process. In the balance between due process and the pressures of new criminal filings, dismissals exacerbate tensions between police and courts. Finally, the role of U.S. Attorneys and probation officers in guilty pleas, convictions and acquittals reported in table 6.13, largely replicate the results reported in table 6.10.

Conclusion

There are two apparent, if paradoxical, themes to emerge: judges remain the professional core of judicial decision-making. But, it is also clear that the organizational structure of courts has an impact on the process and outcome of those decisions. Judicial productivity as measured by the number of terminations per judge, has—with a few historically explainable exceptions—remained remarkably stable and has, if anything, increased during the last decade. At the same time, however, an elaborate organizational support structure has emerged especially since 1970. It has become an essential factor for insuring productivity.

Is it accurate, then, to speak of judges as key actors and the rest of the nonjudicial employees as "organizational support"? We believe not. This imagery continues the same myth of central professional service and nonprofessional support that has dominated the medical model: the doctors are the key actors, and everybody else—including the organizational structure of hospitals—is there merely to facilitate their work (see, e.g., Freidson 1971). But, then, is the traditional model of professional-judicial dominance in courts still valid?

We believe that there is evidence to show that the relationship between professional staff and organizational structure is not one of support or dependence but rather one of interdependence. The interrelationships between various elements of the internal organizational structure of courts discloses a network of simultaneous relations and interdependencies such that it is difficult to speak any longer of "organizational support" or of a division between professional and nonprofessional labor. Since 1970, magistrates have assumed an ever larger role in the affairs of district courts. Probation officers, trained in the social sciences such as sociology and psychology, participate decisively in criminal proceedings and help to determine their outcome. Law clerks have become more and more like associates of judges, rather than subordinates or apprentices. The total number of positions in courts has grown tremendously and is highly correlated with other structural variables. These interrelationships, as we have demonstrated, point to the emergence of a highly elaborated network of organized activities that has relatively unique characteristics and does not any longer fit the traditional model of the professional work organization. Nor does it fit the model of bureaucracy with a simple hierarchy and division of labor, formal rules, regulations and career lines.[5]

The evidence for interdependence between the elements of the organizational structure of courts, including judges, is even more striking when we look at their combined effects on the process and outcome of decision-making. Clearly, civil and criminal terminations are strongly determined not only by the work of judges, but by the organizational factors we have considered. Thus, not only are decisions (terminations), as such, influenced by factors other than judges, but the stages in decision-making are themselves differentially affected by structural variables. In civil dispositions, more of all personnel resources go into no action and pretrial dispositions than into trials. Types of cases such as civil rights, prisoner petitions, labor and corporate cases receive differential attention from judicial and nonjudicial personnel alike.

In criminal dispositions, judges may have the final word in dismissals and in trials leading to convictions, but they decidedly take the back seat when it comes to guilty pleas where probation officers, magistrates, and U.S. Attorneys dominate the process. And, it must be remembered that guilty pleas account for a very high proportion of criminal dispositions.

We have also found considerable evidence that shows that trials are more likely in geographically dispersed—more rural—districts and that, conversely, no actions are more likely in metropolitan courts. Strictly speaking, geographical dispersion is an indicator of organizational structure since the dispersion of court location is a form of functional decentralization. But, this variable also captures environmental factors because dispersed courts tend to be located in areas of low population density. This analysis, then, reveals a pattern where caseload pressure (especially evident in corporate and labor cases that are, after all, somewhat more likely in urban settings) coupled with "local legal culture" (Church 1985) induce a higher rate of settlements and no actions. On the other hand, smaller, nonurban courts may still be more hospitable to traditional practices, in large measure because fewer pressures make it feasible.

Finally, we analyzed some of the causes and consequences of the time interval between filing and disposition. While demand is clearly a factor in delay on the civil side, it has a less apparent effect on criminal cases. We believe that criminal dispositions are driven by the state's law-and-order logic represented mainly by U.S. Attorneys. Interestingly, the antidote to delay on both the civil and criminal side is the contribution of magistrates—a finding that should be of interest to policymakers and judges alike.

Delay, as measured by time interval, does have a significant effect on the rate of dismissals in criminal cases. This finding underscores the age-old complaint by the law enforcement community that their work may be undone by that of judges and courts. At a deeper level, however, our findings suggest that there may be a structural contradiction between the interests of crime control and due process—a point where we began this journey. The resources poured into law enforcement are, to some extent, wasted if courts are not adequately staffed and thus respond to overload by dismissing cases. It is, of course, also possible that criminal cases generated by an overzealous law enforcement effort may not pass the standard of due process. Clearly, these themes point toward the need for more research on whether it is lack of resources or high judicial standards (or both) which explain dismissals.

All told, modern judicial decision-making is inseparable from the organizational matrix in which it is embedded. But, that does not mean *pari passu* that judges are bureaucrats or that the judiciary is being bureaucratized. The growth and complexity of the organizational structure of courts is an undeniable development. But there are few signs that such growth is bureaucratic in the sense of Weber's model. Judicial case management has clearly played an important role in the rise of no-action and pretrial dispositions. Yet, the mandatory settlement conference or other pretrial mechanisms of dispute resolution are not necessarily "bureaucratic" since they involve a host of *informal* procedures that deviate from the bureaucratic *and* from the formal adversary-adjudicatory model alike. What is perhaps more crucial, as Menkel-Meadow (1985) suggests, is *how* these conferences are conducted, what mix of formal rational and informal-social elements they use, and what innovative alternatives they admit into their arsenal of conflict resolution techniques.

If modern judges have become "managerial" and rationalized, this does not necessarily mean they are "bureaucratic." Their orientation and policies may have changed from that of formal adjudicators of cases to that of informal processors of disputes (Kritzer 1982, 20; see also Villmoare 1982). From that perspective, one may wonder whether a high and variegated caseload will not fundamentally alter the role of judges as well as the traditional structure of courts. Our data support the notion that the caseload demand on courts is associated with a more rationalized disposition process. Specifically, we have demonstrated that civil filings and demand are strongly related to no action and to pretrial dispositions in district courts, and that criminal filings are strongly related to dismissals and guilty-pleas.

Our findings in the present chapter make it clear that none of these types of dispositions occur without the participation of the various actors and groups composing courts, from judges, law clerks and magistrates to probation officers, lawyers and U.S. Attorneys. It is in this sense, then, that courts are responding to environmental pressures by moving away from the traditional professional model of adjudication associated with the adversary process. But, they have also moved away from bureaucratic procedures since formal hierarchies are yielding to new forms of participation, teamwork, and cooperation between a growing diversity of actors and groups. We shall consider the larger consequences of these new organizational phenomena in the concluding chapter. Before engaging in such an evaluation, however, let us take a closer look at the one external actor in the courts' environment that may be the proximate cause of much of this process of transformation, the federal government.

CHAPTER 7

*

The Growing Shadow of the Federal Government

The organizational history of the federal district courts is closely intertwined with the expanding role of the government in the twentieth century. In this chapter, we recast this theme and focus on the way in which the government shapes the internal agenda of federal district courts through the jurisdictional composition of civil cases. The growing proportion of U.S. cases on the docket of federal courts in the twentieth century is, however, part of a much larger change in the state's role to administer, regulate, and enforce policy: U.S. cases capture the change in the state's role from a relatively passive to an active participant in the political economy, the subject of this chapter.

Yet, viewed from inside the administrative agency system, courts only participate in the top layers of this regulatory avalanche (Miller 1976; Davis 1977; Horwitz 1977; Freedman 1978). By 1976 there were sixty administrative agencies, not including the numerous regulatory functions performed by the executive. The number of decisions rendered by such agencies far outranked that of courts and, no doubt, had a more direct effect on the lives of most citizens. To take but one example, the Federal Communications Commission issues about 800,000 licenses in a given year, each technically an "adjudication." But, out of those 800,000 actions there will be about 115 hearings, with even fewer cases appealed to the courts (Davis 1977). The development of alternative administrative forums that perform the multiple and paradoxical tasks of dispute resolution, adjudication, social control and norm enforcement makes clear that courts are but one setting for the transaction and legitimation of these activities in contemporary society.

The courts do, however, continue to play a central role in the administrative process through their power of judicial review. That is, as the government's intervention becomes more omnipresent in "postindustrial" society, it casts a more and more visible shadow over the courts. Although the power of judicial review has been vested mainly in the appellate courts of the judicial

159

system and in the U.S. Supreme Court (see, e.g., Choper 1980), district courts do participate in the reexamination of the proceedings of certain administrative agencies and have the power to affirm or overturn an agency's decision on appeal before the court. In this capacity, the types of tasks brought before district courts are stretched in interesting ways and may include the more traditional function of dispute resolution as well as norm enforcement and lawmaking. We have discussed in earlier chapters the ways in which these functions, at times contradictory, are historically embedded in the role and legitimacy of courts. The emergence of an administrative process has, however, shaped these functions in ways that challenge the foundation of this precarious balance and captures yet another modern preoccupation with rationality.

Perhaps nothing reveals the forces of governmental rationalization more dramatically than the expansion of administrative law and its concomitant impact upon the courts. For the transformation of the American political economy from one organized around local elites and competitive markets to one organized around a national, if not international, economic structure and transnational arenas began to reveal the inadequacy of a doctrine of separate powers whereby rule-making, enforcement, and interpretation were carried out under three separate roofs. That this system of laissez-faire government ever worked is open to debate; that it was clearly inadequate by the turn of the century is a point of general consensus.[1]

What made the formation of the Interstate Commerce Commission in 1887, the first federal independent regulatory agency, such a notable departure from traditional practices was the reluctant recognition on the part of the state's managers of the need for standardized, centralized, and rationalized control of interstate commerce (Kolko 1962; but see Wilson 1975).[2] This step, in turn, laid the first building block for the foundation of a "fourth branch" of government, viz. administrative and regulatory agencies that would eventually be "comparable in the scope of its authority and impact of its decision-making to the three more familiar constitutional branches" (Freedman 1978, 6). The expansion of a national administrative presence is captured in masterful detail by Stephen Skowronek (1982) in his study of the transformation of the American state between 1877 and 1920. Whereas political parties and the courts represented formidable obstacles to administrative reform in the last quarter of the nineteenth century, governmental intervention and administrative regulation began to expand dramatically during Theodore Roosevelt's administration. Focusing, among other things, on the political and historical trajectory of the Interstate Commerce Commission, Skowronek (1982, 259-67) sketches the intricate political struggle between the executive and the judiciary over the formation of administrative law and the establishment of procedure. While appeals from most regulatory commissions and administrative agencies were referred directly to the federal appeals courts and, from there, to the Supreme Court, one can say generally that the Progressive period marks the first real expansion of government litigation in the federal courts.

Practically and politically, the growth of administrative law has transformed the composition of the jurisdictional agenda of the federal court's caseload. To document this development and its attendant impact, we will begin by examining the jurisdictional composition of cases filed in the federal district courts from 1910 to 1984. Of particular interest to us here is the spectacular growth of "public law litigation" (Chayes 1976) which has come to dominate the civil docket of federal district courts. Next, we will examine the effects of the changing political, economic, and demographic environment on the jurisdiction of the courts. Finally, we will analyze the joint effects of environment, task structure, and organizational structure on the types of decision-making, controlling for the major categories of jurisdiction. Our purpose here is to isolate and to concretize the implications of the increasing role of government in shaping the task structure and organization of federal district courts.

Jurisdictional Agenda: The Formation and Transformation of the District Courts

In general, we may speak of four broad categories of federal jurisdiction: (1) diversity of citizenship, (2) federal question, (3) U.S. plaintiff, and (4) U.S defendant cases. Federal question and diversity of citizenship are private cases; they are legal questions initiated without the active involvement of another branch of the federal government. While cases raising federal questions may address issues of constitutional or "public" law, they specifically do not involve a suit by or against the government. That is, both diversity and federal question cases are controversies between private parties in which the court is nothing more or less than a formal locale for dispute resolution. As we shall see, this is very close to what the Founding Fathers had in mind for the courts. By contrast, U.S. cases are disputes that arise when either the government is being sued (U.S. defendant) or is suing a private party (U.S. plaintiff), often over the interpretation and meaning of an administrative guideline.

The historical and contemporary relationship between the jurisdictional origins of these cases itself tells a story about the court's role in the organization and legitimation of the American political economy. In the last seventy-five years, public law litigation has increased dramatically, reaching a high point with the civil rights litigation of the 1960s and 1970s that contributed to a 600-percent increase in federal question cases. Civil suits by and against the United States showed a sharp rise, as well, with a 200-percent increase in U.S. cases occurring during the same two decades. Yet, in 1789, at the time of the court's establishment, the notion of a suit against the government was unthinkable, even though provisions were made for the U.S. government to bring suit in federal court (Hart and Wechsler 1953). By contrast, it was almost universally agreed that cases involving diversity of state citizenship should be tried in federal courts. Today, however, such cases are the center of reformers' attention who propose that diversity of citizenship cases, which now largely result from personal injuries, be turned over to state courts to relieve federal courts of time-consuming business (see chap. 4; also see Friendly 1973; Burger 1976; *The Third Branch: Bulletin of the Federal Courts* January 1976, February 1977, January 1978, February 1979). In short, one sees in the history of the court a transformation in the jurisdictional basis of its demands. In keeping with this point, we will begin by considering the basis of private jurisdiction, specifically diversity of citizenship, followed by federal question cases. We will then turn to a more detailed discussion of the growth of U.S. cases.

Diversity of citizenship. In light of the pressing problems of establishing nationhood, the future role and jurisdiction of the Judicial Branch was a relatively minor issue for the Founding Fathers. Yet, these were men of business and property with a keen sense of the future economic possibilities of the United States and the legal needs that this historical destiny entailed. Hence, the scope of the court's jurisdiction was debated and originally established on the basis of an optimistic belief in the possibilities for economic growth and expansion (Frank 1948).

In many respects, the collective conscience of the Founding Fathers bridged the worlds of an industrial and an agricultural society in which the role of land and property took center stage (Wolfe 1977). Thus, the relatively "static" common law conception of property that had its origins in a sovereign's control was gradually usurped by a more dynamic conception as new possibilities for economic development unfolded.

Early questions of American economic development revolved around new interpretations of property. Gradually, as the economy evolved from agrarian to mercantilist and then to capitalist, questions of land rights, water rights, dam usage, and eminent domain all became equally pressing issues. In the area of water rights, questions were posed in terms of upstream-downstream rights and to what extent those upstream were legally responsible to those below them. As dams were built, they had the inevitable effect of obstructing passage and thereby raised questions of legal responsibility. Finally, as land was taken over by the government for the building of roads, canals, and later, railroads, the need for legal clarification and responsibility in the context of a developing economy was again required. Morton Horwitz (1977) has given a detailed account of the legal permutations of these issues and their attendant impact upon the development of the American economy. In general, he shows that there is a trend toward guaranteeing "certainty and predictability to those who invested in economic development" (Horwitz 1977, 43; Wiebe 1967) that entailed numerous reinterpretations of common law doctrine (but see Commons 1968; Tushnet 1978). What does clearly emerge from this history is the centrality of property disputes in the earliest stages of American economic development.

Hence, it is hardly surprising that the Founding Fathers insured that cases involving land disputes across state borders (i.e., "diversity of citizenship") would be heard by federal court judges. Diversity of citizenship as a basis of federal jurisdiction was, more importantly, established in an attempt to protect creditors of various states (Friendly 1973). Since the early years of this nation's expansion revolved around the purchase and sale of large property holdings, border disputes (i.e., diversity cases) potentially affected landowners across state lines. Moreover, there was a general lack of confidence in state judges to be objective in their judgments of citizens from another state, a concern that was warranted when the concept of the United States as a nation was new. But to avoid the possibility of trivial cases being tried in federal courts, jurisdiction was restricted to those cases in which there was at least five hundred dollars in dispute (Hart and Wechsler 1953).

The concerns of the Founding Fathers were justified; during the early years of the court's existence (1790–1815) diversity cases constituted the largest number of cases heard by the lower federal courts and appealed to the Supreme Court. Of course, it should be kept in mind that "the whole Federal judicial system from 1790 to 1815 gave almost its entire attention to the settlement of the simplest types of commercial and property disputes" (Frank 1948, 18).

Federal questions. The Judiciary Act of 1789 did not establish the use of judicial power for most cases arising under the Constitution or laws of the United States. Rather, private litigants turned to state courts for protection of federal claims in the first instance. Indeed, civil rights cases, which form a notable portion of federal question cases, did not become a focal point of the court's agenda until quite recently; in part this is due to the fact that such cases were beyond the district court's jurisdictions. In a larger sense, however, the lack of concern with guaranteeing a relatively more prestigious forum for hearing such cases was in general keeping with late eighteenth century conceptions of the role of the state in protecting citizens' rights that was anchored in a strong federalist tradition. As Alan Wolfe (1977) has suggested, an important role of the state in the earliest stages of capitalist development was to openly repress dissent from below. Because demands for an ordered society outweighed others, it stands to reason that the Founding Fathers skirted the problem of securing the use of federal courts for cases involving protection of constitutional rights. Put differently, in the balance between the state's economic and democratic roles, the agenda for capitalist accumulation won out.

The steps through which federal questions gradually entered the federal court's docket further illustrates this point. In the court's earliest period, federal question cases were limited to admiralty, bankruptcy, patents, and copyright cases (Friendly 1973). Of these, admiralty was the only category of primary concern to the framers of the Constitution. Like diversity cases, admiralty questions were a reflection of the principal modes of commerce and trade in the early years of nationhood. And, admiralty cases represented a significant portion of the federal docket in the years between 1790 and 1815. The leaders of the shipping industry, a principal economic group, had the political clout to demand a relatively prestigious forum where their cases could be litigated.

The full impact of this basis for federal jurisdiction was solidified after the Civil War (Pole 1978). It was not until the Reconstruction Period "that the basic change was made whereby the national courts became the primary forum for the vindication of Federal rights" (Hart and Wechsler 1953, 727) , an important strategy during the first wave of civil rights litigation that was made possible by the passage of the Thirteenth, Fourteenth and Fifteenth Amendments. Like the advocates of federal jurisdiction before them, there was an assumption that "better," more equitable justice might be delivered by a presidentially appointed, rather than a locally selected, judge. Furthermore, the Removal Act of 1875 gave tremendous additional power to the federal district courts by permitting cases that raise questions of federal rights to be tried in a federal court (Friedman 1973, 337).

After the Civil War, then, the practice of district court litigation over federal laws was established. Nevertheless, it was not until the 1960s that the civil rights movement achieved the political clout to litigate effectively (Piven and Cloward 1977). Thus, in 1961 there were about 1,270 private civil rights cases; by 1972, 5,482 civil rights cases (not including prisoner petitions) were filed in the federal district courts. This represented an increase of 332 percent in an eleven-year period. The impact of this development is further revealed in the findings shown in table 7.1. By 1970, federal question cases were over 40 percent of the civil docket, representing a 283-percent increase from 1960 to 1970. Again, many of these cases were the product of civil rights controversies.

Table 7.1 also shows the number, percentage, and percentage change of diversity and federal question cases from 1940 to 1987, as well as the number of all private jurisdictional filings from 1910 to 1987 excluding cases of local jurisdiction. A number of relevant points can be gleaned from the figures

Table 7.1
Jurisdictional Origin of Private Civil Cases
in U.S. District Courts, 1910-1987

Private Cases

Year	Diversity of Citizenship Number	Percent of Civil Cases	Federal Question Number	Percent of Civil Cases	Total Number	Percent of Civil Cases
1910	—	—	—	—	10,678	77.4*
1920	—	—	—	—	16,383	74.1
1930	—	—	—	—	23,391	48.4
1940***	7,254**	29.8	4,491**	18.5	11,745	48.3
1950	13,124	31.4	6,775	16.2	19,899	47.7
1960	17,024	36.3	9,088	19.4	26,112	55.7
1970	22,854	27.6	34,846	42.2	57,700	69.8
1980	39,315	23.4	64,928	38.7	104,243	62.1
1987	67,071	28.1	99,301	41.6	166,372	69.6

	Percent Change Diversity	Percent Change Federal Question	Percent Change Total Private Cases
1910-20	—	—	53.4
1920-30	—	—	42.8
1930-40	—	—	−99.2
1940-50	80.9	50.9	69.4
1950-60	29.7	34.1	31.2
1960-70	34.2	283.4	121.0
1970-80	72.0	86.3	80.1
1980-87	70.6	52.9	59.6

* Percent of total civil filings.
** Not available before 1940.
*** 1940-1984 excludes admiralty cases and general local jurisdiction.

reported in this table. Diversity cases represent a fairly significant proportion of the court's workload, though there is a noticeable decline in the percentage of such cases in 1980, as is true of federal question and, indeed, all private cases.

Today, American economic development is far removed from its agrarian origins; yet, the effect of diversity cases is still felt, though most of these matters are the result of personal injury and contract disputes. There is a certain irony here that should not be overlooked. The guarantee that America's elite of the early nineteenth century could take its controversies to federal court has today left judges with what is viewed as an unwanted burden of minor matters. That is, the development of economic relations far beyond the borders of states has diminished the importance of diversity of citizenship.

The traditions of the courts, however, are not easily changed. Strategies have been introduced to minimize the burden of diversity cases by increasing the financial basis necessary for federal court filing, recently raised again from $10,000 to $50,000. [Comparing the rate at which such cases increased from 1950 to 1960 (30 percent) and 1960 to 1970 (34 percent) suggests that increasing the amount in controversy is one alternative for incremental change.] Of course, a more sweeping and drastic reform would be to return such cases to state jurisdiction; but, this strategy raises all of the controversial points attendant upon reform of the practices of litigating personal injury cases. Hence, Congress will no doubt continue to increase the financial basis of federal jurisdiction for such cases while skirting the larger questions.

Turning to the figures shown for federal question cases also confirms a point developed in chap. 3. District court jurisdiction over federal question cases, and particularly civil rights controversies, is clearly an important part of the court's work in absolute numbers, although the rate of change has slowed down since 1980. The court's role in this area is, however, only partially understood if we focus on private jurisdiction. Protection and enforcement of civil rights has also become a more direct responsibility of the U.S. government (Garrow 1986), as the increase in U.S. cases documents.

United States cases. The framers' conception of U.S. cases was very narrow: suits to collect federal revenue; cases where a state attempted to challenge the work of a federal officer; suits to protect U.S. lands; and suits to enforce U.S. contracts (Friendly 1973, 62)—occurrences that were more common in times of war when an unbalanced budget was temporarily acceptable (O'Connor 1973). But, it must be kept in mind that these men were products of the "liberal period, which, for obvious reasons, [desires] as little governmental intervention as possible—since intervention, by definition, interferes with private rights" (Neumann 1957, 168). Furthermore, these were men who understood the need for nonmajoritarian institutions to protect private rights, as the discussion of diversity of citizenship cases illustrates.

The elites who controlled this economy were located along the eastern seaboard where political needs were limited to self-contained areas. Thus, it was quite feasible for judges, through the auspices of courts, to protect these rights within a framework that complemented a doctrine of separate and delegated powers. That is, traditional legal forms of dispute resolution were adequate for guaranteeing a favorable market setting when land expansion and merchant relations formed the basis of the U.S. economy. The economic prerequisites of continuity of power in the hands of an economic elite include a concentrated control over necessary capital, a fairly low rate of economic growth, sufficiently slow product and service innovation, and a geographical area small enough for the elites to administer.

Virtually none of these conditions existed after 1910 (Wiebe 1967; Kolko 1976, 251; Skowronek 1982). As the variable costs of capitalist growth took on more significant proportions, the private sector was, to put it bluntly, less and less willing to take the risks involved. Hence, new demands were placed upon the state. In the tradition of protecting private rights, the state was called upon to absorb the costs of expansion in terms of more direct investments in the private sector and to create a degree of coordination, planning, and control between growing monopolistic enterprises by indirectly absorbing unnecessary competition.

The impetus for the expansion of regulatory commissions and administrative agencies, the "fourth branch" of government, complements the state's mandate to protect private economic rights. As James O. Freedman points out, while "the independent administrative agencies quite obviously were not anticipated by James Madison in *The Federalist*, . . . they are nonmajoritarian institutions of the kind that he regarded as essential to the construction of an effective and stable government" (1978, 77). The earliest experiments with administrative law, and the success of these efforts, constituted a response to the demands on the state to begin planning economic development. Experiments with administrative control and planning—specifically the Interstate Commerce Commission, Federal Trade Commission, and Federal Reserve Bank—took form in response to this historically new demand on the state to insure a viable setting for private capital accumulation.

Yet, this development posed a dynamic set of ideological problems. Commenting, one English observer of American courts has written: "The basic economic policy of the Federal government has, it is true, been the promotion of free competition; but this, paradoxically, has led it to take an increasing role in the regulation of the economic system. The desired end of free competition could only be achieved through the curbing of the abusive practices which result from a policy of laissez-faire" (Wade 1950, 9). Indeed, an important theme of twentieth-century American politics remains the paradoxical demands of large-scale industrial growth, requiring planning, monitoring, and collective action, coupled with nineteenth century values of individualism, governmental passivity, competition, and separation of powers (Hawley 1966).

The underpinnings of this conflict surfaced during the Progressive Era. By the Great Depression of the 1930s they became the centerpiece of political debate. In response to the crisis of the Great Depression, New Dealers built upon the organizational model of the administrative agency and extended its use far beyond the expectations of Progressive Era reformers.

The paradigmatic example of this initial response was the establishment of the Social Security Administration and the National Labor Relations Board, later to be followed by the agencies of the War-on-Poverty years. By the end of the New Deal period, then, administrative procedures spanned the spectrum of governmental activities.[3] That is, after 1935, New Deal programs became "sympathetic to the underprivileged, and to organized labor, and it was pervaded by a general spirit of liberal, humanitarian reform" (Zinn 1966).

Yet, the concept of integrated responsibility for policy-making, enforcement, and review under one administrative umbrella remains controversial. Reflecting this, the courts, in the earliest days of administrative development, commonly limited the tasks delegated to such agencies and, in the process, stripped them of essential powers.[4] In one sense, courts were being asked to respond to an alien process, that is, the constitutionality of decision-making, planning, and control by technical experts. It is hardly surprising that judges responded in the only way they knew by using the powers of judicial review to say "no" to this "hybrid" phenomenon (White 1974; Horwitz 1977). A negative crescendo occurred, of course, by the time of the New Deal when the Supreme Court declared the National Recovery Act unconstitutional. Despite the fanfare of this decision, the New Dealer's contribution to the modern state was to solidify the theory of delegated power and, in so doing, finally, and completely, put the theory of laissez-faire to rest (Kariel 1961). "By the 1950s, delegated power became the single most important principle of the modern capitalist state" (Wolfe 1977, 131). Or, as Lowi has put it, "The administrative process is, in essence, our generation's answer to the inadequacy of judicial and legislative process" (1969, 145).

In sum, the genius of this legal brainchild, i.e., administrative law, has been the discovery that its structure and process can be replicated in nearly all areas of the welfare state. All has not, however, proceeded without problems as the development of administrative regulations, in whatever area of the state's endeavors, is the subject of debate among various interest groups within Congress. Anxious to placate all, the result has been the formation of vague, broad, indeterminate, if not simply confusing, administrative guidelines (Bernstein 1955; Kariel 1961; Davis 1977; Freedman 1978; Horwitz 1977).

It is at this point that the court's role, particularly at the appellate level, becomes one of legal clarification of Congressional intent. In the process, the activity of judicial review has become the subject of debate because the judiciary is put into a more openly activist posture that demands that it solve problems and enforce rules (Chayes 1976; Horwitz 1977; Stewart 1979).[5] That is, it has become the task of courts to figure out "the intent of Congress" when, in many instances, that intent is quite vague. As a result, it is "natural" to see the expansion of judicial activity as a "mere concomitant of the growth of the welfare state" (Horwitz 1977, 5) while, at the same time, maintaining its more traditional functions of dispute resolution and norm enforcement.

Generally, the task of interpretation—or what some might describe as an "imperial judiciary" (see chap. 6)—has fallen to the appellate courts. Indeed, it is commonly assumed that the expansion of administrative practice and procedure has had a limited effect on the agenda and activities of federal district courts. Yet, a cursory examination of the findings reported in table 7.2 suggests otherwise.

Table 7.2
Jurisdictional Origin of U.S. Civil Cases in
U.S. District Courts, 1910-1987

Year	Plaintiff Number	Plaintiff Percent of Civil Cases	Defendant Number	Defendant Percent of Civil Cases	Total Number	Total Percent of Civil Cases
1910	—	—	—	—	3,170	23.0
1920	—	—	—	—	5,726	25.9
1930	—	—	—	—	24,934	51.6
1940	10,415	42.8	2,171	8.9	12,586	51.7
1950	17,726	42.5	4,128	9.8	21,854	52.3
1960	14,934	31.9	5,832	12.4	20,766	44.3
1970	13,310	16.1	11,655	14.1	24,965	30.2
1980	39,810	23.7	23,818	14.2	63,628	37.9
1987	42,653	17.8	29,369	12.3	72,022	30.1

	Percent Change U.S. Plaintiff	Percent Change U.S. Defendant	Percent Change Total U.S. Cases
1910-20	—	—	80.6
1920-30	—	—	335.5
1930-40	—	—	−98.1
1940-50	70.2	90.1	73.6
1950-60	−18.7	41.3	−5.2
1960-70	−12.2	99.8	20.2
1970-80	199.1	104.4	154.9
1980-87	7.1	23.3	13.2

Table 7.2 shows the number of United States cases from 1910 to 1987 along with the number and percentage of U.S. plaintiff and U.S. defendant cases from 1940 to 1987. The impact on the district courts has been notable insofar as the total number of U.S. cases has grown at a marked rate since the turn of the century (1910-87: over 200 percent or 21 fold). In 1910, U.S. cases (3,170) were a fairly rare occurrence; by 1987 (72,022 cases) this is hardly the situation. Of this total, U.S. plaintiff cases represent the largest share, especially between 1940 and 1950 when these cases constituted over 40 percent of all civil cases. While the high rate of legal initiative the U.S. government took in the 1930s and 1940s began to decline, reaching a low point of 16.1 percent in 1970, it grew again, especially by 1980. This trend paralleled the number of suits filed against the government, which saw a slow but steady rise from 8.9 percent in 1940, to 12 percent in 1987, with high points over 14 percent in 1970 and 1980. While the U.S. caseload is still much smaller than the private caseload (see table 7.1), its development must be considered from the point of view of its small beginnings.[6]

The impact of the expansion of administrative law is clearly felt by the district courts. Because the enabling legislation of an agency established by Congress specifies the procedure for review of controversies, it is feasible to sort out the types of U.S. cases that reach the district courts. That is, the forum for adjudication in the first instance may be an administrative law judge within the agency in question, or else the district court, the circuit court and, very occasionally, the Supreme Court. By and large, a notable portion of the U.S. cases that reach the district courts include social security claims, Equal Employment Opportunity Commission (EEOC) cases, some National Labor Relations Board (NLRB) cases, Veterans' Administration cases, and student loan matters—what some might describe as the less weighty issues of the administrative agenda. Indeed, many of these cases have become the routine tasks of magistrates (Seron 1983).

Yet, this does not tell the whole story. By the 1960s, the administrative process was an accepted part of American legal institutions and confronted, like all branches of government, challenges from below generated by the social upheaval of the antiwar and civil rights movements. "Faced with this situation, Americans did what societies often do when social conflict threatens to disturb an existing sense of stability and commonality: they turned to procedural formality to establish a degree of confidence that the government's authority, particularly to the extent that it had the capacity to favor one group at the expense of another, was exercised fairly" (Freedman 1978, 27; Kariel 1961; Balbus 1973; Hay 1975). That is, the courts began to step in and demand that agencies adopt more adversarial techniques; this often took the form of redefining an agency's basis of jurisdiction, standing, and ripeness to sue, thereby giving citizen groups grounds on which to challenge the government's actions. The tendency, then, within agencies toward "judicialization" of their processes, initiated by the Administrative Procedure Act of 1946, led to a strengthening of procedure, the first step of which was to simply make it easier to sue.

The effect of this tendency is reflected in the figures reported in table 7.2. The number of U.S. defendant cases—i.e., suits against the government—increased almost 100 percent from 1960 to 1970, and by over 150 percent from 1970 to 1987. One might justly claim that the "due process revolution" in the criminal area also had its effect upon the administrative arena since the general push, in both, has been in the direction of guaranteeing more and more procedural safeguards. Or, in a larger sense, "the due process revolution of the sixties and seventies can be perceived as an inherent and predictable consequence of the capitalist state's expanding economic role, as welfare groups and corporations alike sought to limit the discretion of the state's administration of its legitimation and accumulation functions" (Grau 1980, 10).

The analysis based on tables 7.1 and 7.2 is, however, limited by the traditional methods of presenting judicial statistics in terms of the dichotomy between private and U.S. cases. This breakdown masks the fact that civil litigation under federal statutes is as much a form of public law litigation as is litigation involving the U.S. government as a party. Thus, by combining U.S. cases and federal question cases, we can show that, in Abram Chayes's (1976, 1304, footnote 93) words, "... much of the business of the federal district courts displays many of the features of public law litigation."[7]

Table 7.3 shows in simple and stark terms that when the three categories of jurisdiction are combined, there has been an increase in the proportion

Table 7.3

The Rise of Public Law Litigation: U.S. and Federal
Question Filings in U.S. District Courts, 1940-87

Public Law Litigation

Year	Number of Filings	Percent of Civil Filings	Percent Change
1940	17,077	70.2	—
1950	28,629	68.6	67.6
1960	29,854	63.7	4.3
1970	59,811	72.4	100.0
1980	128,556	76.6	114.9
1987	171,323	71.7	33.3

of public law litigation of all civil litigation from 63.7 percent in 1960 to 71.7 percent in 1987, with a high of almost 77 percent in 1980. Even more importantly, the rate of change accelerated in 1980. While there was an increase in all three categories of public law litigation in the 1940s, no doubt related in part to the war and its aftermath, the 1950s were a relatively quiet decade, as we have repeatedly noted in other contexts. But, then, in each of the decades since 1960, public law litigation doubled, with a slower growth only since 1980. While diversity litigation has also grown numerically during these years, its proportion of the total civil caseload in federal courts declined between 1960 and the early 1980s (table 7.1).

Thus, public law litigation has risen in an unprecedented fashion and has become a cornerstone of the larger system of public regulation. What is so significant about this shift is that the judiciary is called upon to perform both legislative and executive functions along with its more traditional ones. As the introductory note to Chayes's important article states:

> The law suit (in public law litigation) does not merely clarify the meaning of the law, remitting the parties to private ordering of their affairs, but itself establishes a regime ordering the future interaction of the parties and of the absentees as well, subjecting them to continuing judicial oversight. Such a role for courts, and for judges, is unprecedented and raises serious concerns of legitimacy. (1976, 1281)

To sum up, the government's intervention in economy and society has also shaped the composition of cases within the federal courts. In the nineteenth century this intervention was reflected in a private caseload of diversity of citizenship cases coupled with admiralty, patents, and copyrights. Beginning in the Progressive Era, solidified by the New Deal and reactivated in the 1960s, this intervention has been expressed by a public law caseload that has demanded that judges become the agents of review and enforcement of an ever-growing maze of federal statutes and administrative regulation. Moreover, as the administrative process extends its tentacles into controversial areas, the enacted regulation has become both esoteric and complex, hence demanding an ever more activist role for judges. Put in this position, judges are caught between the demands of deferring to the discretionary authority of technical experts, on the one hand, and the demands of preserving, developing, and maintaining the procedural guarantees of due process of law, on the other. That is, the expansion of the court's public law litigation leaves judges squarely in the middle of the contradictory demands of technocratization and judicialization. Or, as we have described it in earlier chapters, the debate between the proponents of administration and adjudication conjures up the dialectical double-bind of courts in the twentieth century.

The Impact of the Political Economy on the Jurisdiction of Civil Cases

To substantiate this trend in greater detail we will now examine the effect of economic, governmental, and demographic factors on the court's four bases of jurisdiction. The research strategy that follows parallels that developed in earlier chapters. In this section we begin by looking at the effects of environmental factors on the court's caseload, controlling for jurisdictional origin. In the final section, we will examine the relationship between environmental, task, and organizational variables and the disposition (i.e., no actions, pretrials, and trials) of cases by jurisdiction.

Table 7.4 reports the effect of population density, number of corporations, and number of government employees on federal question, diversity, U.S. plaintiff, and U.S. defendant cases for 1950, 1960, and 1970. (Following the approach of earlier chapters, all variables, except population density, are analyzed net of population size.)

Table 7.4a
Environment and Litigation Rate by Jurisdiction, 1950-1970

		Federal Question/Population			Diversity/Population		
		1950	*1960*	*1970*	*1950*	*1960*	*1970*
Population	r	.44	.40	.24	.64	.61	.48
Density	b	7.70-09	1.20-08	1.60-08	3.20-07	9.90-08	7.70-09
	b*	.40****	.45***	.20	.69****	.26***	.10
Number of	r	.45	.39	−.13	−.05	.02	.02
Corporations/	b	4.90-03	7.60-03	1.00-02	−5.50-02	−2.40-03	1.70-03
Population	b*	.38****	.33**	−.15	−.18	−.01	.03
Number of	r	—	−.01	.23	—	.85	.81
Government	b	—	−1.00-03	6.90-04	—	.05	4.90-03
Employees/	b*	—	−.22	.09	—	.71****	.73****
Population							
1/Population	r	−.07	−.10	.03	.04	.10	.30
	b	−1.30	−7.80	29.90	151.60	63.80	62.30
	b*	−.03	−.08	.09	.13	.05	.21**
	R²	.36	.32	.09	.46	.76	.70

The findings reported in this table present another angle for considering the impact of the court's environmental profile on intraorganizational activities. Federal question cases include suits between private parties that raise, in general, disputes involving conflicts over interpretation of what is "right"—that is, values—that may in some instances go to interpretations of the Constitution itself. By contrast, diversity cases are private matters that are, again in a general sense, disputes involving differences of interpretation over a set of factual events. Analytically, federal question cases tend to revolve around issues of norm enforcement while diversity cases raise issues of more straightforward dispute resolution. In many respects, the findings reported in table 7.4a underscore this distinction.

In 1950 and 1960, population density and the number of corporations show a significant impact on federal question cases documenting the permeable boundary between environmental and task demands as well as the relatively stable relationship between court and community that we have documented in earlier chapters. By 1970, however, environmental factors do not show a direct or mediated impact on federal question cases; this finding coincides with the timing of the profound impact of the civil rights movement on the docket that was discussed earlier. That is, the impetus to file these public law cases derives from a politicized awareness of one's rights—or an ideological commitment that is not captured by these environmental variables. The findings for 1970 provide indirect evidence that the pressures of conscious, political action orchestrated by an activist bar may outweigh the effect of environmental pressures.

This point is reenforced if we turn to the findings for diversity cases. Here, we see that environmental factors do explain this category of jurisdiction and that the pattern, in many respects, parallels those found for civil filings reported in chap. 3 (see esp. table 3.2). First, in 1950, population density is the main factor ($b^* = .69$) in an explanation of diversity cases. Second, when the number of government employees is added to the equation in 1960, it becomes a strong ($b^* = .71$) and significant factor in an explanation of these cases. Third, the effect of density disappears whereas the government effect holds for the findings reported for 1970. Together, these findings demonstrate that the court's traditional tasks of dispute resolution continue to pose a demand, even as new pressures are placed on the courts to serve as an arena to resolve deeper moral dilemmas of American society.

The findings reported for U.S. plaintiff and U.S. defendant cases in table 7.4b document, once again, the multiple roles of this branch of government; but, here we may add the task of norm enforcement to that of dispute resolution. From the standpoint of the government itself, U.S. plaintiff cases—suits filed by the government against a private party—have many of the same characteristics as the criminal docket because the government may decide to act or not to act on a particular matter; at the district court level, many of these cases consist of enforcement matters that may range from VA questions to more weighty issues. The activities of the U.S. Attorney's Office and its organizational base, the Department of Justice, are the institutional gate-keepers of disputes where the government decides to sue; they have the pre-rogative to set—and to monitor—this agenda. Thus, it should hardly be a surprise to learn that environmental factors do not contribute much to an explanation of this category of jurisdiction in 1950, 1960, and 1970.

Table 7.4b
Environment and Litigation Rate by Jurisdiction, 1950-1970

		U.S Plaintiff/Population			U.S. Defendant/Population		
		1950	*1960*	*1970*	*1950*	*1960*	*1970*
Population	r	−.12	−.19	.09	.65	.60	.51
Density	b	−3.30-09	−8.70-10	1.30-09	1.30-08	1.40-08	3.30-09
	b*	−.13	−.06	−.06	.67****	.24***	.04
Number of	r	.16	.17	.05	.06	.03	−.05
Corporations/	b	3.00-03	1.00-03	−7.70-05	−9.00-04	3.40-04	1.80-03
Population	b*	.18	.08	0	.07	.01	.03
Number of	r	—	−.21	.32	—	.85	.87
Government	b	—	−5.70-04	6.30 04	—	7.40-.03	6.10-03
Employees/	b*	—	−.22	.32**	—	.72	.85
Population							
1/Population	r	.23	.30	.31	−.01	.11	.15
	b	13.20	16.40	22.30	3.60	11.50	11.90
	b*	.21	.31	.26*	.07	.05	.04
	R²	.09	.17	.18	.43	.77	.76

By contrast, U.S. defendant cases consist of suits by private parties against the United States. This includes "not only claims in contract and torts directly against the government . . . but the multitude of suits to prevent Fed-eral officers or agencies from taking action claimed to be prohibited, or to require them to take action claimed to be demanded by Federal law" (Friendly

1973, 9) that may include land condemnation, deportation, and prisoner petitions. The findings reported in Table 7.4b for U.S. defendant cases parallel
closely those reported for diversity cases. In other words, the pressures that
push toward suits by private parties against the government are associated
with, and explained by, the environmental shifts and complexities of a district, with population density playing a significant role in 1950 and 1960.

In sum, the findings presented in table 7.4 disclose that the political
economy of federal jurisdictions helps to explain the diversity and U.S.
defendant docket. Interestingly, the same factors explain the decision of private parties to sue, regardless of whether they are suing one another or the
government. That the government is treated as just another player in the
political economy documents the neocorporatist or technocratic blending of
private and public waters. U.S. plaintiff cases are not, however, explained by
environmental factors; in this arena, the government itself is the gatekeeper
and exercises considerable leverage to shape policy agendas. Furthermore,
by 1970 federal question cases were not explained by environmental factors,
as political challenges to the court's traditional passivity took hold. Ironically,
perhaps, both the government and an activist bar penetrated the politicization
of the tasks of courts.

The impact of the expansion of the administrative state on the federal
district courts presents a multidimensional picture. Administrative expansion has not only provided an alternative to the legal forum of courts; it has
also been used by executives to articulate political agendas. Yet, the depth of
the government's shadow is not evenly cast. After all, a social security case
and a school desegregation suit are both products of the public law explosion, but they differ in their degree of complexity and, therefore, in their
impact on court resources. Despite the variation in impact, contemporary
functions of courts include the interpretation and clarification of regulatory
guidelines as well as the resolution of disputes. While perhaps the biggest
impact of this twentieth-century development is felt at the appellate level, it
is clear that the district courts have not been immune.

As Wolfe has noted, the "franchise state" (related to the notions of the
welfare state and neocorporatism) "attempted to solve both intra-and inter-
class conflict by granting public power to private agencies" (1977, 9). An
important feature of the franchise state is its "intentionally mixed public and
private character" (p. 112) in which government-corporate linkages (e.g.,
administrative agencies) enjoy "both the administrative autonomy of a private organization and the judicial authority of a public institution" (Sarti, as
quoted by Wolfe 1977, 120). Even as we speak of an explosion in public law
litigation, however, we must also take care to distinguish between important
qualitative dimensions. As we demonstrated in the preceding analyses, the
historical origin of these cases lies in the larger transformation of the political

economy surrounding the court, especially the need to combine and systematize dispute resolution, enforcement, and lawmaking under one administrative roof. Thus, public law litigation (U.S. and federal question cases) is to be distinguished from diversity because the former may simultaneously demand a variety of judicial functions—dispute resolution, enforcement, and policy clarification.

The Consequences of Jurisdiction for Decision-Making

Yet, examination of the public law explosion from the standpoint of the district courts also underscores the fact that not every one of these cases is necessarily inherently complex and appealed for circuit or Supreme Court review. In fact, public law cases may be disposed of through pretrial channels, again stressing the importance of analyzing patterns of litigation from the bottom up. What are the consequences of these differences for judicial decision-making? As before, we will concentrate on a synchronic analysis of various effects on terminations and dispositions.

Table 7.5 shows the effects of three environmental variables—population density, government, and corporations—as well as demand and number of judges on the terminations of U.S. and private cases, net of population size, for 1970. The impact of these independent variables on U.S. and private terminations is remarkably similar. First, of the selected environmental variables, government presence emerges as a key factor in an explanation of these terminations. Second, the per capita demand shows a clear impact on both categories of termination when other variables are controlled. Third, judicial resources show a strong simple correlation with both types of terminations, but are not significant when other factors are added to the equation. Standing back, these findings suggest that governmental and task demands push toward disposition while the key organizational resource, judges, are seemingly marginal. But, before drawing this conclusion it is essential to examine the court's output through a more finegrained lens.

Table 7.6 reports the effect of task and resource variables on the types of disposition by jurisdictional category, net of population, for 1970. The task structure is measured by the total civil and criminal demand on the federal district court; organizational resources are measured by both judicial—number of judges and magistrates—and nonjudicial functions, specifically the impact of the division of labor (number of positions). Finally, geographical dispersion (or the number of places for holding court) is included in this equation; this variable represents, in microcosm, the permeable boundary between the court's environmental and organizational dimensions. Geographical dispersion is inversely correlated with urbanization since more rural dis-

Table 7.5
Effects of the Environment, Demand, and Judges on U.S. and Private Terminations in 1970

	1970 U.S. Terminations/ Population			1970 Private Terminations/ Population		
	r	*b*	*b**	*r*	*b*	*b**
Population Density	.41	−4.50-09	−.05	.47	1.30-08	.04
Corporations/ Population	.04	5.60-03	.07	−.01	3.00-03	.01
Government Employees/ Population	.75	5.70-03	.67****	.75	1.70-02	.60****
Demand/ Population	.71	9.50-02	.46***	.74	3.40-01	.51***
Judges/ Population	.74	−24.60	−.27	.74	−95.00	−.30
1/Population	.27	66.90	.18*	.24	227.80	.19
R^2			.66			.67

tricts must continue to maintain multiple courthouses. Of course, nonmetropolitan courts also tend, on balance, to be less congested. With this in mind, what factors account for the termination of cases?

Private terminations. We have argued that, in many respects, the diversity-personal injury docket is a drag on the district court's more modern role to mediate state enforcement relations. Substantiating this theme, demand remains the primary factor in an explanation of diversity no-actions terminations (b^* = .67) (see table 7.6a). When pressures become too great, lawyers are pushed to settle these cases without, apparently, the input of judicial or nonjudicial support. A consideration of the findings reported for the pretried and tried diversity docket shows that geographical dispersion as well as nonjudicial resources (number of positions) have no significant effect, with the exception of a negative influence of the number of positions on diversity trials. We may speculate that these cases are more likely to receive some attention from the court in more isolated, and thus less congested, settings, but that, even here, the pattern is not clear or strong.

Table 7.6a
Effects of Demand, Organization, and Jurisdiction on
Civil Dispositions in 1970[a]

Private Cases

Diversity/Population

	No Actions			Pretrials			Trials		
	r	*b*	*b**	*r*	*b*	*b**	*r*	*b*	*b**
Judges/ Population	.16	3.00	.09	.18	6.10	.20	.01	3.40	.27
Number of Positions/ Population	.13	−8.90	−.84	.34	−8.90	−.93	.23	−4.90	−1.20*
Magistrates/ Population	.01	22.40	−.18	.09	11.10	.10	−.12	−2.20	−.05
Demand/ Population	.26	4.80-02	.67*	.17	1.90-20	.30	.60	8.40-03	.31
Geographical Dispersion/ Population	.12	.62	−.02	.34	3.20	.09	.37	1.10	08
1/Population	.12	97.50	.74	.40	120.80	1.00*	.39	62.70	1.30**
R^2			.16			.22			.25

[a] These findings should be interpreted with caution due to possible problems of multicollinearity, especially between number of positions and 1/Population.

Turning to federal question dispositions, the findings reported for no-actions parallel those shown for the diversity docket (see table 7.6b). Demand emerges as a strong and significant factor ($b^* = .80$) in an explanation of federal question, no-action terminations. The number of positions also affects no-action dispositions, but again negatively. On balance, these findings suggest that there are notable pressures to have attorneys orchestrate the termination of these cases in their offices, rather than in judges' chambers or courtrooms. Supporting this theme is the notable absence of a judicial effect on the termination of federal question cases.

Rationalizing Justice

Table 7.6b
Effects of Demand, Organization, and Jurisdiction on
Civil Dispositions in 1970

Private Cases

Federal Question/Population

	No Actions			Pretrials			Trials		
	r	b	b^*	r	b	b^*	r	b	b^*
Judges/ Population	.11	1.10	.02	.20	−12.80	−.17	−.01	−3.20	−.28
Number of Positions/ Population	.00	−20.30	−1.10*	.26	3.10	.13	.17	−.43	−.12
Magistrates/ Population	.06	−20.30	−.10	.22	47.60	.18	.00	3.30	.08
Demand/ Population	.26	.10	.80***	.20	.02	.14	.01	4.90-03	.20
Geographical Dispersion/	−.08	−12.10	−.18	.12	2.60	.03	.20	.53	.04
1/Population	−.04	206.50	.91*	.21	26.60	.09	.25	16.80	.37
R^2			.18			.09			.09

A key element of a technocratic model of administration is to construct a permeable boundary between private and public sector activity—to encourage an adaptable, flexible approach to the coordination of work. Of course, this assumption about efficient management contradicts traditional ideas about the advantages of a bureaucratic model and suggests one reason why many arenas of state activity have been resistant to recent discussions of organizational innovation. Yet, the organizational structure of the federal courts gives a certain advantage to modern social engineers of organizational change. Building on a federalist tradition the courts have always had a decentralized structure and, furthermore, a loosely-coupled linkage between private attorneys and judges. The push to file cases in a public forum and to then settle them privately is, ironically, a part of a federalist tradition as well as an emergent neo-corporatist, technocratic strategy. What of U.S. cases? Is the same pattern emerging?

U.S. cases. When the government sues, particularly at the district court level, cases tend to revolve around issues of enforcement that, moreover, are backed by the full weight of the government. The findings reported in table 7.6c underscore this point in a curious way: when trials occur it is in the smaller, upstate, nonmetropolitan courts (judges: $b^* = -.58$; geographical dispersion: $b^* = .40$). In large measure these findings lead us to speculate that the "gatekeeping" role of the U.S. Attorney extends to the informal, nontrial resolution of government matters, especially in metropolitan courts.

Table 7.6c
Effects of Demand, Organization, and Jurisdiction on Civil Dispositions in 1970

U.S. Cases

U.S. Plaintiff/Population

	No Actions			Pretrials			Trials		
	r	b	b^*	r	b	b^*	r	b	b^*
Judges/ Population	.13	−1.85	−.08	.27	.63	.05	.14	−.80	−.58*
Number of Positions/ Population	.30	.46	.06	.27	.08	.02	.41	.33	.77
Magistrates/ Population	−.01	−12.28	−.15	.22	4.39	.10	.10	.46	.09
Demand/ Population	.10	.01	.19	.26	3.48-02	.14	.14	5.70-03	.20
Geographical Dispersion/ Population	.22	−1.06	−.04	.19	2.68	.19	.48	.64	.40**
1/Population	.33	28.68	.31	.18	−.17	.00	.44	−1.85	−.35
R^2			.13			.11			.31

Finally, let us consider the impact of this model on U.S. defendant terminations (table 7.6d). Here, we begin to see the other side of the same coin. Instead of trials being explained by geographical dispersion and by small court size, no actions and pretrials are explained by large court size ($b^* = .94$

and .46, respectively). Similarly, whereas in U.S. plaintiff cases (see table 7.6c), trials produced the highest explained variance ($R^2 = .31$), in U.S. defendant cases it is no actions (.67) and pretrials (.66) that show a higher explained variance. These findings suggest that the government may exert powers to shape its own mode of resolution—trials when this seems appropriate, negotiation when this seems preferable.

Where, then, do judges place their overall energies? Clearly, when the government is being sued in larger and more demanding settings, judges appear to intervene to orchestrate settlement.[8] It is not that judges are not significant in an explanation of dispositions; rather, their work focuses on problem-solving or mediation rather than adjudication when the state and

Table 7.6d
Effects of Demand, Organization, and Jurisdiction on
Civil Dispositions in 1970[a]

U.S. Cases

U.S. Defendant/Population

	No Actions			Pretrials			Trials		
	r	b	b^*	r	b	b^*	r	b	b^*
Judges/ Population	.80	8.94	.94****	.78	33.00	.46*	.43	−.33	−.11
Number of Positions/ Population	.49	−1.24	−.41	.53	4.78	.21	.47	.48	.53
Magistrates/ Population	.52	−3.46	−.10	.54	−13.46	−.05	.22	−1.87	−.18
Demand/ Population	.73	3.70-02	.18	.77	.05	.32	.43	2.30-02	.38
Geographical Dispersion/ Population	−.04	−1.31	−.12	.11	11.64	.14	.22	.11	.03
1/Population	.14	9.93	.27	.18	−76.76	−.27	.34	−1.51	−.13
R^2			.67			.66			.28

private sector actors dispute. Here we see, in a quite concrete way, that the way judges work—through negotiation and settlements—and what judges tend to work on is responsive to the neocorporatist, franchise structure of modern state activities.

In view of the findings presented in tables 7.6a to 7.6d, as well as the previous chapter, we are forced to ask: At what point do we still describe the work of judges as that of adjudication? A number of issues complicate the answer to this question. Most obviously, the legal profession has secured an indispensable position in the steps of legal decision-making, whatever the form of disposition, thus making it difficult to conclude that the inevitable result of the court's dilemma will be the abdication of judges and lawyers and their replacement with low-level technical experts, or a routinized world of law controlled by simplistic rules executed by mindless, insensitive robots.

But, form is also important, especially in courts. If dispute resolution is a process, granted one that may in some instances be orchestrated by judges, then we must recognize that this process has changed dramatically. It is, therefore, no accident that the "politics of informal justice" (Abel 1982) has emerged in recent years as one of the major challenges to the domain of formal justice (see also Nader 1980; Menkel-Meadow 1985). The question remains: Can judicial professionals construe the language of informalism as one of securing continued judicial control over dispute resolution, or might other actors step in, perhaps from below, to claim a role?

Conclusion

The history of federal jurisdiction tells a story about the role of the courts in the legitimation of modern governmental institutions. Federal district courts witnessed a shift in the composition of cases from private to U.S. cases. While U.S. cases do not yet exceed the number of private matters, they have grown at a faster pace in the twentieth century and U.S. defendant cases appear to receive closer attention from judges. Furthermore, the number of U.S. cases and their impact upon the court will not be reversed so long as the franchise state and Congress must continue to expand the government's services and economic involvement. As we suggested in the introduction to this chapter, the growth of U.S. cases is the end product of the expansion of the administrative process.

But the growth of U.S. cases does not simply mean a numerical expansion of the courts' workload; qualitative issues are at work as well. More specifically, our findings suggest that judicial resources are associated with no-action and pretrial U.S. defendant terminations where there is room to experiment with innovative and alternative modes of dispute resolution. At one level, these findings once again make clear that courts obviously do not work as they are supposed to. But the emphasis on organizational-administrative innovation carries an especially important message.

For what is squeezed out of the traditional form of law is a locale for a moral vision and political debate; the administrative process rewards "technical expertise"—specialization, objectivity, and neutrality. There is, then, a very real price that is paid. Rationalization creates politics without Politics; it creates a world in which everything and nothing is political; it creates a world in which political discourse and conflict become illegitimate. As Sheldon Wolin has said, "in a world of organizational politics, men [and women] are no longer exercised by the ancient battle cries of inequality" (1960, 356). Rather, problems may be solved through technical means—technical reforms. With this in mind, let us turn to a review of the overall findings that have emerged from this study and, of equal importance, place these debates over court reform in a larger context. Is it possible to claim or retain a substantive, moral vision in the face of the vagaries of technocratic politics?

CHAPTER 8

*

Conclusion:
From Adjudication to Administration, or
Is the Third Branch Wilting?

In this concluding chapter, first we review briefly our argument and our findings. Though we have not tested a series of scientific hypotheses, we have confronted our argument with historical and empirical data and it is in this sense that we feel we have documented themes, patterns and relations through social research. Following this review, we show, through argumentation, that the shift from adjudication to administration is an expression, or at least a symptom of, a larger transformation of the state in American society. In the third section, we speculate on the limits of rationalization and raise the question whether there can be something like "democratic justice" in a complex society. We ask: Is it possible to develop a conception of judicial reform that goes beyond rationalization and a quest for managerial or technocratic control of courts, by acknowledging the need for both a degree of technical rationality and political democratic input into judicial processes? In considering this question, we will offer a typology of six models of justice, including an extensive discussion of technocratic justice, the central target of this book. Finally we suggest a research agenda that builds upon our work, including possibilities for comparative research.

The central thesis of this book is that there has been a distinctly observable movement toward the rationalization of justice, that is, a progressive transformation in the structure of courts and a shift in the disposition of cases from adjudication to administration. We have traced this process to the increasing demand for adjudicatory services (due to a rise in civil litigation) coupled with constraints on the resources of federal courts.

The method we have used to investigate these processes has been to construct a cause-and-effect chain, establishing various connections between the political economy and ecology of the environment, litigation and prosecution, civil and criminal caseloads, internal court structure, and modes of

185

dispositions and outcomes. The empirical results of our investigation can be summarized by briefly retracing this causal path, but in reverse order, that is, starting with (1) the output, disposition and termination of cases, and proceeding (2) to the internal organization of courts, (3) to the task structure of courts (the input), and finally (4) to the external jurisdictional environment and the historical trends in litigation.

Summary and Findings

A. Dispositions and Outcomes as Dependent Variables

The disposition of cases, especially those types of dispositions that constitute alternatives to the model of full adjudication, are affected significantly by the level of judicial and court resources. In civil cases, no-action and pretrial dispositions are the common modes of disposition; in criminal cases, dismissals and plea bargaining are the common mode. These latter types of dispositions are affected heavily by the fiscal and organizational resources of district courts. In other words, the resources and labor-power of courts are disproportionately devoted to administrative rather than adjudicatory services. We may note some salient findings.

1. The effect of judges is not the only, or even the main factor, in an explanation of terminations. To be sure, an Article III judge is ultimately responsible for the written order that will expedite or terminate a particular case. But the "support staff" of modern judicial personnel plays an important part in this process; nonjudicial personnel are interdependent with judicial personnel and in some instances directly effect decisions and outcomes. In civil dispositions, we show that, besides judges, the number of magistrates plays an important role, especially in more "marginal" types of cases (for example, prisoner petitions) or when it comes to reducing delay (the time from filing to disposition). In criminal dispositions, U.S. Attorneys and probation officers have a central part, especially in guilty pleas, acquittals, and convictions. These findings suggest that the construct "organizational support" may be conceptually inadequate.

2. The type of case category—personal injury or labor, for example—is another factor that influences the effect of court structure on civil dispositions. For example, the effect of court personnel is quite different in prisoner petitions than in civil rights cases, with disproportionate resources devoted to the pretrial stages of litigation in the latter types of cases. Magistrates play a significant role in the trial stage of prisoner petitions, though this is a rare occurrence in any event. Judges and support staff have a significant effect on pretrials in corporate litigation; magistrates, however, play a greater role in

the no-action and pretrial dispositions of labor cases. These patterns underscore the fact that differential resources are available to litigants, with the
effect that some cases, prisoner petitions and labor cases, for example, are
less likely to engage the full attention and resources of the courts than other
types of cases. (These findings are analyzed in detail in chap. 6.)

3. The basis of jurisdiction—private versus U.S.—is an additional factor
that influences the nature of dispositions. For example, demand is a significant factor in private no-action dispositions. By contrast, government cases
are handled differently than private ones, even though the same type of suits
(e.g., tort, real property, and contract) may be involved. Thus, demand is the
driving force in no-action dispositions. In U.S. cases, by contrast, the relative
size and location of the court (rural vs. urban) is a significant factor for both
no-actions and trials.

But within government cases, there are some important differences as
well. Government cases dominate the agenda of federal district courts, in part
a result of the activities and conflicts generated by administrative and regulatory agencies and, more generally, by the executive branch (see chap. 7 for a
detailed discussion). But U.S. defendant cases (which include a large proportion of prisoner and social security cases) have a greater probability of being
disposed of by no action or by pretrial dispositions than U.S. plaintiff cases.
Our data suggest that case complexity is a major factor in this pattern, especially since U.S. plaintiff trials are better explained than pretrials and no
action dispositions, as compared to U.S. defendant dispositions.

4. Task structure variables have an overriding effect on dispositions in
1950, 1960, and 1970. Whether one uses total demand or controls for civil
versus criminal filings, and whether one considers task structure effects alone
or jointly with environmental variables, the various types of dispositions (with
the exception of civil trials in 1970) are affected by the level of filings and of
pending cases in a district. In large part, this finding is the result of a logical
relationship between input and output: the more cases are filed, the more are
terminated. But the combination of new filings and pending cases has a different effect on civil as compared to criminal dispositions. In civil cases,
demand acts to increase the effect of time pressure on decision-making, leading to no-action or pretrial dispositions, especially for certain kinds of cases
such as private cases or labor cases.

In criminal cases, on the other hand, the organizational influence of U.S.
Attorneys and probation plays a special role, though the pressures of pending
cases will occasionally increase the rate of guilty pleas (that is, plea bargaining) and, hence, convictions (see table 6.10).

5. The comparison between the effects of task structure and environmental variables in 1960 and 1970 shows a sharp difference between civil
and criminal dispositions. We interpret this difference as a function of the

crime control model as advocated by the Department of Justice and the U.S. Attorney's Office. It is the government's interest in implementing a "law-and-order" policy that puts direct pressure on courts to expedite criminal disposi-tions, thus displacing adjudicatory services and giving civil cases a lower priority in terms of urgency and scheduling.

6. Supporting this generalization is the fact that delay is related to de-mand in civil cases, but not in criminal cases. Rising demand will increase the number of days from filing to disposition in civil cases. The use of magis-trates, by contrast, will significantly reduce delay in both civil and criminal dispositions.

7. Geographical dispersion is inversely related to the probability that civil cases will be disposed of through no action dispositions (that is, settlement), and directly to the probability that trials will be held in some categories of cases. Geographical dispersion, the number of places at which court is held in a given district, is inversely related to population density and combines, there-fore, both external and internal aspects of court structure. Our analysis shows that smaller, nonurban court settings favor trials whereas no action disposi-tions are more likely in large, concentrated metropolitan courts.

Extrapolating, we believe that geographical dispersion also measures, however crudely, differences in both case pressures and local legal culture. Simply put, smaller, nonurban district courts still tend to be more hospitable to judicial forms of adjudication whereas metropolitan courts, under greater caseload pressures, tend to adopt practices that promote the rationalization of justice. In this sense, then, metropolitan courts might be said to be the trendsetters of change.

B. The Internal Organizational Structure of Courts as a Dependent Variable

Courts are becoming more technocratic organizations. While some aspects of court organization, for example, the clerk's office, exhibit bureaucratic char-acteristics, the overall process of rationalization moves in a technocratic direc-tion (see our review of these debates in chap. 6).

Two sets of findings support this generalization. First, those elements of the internal structure of courts that can be seen as indicators of "bureau-cratic" properties are positively, rather than negatively, related to the indica-tors of the "professional" structure of courts. This positive relationship sug-gests an interdependence of bureaucratic and professional elements that is characteristic of technocratic rather than purely bureaucratic or professional organizations.

Second, the qualitative procedures and practices used to dispose of cases are geared toward flexibility and informalism, that is, negotiation and bar-gaining, mediation, arbitration, pretrial settlements, and dismissals. As a result, formal adversarial procedures are downplayed in the interest of speeding up the disposition process, reducing backlogs, developing mechanisms for avoiding lengthy procedures, especially trials, and generally reducing the pressures on judges. In more innovative settings, pretrial procedures in routine cases are increasingly handled by magistrates. While some courts still have certain "bureaucratic" rules about delegation of authority between judges and magistrates—an arrangement that may reflect in part their traditional social distance—others encourage a team approach that relies upon cooperation and coordination, rather than a radical division of labor and subordination. Our quantitative data on the effects of both judges and magistrates on pretrial procedures suggest a similar picture, namely that both are heavily, and equally, involved in largely managerial, nonadjudicative decision-making. Supporting this important organizational development in modern American courts, our work also shows the following:

1. Overall, the task structure of federal district courts has a strong effect on their organizational structure and resources, but a number of qualifications and specifications remain. The organizational structure of courts, especially the number of judges, total personnel, number of positions, support staff and the size of the clerk's office are strongly affected by the civil litigation rate. Among civil cases, government litigation (especially U.S. defendant cases) has a greater capacity to mobilize resources than private litigation. The nature and complexity of the task thus figure prominently in the size, structure, and resources of courts. This finding is not surprising for the student of organizational sociology. But, it represents a new insight for the student of courts and judicial administration since organizational factors have rarely been taken into account in the sociology of law and judicial administration.

2. The jurisdictional environment of courts also exercises a strong effect on organizational structure and resources. These findings vary, however, when different dimensions of the political, economic, and ecological environment are controlled. Population density has an effect only on the number of judges in 1960 and 1970. The number of per capita corporations in a district is, contrary to expectations, not a determinant of court structure (except the number of judges in 1960). The presence of government agencies (number of per capita government employees), by contrast, is a significant factor in an explanation of organizational variables (except the number of judges in 1960), and remains a powerful determinant when the task structure is controlled.[1]

3. The proportion of resources for the third branch of the total federal budget concretely documents the disparity in fiscal allocations between the judiciary and other agencies of government. The theme is quite clear: from 1910 to 1980, the budget for the judiciary hovered around a half of a percent of the total U.S. budget. Since 1980, the budget has dropped to about one tenth of a percent. By contrast, the budget of the Department of Justice has

been larger than that of the judicial and legislative branches combined: it went from $41.4 million in 1930 to $3.3 billion in 1984. In other words, in 1984 the Justice Department, one agency among many others of the executive branch, had a budget that was more than three and a half times that of the judiciary. While this budgetary difference must, of course, be seen in light of the specific tasks and functions legislated for the law enforcement arm of government, it nevertheless reveals a certain disparity of power and priorities in the overall allocation of resources. As the British Prime Minister William Gladstone said, " 'Budgets are not really matters of arithmetic. They are a record of the choices that a government makes and the values to which it commits its energy'" (Cohen and Rogers 1986, 513; also see Schumpeter 1954).

4. Another indicator of the "values" and "choices" implied by governmental policies is seen in the internal allocation of resources *within* the third branch. Analysis of the third branch's expenditures from 1950 to 1984 shows that the nonjudicial or "support" side of the courts' budget has received a larger share of available moneys than the judicial side. Furthermore, while both of these budget categories have increased in absolute terms, the relative share of each subcategory of judicial expenditures (judicial salaries and fees of jurors and commissioners-magistrates) has tended to decrease since 1950. By contrast, other administrative expenditures have increased since 1970, notably those for the Administrative Office of the U.S. Courts and Federal Judicial Center.

These trends in the budget of the courts show that (1) expenditures for the judiciary as a whole have not kept pace with those of the executive side of law enforcement, that is, the Department of Justice and (2) there has been an internal shift *within* the third branch from adjudicatory to administrative services, with greater emphasis placed on the nonjudicial, organizational capability of courts rather than the professional core of judges and judicial personnel.

C. The Task Structure of Courts as a Dependent Variable

The political, economic, and demographic environments of courts have a strong effect on the task structure of federal district courts. Changes in the jurisdictional environment's political economy explain and predict changes in the courts' dockets (see chap. 3). Four sets of findings deserve special notice in this context.

1. Total per capita demand (new filings and pending cases) is significantly influenced by population density at all three time points of our study, although the effect is strongest in 1950 and weakens in subsequent decades. There is also a significant government effect on demand in 1960.

2. Considering only the incidence of new filings per population, and especially the civil litigation rate, we show that the number of per capita corporations does have an effect in 1950, and population density still plays a role up to 1960. In 1960 and 1970, however, the presence of the government has a pervasive and significant effect on total filings and on the litigation rate, overshadowing the other environmental influences. Thus, the internal relations of the political economy have become more crucial for an explanation of the activities of district courts. The policies and actions of the executive branch emerge as the significant factor in an explanation of the task structure of courts and, more abstractly, of the processes of judicial rationalization, a finding that has surfaced repeatedly at different stages of our analysis.

3. Complex civil filings are more heavily influenced by environmental variables than complex criminal filings (see table 3.3). For students of criminal justice this finding should not be surprising. Research has shown that shifts in operational policies within the Department of Justice or the U.S. attorneys' offices influence directly the types of criminal cases that find their way onto the courts' docket. A policy decision by a U.S. Attorney to enforce drug laws, for example, will be reflected in the courts' docket (see Olson 1984). An affirmative policy decision by the court's criminal justice gate-keepers, our findings indirectly suggest, is more important than the ecological complexion of the district's environment in shaping the types of criminal cases that are filed in federal court.

4. Environmental effects vary across subcategories of civil litigation. Civil rights litigation, prisoner petitions, and personal injury litigation are more strongly influenced by the dynamics of the environment than corporate and labor litigation. While ethnic heterogeneity (proportion of blacks in the population) and government presence play an important role in civil rights litigation and prisoner petitions, net migration appears as an important (but inversely related factor) in personal injury litigation (geographical mobility reduces the probability of people litigating personal injury cases).

In corporate litigation, economic development (industrialization) and governmental activity (legal-governmental sector) do play the most important role. Labor litigation, by contrast, is the most elusive of the civil litigation categories considered here: none of the environmental factors is significant in labor cases, suggesting that in corporate and labor litigation, mediating factors such as bargaining and negotiation intervene more strongly between external determinants and litigation than in other types of cases.

Beyond the unique factors that shape the history of civil cases, these findings underscore the variable influences on court dockets. From a managerial standpoint, these findings concretize the difficulties of developing or imposing uniform procedures in the light of variable demands across the entire system.

5. Finally, general trends in district court caseloads from 1904 to 1985 disclose considerable variation in filings from decade to decade, though civil filings steadily increased since 1940. More importantly, since 1960 the litigation rate has increased dramatically. While this is not a new finding per se, we have refined the analysis of litigation by using the adult population over 18 years of age as the basis for computing the litigation rate. This analysis shows that in federal courts, criminal filings per 100,000 adults have tended to decrease since 1930. By contrast, civil filings per 100,000 adults have increased from 48.9 in 1960, to 103.7 in 1980, that is, it has more than doubled in merely two decades.

Thus, the increase in federal civil litigation in the last quarter century is quite real and constitutes a definite rise in demand for services. Whether this increase in civil litigation by itself creates a managerial problem for courts is a separate question that we have tried to answer by examining the organizational capacity of courts and the nature of judicial dispositions.

Given our empirical evidence, why have there been various efforts to downplay the importance of the increase in litigation (for example, Galanter 1983; Daniels 1985, although focusing mainly on state courts)? In our view these efforts may be seen as attempts to minimize the significance of external pressures on courts and to ascribe the new informal and administrative modes of disposition to internal legal and judicial changes. Our use of the sociology of law, however, provides a method that relates observed legal and judicial change, that is, changes in the form of law, causally and meaningfully to social change.

First, a methodological point. By treating courts as organizations, that is, as structural units rather than as an aggregate of individual persons, cases, or disputes, we have advanced the analysis of judicial decision-making beyond the level of dispute resolution among individual actors. Our structural or organizational approach has two important consequences. First, it shifts the microsocial concerns of dispute processing to more macrosocial and historical questions. In other words, it shifts the analysis from the consumers of law at the individual level, to the institutional level of law and to the structural conditions under which legal actors can expect to have their proverbial "day in court." We have shown, we believe, that this cannot be achieved by using "disputes as the prism through which to view civil courts and their role in society" (Trubek 1980-1981, 487).[2]

In other words, the exclusive focus on individual disputes or cases, while possibly valid for social psychological study, tends to mask the important structural variations that we have observed in the rates and patterns of litigation. It is the analysis of these variations that requires a focus on the macrosocial and structural contexts within which litigation arises.

Moreover, as Robert Kidder (1980-81) points out, the focus on the use of disputes as indicators of a disrupted social equilibrium (the so-called "perceived injurious experience," which is activated at a certain threshold) ignores the use of law and legal institutions for purposes of establishing or changing power relations, that is to say for strategic and proactive purposes, which have nothing to do with norm enforcement, rectifying imbalances, or plain justice. Corporate and governmental litigation are good examples of this. Here, courts themselves become actors in political processes and struggles that have nothing to do with functionalist images of balance and equilibrium. Corporate and governmental litigation can be seen to arise from structural and institutional contexts, legal and historical patterns, and interorganizational dynamics rather than from individual motivations and actions.

A second consequence of our structural approach is that we treat courts themselves as organizational units of analysis, not as a collection of interested parties or actors as, for example, in the notion of the courtroom work group (Eisenstein and Jacob 1977; see also Feeley 1979).[3]

The conceptual narrowing of courts to informal work group behavior is, in part, a question of the level of analysis and the unit of analysis. But it also has serious policy implications. Not only is the de facto operation of informal group norms in judicial processes accepted as a "neutral" social fact, but the operation of informal norms—oriented as they are toward expediency and efficiency in *ad hoc* decision-making—are seen as overriding the normative questions of due process and quality in delivering justice.

The dynamic of the political and economic environment of courts has a powerful effect on the task structure.[4] But having stated this, we hasten to add that the growth and complexity of caseloads are not simply "functions" of environmental complexity as the social developmental model of law maintains (for a critique see Munger 1988). There are two facets to this argument. First, corporations, far from contributing increasingly to civil and corporate litigation, have learned to keep litigation out of the courts because it is protracted, expensive, and unpredictable. Large corporations have developed appropriate staffs of in-house counsel and elaborate relationships with corporate law firms to mediate, negotiate, and settle disputes before they reach the stage of formal litigation, or if they do get into the court system as "cases," to have them settled or dismissed by various forms of pretrial dispositions. Our data provide ample evidence to support this generalization (see also Toharia 1976).

Second, the functionalist social development model of law needs to be modified since it skirts consideration of the role of government in civil litigation. This role manifests itself in various ways—ranging from the effects of regulatory and administrative agency litigation, to a general historical trend, to the particular ways in which government agencies at various levels affect caseloads as well as patterns of judicial decision making, and the ways in which U.S. cases have come to dominate the agenda of U.S district courts. We have traced these tendencies historically and structurally, that is, in terms of the governmental effects on task structure, internal organization, and dispositions. It is quite clear that the executive branch has had an increasing effect on the structure and functioning of the judiciary. Indeed, we believe this trend to be so powerful and pervasive that we are persuaded to speak of a gradual shift in the relations between the executive and judiciary, and a crisis in the rule of law generally, that is, a crisis that is potentially changing the institutional structure of American government and its relation to law. Let us briefly spell out the nature of this conclusion.

The Crisis of the Rule of Law

The crisis of the federal courts constitutes a social problem of major proportions with consequences that can be viewed as a crisis of the rule of law. It is appropriate, therefore, to step back and take a longer view of the dilemma confronting the courts, to examine critically the agenda to reform the judicial system, and to consider some of the few alternatives that remain.

The obvious aspect of the crisis of the American judicial system is that it is increasingly called upon to deal with a growing volume and complexity of demand for service without having the fiscal and organizational capacity to do so. Backlogs, delays, problems of access, cumbersome procedures, unfair outcomes, and general "dissatisfaction with the administration of justice" are only the most immediate symptoms. Although some of these symptoms go back to the turn of the century and to deeper problems, the court system is responding with various attempts to deal with these surface manifestations. The resulting gradual adaptations—under the guise of organizational reform —are leading to changed priorities of internal resource allocation and to changed definitions of effectiveness. For example, there is growing demand for greater speed and higher productivity in the disposition and termination of cases. At the same time, however, the quality of dispositions in terms of "due process" and other criteria of formal justice remain controversial issues, partly because of the perception that "the process is the punishment" (Feeley 1979; 1983). In addition, pressure toward increased speed and productivity leads to changes in the nature of the disputes defined as worthy of judicial attention and review, that is, changes in the accessibility, priorities, and output of courts. Hence, there is a growing acceptance of the necessity of plea bargaining, pretrial and nonjury dispositions, dismissals and discontinuances, and a proliferation of informal alternatives to the formal procedures of adjudication. Among these informal alternatives, usually presented as innovations, are the following: the encouragement of "judge-hosted" settlement by means of mandatory settlement conferences; court annexed, mandatory nonbinding arbitration; lawyer mediation; use of special masters (for example, magistrates and lawyers); summary jury trials and minitrials; and the expanded use of settlement magistrates who develop special expertise in the settlement process (Bucholz et al. 1978; Rebell and Block 1982; Harrington 1985; Provine 1986). Most of these participatory methods of adjudication and case management are aimed at getting the parties to reach a negotiated settlement that can be adopted by the court as a consent decree.

Law and state. At a somewhat deeper level of analysis, the judicial system can be said to be in crisis because its fundamental normative underpinning—the "rule of law"—is in a dialectic contradiction with the changing requirements of the very social, economic, and political structure which brought it into being: the political economy of capitalism. Today, this contradiction has three specific aspects: a conflict between law and order, or law and the state, between law and economy, and—fueling both—a conflict between state and economy. One might express this tripartite constellation also as a multiple conflict between three types of rationality: formal, substantive, and economic-technocratic.

The conflict between law and order is fundamentally a contradiction between judicial and political power, between the principles of due process and the imposition of social control, a tension already recognized by Locke and Hobbes (Neumann 1957, 24; Balbus 1973, 7-15; Diamond 1974). A more concrete, modern version of this conflict is that between judicial and executive prerogatives, that is, a conflict *within* the state that affects the constitutional balance between the branches of government [see, originally, *Federalist Papers*, Nos. 9 and 10 1787; Montesquieu (1748) 1978; see also Grau 1980; Kennedy 1976; Unger 1976].

Recent theories of the state have emphasized the functional conflicts between legitimation (social harmony) and accumulation (economic growth) (Alford and Friedland 1985). Research has focused on these conflicts within the executive branch with some attention to the role of the legislature (Skocpol 1980; Skowronek 1982). The balancing act between the functions of legitimation and accumulation has been referred to as a "legitimation crisis" (Habermas 1975) and has, in James O'Connor's (1973) view, led to the "fiscal crisis of the state" because social service expenditures, required by the need for social harmony, have increasingly tended to outrun the capacity of the state to generate revenues.

While we believe that the *functional conflicts* within the state are important determinants of budget deficits and fiscal crises, our research has focused more on the *structural conflicts* between the branches of government.[5]

In particular, we have focused on the confrontation building up between the judiciary and the executive branch; here we have suggested that the judiciary is winning some intermittent battles, but is gradually losing ground to the executive branch. Though the legitimacy of the liberal democratic state, especially the executive, depends heavily on a strong, independent judiciary, budgetary priorities (in part administered by Congress) affect each branch differently. The executive gets the lion's share; the judiciary is chewing on the bones. These budgetary constraints on the judiciary, especially in view of increasing litigation, tend to transform the judiciary into an administrative agency that carries out more and more the agenda of the executive branch—whether it is through the dominance of government cases in federal courts, the transformation of trial courts into appeals courts (with high accessibility costs), litigation arising from the decisions made by regulatory and administrative agencies, or the rationalization of procedures to keep the courts "functioning."[6]

These changes—encompassing different aspects of the rationalization of justice—undermine the judiciary's capacity to legitimate itself as well as the executive, since the executive increasingly converges with the judiciary, a conflation of political and legal functions similar to the technocratic forms of law in state-socialist societies. One could add here the intermittent political attacks of the executive, especially the Department of Justice, on the independence of the judiciary as well as the perennial attempt to curb judicial activism in favor of judicial restraint, which almost always suits the interests of the Executive. Judicial activism, however, is itself an outgrowth of the problems and failures of regulation which, in turn, was to stabilize the capitalist economy, often against its will as Theda Skocpol (1980) and Fred Block (1977) suggest. (Note that this perspective transcends the one-sided critique of judicial activism [Glazer 1975; Horowitz 1977].)

Over fifty years ago, Max Weber diagnosed the conflict between law and the state not as an abstract tension between two institutional spheres of power, but as a conflict fueled by the historical development of capitalism. He characterized this conflict in terms of a pervasive dualism between formal and substantive justice.

> Formal justice guarantees the maximum freedom for the interested parties to represent their formal legal interest. But because of the unequal distribution of economic power, which the system of formal justice legalizes, this very freedom must time and again produce consequences which are contrary to the substantive postulates of . . . political expediency. (1966, 228)

Law and economy. A second aspect of the dialectic between the rule of law and the political economy is the conflict between formal legal equality and the continued economic and social inequality among various groups, strata, and classes. At one time this appeared as a conflict *within law* insofar as the substantive claims of different interest groups were legitimated by formal law without their being able to achieve an adequate resolution under the provisions of capitalist economic and social relations. But, increasingly, this means that it has also become a conflict *within liberal democracy as a whole* insofar as the promise of democracy is extended to the political and judicial sphere, but withheld from the social and economic sphere. Voting, equality, and the protection of civil rights have few, if any, counterparts in the corporate economy and in the workplace.[7] Economic and social democracy remain unfulfilled ideals.

Again, Weber's insight into the original nineteenth-century connection between law and economy is striking.

> Among those groups who favor formal justice we must include all those political and economic interest groups to whom the stability and predictability of legal procedure are of very great importance, i.e., particularly rational economic and political organizations intended to have a permanent character. Above all, those in possession of economic power look upon a formal rational administration of justice as a guarantee of "freedom." ... (1966, 229)

Weber went on to specify the concrete consequences of this situation for the poor and the close connection between unequal justice and the adversary system.

> ... the high cost of litigation and legal services amounted for those who could not afford to purchase them to a denial of justice. ... This denial of justice was in close conformity with the interests of the propertied, especially capitalistic classes. But such a dual judicial policy of formal adjudication of disputes within the upper class, combined with arbitrariness or de facto denigration of justice for the economically weak, is not always possible. If it cannot be had, capitalistic interests will fare best under a rigorously formal system of adjudication which applies in all cases and operates under the adversary system of procedure. (1966, 230)

> The bourgeois strata have generally tended to be intensely interested in a rational procedural system and therefore in a systematized and unambiguously formal and purposefully constructed substantive law which eliminated both obsolete traditions and arbitrariness and in which rights can have their source exclusively in general objective norms. (1966, 231)

What exactly was the nature of formal law and justice, as expressed in the notion of the "rule of law"?

Empirically, the rule of law had various components. One of them was the guarantee of procedural rights or due process of law which was specifically designed to protect individuals (originally, read: owners of property) from the arbitrary exercise of governmental power. This included the right to be heard by a judge ("having one's day in court"), legal representation, habeas corpus, the separation of prosecution and investigation from adjudication, not having to testify against oneself, the right to be tried by a jury, the right of appeal, and similar specific provisions of due process and the adversary system.

Adjudication, by an independent judiciary, in particular, is pivotal to the notion of rule of law insofar as it is a peaceful process of resolving disputes among private parties under the auspices of formal legal rules and procedures or, as Lon L. Fuller (1981, 91) puts it, a "form of social ordering" based on "presentation of proofs and reasoned arguments."

The traditional model of civil adjudication ideally exhibits the following elements:

1. The lawsuit is bipolar. Litigation is organized as a contest between two individuals or at least two unitary interests, diametrically opposed, to be decided on a winner takes all basis.

2. Litigation is retrospective. The controversy is about an identified set of completed events: whether they occurred, and if so, with what consequences for the legal relations of the parties.

3. Right and remedy are interdependent. The scope of the relief is derived more or less logically from the substantive violation under the general theory that the plaintiff will get compensation measured by the harm caused by the defendant's breach of duty. . . .

4. The lawsuit is a self-contained episode. The impact of the judgment is confined to the parties . . . entry of judgment ends the court's involvement.

5. The process is party initiated and party controlled. The case is organized and the issues defined by exchanges between the parties. Responsibility for fact development is theirs. The trial judge is a neutral arbiter of their interactions who decides questions of law only if they are put in issue by an appropriate move of a party. (Chayes 1976, 1282-83)

Of equal importance is the fact that this bipolar, retrospective, interdependent, self-contained, and party-initiated process historically implied a certain type of organizational arrangement characterized by a traditional and professional structure. In other words, adjudication was a process of dispute resolution that was tied to a historically specific organizational structure. The professional decision of the judge was the outcome of a reasoned, deliberative process of adjudicating disagreement about the facts of a case, based on a general agreement on the validity of substantive and procedural legal rules and on the desirability of a just outcome. The judge was expected to act as the quintessential "professional" facing a complex case to which the special knowledge of the law was to be applied.

In contrast to adjudication, administrative decision-making implies the routine application of technical rules and precedent to particular problematic situations under conditions of agreement on both the facts and the desired outcome (Thompson and Tuden 1959). There is, ideally, no uncertainty in the facts and in the rules. The outcome is a generally unappealable decision or decree. Adjudication and administration, then, require fundamentally different premises for decision-making.

Nevertheless, the analytic distinction may be blurred in actual practice. Adjudication may, in some instances—and perhaps now as a matter of historical tendency—approximate the model of administration via such intermediate steps as mediation, arbitration, or other types of "informal justice" (see Abel 1982). Moreover, adjudication may require the exigencies of administration under other circumstances, such as the proliferation of certain types of cases. This is especially apparent when courts are called upon to resolve questions of public law. Abram Chayes (1976) shows that these cases require a certain type of administrative disposition because they raise a number of issues that do not fit the criteria of traditional adjudication. Thus, public law litigation has the following characteristics:

1. The scope of the lawsuit is not exogenously given but is shaped primarily by the court and parties.

2. The party structure is not rigidly bilateral but sprawling and amorphous.

3. The fact inquiry is not historical and adjudicative but predictive and legislative.

4. Relief is not conceived as compensation for past wrong in a form logically derived from the substantive liability and confined in its impact to the immediate parties; instead, it is forward looking, fashioned ad hoc on flexible and broadly remedial lines, often having important consequences for many persons including absentees.

5. The remedy is not imposed but negotiated.

6. The decree does not terminate judicial involvement in the affair: its administration requires the continuing participation of the court.

7. The judge is not passive, his or her function limited to analysis and statement of governing legal rules; he or she is active, with responsi-

bility not only for credible fact evaluation, but for organizing and shaping
the litigation to ensure a just and viable outcome.

8. The subject matter of the lawsuit is not a dispute between private individuals about private rights, but a grievance about the operation of public
policy. (1976, 1286)

Evidence of the inadequacy of adjudication for public law cases is suggested by at least two, seemingly unrelated, developments: at one extreme
public law litigation has become particularly susceptible to various pretrial
alternatives because the dictates of full scale adjudication are too formal. At
the opposite extreme, public law cases require courts to go far beyond their
traditionally passive role. In one case the judge becomes a low-level manager
of administrative guidelines; at the other extreme the judge becomes the
manager of public policy implementation; but in neither case is the judge
asked to "umpire" a dispute. If, as Chayes estimates (and as we have confirmed in chap. 7), more than three quarters of all civil cases coming before
the federal courts involve questions of public policy and, hence, are apt to
take the form of public law litigation, one may begin to get an idea of the
extent to which the adjudicatory model has already been replaced by something closer to administration, at least with respect to the form of judicial
proceedings (also see Horowitz 1977).

Another general aspect of the rule of law, in addition to adjudication, is
the notion of formal equality before the law that guarantees, in theory, that
everyone is treated alike in the eyes of the law even though not everyone is
alike in terms of social origins and economic standing. Finally, the rule of law
guarantees the independence of law vis-à-vis other governmental powers, such
as the legislative and executive branches, a principle central to the doctrine
of the separation of powers. The autonomy of law, in turn, entails the perhaps
most basic principle of the rule of law: the power of judicial review.[8] This
power implies that legislative policies and executive decisions can, in principle, be appealed and overturned.

Historical Change and Evolving Contradictions. Historically, it can be
argued that the rule of law is a set of abstract institutional norms that are the
joint outcome of the liberal doctrines of industrial capitalism and the struggle for political democracy (see, generally, Wolfe 1977). Liberal democracies
established the rule of law in an attempt to achieve economic stability and
predictability, legal uniformity, political unity, and the legitimation of the
new social order. It is this set of political and economic objectives that can be
said to have created not only a *content of law* generally favorable to private
capitalist interests, but above all the *form of law* so characteristic of liberal
democracies (Unger 1976; Balbus 1977; Horowitz 1977; Tigar and Levy 1977;

Tushnet 1978; Pashukanis 1980). The emergence of formal legal rationality or *legal domination*, as Weber called it, left its mark on corporations and government bureaucracies alike.[9]

Weber demonstrates how legal domination, once an instrument of liberation from "irrational" feudal and traditional social norms, has not only been eminently compatible with, but indispensable for the legitimation of economic inequality under industrial capitalism. Hence, legal domination—the rule of law—has been an important cornerstone of capitalist social relations and economic rationality. Of central significance here has been the institution of the legal contract among private individuals or corporate actors [Maine (1861) 1917; Commons 1924; Kahn-Freund 1949; Renner 1949, esp. 105-58], and especially the labor contract that provided the legal basis for surplus appropriation by private owners of capital, for the authority of management, and for the evolution of labor management relations (Klare 1978; Stone 1981). For legal and judicial administration itself, this push came much later, as the exigencies created by an "old-fashioned," outdated, and cumbersome process were finally conceded to be ineffectual; hence, it was only a matter of time before the courts began to adopt corporate methods of administration.

Most of the preceding considerations on the affinity of formal law and liberal democracy apply essentially to the early stages of capitalist development up to about 1900, that is, they apply to the production and market relations of competitive capitalism. But the changing nature of the capitalist economy has produced a set of new social and historical conditions within which the rule of law is turning from a positive force into a constraint.[10] Thus, the economic growth and concentration of corporations has transformed nineteenth-century market capitalism into a new oligopolistic form with tendencies toward the centralized control of production and markets as well as the internationalization of capital no longer subject of the sovereignty of a particular nation state. The economic dislocations and crises emerging from this development, in turn, gave rise to Keynesian economic policies, notably the policies of state intervention in the economy ranging from tacit cooperation between state and economy, to explicit regulation and control of certain economic activities by the state. However, state intervention is, in the language of functionalism, both functional and dysfunctional for the capitalist economy. It seeks to stabilize and regulate short-term economic cycles and dislocations as, for example, in antitrust intervention to restore competitiveness or prevent complete monopolization, and in the control of recessions. But it is also undermining the long-term development of the capitalist economy by virtue of planning, technocratic regulation and control, and by seeking to create a neocorporatist partnership between the monopoly sector of the economy and the federal government.

The influence of these changes on the rule of law are subtle and complex, but their net effect has been to transform the original marriage between capitalism and formal law into a conflicted and contradictory relationship, with a new partner, the interventionist state, increasingly disturbing the once idyllic union.

There is an instructive parallel between the development of capitalism and the development of law that speaks to the issue of the incremental transformation of quantitative changes into qualitative ones. Private capital turned from a creative innovation into a social problem once its productive capacities had vastly expanded due to new forms of energy and production (for example, the factory system), thus periodically generating recessions, waste, and social dislocations. In a similar way, the rule of law is being transformed, by virtue of the growth of the state, from an instrument of class ascendance and class domination under the guise of relative autonomy into a (as yet somewhat recalcitrant) partner of the other two branches, especially of the executive. Among the consequences for the nature of law are that the separation between private and public law is disappearing (Chayes 1976) and that there is a change in the conception of "rights" from "the embodiment of individual rights to the embodiment of corporatist status" (Grau 1980, 199; see also Fraser 1978). In other words, there is a movement from rights as absolute entitlements to the "weighing of interests" or the "representation" of interests by administrative agencies or corporatist decision-making structures (Klare 1979, 126).

In sum, the modern conflict between formal legal rationality, economic-technocratic rationality, and substantive political rationality has its historical roots in the ideology of the insulation of autonomous law from politics in liberal democracies. The very autonomy of legal procedures, that is, the formal rationality of law, valued by the liberal ethos of early capitalism, is anathema to a democratic political ideal in which everything, including law and the decisions of judges would be referred to popular will and democratic representation. Populist attacks on formal law found their ideological expression in the rise of legal realism around the turn of the century. Sociological jurisprudence sought to establish the significance of the social context of law and to shift the normative emphasis from "legal justice" to "social justice" (Pound 1906, 1968; see also Simon 1968, 4; Black and Mileski 1973, 2). Yet the modern capitalist state, especially its authoritarian and totalitarian incarnations, has mounted an even more ferocious attack on the institutions of formal law, as the example of German fascism shows (Frankel 1941; Neumann 1957; Kirchheimer 1961). And although we still know little about law and justice under state socialism, indications are that there is a tendency toward integrating the legal and political spheres and subordinating law to the policies of the socialist state, for example, a tendency toward the use of law for purposes of decentralized technocratic guidance and control (see, for example, Golunskii, as quoted by Nonet and Selznick 1978, 100; Shelley 1984, 1987; but see Spitzer 1982, 190-200). Thus, while the rule of formal law has not been abolished together with the state, as was hoped by Eugenii B. Pashukanis and other revolutionary legal theorists, its autonomy and formally rational character has certainly been severely limited.

In liberal democracies, the growth of the state has changed the balance between the three branches of government (McConnell 1966; Lowi 1969; Lorch 1969; Miller 1976). It has also brought about a new set of crisis dimensions circumscribed by the so-called "fiscal crisis of the state" itself, on the one hand, and the "tax welfare backlash," on the other. The fiscal crisis of the state manifests itself in an expansion of government services at a time when the objective fiscal resources and conditions for such an expansion are beginning to decline. As James O'Connor puts it:

> ... the capitalistic state must try to fulfill two basic and often mutually contradictory functions—*accumulation* and *legitimization*. This means that the state must try to maintain or create the conditions in which profitable capital accumulation is possible. However the state must also try to maintain or create the conditions for social harmony. A capitalist state that openly uses its coercive forces to help one class accumulate capital at the expense of other classes loses its legitimacy and hence undermines the basis of its loyalty and support. But a state that ignores the necessity of assisting the process of capital accumulation risks drying up the source of its own power, the economy's surplus production capacity and the taxes drawn from this surplus (and other forms of capital). (1973, 6)

The implications of this problem are far-reaching. First, costs of capital development are "socialized" (that is, paid for by the tax paying public, through the state), while profits continue to be "privately appropriated"; this contradiction creates, then, a "structural gap" between expenditures and revenues. Or, put simply, the state tends to spend more than it takes in by taxation. Second, there is an increasing privatization of state powers for special groups, including corporations and other business interests (Offe 1981). Third, the political system must navigate and coordinate these neocorporatist projects, but under the guise of a free-market model.

Reinforcing and compounding the fiscal crisis of the state is the by now widespread phenomenon of the tax welfare backlash that swept Reagan and Thatcher, among others, into office (Wilensky 1976; Ferguson and Rogers 1981, 3-64; but see Peretz 1982). As Harold L. Wilensky argues:

> ... at high levels of economic development the revolution of expectations must be channeled and contained because mass demands for benefits and

services are outrunning the capacity of government to meet them; people are
happy to consume government service but increasingly restive about paying
for them. How to contend with this "tax welfare backlash" is a crucial problem for all democratic governments. (1976, 8)

Although we are not convinced that "people are happy to consume government services," it stands to reason that the tax welfare backlash exacer-
bates the fiscal crisis of the state by forcing (or condoning) budgetary cutbacks
of social services and increased rationalization of those that remain. In addition, the widely shared notion of low productivity in the public sector and
services, in general, receives a new impetus. Hence, there is further pressure
building to transfer business methods from the private to the public sector
and to introduce labor-saving technology and other measures of efficiency,
budget control, and cost effectiveness to public and governmental organizations.

While James O'Connor has a somewhat reified and mechanistic vision of
crisis tendencies and does not spell out the consequences of the fiscal crisis
of the state for the judiciary, it is clear from his analysis that the third branch
is intimately implicated in the state's function of legitimation, that is, the
need to maintain the "conditions for social harmony," and that this function
threatens to be undermined by the fiscal crisis of all state agencies, including
the courts. More specifically, since courts are part of the "political framework"
of the modern state, they are intimately involved in the political processing of
social and economic claims on the government's already embattled budget.
Hence, courts play an integral role in the legitimation of "private appropriation of state power for particular ends" and in the continued maintenance of
favorable conditions for private capital accumulation. Under advanced capitalism, however, the direct role of courts in this process becomes somewhat
tangential as administrative and executive branch agencies take over more
and more of this function, leaving the judicial branch with the complex responsibility of justifying this uncomfortable development.

In sum, if we can assume that legitimation of economic inequality, of
social control of individual criminal activity and collective political violence,
and of government intervention in economy and society are part of the "functions" of the modern capitalist state (albeit contradictory ones), then the brunt
of such an implementation of the role of law falls not only upon the organs of
law enforcement and the executive branch, but also on the courts and the
third branch. Under the doctrine of "judicial review," it is judicial authority
that must ultimately legitimate social control and state intervention in the
name of formal legality and the rule of law. Hence, the implementation of the
rule of law is seriously strained as it is increasingly called upon to operate on
behalf of the state as a whole, yet carries the historical baggage of autonomous action under the guise of separation of powers. In addition, there are

the fiscal problems of the courts that are shared with the state as, together, they face the relative decline of their resources and the progressive rationalization of their service-oriented structure.

In judicial administration this strain works to move legal domination from the professional judicial form to technocratic forms, from adjudication to administration, from judicial review within the courts to administrative review within independent agencies. Most importantly, the internal structure of the judiciary is changing. The models of executive and corporate forms of decision-making are gradually finding their way into the judicial system. Ideological pressures emerge to treat the doctrine of the separation of powers and of judicial autonomy as a benign myth that has outlived its usefulness, to openly acknowledge the increasing integration of judicial and executive functions or of law and politics, and to move toward a new legal realism and positivism that subordinates formal justice to the substantive reguirements of political capitalism (Unger 1976; Nonet and Selznick 1978). Eventually, this process would unify the disparate aspects of adversary procedure into an "administrative judicial" system, and it would put an end to the belief that "judicial activism" and judicial policy-making are but temporary aberrations of the Warren Court of the 1960s (Cox 1976; *New York Times*, 24 April 1977).

None of these developments occur without a struggle, for each change and reform more and more exposes the contradictory strains of liberal legalism. Hence, many reforms that are introduced into judicial administration take on a hybrid quality, a deference to traditional ways of doing things that is not directly shared by other public or private organizations; yet, an administrative rationality does threaten to undermine those traditional ways.[11] The operation of these pressures has been documented particularly for the criminal justice system (Skolnick 1966; Blumberg 1967; Packer 1968; Balbus 1973; Hartje 1975; Sikes 1975; Quinney 1977). By contrast, a primary purpose of this study has been to show that the process of rising pressures and reformist adaptations has consequences also for civil law and procedure, as well as for the entire field of judicial administration, especially at the federal level. Currently, state and urban trial courts deal predominantly with criminal cases and certain minor civil cases (Jacob 1972). By contrast, as we have shown, federal courts increasingly deal with complex civil litigation involving large corporations, national organizations, administrative agencies, and the U.S. government. Other adaptive strategies, advocated by many economists of law, are to remove individual civil litigation, such as automobile accidents and certain types of personal injury cases (Calabresi 1970), from the judicial system to the "administrative" systems of insurance companies and other forms of "administrative justice" (Nonet 1969).

The distinction between civil and criminal law is gradually being eroded by the proliferation of the "civil offense," a hybridization of civil and criminal forms of law. In "civil offenses," regulatory offenses, or other types of non-criminal violations, administrative agencies, and even private entities, are "granted the power not only to enforce and adjudicate, but to impose penalties sometimes subject only to limited judicial review" (Freiberg and O'Malley 1984, 377). Minor disputes are shifted to extrajudicial or informal forums of dispute resolution (Abel 1982). There is a growing movement to delegalize certain types of disputes in the interest of alleviating the burdens of the court system (Harrington 1982). There are long-standing proposals and some recent reform activity to remove diversity cases involving disputes between the residents of different states from federal to state jurisdiction (ALI Report 1934; Hart and Wechsler 1953; McGowan 1969; Friendly 1973). A recent court reform bill has raised the monetary limit in diversity litigation in federal courts from $10,000 to $50,000.

Most importantly, however, federal courts must deal increasingly with issues of national social and economic policy and thus are called upon to respond to the structural problems generated, on the one hand, by economic concentration, monopolization, and international expansion and, on the other, by the popular demand for the protection of entitlements. In other words, the federal courts are confronted with the precarious task of mediating the contradictions between the interventionist but fiscally unstable government and the unpredictable economy, a balancing act that is likely to become more difficult as the contradictions of the capitalist political economy as a whole continue to evolve. It is not surprising, then, to hear voices of caution suggesting that the courts have taken on more than they can handle, that they should withdraw from political involvement and practice "judicial restraint" (Horowitz 1977; Berger 1977).

In the preceding pages we have provided a brief sketch of the development of the sociohistorical context of the crisis of the rule of law. Particular attention has been given to the way in which law and the judiciary are imbedded and implicated in the crisis of advanced capitalism and the modern state. A central element of the latest institutional responses of economy, state, and judiciary to these crisis conditions has been the emergence of neo-corporatist and technocratic strategies of rationalization, conflict containment, and *ad hoc* adaptation. These responses, we argue, combine to undermine and transform the rule of law and the independence of the judiciary.

Responses to Crisis: Six Models of Justice

If our analysis of the crisis of the rule of law has any validity, the question arises as to what is being done about it or what can or should be done. There is obviously no easy answer to these questions since the nature of the crisis is a historically changing phenomenon, hence subject to varying perceptions and multiple interpretations. However, one way to deal with this complexity is to identify some of the dominant perspectives and value orientations that have animated the debate on legal and judicial reform, a debate that is largely constituted by the various interpretations of the crisis of the judiciary and the rule of law, including those that deny that there is a crisis at all.

In the following section, we propose to categorize these perspectives and value orientations in terms of six possible models of justice: traditional, professional, bureaucratic, technocratic, economic, and democratic.[12] At various points, we have considered dimensions of the traditional, professional, bureaucratic, and technocratic model; in closing, it is useful to distill their salient elements. Economic and democratic models represent more recent conceptualizations, though they draw upon long-standing, albeit different, political traditions.

Each model contains a particular vision of the crisis, a particular interest or value orientation, and a set of remedies or strategies for crisis management. In this context, our description of the crisis of the rule of law does *not* rely on developmental or neoevolutionary assumptions about the nature of sociolegal change, as, for example, in Niklas Luhmann 1972; or Juergen Habermas 1975, 1979; Philippe Nonet and Philip Selznick 1978 (see esp. Teubner 1983, for a brilliant and comprehensive "integration" of these assumptions). Instead, we emphasize the historically contradictory (that is, decidedly nonevolutionary) contingencies that characterize late capitalist and postmodern processes of change, in general, and the contextual nature and limits of legal change, in particular. Furthermore, we argue that theories of crisis and the formulation of crisis management policies are inextricably intertwined. It is especially important to analyze systems-theoretical and neofunctionalist descriptions of postmodern legal forms (for example, "responsive" and "reflexive" law) as responses to perceived crises and hence, as efforts to contribute to crisis management by stressing the need for system integration; thus, they are not theories explaining change itself. The close link between crisis definition and crisis response can, however, be found in other perspectives as well. We, therefore, characterize the six perspectives as models rather than as theories because they do not constitute a particular developmental or evolutionary sequence. Rather, they coexist today as choices for social and legal policies. Finally, we want to stress the need for confronting these models with the empirical reality of today's legal institutions and hence, the need for pushing them in the direction of more grounded theoretical development and systematic research.

The traditional model of justice. The traditional model is, admittedly, a residual form, similar to Weber's categories of traditional authority, which includes patriarchal, patrimonial, and feudal forms. The points of reference of the traditional model are wide-ranging and include kinship based "archaic law" (Luhman 1972), "repressive law" designed to legitimate an emerging political system (Nonet and Selznick 1978), "preconventional law" (Habermas 1975), case-oriented substantive legal irrationality that Weber, besides Khadi justice, ascribed to some extent to Anglo-Saxon common law (Rheinstein 1966, xlviii), "populist justice" based on a totalistic conception of law and society (Cain 1985, 350, 360), and other forms of premodern law. In the America context, premodern, preprofessional law can be seen as an aspect of the political sphere and serving mainly to legitimate traditional social and political structures of domination (see our description of the initial phase of American legal and judicial development in chap. 1).

For present purposes, the significance of the traditional model of justice is limited, but it does imply that there is no generalized perception of any crisis conditions and, perhaps, no objective occasion for such a perception. Traditional legal and judicial elites are centrally interested in maintaining the legal *status quo*. They, therefore, define any problems of overload, capacity, or value change as essentially temporary and external to the legal and political system, that is seen as being guided by the legitimate elite interests and "reasons of state." The system adequately muddles through with small incremental changes and responses, but it basically absorbs any problems that might emerge. Judicial output simply expands and contracts with the demand placed on the system.[13]

The professional model of justice. The professional model is, of course, the classical reference point for discussion of formal justice or autonomous law; this model expresses "its rules by the use of abstract concepts created by legal thought itself and conceived of as constituting a complete system" (Rheinstein 1966, L). It is the centerpiece of Herbert L. Packer's (1968) "due process" model. The rise of legal professionalism in Europe and America in the last half of the nineteenth century was closely linked to the ascendance of this type of formal-legal rationality. Thus, the legal profession has had a pivotal interest in reinforcing the liberal-democratic principle of the constitutional separation of powers, especially the independence of the judiciary, principles that had a strong effect even on common law legal systems.

In this context, crisis conditions are perceived to originate from forces undermining legal-professional authority, including overload of the system; inadequate working conditions for judges (for example, inadequate support staff); and insufficient legislative restrictions and protections on the jurisdiction of courts.[14]

This model of the "crisis" conditions of courts is given voice and animated by judges and spokespersons for the courts and the third branch in the narrow sense (that is, it excludes prosecutors, defense counsel, and the private bar—albeit for different reasons). Thus, there is a perceived need for the expansion of judgeships in the interest of strengthening the professional core of the third branch, but not to the point of diluting professional-collegial authority. To enhance judicial authority and to limit federal jurisdiction, changes are proposed in the legal arena; for example, delegalization and decriminalization of certain areas of law; removal of jurisdiction ("standing") from federal to state courts (for example, diversity jurisdiction), and other changes or limitations of jurisdiction, as well as the introduction of certain informal alternatives to adjudication and the elimination of trivial or "frivolous" cases.

These reform proposals, however, leave the professional-judicial structure of work and authority basically intact. Judges remain at the top of the professional-collegial hierarchy, both in terms of work arrangements and of the appeals and review process based on the organization of superior/appellate and inferior/trial courts. More fundamentally, doctrinal and case-related issues of legal policy have primacy over issues of judicial administration and system management.[15]

As we noted, the professional model may have an affinity with both formal rationality (autonomous and code law) as well as substantive irrationality (the case orientation of common law). Under either legal system, however, the professional model is rather unresponsive to the problems of access to justice by clients; to problems of structural (vs. individual) inequity and injustice, especially in class-stratified societies; and, generally, to systemic problems of cost, productivity and delay and to the turbulence of the extrajudicial environment (see also Cain 1985, 348). It is, therefore, not surprising to find that the model of professional justice has little capacity for "crisis management." The doctrinal orientation of legal professionals tends to restrict their vision to the individual case or precedent and reduce their ability to perceive structural problems in the justice system at large.[16]

The bureaucratic model of justice. Historically, the bureaucratic model of justice in the United States has its origins in the administrative context where, interestingly, there has been a pull toward the judicialization of administrative agencies [see, for example, Mashaw's (1983, 31) distinction between bureaucratic rationality, professional treatment, and moral judgment]. Yet, many observers fear that the "bureaucratization of justice" will find its way into the third branch; of greater importance, there is an expressed fear that the cure is worse than the ills it is designed to address (see our discussion of this issue in chap. 6). In line with these developments, there is a concern about delegation of judicial authority to lower levels of an essentially managerial hierarchy, (that is, to nonjudicial, paralegal, and administrative personnel) so that the support staff performs the traditional functions of judges. Conversely, there is a fear that the roles and activities of judges may become bureaucratized as judges are called upon to manage cases (Blumberg 1967, 117; 169; Resnik 1982).

The basic thrust of the bureaucratic justice model, insofar as it exists at all in courts, is not to expand judicial labor power, but rather to expand administrative support services under the principle of bifurcation of bureaucratic and professional functions. On the bureaucratic side, accuracy and efficiency are emphasized along with concepts of program implementation, hierarchical structure, and information processing (Mashaw 1983, 31) while the work of judges, the professional core, is left untouched. In many respects, this model has informed the formation and development of the Administrative Office of the U.S. Courts and thus continues to be a relevant, if somewhat antiquated, point of reference in the debates over court reform (see chap. 6). As we have noted, it is basically a model for administrative agencies rather than for courts of law. Like the professional model, the bureaucratic model is too rigid and unresponsive to external turbulence. Because this model assumes a relatively stable and routinized or routinizable environment, it is not capable of engaging in crisis management.[17]

Maureen Cain (1985, 353) distinguishes between two subtypes of bureaucratic justice or "incorporated justice": one is located in "state-authorized institutions", for example, administrative agencies (Nonet 1969; Blegvad 1973; Hetzler 1982) and the other is located in "private sites" such as private corporations or associations (Scott 1965; Macaulay 1966; Selznick 1969; Evan 1976). Both subtypes of bureaucratic justice are based on a hierarchical structure of accountability and treat experts as nonaccountable or politically neutral (Cain 1985, 350). In Weber's terms, both constitute a form of substantive rationality that "is guided by the principles of an ideological system other than that of the law itself (ethics, religion, power politics, etc.)" (Rheinstein 1966, L). This substantive rationality or "re-materialization" of law is characterized by "particularism, result orientation, an instrumentalist social policy approach, and the increasing legalization of formerly autonomous social processes" (Teubner 1983, pp. 267-68). The bureaucratic justice of welfare-state institutions is thus a prime example of this model. Its severe limitations, if not inappropriateness, for dealing with the problems of courts should be amply evident.[18]

Given the blindness or unresponsiveness of both professional and bureaucratic models of justice to rapid change, turbulence, complexity, uncertainty, and crisis conditions in the legal judicial environment, and given their acknowledged resistance to innovation, the question arises: What other policy options and reform strategies are available? As we have suggested throughout this book, the technocratic model of justice transcends many of the limitations of the professional and bureaucratic model. Here, then, it is appropriate to review its more salient features.

The technocratic model of justice. The technocratic model of justice avoids the worst features of both the professional and bureaucratic models and promises to increase productivity, contain costs, reduce backlogs and delays, and improve the "responsiveness" and crisis management capacity of the system as a whole.[19]

The central policy orientation of the technocratic model is the attempt to increase the *flexibility* of the judicial system. Technocratic rationality favors not only technical rationalization (for example, by computerization), but also new forms of social rationalization. These new forms are noteworthy for their deviation from, or contrast to, both bureaucratic and professional forms of control. Thus, the social engineering aspect of technocratic strategies includes the following elements: informalism in work and authority relations; a lower level of category consciousness, that is, weak and permeable boundaries between cognitive categories, spheres of competence, and social roles; a hands-on emphasis on research and development as a strategy for sharing information and coordinating work, education, and training; a certain degree of loose coupling and structural flexibility among subunits; increased linkages and interdependence between courts and other subunits of the justice system; and the propagation of an ethos of trust and loyalty as aspects of a common legal culture, similar to the new emphasis on clan-like organization and corporate culture in the business world.

Examples of the tactical corollaries of a flexible approach to crisis management in the justice system include many of the familiar reforms and innovations we have discussed throughout this book. Because it is the constellation of these forces that points toward the technocratic model, it is useful to review them together. They include:

1. Expanding the judicial apparatus, including new judgeships, but also reorganizing the work and authority structure of courts (for example, use of magistrates, teams, and court work groups).

2. Introducing technical innovations, specifically new technologies that change the nature of work, (for example, statistical measurement of judicial output, data processing in the clerk's office, and video technology in court proceedings).

3. Changing the decision-making process and the adversary (professional) model based on adjudicatory services, including full due process, adjudication, and juries. The main element is an increased emphasis on informal techniques such as settlement conferences; pretrial activity to reduce the use of juries; negotiation, mediation, arbitration; plea bargaining and dismissals in criminal cases; experimentation with settlement strategies at the appeals court level; and various forms of participatory adjudication.

4. Introducing alternative forms of dispute resolution outside the formal court system (for example, neighborhood justice centers); early intervention by mediators; and conflict resolution and dispute settlement techniques instituted in organizations and work settings.

5. Expanding the research and training functions and apparatus of the federal judiciary (see, for example, the functions of the Federal Judicial Center and its role in training new judges and other court personnel, or engaging in research on the judicial system).

6. Moving toward systemic solutions whereby courts and judges become part of a larger system involving law enforcement (police and prosecution), jails and probation, and the private bar (changes in law school training). Adopting a new technical, systemic calculus of cost benefit analysis, productivity and input/output ratios of the justice system as a whole, rather than just of courts and judges.

These proposals for change can be illuminated by contrasting the nature of professional service with that of commodity production. Professional service is characterized by an identity of process and product whereas commodity production separates process from product. In the latter case, it is possible to rationalize the process of production (through mechanization, automation, and various productivity measures) without affecting the nature and quality of the product. If the process is changed, for whatever reason, the service—as a product of that activity—is also changed. Hence, the technocratic rationalization of adjudicatory services changes the nature of these services themselves, that is, it changes the outcome of judicial decision-making and may even contribute to a process of deprofessionalization. When judges host settlement conferences and engage in other forms of "case management," for example, their role is arguably changed from adjudication to administration.

A basic requirement for the success of technocratic strategies is a cooperative judiciary and a close alliance, if not coalition and integration, between law and the technocratic politics of the state (Unger 1976; Fraser 1978; Nonet and Selznick 1978; Klare 1979; Grau 1980; Schreiber 1980; Villmoare 1982). This cooperation is emerging in the United States, as it has been in many Western political economies, but it takes on particularly complicated forms in the American context. The dualism of formal justice versus substantive political rationality, so eloquently diagnosed and described by Weber (1966), Roberto Unger (1976), and others must, therefore, be redefined in terms of a dialectical movement toward the resolution (or mediation) of the contradiction between formal law and technocratic politics.

The first observable step of this process is that law and the administration of justice are being modified to fit the needs of the newly emerging technocratic rationality bent on containing and preventing crises by "purposive" (specially targeted) strategies and "responsive" crisis management. Hence, the autonomy of law is no longer desirable, but rather becomes an obstacle to the efficient implementation of policy and planning. Technocratic strategies do not see any virtue in an independent judiciary and thus contribute to its gradual decline. The judiciary changes from a labor-intensive, professional service organization to a more capital-intensive, computerized governmental and administrative structure staffed by technical experts and programmed to implement the political requirements of legitimation and social regulation.

A proviso is in order: just as others have documented the contradictory strains between formal justice and substantive political rationality, so we must also consider the contradictory forces confronting this more recent political development, that is, that between formal law and technocratic politics. In other words, none of these more recent developments, that is, the transformation of courts from labor intensive to more capital-intensive organizations, from professional to technocratic decisionmaking, occurs without a struggle. At each turn in the road, vested interests, armed with powerful ideological weapons and *de facto* authority, continue to seek to maintain their claim to legitimate traditional and professional control.

As should by now be obvious, the technocratic model of justice does not represent a return to the substantive rationality of the welfare state, but rather a transcendence of Weber's categories of formal versus substantive rationality in the direction of technocratic rationality (Heydebrand 1984). We believe that this new type of rationality includes both "responsive law" and "reflexive rationality." This new amalgam of different elements of rationality is, however, not without its internal contradictions. As Gunther Teubner puts it: "Reflexive law is characterized by a new kind of legal self-restraint. Instead of taking over regulatory responsibility for the outcome of social processes, reflexive law restricts itself to the installation, correction, and redefinition of democratic self-regulatory mechanisms" (1983, 239). In addition, Teubner argues, "Reflexive law resembles liberal and neo-liberal concepts of the role of law" (pp. 254, 983), an element that reveals some affinity between the technocratic and the economic model of justice, to be discussed presently. The presence of "democratic self-regulatory mechanisms" and other forms of democratic participation inherent in the technocratic model suggests, however, the coexistence of contradictory elements and points to the unstable, temporary, and *ad hoc* character of technocratic strategies. This instability may generate fruitful and productive conditions that could conceivably prefigure the emergence of a democratic model of justice. Before turning to this, however, it is important to explore briefly a recent variation on a very old, libertarian theme that is, after all, also an element of technocracy.

The economic or market model of justice. In many ways, the economic model of justice represents a regression of legal rationality to premodern and preconventional utilitarian premises. The main element of this model is that legal protection and judicial services are not rights guaranteed by the state and paid for by taxes, but a private good to be purchased according to an economic calculus. This calculus includes the interests of the parties, estimates of costs and benefits, and similar variables measuring the relative "utility" of justice (Landes 1971; Posner 1972, 1985). Here, the judiciary becomes a semi-private or privatized service institution that entails certain basic changes in the nature of adjudicatory services:

1. the treatment of litigating parties as customers rather than as clients with particular needs or as citizens with substantive and procedural civil rights;

2. a limited range of judicial services is offered to these customers, largely determined by their ability to pay.[20]

3. the establishment of economic mechanisms of self-regulation like no fault accident or divorce proceedings, decriminalization of certain types of offenses (victimless crimes), or the civilianization of certain criminal offenses.

4. the use of competitive mechanisms to allocate various elements of the scarce resource "justice."

According to Richard Posner, judicial services (hearings, trials, decisions, and appeals) can be thought of as a

> product that the parties (in the first instance, the plaintiff) "buy" when they decide to bring a suit or to continue with a suit that they have already brought, and that the court therefore "sells" to them. The amount of judicial services supplied can therefore be thought of as the intersection of the demand for and the supply of those services. (1985, 7-8)

In light of this rationale, it would be absurd, Posner argues, not to charge—beyond a trivial fee—for the use of this service. If there is a charge for judicial services, then one can limit the cases that come into courts, insure the pres-tige of the institution, and improve the quality of the services delivered—justice. Posner concludes as follows:

> ... the model of judicial supply ... is more accurate than a model which assumes that the supply of federal judicial services is infinitely elastic. We are long past the point where new increments of demand for federal judicial

services could be met, with no impairment of quality, simply by adding more judges at existing salary levels. It has proved necessary to add many (but not enough) judges, to create a large judicial bureaucracy, . . . to curtail oral argument drastically, to reduce the average quality of judicial opinions . . . and in these and other ways to lower the quality of federal justice. Combined with unremitting case load growth, the commitment of the federal court system to accommodating all increments of demand without increasing the price of access to the system has forced the system to operate in a region of sharply increased costs, of which the purely budgetary dimension is the least significant. (1985, 129)

Although Posner urges the adoption of the neoliberal economic model of justice as a cure for the ills of the federal judiciary, it is one that is clearly not viable in the context of democratic institutions and constitutional protections [see also Polinsky's (1974) warning against the economic analysis of law as a "potentially defective product"]. The "free-market" creed implied by the model may appeal to certain members of the private bar who believe that limits on punitive damages and restrictions on lawyers' fees are sinister incursions of the government on their and their clients' rights. Nevertheless, most lawyers would ultimately defend those rights in terms of constitutional principles rather than of the law of supply and demand.

Echoing C. Wright Mills, we have tried to identify the range of "public issues" that affect the justice system. Many of these elements point toward a conservative, if not repressive, apparatus that administers and privatizes dispute resolution. Technocratic administration, we have suggested, captures the essential elements of this trend. An economic market model is its even more conservative variant in a neo-liberal guise. Yet, there are elements within these forms that point counterfactually toward a democratic model of justice that it is our responsibility to clarify as well.

The democratic model of justice. Though it is difficult to define a model of democratic justice, we believe that it is possible to articulate the "range of public issues" that must be addressed in such an endeavor. These issues for dialogue include:

1. ease of access to justice;

2. control of the professional dominance of lawyers;

3. control of the bureaucratic and technocratic preoccupation with systemic efficiency to the exclusion of political issues;

4. an independent judiciary that is elected for life yet that remains politically sensitive;

5. the treatment of individual cases as potential class actions;

6. institutional mechanisms to protect courts from the influence of the state, large corporate actors, and other forms of interest aggregation:

7. lay participation by members of the community in the process of adjudication;

8. guidance by a substantive rationality, oriented toward explicitly democratic goals, institutionalized in substantive civil rights and procedural guarantees.

Clearly, this is a largely Utopian view of justice. It is based on communitarian and left-libertarian concepts of law and could well be called "democratic collectivist" (see Rothschild Whitt 1979, who provides a useful description although without spelling out the legal and juridical implications of her organizational model).

Maureen Cain (1985, 342, 360) argues convincingly that a strict distinction must be made between "collective justice"—a concept close to the democratic model—and "populist justice" or other forms of informal justice that are repressive and reactionary. While the ideal of democratic-collectivist justice dispenses with the formalism of professional justice, and while Cain's "collective justice" is explicitly working-class based, both are informed by "objective rules derived from emergent moral/political theory" and have a democratic, "non-gendered" internal organization (1985, 350).

It is crucial to understand that the realization of a democratic-collectivist type of law and justice presupposes a fundamental critique of the *form of law* (Balbus 1977). As Richard Abel (1980, 828) puts it, "... We must broaden the meaning of justice itself by stepping outside the ideology through which legal institutions seek legitimation. ..." Furthermore, construction of such a legal-judicial reality would demand the creation of a "post-conventional" legal environment (Habermas 1979, 157-58) and of an "ideal speech situation," which only a fully democratic society could guarantee (see also Walzer 1983).

The democratic-collectivist model envisaged here is, indeed, antithetical to all other models just described. It treats justice as a civil right rather than as a private good or commodity; it has a decidedly political dimension rather than the technical calculus of technocratic justice; it circumvents (or controls) the dysfunctions and problems of the conventional professional model of justice which—like the economic model—has relatively high access costs and, in addition, suffers from the tendency of professional services to degenerate into the exercise of illegitimate power or professional dominance; and, it replaces the hierarchical dimension of bureaucratic justice by a new, participatory, egalitarian dimension in which relevant interests in the community or society are democratically (rather than merely pluralistically) represented in the process of adjudication.

A central element in the democratic model of justice is the communicatory or dialogical concept of moral legal reasoning and adjudication (Gilligan 1982; Cain 1985; Menkel Meadow 1985). This concept emphasizes negotiation, communication, participation, and dialogue, that is, a continuing relationship between the disputing parties, rather than confrontation and the application of logical and formal-legal principles. The dialogical concept of adjudication has, however, a problematic side that needs to be dealt with further: the notion of participation in dispute resolution presupposes an ideal speech situation, that is, the possibility of undistorted communication and the absence of domination and hierarchy (Habermas 1979, chap. 1). Moreover, the concept seems to imply the undesirability of social conflicts, legal disputes, and confrontations.

These presuppositions or assumptions may not be warranted in many disputes reaching the courts. It is precisely the inequality of power in the disputing relationship that may lead plaintiffs to demand their "day in court." Because the dispute may have run its course and does not lead anywhere, and because the socially more powerful defendants may obstruct conflict resolution or demand settlement on their terms, the plaintiff may wish to talk not to the other party but to a "higher authority," that is, the judge. The dialogical concept of justice may, therefore, complement the dynamics of the early stages of disputing. At later stages, however, the democratic model may require the presence of a public authority whose task may be to insure that there is an adaquate equalization of power between the disputing parties. Indeed, in some circumstances, the agreement on rules may be an appropriate solution to a particular dispute.

In short, the dialogical concept implies participation, communication, and ongoing interaction—which may be facilitated publicly if the parties are unable to achieve them voluntarily. The key issue is that the formalism of the adversary-professional model is transformed into a new form of substantive, even "reflexive" justice that is responsive to the political and cultural needs of the community.[21]

In essence, one may trace a movement toward democratization to the extent that

> [l]aw in the western world—both at the level of the judicial process and at the level of legislation—is asked to overcome its abstraction and its underlying individualism, to take into account extra-legal powers and social inequalities, to investigate total social situations, to make orders that require new powers and new attitudes on the part of courts, to cease treating the "public interest" as an unruly horse or, at best, as just another private interest to be weighed against the rights of individuals, to recognize instead a moral hierarchy of interests, to turn its attention from the past actions, immediate interests, and

abstract rights of the parties before the court to the social context, the social implications and the future consequences of such actions as a general class. (Kamenka and Tay 1975, 130)

Conclusion

Implicitly, the proponents of various models of justice generally disagree on the nature of the crisis. Yet, there is a debate over what is the most adequate response to the crisis of the judiciary. While we have not proposed a definite program of crisis management, we believe that we have clarified the scope of the debate. The main policy disagreement focuses on the relative merits of the professional versus the technocratic models of justice. We believe we have presented strong evidence for the historical ascendance of the latter and of the gradual erosion of the former.

Yet, while the shift from adjudication to administration is a powerful one, it is not inevitable. Various conditions may emerge that could weaken the technocratic tendencies we described and, instead, stress and revitalize professional-judicial control over adjudicatory services. The contradictory character of technocratic strategies may, however, also lead in altogether new directions that cannot be envisioned fully. Indeed, one of the main consequences of technocratic justice is that it removes existing barriers to change and reform: it undermines formal law and erodes the professional model of justice. By contrast, the democratic kernel in the current flurry of reform and change seems precarious and endangered.

Regardless of the policy position one takes on these issues, however, it is useful to sort out the premises of proposed change; therefore, we believe that more intellectual work in the empirical mode is needed in order to confront the models of justice just outlined within the context of current activities in courts. The trend of increasing litigation in the federal courts bears watching, especially in comparison to trends in state courts and those in other societies and legal systems. The specific effects of corporate and governmental forces on the nature and outcome of adjudication need to be studied by analyzing the qualitative process of decision-making itself, not just the quantitative statistical outcomes, as we have done.

The various policies of reducing the jurisdictional burden on courts need to be looked at from a critical legal perspective so as to provide a basis for judging their constitutional consequences. The strategies of technocratic justice—information and management systems as well as informal and flexible settlement strategies, case management, arbitration—need to be studied comparatively and cross-nationally so as to establish the limits of what is technically possible and what is legally necessary. In other words, the legal and political consequences of the use of these techniques must be analyzed critically so that the ideologies by which legal institutions seek to legitimate themselves do not become blinders and fetters on free inquiry.

We hope to participate in this process; "suggestions for further research" should not remain empty, ritualistic gestures but, instead, impart a commitment to contribute constructively to the debate over the future of the judiciary. Most importantly, we invite the participants themselves—judges, attorneys, magistrates, law clerks, court executives, managers, and others—to contribute to the ongoing debate by critically responding to and commenting on the models and alternatives articulated here.

APPENDIX A

*

The Empirical Study of Courts:
A Methodological Note

There is no dearth of empirical studies of courts, judges, and the judicial process. Following the traditional academic division of labor, law and the courts have been studied from a variety of viewpoints and disciplinary frameworks, notably anthropology, economics, law, politics, and sociology. These approaches differ in terms of their substantive concepts, their choice of an explanatory principle or proposition, and their level and unit of analysis. Most of the relevant empirical studies, however, share the concerns of modern social science with description and explanation, even though normative statements and critical interpretation do find their way into the study of courts (see, for example, Posner 1985). In general, then, the dominant perspectives on law and the judicial system have certain characteristic methodological consequences. Before turning to a discussion of the methods used in the present study, it may be useful, therefore, to review briefly some of the major perspectives relevant to the study of courts.

A Review of the Literature

In the social sciences, two traditions have tended to dominate the study of courts: an older, behaviorist approach focusing on the study of how judges and lawyers act in their roles as officers of the court and, more recently, a reductionist perspective emphasizing individual disputes, cases, and decisions in the study of court activity.

Both approaches challenge the traditional legal academic perspective to the extent that they look at actual behaviors, rather than the law as announced by the judge. More subtly, however, both perspectives also adopt the normative underpinnings of relations between lawyers or judges as officers of the court and clients who are individuals or organizations with grievances to be resolved by this institution (see Abel 1980), that is, they adopt the insider's

221

definition of what constitutes the slice of reality to be studied and documented. As a result, then, one may trace a tendency to reduce the study of
courts to the ahistorical study of individual behavior. This stance has important consequences for shielding researchers from developing a critical analysis of the consequences of changes in the organization of courts. Let us
elaborate on these points.

The behaviorist emphasis grows out of the realist legal tradition. It is
assumed that law and the judicial system are what courts, judges, and other
legal actors *do*, regardless of the goals, legitimacy, constitutionality, and effectiveness of the behavior in question (Black 1976; Feeley 1976; Sarat 1985;
but see Nonet 1976). For example, in describing the operations of a New
Haven lower criminal court, Malcolm Feeley (1979) is concerned with what
the participants actually do and how they perceive what is being done. The
study concludes that the "process is the punishment" because of the existence of certain negative perceptions of, and reactions to, formal adversary
procedures. Procedural complexities are seen as standing in the way of achieving substantive justice, and the degree of individual satisfaction with the
administration of justice is treated as a measure of its effectiveness. Similarly,
the practice of plea bargaining is now almost completely accepted as a necessary part of criminal court proceedings even though its constitutionality is
questioned by some (Blumberg 1967; Alschuler 1968; Kipnis 1979; see also
Skolnick, 1966, 1967; Cole 1970). That the abrogation of formal procedures
and due process in the interest of efficiency and substantive outcomes might
be in conflict with standards of quality and formal justice is deemed of sec-
ondary importance or simply irrelevant. Indeed, the new informal or substantive justice is often declared to be of higher quality, presumably because it
satisfies the participants and would not exist if it were not superior. Besides,
it is now an established reality, hence the controversy is seen as turning on a
moot point (Casper 1979). The crucial methodological issue, however, is that
the development of plea bargaining and other informal practices, regardless
of their origin and initial rationale, are now seen as "functional" for the maintenance of the system. To measure such informal adaptations against some
"vague goals" such as due process or constitutional protections would, it is
argued, introduce value judgments into research and would, therefore, be
unscientific and ideologically biased (Feeley 1976, 498-500).

A second point is that there has been a tendency to conceptualize legal
phenomena from an individualistic perspective that tends to reduce litigation, dispute resolution, and the organization of courts to the level of individual transactions isolated from the larger social and organizational context.
This tendency has two aspects: the practice of focusing on the individual
"case," and the reduction of the organizational structure of courts to the
model of individual legal and judicial decision-making. Both aspects are

joined, as it were, in their affinity to the professional model of legal practice where the set of decisions relevant to a "case" is the unit of analysis.

As to the first aspect, the "case" approach exemplifies the deterministic and casuistic form of legal reasoning in contrast to the dominant social science pattern of thinking in terms of probability distributions.[1] But there is more involved: the case approach typically does not see the forest for the trees. As Charles Grau puts it, "Individualized treatment of each 'case' hampers the development of a consciousness that reorganizes the systematic causes of deprivation and domination. Courts recognize narrowly defined legal issues that may bear little resemblance to underlying social issues" (1980, 205). Similarly, in a critique of current empirical studies of civil litigation and dispute resolution, Robert Kidder states that

> the notion of the dispute has typically included a focus on the individual as the key actor. Just as Western law has isolated the individual as the paramount possessor of legal rights, and has deemphasized obligations toward traditional groups ... in its handling of formal legal disputes, so the anthropologists emphasized the individual as the object of attention in the study of disputing in non-Western society. (1980-81. 719-20)

The second aspect of methodological individualism to be noted here refers to a lingering resistance against conceptualizing *structural* and *relational* phenomena as scientific objects, that is, to the tendency to reduce organizational realities to individual behavior-in-organizations. For example, much of the political science literature on courts and the judicial system in modern society used to be concerned with the behavioral aspects and processes of judicial decisionmaking, the sociopolitical background and the selection of judges, and the "output" of judicial decisions (see, for example, Scigliano 1962; Jahnige and Goldman 1968; Murphy and Pritchett 1974; Goldman and Sarat, 1978). Courts were treated as extensions of the semifeudal prerogatives of judges (as, for example, in "the court has decided. ..."). Sometimes courts are treated as small work groups composed of lawyers and subject to newly emerging determinants and impersonal dynamics (Ulmer 1971; Mohr 1976; Eisenstein and Jacob 1977; Goldman and Sarat 1978, chap. 14; Nardulli 1978). Modern research on courts and their alternatives, however, increasingly emphasizes organizational and institutional processes (for example, see Balbus 1973; Seron 1978; Sheskin 1981; Harrington 1985).

Another form of reductionist thinking and methodological individualism appears in the "economic analysis of law," an approach that treats legal behavior as an aspect of economic rationality based on the calculus of costs, gains, utilities, and exchange (Calabresi 1970; Landes 1971; Posner 1972; Feeley 1976, 517-519; but see Polinsky 1974; and for a more extensive discussion of the economic or market model of justice, see chap. 8).

   Law and the courts are often portrayed as institutions that are functional
for the integration of society, without considering their problematic nature
as structures of political rule and social power as well as their potentially
contradictory relationship to state and economy (Bredemeier 1962; but see
Hay 1975; Grau 1980, 199-204; Sheskin 1981, 79). As Kidder puts it with
special reference to the transmission of functionalism from anthropology to
the sociology of law and political science:

> The functionalist assumption, or pressure-cooker model, is that each dispute
> is a discreet disruption which can be rectified if given appropriate and timely
> treatment. . . . but there is very little recognition . . . that "accumulated" griev-
> ances may represent systematic inequalities, institutionalized asymetrical
> developments in a society's relationships. (1980-81, 719)

Moreover, legal anthropologists "usually treated the disputing process as cen-
tering on local analogues to the Western plaintiff and defendant. They rarely
treated the process as a corporate or political action—as an element in shifting
relationships between groups, as battlegrounds in strategic maneuvering to
reorder power relationships and upset disadvantageous 'balances' " (Kidder
1980-81, 720).
   A corollary of the functionalist approach is a certain ahistoricism. Neo-
functionalism is interested in the consequences of social patterns for the
integration of social systems, not in their origins. As a result, the operation of
legal and judicial processes are analyzed in isolation from the sociohistorical
context and from social and economic trends. A well-known exception is the
type of study Lawrence M. Friedman and Robert V. Percival (1976) conducted
of two California county courts, but this exception accentuates the "rule" in
that the "history" of law and the system tend to be clearly segregated from the
otherwise functionalist framework of empirical studies (Hurst 1950, 1980-81;
Friedman 1973; Daniels 1984; Genovese 1985; but see Munger 1988, as well
as the results of the Conference on the Longitudinal Study of Trial Courts,
Buffalo, 1987).
   Law and the judicial system are often conceptualized in a contradictory
form when it comes to the relationship between law and politics. Law is often
seen from *within* the dominant legal perspective, namely as autonomous
vis-à-vis the other branches of government and independent of the political
economy of capitalism. At the same time, however, there is a recognition of
"political influences" on, and the political role of, the judiciary. This political
factor is seen as a transhistorical, near-universal given of the reality of courts
and judicial behavior (see, for example, Shapiro 1980). This view, too, is one
of the domain assumptions of legal realism and certain strands in political
science and adds to "jurisprudential sociology" the parallel concept of "political jurisprudence." As Walter F. Murphy and C. Herman Pritchett put it:

Now ... it is generally understood not only that American judges have important responsibilities in creating public policy but also that they have always had such a role. The decisions of the Supreme Court under the chief justiceship of John Marshall were no less "political" than those of the Court under Charles Evans Hughes, Earl Warren, or Warren Burger. (1974, 3)

However, here, too, it appears to be necessary to challenge the conservative maxim that "there is nothing new under the sun" and that things have "always" been a certain way. As long as the intrusion of politics into law could be treated as an aspect of human nature, as an accident of history, or as an informal deviation from the norm of legal and judicial autonomy, there was no need to confront the possibility of a real constitutional shift from the separation of powers to their relative integration. But insofar as state intervention and the integration of law and politics under "purposive-responsive" law begins to be a systematic and normal feature of contemporary society, constitutional issues are apt to assume a new urgency not only for legal phisosophy, but for the very real and political adjudication of the competing claims of technocratic and democratic theory. We must therefore acknowledge the historical possibility that the changing context of law and the changing socioeconomic and political environment of courts raises a fundamental question: Under what conditions might autonomous law be replaced by responsive-purposive law (Nonet and Selznick 1978) or "reflexive law" (Teubner 1983), eroded by bureaucratic law (Unger 1976), or superseded by the technocratic administration of justice (Heydebrand 1979)?

Finally, as the preceding discussion points suggest, there is often an uncritical acceptance of the traditional modes of analysis without consideration of the possibility that the theories and modes of analysis are themselves historical and ideological products of the development of the contradictions between state, law, and economy (for useful discussions of ideology, see Hunt 1985; Law and Society Review 1988). It is especially this latter point that underlines the difficulty of grasping nonfunctional, dysfunctional, incompatible, or contradictory tendencies in the historical transformation of the rule of law. This is particularly true of the myriad studies and analyses that propose administrative and managerial reforms of the judicial system without being fully aware of the value-oriented or policy-oriented, in short ideological, nature of their nominally positivist (that is, neutral, objective, value-free) conceptual framework (for critical reviews of court reform efforts, see Feeley 1983; Harrington 1985, chap. 1). With these considerations in mind, let us turn to a discussion of our approach to the study of trial courts and the changes in the forms of adjudication. These new forms of law, we argue, will be revealed by tracing the causal chain between the jurisdictional environment of courts and the distributions and probabilities of types of cases ultimately receiving a certain treatment or disposition.

On the Organizational Ecology of Courts

The methodological tradition informing the quantitative part of our analysis is rooted in the human ecology perspective of Amos Hawley (1950, 1968) and Otis D. Duncan and Leo F. Schnore (1959). This perspective has recently spawned a number of different approaches to the ecological analysis of organizational environments (Hannan and Freeman 1977, 1983; Aldrich 1979; Carroll 1984; Bidwell and Kasarda 1985). Although almost all of these authors focus on private corporations and their markets rather than public, governmental organizations like courts of law, their attempts to conceptualize the dynamics of organizational environments have been uncommonly innovative and fruitful.

The basic thrust of the ecological analysis of organizations is to establish a causal or functional link between the characteristics of organizations and those of their environments. This linkage can be studied at different analytic levels, one of which has been the analysis of the relational or interorganizational characteristics of the organizational environment (Litwak and Hylton 1962; Warren 1967; Benson 1975). Recent work on the population ecology of organizations constitutes another subtype of ecological analysis that focuses on whole populations or aggregates of organizations as if they were biological species (Hannan and Freeman 1977, 1983; Aldrich 1979). In this approach, the "natural" selection of certain organizations by the (favorable or unfavorable) characteristics or dynamics of their environment constitutes the central concern, in contrast to the (more or less "rational") adaptive responses of organizational managers to environmental change.[2]

The present approach, while clearly part of the ecological tradition, differs from the interorganizational, population-ecology and developmental perspectives in three important ways. First, in contrast to the interorganizational or *relational* characteristics of organizational environments, we are focusing on the *aggregate* characteristics of organizational environments in their effect on our population of courts (for this distinction, see Heydebrand 1973, 14; 1977, 773; see also Seron 1978, 34). While certain aggregate characteristics can be defined as relational in their impact (for example, government employees as representing the presence of government agencies), the analysis is based on measures of environmental characteristics derived from census data of counties and then aggregated to the level of the jurisdiction of district courts.[3]

The second difference between our subtype of ecological analysis and the others concerns the nature of the organizational environment we are dealing with: jurisdictions. In contrast to open-ended environments such as markets or potential client populations of service organizations (for example, hospitals), court jurisdictions have distinct geographical boundaries that are authoritatively established by acts of Congress and that delimit the judicial and administrative validity of court actions. Only certain types of cases can arise within a given jurisdiction, and only certain kinds of decisions apply within its boundaries. Moreover, since courts, like many governmental units, are not autonomous with respect to their institutional environments, they do not fall within the ecological framework of selection and adaptation. Thus, while the population ecology model may be helpful for analyzing the fate of small- and medium-size businesses in competitive markets, it is only of limited usefulness for the case of nonprofit service or governmental units (unless one cares to define all governmental organizations as part of a specialized or protected niche at a higher level of abstraction).

Third, the present approach differs in its orientation from the classical human ecology and the population-ecology models in preferring historically and critically informed modes of sociological explanation to "naturalist," Darwinist, evolutionary, or functionalist ones. Thus, as Otis Duncan and Leo F. Schnore argue,

> the ecologist takes the aggregate as his frame of reference and deliberately sets out to account for the forms that social organization assumes in response to varying demographic, technological, and environmental pressures. (1959, 144)

Clearly, the concept of "response to pressures" is central to the functionalist and systems-theoretical language of ecology. Moreover, Michael Hannan and John Freeman (1977, 938) show how Amos Hawley uses the principle of isomorphism to explain the relative fit between organizations and environments. This principle states that "in each distinguishable environmental configuration one finds, in equilibrium, only that organizational form optimally adapted to the demands of the environment" (p. 939; see also DiMaggio and Powell 1983). Furthermore, Hannan and Freeman "doubt that the major features of the world of organizations arise through learning or adaptation" (1977, 957); hence, they opt for an "evolutionary explanation of the principle of isomorphism," which in turn is seen as embedded "within an explicit selection framework."

By contrast, the present approach begins with an analysis of the historical contingencies of advanced capitalism and its changing relationship to the modern state apparatus in seeking to explain the fate of courts as governmental organizations, their persistence, growth, and transformation over time, and their precarious status in view of the exigencies of the larger political economy (Wamsley and Zald 1973; Benson 1975). In other words, we are expanding the meaning of "ecological" by placing it into the context of a historically changing and dynamically structured (often contradictory) political economy. This conception differs from the notion of a "natural" ecological environment in that it views the structure of the surrounding political economy as the often unintended result of a complex set of specific, concrete, historical decisions of economic and political actors who, at the structural level, can of course be collectivities, organizations, institutions, or power structures.

Nevertheless, our approach shares with organizational ecology an emphasis on structural phenomena and explanations. "The organization is seen in its environmental context, depending on external resources for sustenance. Environmental conditions constrain the organization and shape organizational structure; however, internal constraints such as size and technology also affect its structure" (Carroll 1984, 73). Therefore, the methodological resources of ecological analysis recommend themselves for the purpose at hand and are, indeed, indispensable for a systematic, empirical, and comparative analysis of the effect of jurisdictional environments on courts.

Institutional versus Politico-economic Environments of Courts

Given our emphasis on the environmental context of courts, the question may be raised as to what extent the institutionalist perspective might be applicable to our analysis. The institutionalist approach argues that "organizations are structured by phenomena in their environment and tend to become isomorphic with them " (Meyer and Rowan 1983, 28; see also DiMaggio and Powell 1983). "Isomorphism with environmental institutions has some crucial consequences for organizations: (a) they incorporate elements that are legitimated externally, rather than in terms of efficiency; (b) they employ external or ceremonial assessment criteria to define the value of structural elements; and (c) dependence on externally fixed institutions reduces turbulence and maintains stability" (Meyer and Rowan 1983, 30).

On the face of it, the institutional approach seems to be relevant to our study in two senses. First, the logic of efficiency, productivity, and cost-effectiveness could be seen as part of the cultural logic of capitalism ready to penetrate not only private business and corporate management, but professional service delivery and the work of governmental agencies. In that sense, then, one could argue for the validity of an institutional perspective since the dominant economic norms of the larger environment seek to institutionalize themselves in all organizations within their sphere of influence (see Alford and Friedland 1985, for a comprehensive discussion of the logics of capitalism and bureaucratic rationalization; see also Fainstein and Fainstein 1980). Indeed, part of our research task has been to examine the impact of an economic calculus, in the form of a preoccupation with managerialism, efficiency, or speed and, in this sense, the institutional approach makes an important contribution. With the institutionalist school we may ask: How does a preoccupation with the rationalization of organizational processes manifest itself in courts of law?

But, we part company with the institutionalist school in our conceptualization of the possibilities for reorganization posed by rationalization. More specifically, the institutional school grows out of a neo-Weberian framework where rationalization, once in place, is taken as a near-universal, all-pervasive, undirectional trend toward bureaucratization that takes on a life of its own (viz. the "iron cage"). By contrast, we take a neo-Marxist approach to the concept of rationalization and attempt to weigh the historical contingencies that affect bureaucratization as but one form of reconstituting organizational relations; that is, we take the imprint of rationality as problematic. The analytic power of approaching this phenomenon as problematic, rather than as a given, is suggested by the limitations of the institutional school to capture persuasively the overriding quest for structural flexibility that may eventually undermine bureaucratic rationalization in light of the turbulent environment of modern corporations and governments.

Second, there is a tendency within this school to collapse the "environment" into one, unified field of "environmental institutions." While the district courts studied here are, indeed, a constitutive part of the federal judicial system, this is not the only, or necessarily the most important environmental factor at work. Thus, a part of what courts are about is derived from the Constitution (Art. III) and congressional action, including legislation that establishes rules of procedure (see, for example, *The Federal Rules of Civil Procedure*) and a common organizational core. But these important commonalities apply to the institutional structure of district courts, *not* to their highly variable social, political, and economic environments that may, in fact, pose a quite different set of demands on these organizations. The institutional school does not distinguish between multiple, various, and possibly contradictory environments at work.

To be sure, a nominal distinction has been made between technical and sociocultural environments, the first referring to the task environment of organizational resources, information, markets, and the coordination and control of technical performance, the second to the institutionalization of norms and rules (Scott 1983, 1987). But as soon as the distinction is made, it is qualified to the point of being meaningless. For example, it is argued that

> institutionalized rules closely resemble technical rules; ... it may be quite difficult to distinguish between technical and social/cultural environments because the latter often develop norms and rules that appear to govern a technical process; ... for all these reasons, it is difficult to draw a sharp distinction between technical environments, on the one hand, and social/cultural environments, on the other." (Scott 1983, 160)

Thus, there is no possibility of testing or verification. If one wanted to test a hypothesis based on the distinction between technical and social/cultural environments, it would not be falsifiable because the latter environment could always be seen as including or determining the former. In other words, we are left with a distinction that has operationally no consequences. Indeed, the encompassing monolithic notion of the institutionalized environment is well captured by Paul DiMaggio and Walter Powell's definition of the "organizational field."

> By organizational field, we mean those organizations that, in the aggregate, constitute a recognized area of institutional life: key suppliers, resource and product consumers, regulatory agencies and other organizations that produce similar services and products. The virtue of this unit of analysis is that it directs our attention not simply to competing firms, as does the population approach of Hannan and Freeman (1977), or to networks of organizations that actually interact, as does the interorganizational network approach of Lauman et al (1978), but to the totality of relevant actors. (1983, 148)

What implications do these considerations have for our approach? The social and politico-economic environment of courts, we argue, is not the same as the institutional system of the federal judiciary. The manifest difference between these two types of environments suggests that the institutional approach is in danger of confusing the institutional environment of systems theory with the concrete larger social structure (that is, here, the federal judiciary with the organizational environments from which the courts are analytically independent). Thus, from an institutional perspective, the norms of the system pervade and "determine" the cultural and structural elements of the focal organization. This proposition flows from the assumption that every system belongs to a larger system and that a given system, therefore, constitutes the environment for its subsystems. Causal or statistical analysis is, therefore, inappropriate because there are no empirical (only logical) boundaries between system and subsystem (see Parsons 1971; Heydebrand 1972). As Meyer and Rowan put it, "according to the institutional conception as developed here, organizations tend to disappear as distinct and bounded units" (1983, 28).

But, from our point of view organizations are clearly distinct from other organizations in their environment. As units of analysis, such organizations are independent of the kinds of analytic and structural properties that characterize their aggregate or interorganizational environment. It is, therefore, possible to estimate, by statistical means, the effect of the environmental characteristics on the task structure and activities of the focal organization. Thus, causal models of the effect of the environment on the task structure and other aspects of the organization are meaningful from our vantage point, but meaningless, indeed, tautological from the standpoint of the institutionalists.

There are at least four other reasons why we feel that the institutionalist perspective is too structuralist and deterministic for our purposes. The first two are specific to the organizations under study, federal district courts, while the other two are troubling at a more general level. As to the specific features of courts, first, each district court promulgates its own local rules which specify its actual operating procedures. Second, federal statutes and federal law are themselves activated or mobilized only at the point where they are formally invoked by a plaintiff, a defendant, or a prosecutor. That is, they are passive or latent aspects of law unless and until mobilized by a dispute and its legal form, the lawsuit (Black 1973; Sarat and Grossman 1975). It is the sources of that mobilization of law that we are concerned to study when we trace the effect of the jurisdictional environment on litigation and caseloads in the federal courts.

More generally, however, conflicts and contradictions within the systemic-institutional environment or "organizational field" cannot easily be grasped by institutionalist theory since it rests its case on the continuous operation of comprehensive cognitive and cultural norms that act as determinants of structure and practices in a particular organizational domain. It is assumed that whatever characterizes the cultural maps of these systemic environments appears in more or less perfectly reproduced form in the subunits of that environment. The invocation of "structural inconsistencies" and environmental pluralism (Meyer and Rowan 1983, 37-38) does not seem to be an adequate solution since it contradicts, or else waters down, the general framework of institutionalism itself. It shares this problem with structural-functionalism, in general, and Parsonian systems theory, in particular.

Finally, the origin and change of the cultural domain itself are not easily explainable by institutionalist theory. Structural convergence and increasing homogeneity (the "iron cage") are the dominant consequences of the theory. But there is typically no account of (1) how the institutional field or domain originated historically (but see Tolbert and Zucker 1983); (2) how it might change historically in directions other than isomorphism, for example, through diversification as an adaptation to uncertainty and risk, as is true of economic markets; (3) why there is not greater or total uniformity, standardization, or homogeneity in organizational fields and systems; (4) whether forces other than norms (for example , structural interests, power, and profit) might account for the convergence. We would argue that organizational and societal contradictions as well as the historical indeterminacy of collective social action and social movements could largely account for divergent change and the absence of complete, one-dimensional, monolithic institutionization.

Echoing the notion of "structural inconsistencies," DiMaggio and Powell (1983) have elaborated the concept of "coercive isomorphism." But the introduction of "coercion" into the logic of institutionalization significantly changes the terms of the theoretical framework which is based on the diffusion and voluntary adoption of norms, or at least, the homogenizing processes of socialization and institutionalization. Introducing the exercise of power and coercion as a backup for a normative or structuralist determinism vitiates the "cultural logic" argument, just as it did for Talcott Parsons and, in another context, for Louis Althusser (Heydebrand 1972; 1981). In sum, the inclusion of "structural inconsistencies" and "coercion" into the institutionalist framework relaxes its assumptions and weakens its theoretical cohesion.

Let us now turn to the specifics of our own research procedures as manifest in the six data chapters of this book.

A Research Agenda

The methods used in the empirical part of this study flow from the theoretical framework we have adopted to address the issue of the rationalization of justice in federal district courts. Wherever possible, we have sought to provide a historical context for the phenomena under investigation, including descriptive statistics on caseloads and related matters from the beginning of this century to the current decade. As to the structural analysis of environmental effects on task structure, organization, and output of courts between 1950 and 1970, a few methodological comments may be useful. Our main purpose in this analysis is to establish a meaningful connection between these four conceptually distinct phenomena or blocks of variables relevant to courts of law.

First, we contribute to an explanation of the "output" of federal district courts: the frequency of different types of terminations and dispositions of cases that are filed in these courts. We take the probability that certain kinds of cases come to trial as seriously as the probability that they do not come to trial and are disposed of at the pretrial stage or through "no action" (see also Landes 1971). These latter two categories of disposition frequently involve a consent decree or an informal settlement between two litigating parties. Similarly, "dismissals" or "guilty-pleas" in criminal cases constitute types of dispositions that point to informal bargaining and negotiation rather than a full-fledged trial by judge or jury. Thus, we take all nontrial dispositions to be indicators of the rationalization of justice. This point requires some clarification. First, in making this claim we are not necessarily arguing that cases will *a priori* move through the courts more quickly or, for that matter, that judges are less involved with the disposition process. Rather, what we are claiming is that the nature of judicial involvement in a case disposed of through dismissal or pretrial is qualitatively different from that of a trial. As other qualitative research indicates—and shifts in court rules legitimate—the forms of pretrial permit judges to orchestrate *proactively* the settlement of a case. This represents a notable shift in the principles of traditional forms of adjudication and, from the standpoint of this tradition, an attempt to impose a more rational approach to judicial work. Second, rationalization—as used in this context—applies to the mode of completing work and should be distinguished, as well, from the *formalization* of trial practice (see, for example, Langbein 1983) through more articulate rules of evidence or standards for jury selection. Strictly speaking, our data on dispositions refer to the stage in the adjudication process at which a particular case is disposed of rather than the exact method of disposition or the degree of judicial involvement. Such detailed data are not available except by examining each individual case record. Nevertheless, we believe our operational definition of "rationalization" as a deviation from fullfledged adjudication has adequate construct validity. As just noted, it is based on a large and growing qualitative literature describing various facets of the form of law as practiced in modern courts, viz. processes of dispute resolution, litigation, plea bargaining, and judicial and administrative decision-making (see, for example, *Law and Society Review* 1979, Special Issue, Plea-Bargaining; *Law and Society Review* 1980-81, Special Issue, Dispute Processing and Civil Litigation; Boyum and Mather 1983).

One part of this literature deals with alternatives to courts and formal dispute resolution, for example, neighborhood justice centers (Harrington 1985). By contrast, we are concerned here with the internal transformation of courts and of the adjudication process. This transformation involves a movement from formal-legal procedures to informal bargaining and negotiation, from formal to substantive justice, in short, from adjudication to case-management and technocratic administration (Heydebrand, 1974; Clark 1982; Resnik 1982; 1984; Provine 1986). It represents a rationalization of the *form of law* in the interest of speed, efficiency, flexibility, productivity, and cost-effectiveness.

Second, we use a central hypothesis in the sociology of law to argue that organizational and other social, political, and economic factors outside judicial decision-making proper, but nevertheless relevant to courts and to the form of law, do affect adjudication even though they do not fully determine it. We therefore use indicators of organizational structure as intervening variables to show that the form of law is not fully autonomous, but only relatively autonomous with respect to the sociological context within which it is practiced (for similar approaches, see Eisenstein and Jacob 1977; Nardulli 1978, 1979; Henderson, Guynes, and Baar 1981; Neubauer and Ryan 1982; Zatz and Lizotte 1985; Luskin and Dixon 1986; Luskin and Luskin 1987; Fleming, Nardulli, and Eisenstein 1987; Eisenstein, Flemming, and Nardulli 1988; Dixon 1988).

A third consideration is that the frequency of terminations and dispositions is clearly influenced by the volume of filings of cases that come to the court from its jurisdictional environment. We have, therefore, constructed a third set of variables: the caseload, demand, or task structure that we hypothesize to be strongly related to the dispositions, as input can be said to be related to output on technical grounds.

There is another theoretical question, however, that must be raised: To what extent is the organizational structure of courts influenced by the task structure and, ultimately, by the environment of courts? In one sense, we could expect some kind of historical or even institutional imperative to operate here. As noted before, the organization of courts and the authority of Art. III judges is established by the Constitution and by what Congress deems necessary from time to time, that is, by legislative action. Thus, Art. III judges have certain defined jurisdictional powers. They also have, as a rule, two law clerks, a deputy court clerk, and a secretary. In this sense then, the organization of courts seems to be a matter of tradition, historical circumstance, legislative rule, and institutional inertia.

Courts, however, are not just one-judge courtrooms, but have grown to become relatively complex organizations composed of judges, magistrates, law clerks, bankruptcy judges, and "support" staff. New judgeships are authorized not just on the basis of average caseloads confronting a given court, but also on the basis of the size of the population residing in the court's jurisdictional district. It is, therefore, reasonable and theoretically justified to ask: What effect does the task structure of the court have on its internal organization? Moreover, is it just growing population size that influences the allocation of new judgeships, magistrate positions, and nonjudicial personnel, or does the social, economic, and political complexity of the jurisdictional district also play a role? Doesn't it stand to reason that the Districts of Southern New York (Manhattan) and Washington, D.C. are more differentiated and generate a more complex caseload than the District of Wyoming or even Southern California, thereby producing however, indirectly, a more complex type of court organization to deal with the difference in demand?

It is this sociological question that leads us to conceptualize a fourth set of variables, namely those that characterize the structure and complexity of the jurisdictional environment itself. These variables, then, are ultimately our "independent variables" in the study of the form of law and courts. There is ample precedent for such an approach as a general theoretical issue (Durkheim 1964; Weber 1966; Trubek 1972; Abel 1973; Friedman 1975; Hunt 1978; Goldman and Jahnige 1985; Jacob 1986;). There is also precedent for it as an assumption with a high degree of plausibility (Frankfurter and Landis 1928; American Law Institute 1934, pt. 2, 50; Hart and Wechsler 1953; Peltason 1955; Casper and Posner 1974) or as an empirically testable proposition (Schwartz and Miller 1964; Richardson and Vines 1970; Grossman and Sarat 1975; Atkins and Glick, 1976; Friedman and Percival 1976; Toharia 1976;

Lempert 1978; Mcintosh 1983). Only the most doctrinaire defender of the autonomy of law and formal justice might raise questions as to the relevance of external, nonlegal, and sociological variables for the explanation of the task structure, organization, and output of courts. While we are far from arguing for a total determination of legal form by nonlegal variables, we are nevertheless proposing to study the theoretically posed connection by empirical means, that is, in terms of the correlations among the four sets of variables just outlined, based on the total population of district courts. Correlations do not prove causation, of course. But a theoretically plausible causal structure is a prerequisite for the interpretation of empirical uniformities and statistical relationships between blocks of variables. We therefore rely on the analytic power of our model to make sense of the observed relationships between the operational definitions of various concepts as well as among the four different levels of variables where dispositions are the dependent variable, environment the independent variable, and task structure and organization the intervening variables. Our model does not consider the possible feedback effects of courts on their environments (cf. Galanter 1983).[4]

The time frame and other details of our analysis require some additional comments. County census data were obtained to construct environmental profiles for each of the district courts for 1950, 1960, and 1970, using the eighty-four original U.S. districts of 1950 as a base. These data were recoded and aggregated for each district from the counties making up that district.[5]

Data pertaining to the task structure, organization, and output of courts were obtained from the Administrative Office of the U.S. Courts for 1950, 1960, and 1973, the year 1973 representing a compromise between an incomplete data set for 1970 and a better, more complete, but later one for 1973. Data on the number of lawyers practicing in each district were obtained from the 1971 *Lawyer Statistical Report*. Data on the number of corporate mergers were obtained for 1960 and 1970 from the National Conference Board's monthly publication, *Announcements of Mergers and Acquisitions*. We have no reason to believe that the slight variance in years for which data were used affects the reliability of our analysis or the validity of our findings.

Our data sets thus span two decades (1950-70) and permit a relatively systematic comparison between the "quiet" 1950s and the "turbulent" 1960s. The year 1960, in particular, marks the beginning of the dramatic and sustained upsurge in civil litigation in the federal courts. At the same time, the 1960s saw the rise of what we have called the "technocratic administration of justice" (see chap. 1), spurred in part by conscious efforts by the Justice Department to "maintain an effective judiciary" (Meador 1982). The analysis of these efforts and their consequences for the rationalization of justice is, of course, central to our whole argument.

Finally, a word about the rationale for selecting certain kinds of environmental variables and not others in order to estimate the effect of the surrounding political economy on the task structure and organization of courts. Given the limitations of census data for the kind of analysis we were contemplating, we decided to concentrate on three groups of environmental variables.

The *demographic* variables are obvious choices since population size and density are fundamental indicators of the human infrastructure making up a district. The proportion of black population serves as an indicator of ethnic heterogeneity, an important factor in view of the surge in civil rights litigation in the 1960s. Net migration serves to complement other aspects of population dynamics.

The choice of *economic* and *governmental* variables was dictated by our effort to construct a theoretically meaningful profile of the political economy surrounding a given court. Among the economic variables, for most analyses we selected two that would indicate the level of overall economic activity in a district: the number of corporations with more than one hundred employees and the number of corporate mergers (a proxy for oligopolistic tendencies). In two analyses (tables 3.4 and 3.8) we were able to use a slightly expanded model which is explained in the text.

The "political" leg of the political economy is represented by the number of government employees in each district. This variable includes employees at all levels of government, federal, state, and local. It serves as an indicator of the presence of governmental structures and agencies in a district. In some analyses, we also used the number of federal government employees and Justice Department employees as separate, more specialized indicators of the presence of federal governmental agencies.

Finally, a crucial variable included was the number of lawyers practicing in a given district. The causal meaning of such a variable is, however, difficult to establish since litigation may require, as well as be generated by, lawyers. We, therefore, have used this variable only sparingly and very selectively.

All other indicators of the task structure, organization, and output of the district courts are listed in Appendix B and are self-explanatory or are discussed in text.[6]

A Note on Critical Sociology

We have raised some critical questions about the methodological and theoretical limitations of some of the extant empirical literature on courts, as well as of the ecological and institutionalist approaches to the study of organizations. In the first case, we have been concerned with the need to transcend the individualist and behaviorist bias in the analysis of judicial decision-making, whereas in the second case our critique has focused on the ahistorical and deterministic character of organizational ecology and institutional analysis and on the possibility of extending their potential and their concrete applicability to the historically specific dynamics of courts. We also feel that the absence of a critical perspective in both traditions imposes unnecessary limitations on the explanatory and interpretive power of social science research.

Since the charge of normative or theoretical bias is often perceived to have a boomerang effect, let us hasten to add three considerations by way of concluding this methodological discussion. First, we do propose to take a critical perspective on studying the form of law and the technocratic tendencies of the judicial system. Generally, a critical approach is less interested in negating or rejecting extant theories than in locating and interpreting them in relation to their historical context and their knowledge interest, for example, explanation, interpretation, or emancipation (Habermas 1971). But such an approach also seeks to go beyond normal scientific criticism of theories in terms of their testability and falsifiability (Popper 1959). In the social world, we believe, scientific procedures must be informed by the understandings of participants of social processes and by the members of social groups, not just by the "objective" categories of the observer. Native and local theories of how things work thus become data in their own right. Moreover, social structures are seen as both constraining and constituting social practices, a viewpoint that transcends the dichotomies of society versus individual, system versus action, and structure versus process (Bourdieu 1977; Bhaskar 1979; Giddens 1984).

Most importantly, critical theory claims to have an emancipatory knowledge interest that moves beyond understanding and explanation toward critique and practice (Habermas 1971; Heydebrand 1983). In other words, critical interpretation is not substituted for understanding and explanation, but rather added to the research enterprise so as to provide a basis and context for evaluating the limitations of theory and method. Thus, we do not propose to abandon method and the empirical mode of doing intellectual work. The frequently encountered hostility of conventional positivist and behaviorist reactions to critical social theory misses that point.

Second, we do not believe that all ideological or value-relevant positions are equally valid. As Lucien Goldman put it:

> Viewed in terms of their effect on scientific thought, *different perspectives and ideologies do not exist on the same plane.* Some value-judgments permit a better understanding of reality than others. When it is a question of determining which of two conflicting sociologies has the greater scientific value, the first step is to ask which of them *permits the understanding of the other as a social and human phenomenon, reveals its infrastructure and*

clarifies, by means of an immanent critical principle, its inconsistencies and its limitations. (emphasis in original; 1969, p. 52)

Goldman's insight is particularly important in sorting out critical versus affirmative perspectives on the managerial strategies of court reform. While efforts to alleviate the problems of the courts are often well-meaning and constructive, they typically do not evaluate their own normative orientations and, hence, have no analytical handle on the contest between opposing models of justice. By contrast, we believe we are showing why currently the techno-cratic model tends to eclipse the adversary model of justice, and, simultane-ously, the progressive and regressive elements contained in this new form.

Third, we do not believe that a critical analysis of social phenomena invalidates their status as scientific objects; on the contrary, a critical analysis can illuminate both the "real" problems of a given phenomenon and the theo-retical framework within which the definition, analysis, and proposed resolu-tion of the problem is couched. It is in this sense that the term *critical* refers not so much to the negation or rejection of the status quo, as to the notion of determining the contradictions and limits both of the object of analysis and of the instruments of analysis. By treating technocratic court reform itself as a type of rationalization that changes the form of law, we believe this study pursues an alternative course of explanation and interpretation from that of most other empirical research on judicial administration and the courts.

Part of the present approach then, entails a reexamination of what it means to study *forms of law* (Kamenka and Tay 1975; Balbus 1977). Hence, our general strategy is to examine the gradual transformation of the rule of law by investigating changes in the *form of law* and judicial administration rather than focusing on changes in the *content of law.* This means, to repeat, that we are not engaging in a legal analysis of the decisions of judges and the way they translate into substantive policies, even though the rationalization and transformation of substantive law and procedure is an important aspect of the historical changes considered (see esp. Neuman 1957, 22-68; Weber 1966, 224-55; 301-21; Trubek 1972; Kennedy 1976; Horwitz 1977). Rather, we focus on the procedures and organizational processes that are the institu-tional expression of the rule of law. It is this set of institutional and organiza-tional processes which, we argue, must be examined in order to ascertain the hypothesized transformation of the legal form under the impact of environ-mental change and technocratic politics.

Accordingly, we examine the processes of adjudication and administra-tion with a full appreciation of their structural, historical and organizational complexity, using courts and their jurisdictional environments rather than individual transactions as the unit of analysis. Similarly, instead of restricting ourselves to individual cases of litigation and judicial decision-making, we focus on the rates of litigation, filings, dispositions, and terminations in courts. In our analysis of the process of rationalization we attempt to bring a historical perspective to bear on the dynamics involved in this process. This requires systematic attention not only to the quantitative aspect of the operation and environment of courts, but also to the qualitative changes as well as the policies and programs advocated by judicial, legal, and administrative decisionmakers.

APPENDIX B

*

Data Sources

Variables	*Source*
All economic and demographic variables, except number of mergers	U.S. Bureau of the Census, *County and City Data Tapes*, 1952, 1962, 1972
Number of mergers	National Industrial Conference Board, 1960, 1970
Number of government employees	U.S. Bureau of the Census, 1962, 1972
Number of lawyers	American Bar Foundation, 1972
Number of federal civilian employees and Justice Department employees	U.S. Civil Service Commission, 1971
Number of U.S. Attorneys	U.S. Department of Justice, U.S. Attorney's Office Statistical Report, 1973
Court data, 1904-30	Annual Report of the U.S. Attorney and American Law Institute, 1934 also see tables *infra*.
All court data after 1940	Administrative Office of the U.S. Courts

Note: Where appropriate, other data sources are reported in text.

Court Cases Cited

Bell v. Wolfish, 441 U.S. 521 (1979)
Bordenkircker v. Hays, 434 U.S. 357 (1978)
Bradley v. United States, 397 U.S. 742 (1970)
Brown v. Board of Education of Topeka, 347 U.S. (1954)
Chandler v. Judicial Council, 398 U.S. 74, 86 (1969)
Colgrove v. Battin, 413 U.S. 149 (1973)
Cooper v. Pate, 378 U.S. 546 (1964)
Escobedo v. Illinois, 378 U.S. 478 (1964)
Gideon v. Wainwright, 372 U.S. 336; Sup. Ct. 792 (1963)
Hallinger v. Davis, 146 U.S. 314 (1964)
Mapp v. Ohio, 367 U.S. 643 (1961)
Marbury v. Madison, 1 Cranch 137 (1803)
Miranda v. Arizona, 384 U.S. 436 (1966)
Monell v. New York City Department of Social Services, 436 U.S. 658 (1978)
Monroe v. Pape, 365 U.S. 167 (1961)
Munn v. Illinois, 194 U.S. 113 (1976)
North Carolina v. Alford, 400 U.S. 25 (1970)
Palko v. Connecticut, 302 U.S. 790 (1937)
Parker v. North Carolina, 397 U.S. 790 (1970)
Santobello v. New York, 404 U.S. 257 (1971)
Thompson v. Utah, 170 U.S. 343 (1898)
William v. Florida, 399 U.S. 78 (1970)

Notes

Introduction

1. Elaborating, Theda Skocpol (1985) suggests that this angle of macroscopic vision on state activity grows out of a Tocquevillian tradition. While we would agree with her that this perspective should be distinguished from one that begins with an analysis of policies, reforms, or "goal-oriented activities," an organizational perspective for understanding state activity is also a distinctly Weberian contribution.

2. For a further discussion of the methodological possibilities and problems in the analysis of courts as organizations, see Appendix A where we elaborate and present the specific methodological considerations that informed this project.

3. A much more detailed discussion of the methodology of this project is contained in Appendix A where we also discuss the extension of a longitudinal and ecological model for analyzing organizations.

Chapter 1

1. One could apply James Thompson's (1967) typology of organizational technologies to courts and argue that the unique characteristic of dispute institutions is their linking of many diverse actors, i.e., that courts have a mediating technology much like that of a post office or a telephone network (Henderson et. al 1981). But while mediation and linking are certainly involved, mediating technologies have variable inputs but uniform outputs (Scott 1981, 38). Courts, on the other hand, have both variable inputs and outputs. It is, therefore, better to use a less mechanical metaphor for describing the work of courts. Thus, Thompson's notion of an intensive technology, or a concept without any built-in reference to "technology" would be preferable. Intensive technology in the present context could be defined as a social technique or method involving intensive interaction with, and feedback from, the social object (clients, litigants, defendants). These processes themselves contribute to the selection of treatments used to produce certain desired changes in the object, a typical part of the professional model of service.

2. However, in a critique of the revised ABA Standards, which essentially constitute an updating and elaboration of the ideas of Roscoe Pound and Arthur Vanderbilt, David J. Saari (1976, 19) shows them to be "based largely on a bureaucratic and closed system model of management" that has changed little since 1938. Instead, Saari, in a more technocratic vein, advocates an open systems model as being more adequate for modern court organization (see also Gallas 1976).

3. See the Fed. R. Civ. P. 16 advisory committee note; this is the first amendment to the rule since 1938.

Chapter 2

1. We are aware of the importance of distinguishing between state and federal court statistics. Others have suggested that a longitudinal analysis of state court statistics does not show a rise in litigation. The federal court picture appears, however, to be different from that of most states; indeed, work on appellate courts also discloses a relative increase in filings (see Baum, et. al. 1981-1982).

2. For readers less familiar with organizational literature, task structure describes the assignment of responsibilities within a given organization and may, generally, be measured in terms of volume (i.e., sheer number), variability (i.e., variation in level of demand for service), and complexity (i.e., the number of different subtasks and the degree of skill reguired to execute the task). In this study, the court's caseload is the indicator used to measure the organization's task structure. For a further discussion of the organizational literature, see Richard Hall 1987.

3. While some data on the filings of court cases are available for the end of the nineteenth century, notably since 1871, such data were not collected systematically for all district courts until 1904. The main sources for these data from 1904 to 1930 are the U.S. Attorney General's Office, and data collected by the Wickersham Commission on Law Observance and Enforcement appointed in 1929. One report issuing from this commission, "A Study of the Business of the Federal Courts" (American Law Institute 1934), is the most important source of historical statistics on the federal judiciary available. After 1938, the Administrative Office of the U.S. Courts took over data collection from the Justice Department. Traditionally, these data have been published as part of the Proceedings of the Judicial Conference, but they are also available in separate annual reports of the Director of the Administrative Office of the U.S. Courts.

4. The problem of standardizing case filings is an extremely complex one because of the difficulty of determining the appropriate denominator. For example, in examining the rate of increase in personal injury cases one may want to standardize by using population size as well as number of insurance claims. For a further discussion of this issue, see Richard O. Lempert 1978.

5. For a more detailed discussion, see ch. 3 where we examine the sociopolitical impact of various movements on the composition of civil cases in federal district

courts. For example, the rise of civil rights cases is related to developments in the black community and its strategy to use the courts as a mechanism of social change. Similar developments are seen in the evolution of labor cases during the 1930s or prisoner rights cases during the 1960s and 1970s. For a discussion of the legal dimensions of these developments, see Henry J. Friendly 1973, 15-55; Handler 1978.

6. Though there are of course exceptions, civil filings in local and state courts may involve relatively small matters which may lend themselves to routine decision-making and the administrative rationalization of dispositions (Friedman and Percival 1976). By contrast, in federal courts, civil filings tend to be weightier, often involving complex civil rights or antitrust issues, larger sums of money, and big organizations, including the government (see also Flanders 1977, 73).

7. We will show in chapter 8 that the U.S. government is a dominant party in federal courts and that U.S. cases receive a disproportionate share of the courts' attention. Analytically, this shift in jurisdiction suggests a more fundamental change and erosion of a distinct division of labor, or separation of powers, between the executive and judicial branches.

8. For various reasons, many cases may not be disposed of during the same year in which they are filed. Foremost among them is the time involved at certain stages of the litigation process, particularly the time it takes lawyers to prepare the case, and, in many instances, the time it takes judges to reach a decision. Court managers also believe that judges' determination and policies to "manage" cases expeditiously is a factor in the speed with which cases move to disposition (Flanders 1977; Bender and Strecker 1978; Connolly et al. 1978). The issue is, however, a complex one and continues to raise the specter of a conflict between speed and quality of justice, managerial protestations to the contrary notwithstanding (Flanders 1977, 68).

9. It may be too simple to use backlog as a measure of complexity. Increased backlog may be measuring increasing demands coupled with decreasing or constant resources. For a further discussion of the fiscal constraints on the judicial system, see chapter 4.

10. As one reviewer pointed out, this decrease may be a function of a large increase in filings, with the disposition rate remaining constant.

Chapter 3

1. Only for per capita personal income and per capita property value did the correlations decrease over time (1902-72) from moderately strong to weak and negative values (Grossman and Sarat 1975, 339). While suggestive, this study cannot be considered conclusive on this point due to a number of methodological problems. In measuring demand, the authors used the litigation rate rather than the actual number of cases filed. Since population is highly correlated with such variables as industrialization, urbanization, and other population variables, using it on both sides of a regression

equation (once in the numerator and once in the denominator) may introduce instabil-
ities as well as negative relationships due to the problem of dependency (Freeman and
Kronenfeld 1973). Another problem in their analysis is the use of data aggregated on
the basis of states, rather than actual district court jurisdictions. While some jurisdictional boundaries are coextensive with those of states, especially the nonindustrial and
nonurban ones, this is by no means true for all federal district courts.

2. All variables are analyzed as rates where the denominator is consistently the
population size of a district; thus, corporations refers to corporations divided by the
population size of a district. For a further discussion of this technique, see Glenn
Firebaugh and Jack Gibbs 1985.

3. Note that data on the number of government employees per district were not
available in 1950.

4. Using the same procedure as that shown in tables 3.1 and 3.2, variables are
ratio measures where merger and black population is divided by population. Net migration, already a composite measure of population, is not divided by population.

5. Patent and tax cases also may come within the jurisdiction of specialized courts—
the Courts of Customs and Patents, and the Tax Court, respectively. The decision of
locale of litigation is left to the parties. The choice of removal of such cases from the
federal courts to specialized courts was, in part, a response to the complexity of such
cases and to the expert knowledge that they often reguire. This is particularly true in
the area of patents where highly esoteric, scientific knowledge is mandatory to the
decision-making process. This point supports the importance of complexity of demands
as an issue for courts and also suggests why environmental factors account for less of
the variance in corporate cases as compared to other categories of civil matters (see
also Friendly, 1973).

6. Using the model shown in table 3.3 for complex civil and criminal cases, the
standardized regression coefficient of 1/population with corporate cases is .97 and
explains 98 percent of the variance. This means that 1/population takes out any spurious contribution from the common presence of 1/population in the independent or
dependent variables. In light of this relationship, it is reasonable to employ a component rather than a ratio variable regression model.

In taking this step, it is also possible to use z-score measures, which are not feasible in a ratio variable model. Thus, industrialization is a z-score variable composed of
the (1) number of corporations with more than one hundred employees, (2) number of
mergers, (3) retail-wholesale trade, and (4) number of white-collar workers in a district.
Legal-governmental sector is a z-score variable that is composed of the (1) number of
lawyers and (2) number of government workers in a district. Socioeconomic level is a
z-score variable composed of (1) median education and (2) median income. Statistical
tests of significance were omitted in this analysis.

7. The high intercorrelation among the independent variables creates a problem
of multicollinearity. This is true for each of the tables in the remainder of this chapter.
We have, generally, tried to deal with this problem by carefully selecting only a few
independent variables at a time for analysis.

8. In fact, it is during this period that education became the American panacea; that the phrase "equality of opportunity" was coined; and that the federal government passed the first Morrill Act granting aid to land grant colleges (Veysey 1965; Brubacher and Rudy 1976). The new demands of a potentially cohesive working class have taken various turns along the path for ever more democratic rights (see Piven and Cloward 1977; Handler 1979).

9. Of course, one might hypothesize that the policies of the Reagan Justice Department would have a significant effect on the civil rights agenda.

10. For a further discussion of this theme, see chapter 7 where we consider the implication of a shift in U.S. and private cases for the federal district courts.

11. A more detailed chronology of the legal unfolding of prisoner petitions can be found in Ronald Goldfarb (1975), and Ronald Goldfarb and Linda R. Singer (1973).

12. Amnesty International has cited the prison at Marion, Illinois, for violation of basic human rights; see *U.S. News and World Report*, 27 July 1987.

13. See *Miranda v. Arizona*, 384 U.S. 436 (1966); *Escobedo v. Illinois*, 378 U.S. 478 (1964); and *Mapp v. Ohio*, 367 U.S. 643 (1961).

14. See *Cooper v. Pate*, 378 U.S. 546 (1964).

15. As of 1988, the lowest amount for diversity cases is fifty-thousand dollars. For a more detailed discussion of diversity cases, see chapter 7.

16. Note that the model used in table 3.4 for corporate cases is also used in table 3.8. (The standardized regression coefficient between 1/population and personal injury cases is .97 and contributes to 96 percent of the variance.) For an explanation of the rationale behind this decision, see n. 6 *supra*.

Chapter 4

1. The figures shown in tables 4.1 and 4.2 have not been corrected for inflation using the Consumer Price Index. Since we also show each allocation as a percentage of the total U.S. budget as well as the percentage change within each category from decade to decade, an equalizing factor has been incorporated into the construction of these tables. That is, the use of percentages permits us to compare across decades for increases or decreases in the budgetary allocations under consideration.

2. The decrease in the percentage of judicial salaries (table 4.2, row 6) from 1970 (18.2 percent) to 1980 (8.8 percent) and 1984 (8.3 percent), paralleling the relative decline of expenses for the jury system and salaries of support staff, resulted in part from the unprecedented increase (351 percent) of the total base from 1970 to 1980 (row 1), much of which derives from a large increase in "other," new expenditures (rows 20 and 22).

3. *The Third Branch* is a monthly publication of the Federal Judicial Center, which surveys relevant developments in the federal courts. Since December 1975, we have

compiled a coded file of this publication for keeping a pulse on issues being considered for change. We cite various issues where relevant.

4. Note that the unstandardized coefficient for government employees also shows a change in direction and impact from 1960 to 1970.

5. Please note that these data are only available for 1970.

6. For a further discussion of magistrates' statutory authority, see Carroll Seron 1985. Briefly, however, pretrial matters may be divided into dispositive and nondispositive motions. Whereas a dispositive motion (e.g., summary judgement motion) refers to an action that may terminate the case, a nondispositive motion (e.g., discovery) covers those activities that are generally viewed as preparation for trial. By statute, magistrates may "hear and recommend" action to a judge on a dispositive motion, but they may decide a nondispositive motion subject to *de novo* hearing by the judge. Seron's work (1985, 93-111) suggests that when magistrates work on dispositive motions they are rarely challenged and, if challenged, rarely reversed by the assigned judge. Furthermore, her findings show that when magistrates decide nondispositive motions the decisions are rarely challenged.

7. Also confirmed by interviews with district court judges in the Eastern and Southern districts of New York, July and August 1974.

Chapter 5

1. Traditionally, students of courts have focused on either the civil or criminal side of courts and caseloads as relatively distinct and separate spheres. In this study we are concerned with analyzing the overall task structure and organization of federal district courts. The analysis of the courts' task structure (see chaps. 2 and 3) shows that the courts' demands are primarily driven by the civil docket. Nevertheless, we are concerned with explaining the extent to which this pressure gives priority to civil case dispositions. In order to measure overall task volume we therefore selected total demand (civil and criminal filings and pending cases) as our main indicator. In line with this approach, we then break out the analysis of civil and criminal terminations (see chaps. 5 and 6).

2. Codification in the case of education, or social service in general, usually took place through the development of a specialized university course, thereby setting apart the elect from the nonelect, the expert from the layperson. For a general history see Lawrence Veysey 1965; Jeffrey Berlant 1975; Thomas Haskell 1977; Magali Sarfatti Larson 1977. In the case of law, the process was somewhat different since this knowledge-base already existed and was to be transformed. In this endeavor, Harvard Law School set the standard (see Schlegel 1979, 1985).

3. The large number of jury trials in 1930 (9,352) is again the effect of prohibition.

4. Recent work on the history of plea bargaining and criminal procedure supports this point (see, e.g., Alschuler 1979; Haller 1979; Langbein 1979), and hence confirms

that caseload pressures are not the only explanation for the development of plea bargaining.

5. It is also important to note the socioeconomic background of these new professionals that was, by and large, blue collar (Platt and Pollock 1974; Haller 1979). In general, the criminal bar is relatively specialized and separate from other arenas of legal practice and is looked upon with some degree of condescension by the legal elite (Auerbach 1976; Heinz and Lauman 1982).

6. Note, these data are not available for 1950. Additionally, the simple correlation between demand and judges is .90 in 1970; this strong correlation may be creating some problems of multicollinearity in this equation.

Chapter 6

1. Productivity, like other aspects of efficiency, is best studied in comparative perspective, with rigorous controls on the independent variables that might affect it and with an adequate sample of the relevant unit of analysis. In the present case, the independent variation of the number of judges, nonjudicial personnel, volume, complexity of cases, and historical time periods, permit only a relatively crude examination of this issue.

2. It should be stressed that these figures do not mean district judges have sixteen or thirty-six employees at their disposal. The ratios merely indicate the changes in the total organizational system of the federal judiciary, taken as a whole, including appeals courts, the Supreme Court, and various agencies such as the Administrative Office and Federal Judicial Center. But the figures are not far off even for district courts. In 1988, the contingent of 575 district judges constitutes almost 3 percent of the total number of 20,743 federal judicial and nonjudicial employees. In the largest metropolitan district courts the figure is closer to 10 percent. In 1984, the total personnel ratio of judicial to nonjudicial personnel in the twenty-one largest district courts was 501 to 5,055, that is, a ratio of about 1 to 10 (Eldridge 1984; 5, table 1). The average for these courts was 24 judicial to 241 nonjudicial positions, again a 1 to 10 ratio (ibid.) "Overall," the research director of the Federal Judicial Center, William Eldridge, concludes,

> the 501 judicial positions—that is, judges, magistrates, and bankruptcy judges—account for only nine percent of the personnel. For each visible judicial officer, ten other persons are involved in court operations. Actually, even more persons may well be involved. Each district court is a unit in the federal court system; each court has a substantial degree of autonomy in the way it operates, but all the units share responsibility for the effective operation of the system of which they are parts. Discharge of that shared responsibility is another of the rarely perceived aspects of federal court activity (1984, 4).

In other words, systemic and interorganizational functions that need to be performed must ultimately also be figured into the calculation of productivity.

3. An exception to this argument could be seen in the parallel movement of judicial productivity and nonjudicial personnel growth from 1940 to 1950. However, it

stands to reason that the growth in employees from 1940 to 1950 represented a lagged response to the inordinately high caseloads of earlier years.

4. There are ten salary steps within each of fifteen grades. The higher the average grade-step the greater the skill within the nonjudicial sector of the district court labor force.

5. For the district courts analyzed here to be "bureaucratic" it would have been necessary to find significant inverse relationships between the professional staff, that is, judges and possibly magistrates, and the other organizational variables considered. Our data show relatively strong positive relationships between "professional" and "bureaucratic" elements, even though the analysis uses only zero-order relationships. A more conclusive analysis would have to be based on multiple regression and other multivariate techniques, controlling at a minimum for size and complexity. For a discussion of the conceptual and theoretical issues involved, see Richard Hall 1968; and, generally, Wolf Heydebrand 1973, chaps. 13, 24, 25, 27, 28.

Chapter 7

1. In his discussion of legal rationalization, Max Weber (1966) refers to the Anglo-American case as a "problem" because it does not fit his model of development and modernization. While there is much truth to this (see also Trubek 1972a), the rise of administrative law, as a separate and distinct field, suggests some answers to Weber's question. That is, administrative law is a system of written rules, executed by officials, who are part of a larger hierarchical arrangement of authority. While it is true that judicial review and hence an element of irrationality (interpretation) remains, it is also the case that judicial review is the exception and not the rule, in practice.

2. The history of the Interstate Commerce Commission (ICC) has been told many times and need not be repeated here (see Kolko 1962; Freedman 1978; Skowronek 1982). Its formation as an organ of the state does tell, in mute, the unfolding of administrative relations, a few points of which are worth reviewing for the reader not familiar with the details. The central place of the railroads in the industrial revolution is well known. It was both a conveyor and a means for capitalist growth. For its expansion symbolized links between east and west, and north and south. But as railroads expanded across state lines the inevitable problem of price control and guidelines developed, a question that the common law and constitutional law were inadequate to address. In 1877, the Supreme Court finally, though reluctantly, ruled that regulation of private property did not violate due process rights when the property in question was to be used for the "common" good. The Court also held that such regulation should be controlled by the several states rather than the federal government—making the impact of its earlier decision hopelessly ineffectual [*Munn v. Illinois*, 94 U.S. 113 (1987)]. Thus, the most progressive state commissions were soon controlled by the railroad industry. But the need for political control, rationalization, and predictability of the economy also became increasingly clear to the controllers of this and other modern industries, particularly banking and trade. "Expansion and competition, and with them instability

and economic crises, had become the essential hallmarks of the main branches of the American economic structure during the first half of modern American history" (Kolko 1976; 7; also see Wiebe 1967; 48-53). The by-word of reform, federal controls, was gradually accepted as a necessary step if private interests were to maintain a hegemonic position in the American economy. The pressure from reformers and industrialists coupled with the ineffectual decisions of the Court pushed the Congress to act. The ICC, establishing the first independent agency in American history at the federal level, was written into law in 1887.

The Act formally asserted that the ICC was to have control under the auspices of a federal commission. The task of this commission was to control railroad prices and to prevent discriminatory practices. But its power to do so was notoriously weak; the enforcement of controls established by the commission was voluntary on the part of the railroad unless the government sought an injunction against the railroad for eventual review by the court. In other words, the "burden of proof" was placed on the ICC, thus leaving the final test to the courts.

Following the example of the ICC, the Federal Reserve Board (1913) and the Federal Trade Commission (1906) were, like the ICC, established to administer and to regulate banking and unfair competition, respectively. Moreover, the structure of these agencies complemented the ICC as did their respective roles in monitoring potential economic crises. But in one critical way the reforms that introduced larger agencies learned from the errors of the ICC experience. The enabling legislation of the ICC specified in overelaborate detail and concrete language the scope and responsibilities of the Commission; that error was not repeated. The major transformation in the enabling legislation of future agencies was the use of broad and abstract language. For example, in the case of the FTC it controls an abstract category of behavior, commerce, an abstract category of adherence, competition, and an abstract guideline, fairness (Lowi 1969). It opens the way, therefore, for a new role for the law, business and legal advice by agencies of the state to the private sector as laws become a "*series of instructions to administrators rather than a series of commands to citizens*" (Lowi 1969; 144; emphasis in original; also see Freedman 1978). In sum, by 1913 the most important business groups had secured essential legislation for the political control of potential economic crises and in the process affected the future composition of the docket of the district courts.

3. Whether or not the New Deal is a qualitative break from the Progressive Era, or a continuation of that initiative, is a subject of much debate among historians [see chap.7, n.2, *infra*; also see Hofstadter (1955)]. The recent work of many social historians has moved in the very interesting direction of considering the role of organizations and bureaucracy as an overarching theme of the twentieth century, a point that is, of course, consonant with Weber. What is interesting in this regard is that it suggests that Progressive Era/New Deal distinctions are less relevant than the discovery of new types of organizing structures. For a further discussion, see Galambos (1970).

4. As we have shown in the discussion of the ICC, the Court's initial response to the powers of the ICC was to narrow the scope of its authority in keeping with the traditional meaning of separation of powers. Gradually, however, that position changed in response to the needs of administrative rationality. For a further discussion of this

point, see Lawrence M. Friedman (1973), G. Edward White (1974), Arthur S. Miller (1976), James D. Freedman (1978),Richard Stewart (1979), Stephen Skowronek (1982).

5. To quote the Administrative Procedure Act of 1946, "Any person suffering legal wrong because of any agency action, or adversely affected or aggrieved by such action within the meaning of any relevant statute, shall be entitled to judicial review thereof," (sec. 10a).

6. The large number of U.S. cases in 1950 is the result of the closing of the Office of Price Administration; all cases from this agency were turned over to the U.S. Attorney and thus put a significant burden on the court (*Judicial Conference Report* 1947, 1951). However, most of the cases were cleared off the docket by 1952. The explosive effect of these cases on the court dramatically reveals how Congress' actions can alter the effect of court demands. Indicative of this problem, one of former Chief Justice Burger's reform suggestions has been to include a monitoring device (legal impact evaluation) in each piece of administrative regulation to gauge its future impact on the courts; thus far, this discussion remains in limbo (see also Boyum and Krislov 1980).

7. The composition of federal question cases suggests that the construction of "public law litigation" as an exclusive category is justified. In 1986, 80.8 percent of the 98,747 federal question cases were "actions under statutes," including antitrust, commerce, banks and banking, bankruptcy, oil rights, the Economic Stabilization Act, environmental matters, deportation, prisoner petitions, forfeiture and penalty, labor laws, protected property rights, securities, commodities, and exchanges, social security laws, state reapportionment suits, tax suits, customer challenge, Freedom of Information Act, and constitutionality of state statutes. Less than 20 percent of federal question cases were contract, real property, and tort actions, the typical categories of private cases.

8. Note the strong direct relationship between demand and no actions ($r = .73$) and pretrials ($r = .77$) as well as the weak relationships with geographical dispersion ($r = .04$, $r = .11$, respectively).

Chapter 8

1. The population base of a jurisdiction is still used for measuring the need for judgeships, even though it is no longer as strong a factor as it was thirty years ago. Our data suggest that factors other than population should be used as guidelines for determining the need for judges.

2. For purposes of studying courts, the choice of disputes rather than institutional structures as the unit of analysis (the central methodological approach of the Civil Litigation Research Project, see *Law and Society Review*, 1980-81) implies an individualist, reductionist bias since the focus of disputes and litigious behavior entails a reduction of social conflict and legal disputes to questions of individual motivation (Grau 1980; Kidder 1980-81).

3. For example, central to James Eisenstein and Herbert Jacob's approach is the conception of courts as courtrooms, of courtrooms as small groups, and of the "iden-

tity of the courtroom" as an interactional network with varying degrees of cohesion, familiarity, cooperation, and stability under the formal leadership of a particular judge. The theoretical viewpoint of these authors is based on the language of small groups research of the 1950s that has little to do with courts as organizations. There is no concept or measure of structure, surprisingly not even the notion of "negotiated order" (Strauss 1963).

4. This conclusion clearly refutes Joel E. Grossman and Austin Sarat's (1975, 344) assertion of "the relative unimportance of external, environmental factors." We have suggested elsewhere some of the reasons why Grossman and Sarat failed to establish any significant environmental effects (Heydebrand 1977, 810, n. 25).

5. Ralph Milliband (1969, 45-55), has identified different structural elements of modern state systems: the government, the administration, military and police, the judiciary, subcentral government, and legislative bodies. One need not accept his instrumentalist and conflict-theoretical interpretation of the state system to find such a specification of "the" state useful. Nevertheless, other versions of the instrumentalist view in mainstream political science, jurisprudence, and sociology still hold that the state, in general, tends to be captured by elite interests and that the judiciary, in particular, is—and always has been—captured by the managerial and political interests of executive, legislative, and other political constituencies. Any appeal to the normative foundations of the rule of law and the idea of an independent judiciary and of the separation of powers is, from this perspective, often greeted with a mixture of incredulity and cynicism. Consequently, the notion of a crisis of legitimacy of the judiciary or of the modern state is sometimes rejected as too naive and romantic. Similarly, the notion of the capture of the judiciary by the interests of the modern centralized state is seen as not particularly newsworthy (but see Skowronek 1982; Skocpol 1985). We would argue that the relationships between law, courts, politics, and the state are historically contingent, i.e., that legal autonomy and judicial independence are empirically variable phenomena that can be taken for granted in some periods and contexts, but may be threatened in others.

6. In addition, there is, of course, the appropriation of judicial functions by administrative agencies where they take the form of "administrative" or "bureaucratic" justice (Nonet 1969; Mashaw 1983).

7. It should be noted that, of late, there has been some interest in reorganizing the production process of American industries by introducing work teams and other, more democratic managerial techniques. At the same time, however, it is significant to note that demands for such changes in the American factory system are not only originating from unions or rank and file workers, as is a common situation among Western European workers, but also from management itself. One must question, then, the underlying impetus and interest in such changes and the degree to which they are conceived to be truly democratic. As Lester Thurow (1980) has pointed out, it is somewhat ironic that a country that prides itself on being the inspiration for modern democracies and individualism also has the highest ratio of management to workers of any advanced industrialized country in the world (see also Zwerdling 1978a, 1978b).

8. There is some debate among scholars as to whether or not the Founding Fathers clearly intended, in their writing of the Constitution, that the courts should appropriate the role of judicial review of legislative and executive actions. However, by the time Marshall became Chief Justice indications were clearly pointing in this direction; the position presented on judicial review contained in *Marbury v. Madison* was, in essence, a formal statement of a highly probable development.

9. Interestingly, as Max Weber goes on to point out, formal legal rationality did not, in its earliest form, directly shape the form of law or legal administration (i.e., the organization of courts).

10. Here we touch upon the rule of law as a constraint from the standpoint of advanced economic development, especially the interests of large, transnational corporations and new high-tech ventures. Of course, it should not be forgotten that the demands created by the rule of law, in terms of fundamental democratic rights, take on new and extended meaning as well as more marginal groups and strata demand their protection; this development, too, while beginning as a positive force, becomes a "constraint" as the limitations of legitimation are more and more put to the test (see esp. Wolfe 1977).

11. But see Arthur Stinchcombe's (1965) study of organizational innovations in the railroad industry and his observation that the point of formation of an organization is the critical factor in explaining the structure and further process of change in organizations.

12. The typology offered here has its origins in a previous attempt to categorize the different responses to the crisis of judicial institutions. For the distinction among professional, bureaucratic, and technocratic responses, see Wolf Heydebrand 1977, 1979, 1982.

13. This has, of course, happened before, for example, during the Prohibition Era in the 1920s when the federal judicial system was confronted with a large sudden increase of cases, although they were mainly routine cases.

14. Liberal legislation in the areas of civil rights and administrative law, for example, is seen to contribute to a litigation explosion and, hence, to an overburdening of the third branch.

15. Clerical and managerial "support" services are tolerated, even expanded, as long as the decision-making power remains in the hands of judicial professionals rather than being delegated to nonprofessionals or administrators. Law clerks, the *bona fide* newest members of the legal-judicial status group, may be given a role in drafting or writing opinions, but supervision is still present. This apprentice system functions essentially as an integral part of what judges and legal professionals perceive as the prerogatives of a professionally autonomous, self-governing, self-regulating status group.

16. Where judges are found to have such a "systemic" or administrative orientation, they often have a career background in prosecution or enforcement, for example, in the U.S. Attorney's office or other divisions of the Department of Justice.

17. Two examples of possible bureaucratization stand out in federal courts.

(1) Magistrates are taking over some of the functions of judges, especially pretrial work, preparation of cases, but also decisions in routine cases, for example, social security claims. As we have indicated, this began in 1968-70 and has expanded dramatically, although not without some opposition from judges (see Seron 1985)

(2) Court administrators/executives are introduced to actively take over the functions of court management and judicial administration: budget, personnel, public relations; data processing; reorganization of the clerk's office; expansion of clerical services; and paralegal functions. Judicial administration is strictly separated from the judicial functions of judges such as hearings, adjudication, decisions, dealings with juries, and writing opinions. Circuit executives were first introduced in 1970-71 to manage appeals courts and to supervise administratively the district courts. However, in district courts, judicial executives were introduced only experimentally in six out of ninety-seven district courts in the last few years due, in part, to the strong resistance from district court judges.

18. Philippe Nonet and Philip Selznick's (1978, 16 22) typologies of law and formal organization are inconsistent on this point since bureaucratic organization is seen as corresponding to autonomous law (based on formal rationality), whereas "post-bureaucratic" organization and "responsive law" are based on substantive ("material") rationality. See also Gunther Teubner's (1983, 253, 257) distinction among formal, substantive, and reflexive legal rationality and his critique of Nonet and Selznick.

19. The affinity of the model to neocorporatist tendencies is unmistakable, but cannot be pursued here (see Heydebrand 1985).

20. On this point, the adversary system, under the professional model of justice, shares certain aspects of the economic model.

21. The problem of a model consciously emphasizing a form of political justice requires further discussion, a project that cannot be pursued in the present context. Democratic justice is a form of political justice, but it must be conceptualized in a way that is different from the political justice of fascist and state-socialist legal systems. A second issue to be discussed in greater detail elsewhere is the presence of "democratic" elements in the new, informal, participatory strategies of the technocratic model of justice. The problem here is to develop these elements further without getting stuck in the authoritarian potential of the technocratic model. Still another issue to be clarified is the traditional opposition of the dominant professional-adversary model to any notion of democracy. Constitutionally, the third branch is insulated from any democratic accountability and can be influenced democratically only by virtue of the power of the other two branches to nominate and appoint judges, including the composition of the Supreme Court. Judicial independence from democratic politics (in the direct sense of political influence on judicial decision-making) has always been seen as a virtue of the Constitution, but it has also been attacked on semi-populist grounds since the Progressive Era. Thus, the populist impulse behind legal realism has been translated into various criticisms of the conventional notion of for-

mal, autonomous law and has led to the formulation of a concept of social or socialized justice [see Nonet and Selznick (1978) for a discussion and references]. While
we would argue that the social justice model is today part of the technocratic model,
the "social justice" component points to the broader concept of democratic (rather
than populist) justice that could conceivably be present—in embryonic form—in the
current technocratic model.

Appendix A

1. It would be instructive in this context to examine the legal and political controversies surrounding public law litigation, class action suits, the use of statistics for
purposes of evidence, and the doctrine of "standing"—an inquiry we cannot pursue
further at this point (but see, generally, Chayes 1976; Goldstein 1985).

2. In his review of recent developments in organizational ecology, Glenn R. Carroll
(1984) identifies two additional subtypes, organizational demography and the macroevolutionary approach of community ecology. Organizational demography "typically
uses a developmental approach to study evolution" (p. 72). It "involves the study of
demographic events and life-cycle processes across individual organizations" (ibid.).
The macroevolutionary approach, focusing on organizational populations in macro-
settings like cities or whole societies," is primarily concerned with the emergence and
disappearance of organizational forms" (ibid.). Charles E. Bidwell and John D. Kasarda
(1985) have attempted to formulate the most ambitious ecological theory of structuring in organizations that seeks to bridge the developmental and community approaches.
However, the theory is pitched at such an abstract level that it is not immediately clear
how it might contribute to the understanding of concrete cases or historically specific
instances of organization—environment interactions. More problematic for our concerns
is the fact that this theory relies on "calculative behavior as the driving force of the structuring process" and is therefore "limited to economic organizations" (p. 29). The claim
to the possibility of extension to other kinds of organizations is, at this point, unsubstan-
tiated. Moreover, the authors explicitly reject "critical theory in sociology and in the
study of formal organizations" (p. xviii) under the mistaken assumption that since, for
critical theorists, "the forms and activities of organizations are historically specific—
embedded, for example, in one or another of the historical modes of production," their
analysis is limited to case studies and questions the validity of general propositions"
(ibid.). This assumption overlooks not only the internal dynamics of historical modes
of production, but also the feasibility of propositional analysis based on quantitative
data and methods applicable to particular internal periods and processes (see, e.g.,
Heydebrand and Seron 1981; Griffin, Devine, and Wallace 1982; Wright and Singelmann
1982; or much of "cliometrics" and other methods of historical sociology). By contrast,
we feel it is a serious limitation of scientific method to treat political, economic, and
historical change as a form of "residual" heterogeneity, variability or, generally, "pertur-
bation" in the organizational environment (Kasarda and Bidwell 1984, 52-62, 99-104).

3. Aggregate characteristics are, of course, related to what Paul F. Lazarsfeld and
Herbert Menzel (1980, 511) have defined as analytic and structural "collective properties." Analytic "properties of collectives are obtained by performing some mathematical

operation upon some property of each single member" (ibid.). In our case, for example, median education, median income, percent of blacks in the population, and percent of white collar and the like are analytic properties of the districts. Structural properties of collectives are "obtained by performing some operation on data about the relation of each member to some or all of the others" (ibid.). Both the number of corporations, and the number of corporate mergers come close to being structural properties in that they measure the level of economic concentration or activity in a district. Population density (the number of people per square mile), total volume of wholesale and retail trade, and net migration are similarly "structural" in that they describe the relations between different aspects of the district court's environment.

4. For a largely unsuccessful attempt to analyze the cross-lagged environmental effects at Time 1 on organizational variables at Time 2, see Heydebrand 1977, 806-11.

5. The number of districts changed from 84 in 1950, to 94 in 1970 and, indeed, in 1986. In order to be able to make exact comparisons over time, it was necessary to collapse some districts and reconstitute others into their original form. This procedure does not affect the logic of measuring the effects of the jurisdictional environment on the district court. The district changes and additions are as follows:

1950	1960	1970
California North	California North	California North California East (combined)
California South	California South	California South California Central (combined)
Florida South	Florida South	Florida South Florida Middle (combined)
Louisiana East	Louisiana East	Louisiana East Louisiana Middle (combined)
South Carolina East South Carolina West	South Carolina East South Carolina West	South Carolina (combined)

6. The preceding discussion refers to the component form of our variables, that is, the raw numbers of census data aggregated to the district level, as well as the caseload, disposition, and personnel data from the Administrative Office of the U.S. Courts. In the actual regression analysis, starting with table 3.1, we are using ratio variables, that is, all components are divided by the total population of the district. Thus, the number of government employees becomes the *per capita* government employment, civil filings becomes civil filings per population or the litigation rate, and so on. As a result, the entire analysis is standardized by the total population of each district. For further discussion, see chap.3, n.2; the footnotes to table 3.1; and Glenn Firebaugh and Jack Gibbs 1985.

References

Abel, Richard. 1973. "A Comparative Theory of Dispute Institutions in Society." 8 *Law and Society Review*, 217.

_____. 1977. "Law Books and Books about Law." in L. M. Friedman and S. Macaulay (eds.) *Law and the Behavioral Sciences*, 2d ed., Indianapolis: The Bobbs-Merrill Co.

_____. 1979. "Socializing the Legal Profession." *Law & Policy Quarterly*, 1 January 1979.

_____. 1980. "Redirecting Social Studies of Law." 14 *Law and Society Review*, 805.

_____. 1981. "Legal Services," in M. Micklin and M. Olsen (eds.) *Handbook of Applied Sociology*. New York: Praeger Publishers, Inc.

_____. 1982 *The Politics of Informal Justice*, Abel (ed.) New York: Academic Press.

Abraham, Henry J. 1986. *The Judicial Process*, 4th ed. New York: Oxford University Press.

Ackerman, Frank, and Andrew Zimbalist. 1976. "Capitalism and Inequality in the United States," in Richard C. Edwards, et al. (eds.) *The Capitalist System*. Englewood Cliffs, N.J.: Prentice-Hall.

Administrative Office of the U.S. Courts. (1950, 1960, 1964, 1971, 1980, 1988). *Annual Reports of the Director*. Washington D.C.

Aldrich, Howard E., and Albert J. Reiss, Jr. 1976. "Continuities in the Study of Ecological Succession: Changes in the Race Composition of Neighborhoods and their Businesses." 81 *American Journal of Sociology*, 846.

_____, and Jeffrey Pfeffer. 1976. "Environment of Organizations." 2 *Annual Review of Sociology,*, 79.

_____. and Sergio Mindlin. 1978. "Uncertainity and Dependence: Two Perspectives on Environment," in L. Karpik (ed.) *Organization and Environment*. Beverly Hills: Sage.

261

———— . 1979. *Organizations and Environments*. Englewood Cliffs, N.J.: Prentice-Hall.

Alford, Robert. 1975. *Health Care Politics: Ideological and Interest Group Barriers to Reform*. Chicago: University of Chicago Press.

———— , and Roger Friedland. 1985. *Powers of Theory: Capitalism, the State, and Democracy*. Cambridge: Cambridge University Press.

Alschuler, Albert. 1968. "The Prosecutor's Role in Plea Bargaining." 36 *University of Chicago Law Review*, 50.

———— . 1975. "The Defense Attorney's Role in Plea Bargaining." 84 *Yale Law Journal*, 1179.

———— .1979. "Plea Bargaining and Its History." 13 *Law and Society Review* (Winter).

———— . 1986. "Mediation with a Mugger: Concerning the Shortage of Adjudicatory Services and the Need for a Two-Tier Trial System in Civil Cases." 99 *Harvard Law Review*, 1808.

American Bar Association. 1974. *American Bar Association, Commission On Judicial Administration. Standards Relating to Court Organization*. Chicago.

American Friends Service Committee. 1971. *Struggle for Justice*. New York: Hill and Wang.

American Law Institute, 1934. *A Study of the Business of the Federal Courts*. Philadelphia.

Anderson, Theodore, and Seymour Warkov 1961. "Organizational Size and Functional Complexity: A Study of Administration in Hospitals." 26 *American Sociological Review*, 23.

Aspin, Leslie. 1966."A Study of Reinstatement under the National Labor Relation Act." Ph.D. Diss. Department of Economics, MIT.

Atkins, Burton M., and Henry R. Glick. 1976. "Environmental and Structural Variables as Determinants of Issues in State Courts of Last Resort." 20 *American Journal of Political Science*, 97.

Auerbach, Jerold S. 1976. *Unequal Justice: Lawyers and Social Change in Modern America*. New York: Oxford University Press.

———— . 1983. *Justice without Law*. New York: Oxford University Press.

Aumann, Francis Robert. 1940. *The Changing American Legal System*. Columbus: Ohio State University Press.

Baar, Carl. 1975. *Separate but Subservient: Court Budgeting in the American States*. Lexington, Mass.: Lexington Books.

Bachrach, P., and M. Baratz. 1962. "Two Faces of Power." 61 *American Political Science Review*, 947.

Balbus, Issac D. 1971. "The Concept of Interest in Pluralist and Marxian Analysis." 1 *Politics and Society*, 151.

_____. 1972. "The Negation of the Negation: Theory of Capitalism Within an Historical Theory of Social Change." 3 *Politics and Society*, 49.

_____. 1973. *The Dialectics of Legal Repression: Black Rebels before the American Criminal Courts*. New York: Russell Sage Foundation.

_____. 1977. "Commodity Form and Legal Form." 11 *Law and Society Review*, 571.

Barkan, Steven E. 1977. "Political Trials and the *Pro se* Defendant in the Adversary System." 24 *Social Problems*, 324.

Baum, Lawrence, Sheldon Goldman, and Austin Sarat. 1981-82. "Research Note: The Evolution of Litigation in the Federal Courts of Appeals." 16 *Law and Society Review*, 2.

Beard, Charles A. 1913. *An Economic Interpretation of the Constitution of the United States*. New York: Macmillan Publishing Co.

Beirne, Piers. 1975. "Marxism and the Sociology of Law: Theory or Practice?" 2 *British Journal of Law and Society* (Summer).

Bell, Daniel. 1973. *The Coming of Post-Industrial Society*. New York: Basic Books.

Bender, Rolf, and Christoph Strecker. 1978. "Access to Justice in the Federal Republic of Germany," in M. Cappelletti and B. Garth (eds.) *Access to Justice*, vol. 1, bk. 2. Leyden: Sijthoff and Nordhoff, and Milan: Giuffre.

Bendix, Reinhardt, and Guenther Roth. 1971. *Scholarship and Partisanship: Essays on Max Weber*. Berkeley: University of California Press.

Benson, Kenneth F. 1975. "The Interorganizational Network as a Political Economy." 20 *Administrative Science Quarterly*, 229.

Berger, Raoul. 1977. *Government by Judiciary*. Cambridge: Harvard University Press.

Berkson, Larry, and Steven Hays. 1975. "The Court Managers: An Exploratory Study of Backgrounds and Attitudes." Master's thesis, University of Florida.

_____, and Susan Carbon. 1976. *Managing the State Courts*. St. Paul: West Publishing Co.

_____. 1978. *Court Unification: History, Politics, and Implementation*. Washington, D.C.: U.S. Government Printing Office.

Berlant, Jeffrey L. 1975. *Profession and Monopoly: A Study of Medicine in the United States and Great Britain*. Berkeley: University of California Press.

Berle, Adolf A., and Gardner C. Means. 1932. *The Modern Corporation and Private Property*. New York: Macmillan Publishing Co., Inc.

Bernstein, Barton. 1968. "The New Deal: The Conservative Achievement of Liberal Reform," in B. Bernstein (ed.) *Towards a New Past: Dissenting Essays in American History.* New York: Random House.

Bernstein, Marver. 1955. *Regulating Business by Independent Commission.* Princeton: Princeton University Press.

Bhaskar, Roy. 1979. *The Possibility of Naturalism.* Brighton: Harvester.

Bickel, Alexander. 1962. *The Least Dangerous Branch: The Supreme Court at the Bar of Politics.* Indianapolis: The Bobbs-Merrill Co.

Bidwell, Charles E., and John D. Kasarda. 1985. *The Organization and its Ecosystem: A Theory of Structuring in Organizations.* Greenwich, Conn.: JAI Press.

Bird, Susan W. 1975. "The Assignment of Cases to Federal District Court Judges." 27 *Stanford Law Review,* 1975.

Black, Donald J. 1973a. "The Boundaries of Legal Sociology," in D. Black and M. Mileski (eds.) *The Social Organization of Law.* New York: Seminar Press.

———. 1973b. "The Mobilization of Law." 2 *Journal of Legal Studies,* 125.

———. 1976. *The Behavior of Law.* New York: Academic Press.

———, and M. Mileski (eds.). *The Social Organization of Law.* New York: Seminar Press.

Blau, Peter, Wolf Heydebrand, and Robert Stauffer. 1966. "The Structure of Small Bureaucracies." 31 *American Sociological Review,* 197.

Blegvad, Britt-Mari. 1983. "Accessibility and Dispute Treatment: The Case of the Consumer in Denmark," in M. Cain and K. Kulcsar (eds.) *Disputes and the Law.* Budapest: Akademiai Kiado.

Block, Fred. 1977. "The Ruling Class Does Not Rule: Notes on the Marxist Theory of the State." 7 *Socialist Review* 6.

Blumberg, Abraham S. 1967. *Criminal Justice.* Chicago: Quadrangle Books.

———. 1970. *The Scales of Justice.* Chicago: Aldine Publishing Company.

Bottomore, Tom. 1964. *Classes in Modern Society.* New York: Basic Books.

Bourdieu, Pierre. 1977. *Outline of a Theory of Practice.* Cambridge: Cambridge University Press.

Boyum, Keith D., and Samuel Krislov (eds.). 1980. *Forecasting the Impact of Legislation on Courts.* Washington, D.C.: National Academy Press.

———, and Lynn Mather. 1983. (eds.) *Empirical Theory of Courts.* New York: Longman Press.

Boyer, Paul, and Stephen Nissenbaum. 1974. *Salem Possessed: The Social Origins of Witchcraft.* Cambridge: Harvard University Press.

Braverman, Harry. 1974. *Labor and Monopoly Capital*. New York: Monthly Review Press.

Bredemeier, Harry C. 1962. "Law as an Integrative Mechanism," in W. Evan (ed.) *Law and Society*. Glencoe, Ill: Free Press.

Brereton, David, and Jonathan D. Casper. 1981-82. "Does it Pay to Plead Guilty? Differential Sentencing and the Functioning of Criminal Courts." 16 *Law and Society Review*, 45.

Breyer, Stephen E., and Richard B. Stewart. 1979. *Administrative Law and Regulatory Policy*. Boston: Little, Brown and Company.

Brubacher, J., and W. Rudy. 1976. *Higher Education in Transition: A History of American Colleges and Universities, 1636-1968*. New York: Harper & Row, Publishers.

Bucholz, R.E., et al. 1978. "The Remedial Process in Institutional Reform." 29 *Columbia Law Review*, 893.

Burbank, Stephen. 1982. "The Rules Enabling Act of 1934." 130 *University of Pennsylvania Law Review*, 1015.

Budget of the United States Government, FY 1922, 1932, 1942, 1952, 1962, 1972, 1984. Washington, D.C.: Government Printing Office.

Burger, Warren E. 1971. "Remarks on the State of the Federal Judiciary," in J. II. James (ed.), *Crisis in the Courts*. New York: David McKay Co., Inc.

———. 1972. "The State of the Federal Judiciary." 58 *American Bar Association Journal*, 1049.

———. 1976. "Agenda for 2000 A.D.—Need for Systematic Anticipation." Keynote address at the National Conference on the Causes of Popular Dissatisfaction with the Administration of Justice, St. Paul, Minnesota.

Burnstein, Irving. 1971. *The Turbulent Years*. Boston: Houghton Mifflin Company.

Cahill, Fred V. 1952. *Judicial Legislation: A Study in American Legal Theory*. New York: Ronald Press Company.

Cain, Maureen. 1985. "Beyond Informal Justice." 9 *Contemporary Crises*, 335.

Calabresi, Guido. 1970. *The Cost of Accidents: A Legal and Economic Analysis*. New Haven: Yale University Press.

Callan, Sam W. 1979. "An Experience in Justice Without Plea Negotiation." 13 *Law and Society Review*, 327.

Cannon, Mark. 1975. "An Administrator's View of the Supreme Court." 22 *Federal Bar News* (April 1975).

Carroll, Glen R. 1984. "Organizational Ecology." 10 *Annual Review of Sociology*, 71.

———. 1985. "Concentration and Specialization: Dynamics of Niche Width in Populations of Organizations." 90 *American Journal of Sociology*, 1262.

Casper, Jonathan D. 1972. *American Criminal Justice: The Defendant's Perspective.* Washington, D.C.: U.S. Government Printing Office.

――――. 1979. "Reformers vs. Abolitionists: Some Notes for Further Research on Plea Bargaining." 13 *Law and Society Review,* 567.

Casper, Gerhard, and Posner, Richard A. 1974. "A Study of the Supreme Court's Caseload." 3 *Journal of Legal Studies,* 339.

Castels, Manuel. 1980. *The Economic Crisis and American Society.* Princeton, N.J.: Princeton University Press.

Chandler, Alfred D. 1977. *The Visible Hand.* Cambridge: Harvard University Press.

Chandler, Henry P. 1963. "Some Main Advances in the Federal Judicial System: 1922-1947." 31 *Federal Rules Decisions, 1.*

Chase, Harold W. 1972. *Federal Judges: The Appointing Process.* Minneapolis: The University of Minnesota Press.

Chayes, Abram. 1976. "The Role of the Judge in Public Law Litigation." 89 *Harvard Law Review,* 1281.

Child, John. 1973. "Strategies of Control and Organizational Behavior." 18 *Administrative Science Quarterly,* 1.

Choper, Jesse H. 1980. *Judicial Review and the National Political Process: A Functional Reconsideration of the Role of the Supreme Court.* Chicago: University of Chicago Press.

Church, Thomas W., Jr. 1976. "Plea Bargains, Concessions and the Courts: Analysis of a Quasi-Experiment." 10 *Law and Society Review,* 377.

――――. 1985. "Examining Local Legal Culture." 1985 *American Bar Foundation Research Journal,* 449.

――――, et al. 1979. "Justice Delayed: The Pace of Litigation in Urban Trial Courts." Williamsburg, Va.: National Center for State Courts.

Clark, David. 1981. "Adjudication to Administration: A Statistical Analysis of Federal District Courts in the Twentieth Century." 55 *Southern California Law Review,* 65.

Cohen, Joshua, and Joel Rogers. 1983. *On Democracy.* New York: Penguin.

――――. 1986. "The True Cost of Intervention." 242 *The Nation* (12 April), 513.

Cole, George F. 1970. "The Decision to Prosecute." 4 *Law and Society Review,* 331.

――――, 1973. *Politics and the Administration of Justice.* Beverly Hills: Sage.

Commager, Henry Steele. 1950. *The American Mind: An Interpretation of American Thought and Character Since the 1880's.* New Haven, Conn.: Yale University Press.

Commons, John R. 1924. *Legal Foundations of Capitalism.* New York: MacMillan and Company.

Congressional Record. 94 (II), 80th Congress, 2nd Session.

Connolly, Paul R., Edith Holloman, and Michael H. Kuhlman. 1978. "Judicial Controls and the Civil Litigative Process: Discovery." Washington, D.C.: Federal Judicial Center.

Connolly, William. 1969. "The Challenge to Pluralist Theory," in W. Connolly (ed.) *The Bias of Pluralism.* Chicago: Aldine, Atherton.

Cook, Beverly B. 1970. "The Politics of Piecemeal Reform of Kansas Courts." 53 *Judicature,* 274.

———. 1971. "The Socialization of New Federal Judges: Impact on District Court Business." 1971 *Washington University Law Quarterly,* 253.

Cox, Archibald. 1976. *The Role of the Supreme Court in American Government.* New York: Oxford University Press.

Crenson, Matthew A. 1975. *The Federal Machine: Beginning of Bureaucracy in Jacksonian America.* Baltimore: The John Hopkins University Press.

Cunningham, H. Stuart. 1980. "Determining Judgeship Needs: A Study of the Process of Creating Federal Judgeships." Unpublished.

Cyert, Richard, and James March. 1963. *A Behavioral Theory of the Firm.* Englewood Cliffs, N.J.: Prentice-Hall.

Dahrendorf, Ralf. 1959. *Class and Class Conflict in Industrial Society.* Stanford: Stanford University Press.

Daniels, Stephen. 1984. "Ladders and Bushes: The Problem of Caseload and Studying Courts Over Time." 1984 *American Bar Foundation Research Journal,* 751.

———. 1985. "We Are Not a Litigious Society." 18 *Judges Journal* (Spring).

Danielson, Michael N. 1976. *The Politics of Exclusion.* New York: Columbia University Press.

Davis, James. 1979. "The Sentencing Disposition of New York Lower Court Criminal Judges." Ph.D. Diss. Department of Sociology, New York University.

Davis, K. C. 1977. *Discretionary Justice: A Preliminary Inquiry.* Urbana: University of Illinois Press.

Denzin, Norman K. 1978. *The Research Act.* New York: McGraw-Hill Book Company.

Diamond, Stanley. 1974. "The Rule of Law versus the Order of Custom," in S. Diamond (ed.) *In Search of the Primitive.* New Brunswick, N.J.: Dutton.

DiMaggio, Paul, and Walter Powell. 1983. "The Iron Cage Revisited: Institutional Isomorphism and Collective Rationality in Organizational Fields." 48 *American Sociological Review,* 147.

Dixon, Jo. 1988. "The Organizational Context of Criminal Sentencing: Structure, Systems, and Processes." Ph.D. Diss., Department of Sociology, Indiana University.

Dolbeare, Kenneth. 1969. "The Federal Courts and Urban Public Policy: An Exploratory Study (1960-1967)," in J. Grossman and J. Tannenhaus. (eds.) *Frontiers of Judicial Research.* New York: John Wiley & Sons.

Downie, Leonard, Jr. 1971. *Justice Denied: The Case for Reform of the Courts.* New York: Praeger Publishers.

Dubois, Philip. 1982. *The Analysis of Judicial Reform.* Lexington, Mass.: Lexington Books.

_____. 1984. Administrative Structures in Large District Courts. Washington, D.C.: Federal Judicial Center.

Duncan, Otis, and Leo F. Schnore. 1959. "Cultural, Behavioral and Ecological Perspectives in the Study of Organizations." 65 *American Journal of Sociology,* 132.

Durkheim, Emile. 1964. *The Division of Labor in Society.* Glencoe: Free Press.

Edwards, Harry T. 1983. "The Rising Workload and Perceived 'Bureaucracy' of the Federal Courts: A Causation-Based Approach to the Search for Appropriate Remedies." 1983 *Iowa Law Review,* 874.

_____. 1986. "Alternative Dispute Resolution: Panacea or Anathema?" 99 *Harvard Law Review,* 668-684.

Edwards, Richard C. 1975. "The Social Relations of Production in Firm and Labor Market Structure." 5 *Politics and Society.* 83-109.

_____. 1979. *Contested Terrain: The Transformation of the Workplace in the Twentieth Century.* New York: Basic Books.

Ehrenreich, Barbara, and John Ehrenreich. 1977. "The New Left and the Professional-Managerial Class." 11 *Radical America,* 7.

Eisenberg, Theodore, and Stewart Schwab. 1986. "The Reality of Constitutional Tort Litigation." (11 April).

Eisenstein, James. 1973. *Politics and the Legal Process.* New York: Harper & Row Publishers.

_____, Roy B. Flemming, and Peter Nardulli. 1988. *The Contours of Justice: Communities and their Courts.* Boston: Little, Brown and Company.

_____, and Herbert Jacob. 1977. *Felony Justice: An Organizational Analysis of Criminal Courts.* Boston: Little, Brown and Company.

Eldridge, William B. 1984. The District Court Executive Pilot Program. Washington, D.C.: Federal Judicial Center.

Elliott, E. Donald. 1986. "Managerial Judging and the Evolution of Procedure." 53 *University of Chicago Law Review*, 306.

Emery, F. E., and E. L. Trist. 1965. "The Causal Texture of Organizational Environments." 18 *Human Relations*, 21.

Erikson, Kai T. 1966. *Wayward Puritans: A Study in the Sociology of Deviance*. New York: John Wiley & Sons.

Etheridge, Carolyn F. 1973. "Lawyers vs. Indigents: Conflict of Interest in Professional—Client Relations in the Legal Profession," in E. Freidson (ed.) *The Professions and Their Prospects*. Beverly Hills: Sage.

Evan, William. 1976. *Organizational Theory*. New York: Wiley, Interscience.

Fainstein, Norman, and Susan Fainstein. 1980. "The Political Economy of American Bureaucracy," in C. Weiss and A. Barton (eds.) *Making Bureaucracies Work*. Beverly Hills: Sage.

Federal Judicial Center. 1971. 1969-70 Federal District Court Time Study. Washington, D.C.

_____ . 1973. Annual Report of the Federal Judicial Center. Washington, D.C.

Federalist Papers. 1961. Federalist Nos. 9 & 10., 78 New York: Mentor Books.

Feeley, Malcolm. 1976. "The Concept of Laws in Social Science." 10 *Law and Society Review*, 497.

_____ . 1979. "Pleading Guilty in Lower Courts." 13 *Law and Society Review*, 461.

_____ . 1979. *The Process Is the Punishment*. New York: Russell Sage Foundation.

_____ . 1983. *Court Reform on Trial: Why Simple Solutions Fail*. New York: Basic Books.

Felstiner, William C. F. 1974. "Influences of Social Organization on Dispute Processing." 9 *Law and Society Review*, 63.

Ferguson, Thomas, and Joel Rogers, (eds.). 1981. *The Hidden Election*. New York: Pantheon Books.

Firebaugh, Glenn, and Jack Gibbs. 1985. "Ratio Variables." 50 *American Sociological Review*, 713.

Fish, Peter G. 1973. *The Politics of Federal Judicial Administration*. Princeton: Princeton University Press.

Fiss, Owen. 1979. "The Forms of Justice." 93 *Harvard Law Review*, 1.

_____ . 1983. "The Bureaucratization of the Judiciary." 92 *Yale Law Journal*, 1442.

_____ . 1984. "Against Settlement," 93 *Yale Law Journal*, 1083.

Flanders, Steven. 1976. District Courts Studies Project; Interim Report. Washington, D.C.: Federal Judicial Center.

———. 1977. Case Management and Court Management in the United States District Courts. Washington, D.C.: Federal Judicial Center.

———. 1980. "Modelling Court Delay." 2 *Law and Policy Quarterly,* 305.

———. 1984. "Blind Umpires—A Response to Resnik." 35 *Hastings Law Journal,* 505.

Flemming, Roy, Peter Nardulli, and James Eisenstein. 1987. "The Timing of Justice: A Macro-Level Analysis of the Pace of Felony Dispositions in Urban Trial Courts." 9 *Law and Policy,* 179.

Ford Foundation. 1978. *New Approaches to Conflict Resolution.* New York.

Foucault, Michel. 1979. *Discipline and Punish: The Birth of the Prison.* New York: Vintage Books.

Frank, Jerome. 1949. *Courts on Trial: Myth and Reality in American Justice.* Princeton: Princeton University Press.

Frank, John P. 1948. "Historical Bases of the Federal Judicial System." 13 *Law and Contemporary Problems,* 3.

———. 1969. *American Law: The Case for Radical Reform.* London: MacMillan & Co.

Frankel, Ernst. 1941. *The Dual State.* New York: Oxford University Press.

Frankel, Marvin. 1975. "The Search for Truth: An Umpireal View." 123 *University of Pennsylvania Law Review,* 1031.

Frankfurter, Felix, and James M. Landis. 1928. *The Business of the Supreme Court: A Study of the Federal Judicial System.* New York: MacMillan Publishing Co.

Fraser, Andrew. 1978. "The Legal Theory We Need Now." 8 *Socialist Review* (nos. 40-41), 147.

Freedman, James O. 1978. *Crisis and Legitimacy: The Administrative Process and American Government.* Cambridge: Cambridge University Press.

Freeman, Alan. 1978. "Legitimizing Racial Discrimination through Antidiscrimination Law: A Critical Review of Supreme Court Doctrine." 1978 *Minnesota Law Review,* 62.

Freeman, John H., and Jerrold E. Kronenfeld. 1973. "Problems of Definitional Dependency: The Case of Administrative Intensity." 52 *Social Forces,* 108.

Freiberg, Arie, and Pat O'Malley. 1984. "State Intervention and the Civil Offense." 18 *Law and Society Review,* 373.

Freidson, Eliot. 1970. *Professional Dominance: The Social Structure of Medical Care.* New York: Atherton.

———. 1971. *The Profession of Medicine: A Study of the Sociology of Knowledge.* New York: Dodd, Mead & Company.

———. 1986. *Professional Powers: A Study of the Institutionalization of Formal Knowledge.* Chicago: University of Chicago Press.

Friedman, Lawrence M. 1967. "Legal Rules and the Process of Social Change." 19 *Stanford Law Review,* 786.

———. 1973. *A History of American Law.* New York: Simon & Schuster.

———. 1975. *The Legal System.* New York: Russell Sage Foundation.

———. 1979. "Plea Bargaining in Historical Perspective." 13 *Law and Society Review,* 247.

———, and Stewart Macaulay. (eds.) 1977. *Law and the Behavioral Sciences,* 2d ed. Indianapolis: The Bobbs-Merrill Co., Inc.

———, and Robert V. Percival. 1976. "A Tale of Two Courts: Litigation in Alameda and San Benito County." 10 *Law and Society Review,* 267.

Friendly, Henry J. 1973. *Federal Jurisdiction: A General View.* New York: Columbia University Press.

Friesen, Ernest C., Jr., Edward C. Gallas, and Nesta M. Gallas, 1971. *Managing the Courts.* Indianapolis: The Bobbs-Merrill Co.

Fuller, Lon L. 1967. "The Adversary System." Washington, D.C.: The Voice of America Forum Lectures, lecture series 3.

———. 1981. "The Forms and Limits of Adjudication," in K.I. Winston (ed.) *The Principles of Social Order.* Durham, N.C.: Duke University Press.

Galambos, Louis. 1970. "The Emerging Organizational Synthesis in Modern American History." 44 *Business History Review,* 279.

Galanter, Marc. 1974. "Why the 'Haves' Come Out Ahead: Speculation on the Limits of Legal Change." 9 *Law and Society Review,* 95.

———. 1975. "Afterword: Explaining Litigation." 9 *Law and Society Review,* 347.

———. 1977. "Notes on the Future of Social Research in Law," in L. M. Friedman and S. Macaulay (eds.) *Law and the Behavioral Sciences.* Indianapolis: The Bobbs-Merrill Co.

———. 1981. "Justice in Many Rooms" 19 *Journal of Legal Pluralism,* 1.

———. 1983. "Reading the Landscape of Disputes: What We Know and Don't Know (and Think We Know) about our Allegedly Litigious Society." 31 *UCLA Law Review,* 4.

———. 1985. "'. . . Settlement Judge, Not a Trial Judge:' Judicial Mediation in the United States." 12 *Journal of Law and Society,* 1.

————. 1986. "The Emergence of the Judge as a Mediator in Civil Cases." 69 *Judicature*, 257.

Gallas, Geoff. 1976. "The Conventional Wisdom of State Court Administration: A Critical Assessment and an Alternative Approach." 2 *Justice System Journal*, 35.

Garfinkel, Harold. 1956. "Conditions of Successful Degradation Ceremonies." 61 *American Journal of Sociology*, 420.

Garrow, David. 1986. *Bearing the Cross: Martin Luther King Jr. and the Southern Christian Leadership Conference.* New York: William Morrow & Co.

Genovese, Eugene D. 1985. "Law and the Economy in Capitalist America." 1985 *American Bar Foundation Research Journal*, 113.

Giddens, Anthony. 1973. *The Class Structure of Advanced Societies.* New York: Harper & Row Publishers.

————. 1984. *The Constitution of Society.* Berkeley: University of California Press.

Gillespie, Robert W. 1976. "The Production of Court Services: An Analysis of Scale Effects and Other Factors." 5 *The Journal of Legal Studies*, 243.

Gilligan, Carol. 1982. *In a Different Voice: Psychological Theory and Women's Development.* Cambridge: Harvard University Press.

Glaser. William A. 1968. *Pretrial Discovery and the Adversary System.* New York: Russell Sage Foundation.

Glazer, Nathan. 1975. "Toward an Imperial Judiciary." 41 *The Public Interest*, 104.

Goldberg, Stephen B., Eric D. Green, and Frank E.A. Sander, 1986. "Alternative Dispute Resolution Problems and Prospects: Looking to the Future." 69 *Judicature*, 291.

Goldfarb, Ronald. 1975. *Jails: The Ultimate Ghetto of the Criminal Justice System.* New York: Anchor Books.

————, and Linda R. Singer. 1973. *After Conviction.* New York: Simon & Schuster.

Goldman, Jerry, et al. 1976. "Caseload Forecasting Models for Federal District Courts." 5 *Journal of Legal Studies*, 201.

Goldman, Lucien. 1969. *The Human Sciences and Philosophy.* London: Jonathan Cape.

Goldman, Sheldon, and Thomas P. Jahnige. 1985. *The Federal Courts as a Political System* (3rd ed.) New York: Harper & Row, Publishers.

————, and Austin Sarat. (eds.) 1978. *American Court Systems: Readings in Judicial Process and Behavior.* San Francisco: W. H. Freeman.

Goldstein, Richard. 1985. "Two Types of Statistical Errors in Employment Discrimination Cases." 26 *Jurimetrics: Journal of Law, Science, and Technology*, 32.

Graham, Fred P. 1970. *The Due Process Revolution.* New York: Harper & Row, Publishers.

Grau, Charles W. 1978. *Judicial Rulemaking: Administration, Access and Accountability.* Chicago: American Judicature Society.

————. 1980. "Whatever Happened to Politics? A Critique of Structuralist Marxist Accounts of State and Law." 1 *Law and State,* 196.

————, and Arlene Sheskin. 1982. *Ruling Out Delay: The Impact of Ohio's Rules of Superintendence on the Administration of Justice.* Chicago: American Judicature Society.

Greenberg, David. F. 1975. "Problems in Community Corrections." 10 *Issues in Criminology,* 1.

————, and Fay Stender. 1972. "The Prison as a Lawless Agency." 21 *Buffalo Law Review,* 799.

Gregory, Charles O., and Harold A. Katz. 1979. *Labor and the Law.* New York: W. W. Norton & Company, Inc.

Griffin, Larry J., Joel A. Devine, and Michael Wallace, 1982. "Monopoly Capital, Organized Labor, and Military Expenditures in the United States, 1949-1976." 88 *American Journal of Sociology,* 113.

Grossman, Joel B., and Austin Sarat. 1975. "Litigation in the Federal Courts." 9 *Law and Society Review,* 321.

Habermas, Jürgen. 1971. *Knowledge and Human Interests.* Boston: Beacon Press.

————. 1975. *Legitimation Crisis.* Boston: Beacon Press.

————. 1979. *Communication and the Evolution of Society.* Boston: Beacon Press.

Hagan, John, and Ilene Bernstein. 1979. "The Sentence Bargaining of Upperworld and Underworld Crime in Ten Federal District Courts." 13 *Law and Society Review,* 467.

Hall, Richard. 1963. "The Concept of Bureaucracy." 69 *American Journal of Sociology,* 32.

————. 1968. "Professionalization and Bureaucratization." 33 *American Sociological Review,* 92.

————. 1987. *Organizations: Structure, Resources, and Outcomes.* (4th ed.) New Jersey: Prentice-Hall.

Haller, Mark. 1979. "Plea Bargaining: The Nineteenth Century Context." 13 *Law and Society Review,* 273.

Halliday, Terence C. 1987. *Beyond Monopoly: Lawyers, State Crises, and Professional Empowerment.* Chicago: University of Chicago Press.

Handler, Joel F. 1978. *Social Movements and the Legal System: A Theory of Law Reform and Social Change.* New York: Academic Press.

———. 1979. *Protecting the Social Service Client: Legal and Structural Controls on Official Discretion.* New York: Academic Press.

Hannan, Michael, and John Freeman. 1977. "The Population Ecology of Organizations." 82 *American Journal of Sociology,* 929.

———. 1984. "Structural Inertia and Organizational Change." 49 *American Sociological Review,* 149.

Harrington, Christine B. 1982. "Delegalization Reform Movement: A Historical Analysis," in R. Abel (ed.) *The Politics of Informal Justice,* vol. 1. New York: Academic Press.

———. 1984. "The Politics of Participation and Non-participation in Dispute Processes." 6 *Law and Policy,* 203.

———. 1985. *Shadow Justice: The Ideology and Institutionalization of Alternatives to Court.* Westport, Conn.: Greenwood Press.

Hart, Henry, and Herbert Wechsler (eds.) 1953. *The Federal Courts and the Federal System.* Brooklyn: Foundation Press.

Hartje, John. 1975. "The Systems Approach to Criminal Justice Administration." 25 *Buffalo Law Review,* 303.

Hartz, Louis. 1955. *The Liberal Tradition in America.* New York: Harcourt, Brace & World.

Harvard Law Review. 1977. "Note: Plea Bargaining and the Transformation of the Criminal Process." 90 *Harvard Law Review,* 564.

Harvey, David. 1976. "Labor, Capital and Class Struggle Around the Built Environment in Advanced Capitalist Societies." 6 *Politics and Society,* 265.

Haskell, Thomas E. 1977. *The Emergence of Professional Social Science: The American Social Science Association and the Nineteenth Century Crisis of Authority.* Urbana: University of Illinois Press.

Haug, Marie. 1973. "Deprofessionalization: An Alternate Hypothesis for the Future." 20 *Sociological Review Monograph,* 195.

———. 1977. "Computer Technology and the Obsolescence of the Concept of Profession," in M. R. Haug and J. Dofny (eds.) *Work and Technology.* Beverly Hills: Sage.

Hawley, Amos. 1950. *Human Ecology.* New York: Ronald.

———. 1968. "Human Ecology," in D. Sills (ed.) *International Encyclopedia of the Social Sciences,* New York: MacMillan Publishing Co.

Hawley, Ellis. 1966. *The New Deal and the Problem of Monopoly.* Princeton: Princeton University Press.

Hay, Douglas. 1975. "Property, Authority and the Criminal Law," in D. Hay, et al. (eds.) *Albion's Fatal Tree: Crime and Society in Eighteenth Century England.* New York: Pantheon Books.

Heinz, John P., and Edward O. Laumann. 1982. *Chicago Lawyers: The Social Structure of the Bar.* New York: Russell Sage Foundation and Basic Books.

Henderson, Thomas A., et al. 1981. "Organizational Design for Courts," in James A. Kramer (ed.) *Courts and Judges.* Beverly Hills: Sage.

Hensler, Deborah R. 1986. "What We Know and Don't Know About Court-Administered Arbitration." 69 *Judicature*, 270.

Hetzler, Antoinette. 1986. "The Role of Lay Counsels in Democratic Decision Making." 10 *International Journal of the Sociology of Law*, 395.

Heumann, Milton. 1975. "A Note on Plea Bargaining and Case Pressure." 9 *Law and Society Review*, 515.

———— 1977. *Plea Bargaining: The Experiences of Prosecutors, Judges and Defense Attorneys.* Chicago: University of Chicago Press.

Heydebrand, Wolf. 1972. "Review of Talcott Parsons: *The System of Modern Societies.* " *1 Contemporary Sociology*, 387.

————,(ed). 1973. *Comparative Organizations: The Results of Empirical Research.* Englewood Cliffs, N. J.: Prentice-Hall

————. 1973. *Hospital Bureaucracy.* New York: Dunellen Press.

————. 1974. "Adjudication versus Administration: Organizational Structure and Productivity in Federal District Courts: A Research Proposal." New York: Russell Sage Foundation.

————. 1977. "The Context of Public Bureaucracies: An Organizational Analysis of Federal District Courts." 11 *Law and Society Review*, 759.

————. 1979. "The Technocratic Administration of Justice." 2 *Research in Law and Sociology*, 29.

————. 1981. "Marxist Structuralism," in Peter Blau and Robert K. Merton (eds.) *Continuities in Structural Inquiry.* Beverly Hills: Sage.

————. 1982. "Die Technokratisierung des Rechts und der Justizverwaltung." 8 *Jahrbuch für Rechtssoziologie und Rechtstheorie*, 93.

————. 1983. "Technocratic Corporatism: Toward a Theory of Occupational and Organizational Transformation," in R. Hall and R. Quinn (eds.) *Organizational Theory and Public Policy.* Beverly Hills: Sage.

————. 1984. "Technocratic Administration: Beyond Weber's Bureaucracy." Paper presented at the Annual Meetings of the American Sociological Association, San Antonio, Texas.

———. 1985. "Technarchy and Neo-Corporatism: Toward a Theory of Organizational Change Under Advanced Capitalism and Early State Socialism." 6 *Current Perspectives in Social Theory*, 71.

———, and Carroll Seron, 1981. "The Double Bind of the Capitalist Judicial System." 9 *International Journal of the Sociology of Law*, 407.

———. 1986. "The Rising Demand for Court Services: A Structural Explanation of the Caseload of U. S. District Courts." 11 *The Justice System Journal*, 303.

———. 1987. "The Organizational Structure of American Federal Trial Courts: Professional Adjudication versus Technocratic Administration," 2 *International Review of Sociology*, 63.

Higginbotham, Patrick E. 1980. "Bureaucracy—The Carcinoma of the Federal Judiciary." 31 *Alabama Law Review*, 261.

Hirschman, Albert O. 1970. *Exit, Voice and Loyalty*. Cambridge: Harvard University Press.

Hodge, William, Paul Siegel, and Peter Rossi. 1964. "Occupational Prestige in the United States: 1925-1963." 70 *American Journal of Sociology*, 286.

Hoffman, Richard. 1982. "The Bureaucratic Spectre: The Newest Challenge to the Courts." 66 *Judicature*, 60.

Hofstadter, Richard. 1955. *The Age of Reform*. New York: Vintage Books.

Holland, Kenneth M. 1982. "Twilight of Adversariness: Trends in Civil Justice," in Philip Dubois (ed.) *The Analysis of Judicial Reform*. Lexington, Mass.: D. C. Heath & Company.

Holloway, John, and Sol Picciotto, (eds.). 1979. *State and Capital: A Marxist Debate*. Austin: University of Texas Press.

Horowitz, Donald L. 1977. *The Courts and Social Policy*. Washington, D. C.: The Brookings Institution.

Horwitz, Morton. 1977. *The Transformation of American Law: 1780-1860*. Cambridge: Harvard University Press.

Howard, J. Woodford. 1981. *Courts of Appeals in the Federal Judicial System*. Princeton: Princeton University Press.

Hunt, Alan. 1978. *The Sociological Movement in Law*. London: MacMillan & Co.

———. 1985. "The Ideology of Law: Advances and Problems in Recent Applications of the Concept of Ideology to the Analysis of Law." 19 *Law and Society Review*, 11.

Hurst, James Willard. 1950. *The Growth of American Law*. Boston: Little, Brown and Company.

_____ . 1980-81. "The Functions of Courts in the United States: 1950-1980." 15 *Law and Society Review*, 401.

Hyde, Alan. 1983. "The Concept of Legitimation in the Sociology of Law." 1983 *Wisconsin Law Review*, 1.

Institute of Judicial Administration. 1965. *Judicial Education in the United States*. New York: Institute of Judicial Administration.

Irons, Peter H. 1982. *The New Deal Lawyers*. Princeton, N. J.: Princeton University Press.

Israel, Jerry (ed.). 1972. *Building the Organizational Society: Essays on Associational Activities in Modern America*. New York: The Free Press.

Jacob, Herbert. 1972. *Justice in America*. Boston: Little Brown and Company.

Jaffe, Louis I. 1954. "The Effective Limits of Administrative Process: A Reevaluation." 68 *Harvard Law Review*, 67.

_____ . 1965. *Judicial Control of Administrative Action*. Boston: Little, Brown and Company.

Jahnige, Thomas, and Sheldon Goldman (eds.). 1968. *The Federal Judicial System*. New York: Holt, Rinehart and Winston.

James, Howard. 1971. *Crisis in the Courts*. New York: David McKay Co.

Johnson, Earl Jr., et al. 1977. "Outside the Courts: A Survey of Diversion Alternatives in Civil Cases." Denver: National Center for the State Courts.

Judicial Conference Report. 1952. Washington, D.C.: U.S. Government Printing Office.

_____ . 1970. Washington, D.C.: U.S. Government Printing Office.

Kahn-Freund, Otto. 1949. Introduction to *The Institutions of Private Law and their Social Functions*, by Karl Renner. London: Routledge & Kegan Paul.

Kalven, Harry, and Hans Zeisel. 1966. *The American Jury*. Chicago: University of Chicago Press.

Kamenka, Eugene, and Alice Erh-Soon Tay. 1975. "Beyond Bourgeois Individualism: The Contemporary Crisis in Law and Legal Ideology," in E. Kamenka and R. S. Neale (eds.) *Feudalism, Capitalism, and Beyond*. London and Canberra.

Kanter, Rosabeth Moss. 1976. *Men and Women of the Corporation*. New York: The Free Press.

Kariel, Henry S. 1961. *The Decline of American Pluralism*. Stanford: Stanford University Press.

Kasarda, John and Charles Bidwell. 1984. "A Human Ecological Theory of Organizational Structure." in M. Micklin and H. M. Choldin (eds.) *Sociological Human Ecology: Comtemporary Issues and Applicaitons*. Boulder, Col: Westview Press.

Katz, Lewis R., Lawrence Litwin, and Richard Bamberger. 1972. *Justice Is the Crime: Pretrial Delay in Felony Cases*. Cleveland: Case Western Reserve University Press.

Katz, Michael B. 1968. *The Irony of Early School Reform*. Cambridge: Harvard University Press.

———. 1978. "Origins of the Institutional State." 1 *Marxist Perspectives*, 6.

Kaufman, Irving R. 1962. "The Philosophy of Effective Supervision over Litigation." 29 *Federal Rules Decisions*, 207.

Kelman, Mark. 1979. "Choice and Utility." 1979. *University of Wisconsin Law Review*, 769.

Kennedy, Duncan. 1976. "Form and Substance in Private Law Adjudication." 89 *Harvard Law Review*, 1685.

Kerwin, Cornelius M. 1982. "Justice-Impact Statements and Court Management: And Never the Twain Shall Meet," in Philip Dubois (ed.) *The Analysis of Judicial Reform*. Lexington, Mass.: D. C. Heath & Company.

Kidder, Robert. 1980-81. "The End of the Road? Problems in the Analysis of Disputes." 15 *Law and Society Review*, 717.

Kinoy, Arthur. 1983. *Rights on Trial*. Cambirdge: Harvard University Press.

Kipnis, Kenneth. 1979. "Plea Bargaining: A Critic's Rejoinder," 13 *Law and Society Review*, 555.

Kirchheimer, Otto. 1961. *Political Justice: The Use of Legal Procedure for Political Ends*. Princeton, N. J.: Princeton University Press.

Kittrie, Nicholas N. 1971. *The Right to Be Different*. Baltimore: The Johns Hopkins University Press.

Klare, Karl. 1978. "The Judicial Deradicalization of the Wagner Act and the Origins of Modern Legal Consciousness, 1937-1941." 78 *Minnesota Law Review*, 62.

———. 1979. "Law Making as Praxis." 40 *Telos*, 123.

Klein, Fannie, and Ruth J. Witztum. 1973. "Judicial Administration 1972-73." *Annual Survey of American Law*, 717.

Kluger, Richard. 1976. *Simple Justice*. New York: Alfred P. Knopf.

Kohleimer, Louis M. 1969. *The Regulators: Watchdog Agencies and the Public Interest*. New York: Harper & Row, Publishers.

Kolko, Gabriel. 1962. *Wealth and Power in America: An Analysis of Social Class and Income Distribution*. New York: Praeger.

———. 1967. *Triumph of Conservatism*. Chicago: Quadrangle.

———. 1976. *Main Currents in American History*. New York: The Free Press.

Krislov, Samuel. 1968. *The Supreme Court and Political Freedom*. New York: The Free Press.

_____ . 1983. "Theoretical Perspectives on Caseload Studies: A Critique and Beginning," in K. O. Boyum and L. Mather (eds.) *Empirical Studies of Courts*. New York: Longman.

_____ . 1986. "Afterword." 11 *The Justice System Journal*, 360.

Kritzer, Herbert. 1980-81. "Studying Disputes: Learning from the CLRP Experience." 15 *Law and Society Review*, 503.

_____ . 1982. "The Judge's Role in Pretrial Case Processing: Assessing the Need for Change." 66 *Judicature*, 28.

Lambros, Thomas A. 1985. "The Alternatives Movement: Rekindling America's Creative Spirit." 1 *Ohio State Journal in Dispute Resolution*, 3.

Landes, William N. 1971. "An Economic Analysis of the Courts." 14 *Journal of Law and Economics*, 61.

_____ , and Richard Posner. 1979. "Adjudication as a Private Good." 8 *Journal of Legal Studies*, 235.

Langbein, John H. 1979. "Understanding the Short History of Plea Bargaining." 13 *Law and Society Review*, 261.

_____ . 1983. "Shaping the Eighteenth-Century Criminal Trial: A View from the Ryder Series." 50 *The University of Chicago Law Review*, 1.

Larson, Magali Sarfatti. 1977. *The Rise of Professionalism*. Berkeley: University of California Press.

_____ . 1980. "Proletarianization and Educated Labor." 9 *Theory and Society*, 131.

Laumann, Edward, Joseph Galaskiewicz, and Peter Marsden. 1978. "Community Structure as Interorganizational Linkages." 4 *Annual Review of Sociology*, 455.

Law and Society Review. 1979. Special Issue: Plea Bargaining. 13 *Law and Society Review*.

_____ . 1980-81. Special Issue: Dispute Processing and Civil Litigation. 15 *Law and Society Review*.

_____ . 1988. Special Issue: Law and Ideology. 22 *Law and Society Review*.

Law Enforcement Assistance Administration. 1971. *Justice in the States*: Addresses and papers of the National Conference on the Judiciary. St. Paul, Minn.: West Publishing Co.

Lazerson, Mark. 1981. "In the Halls of Justice, the Only Justice is in the Halls," in R. Abel (ed.) *The Politics of Informalism: The American Experience*. New York: Academic Press.

Lazarsfeld, Paul F., and Herbert Menzel. 1980. "On the Relation between Individual and Collective Properties," in A. Etzioni and E. Lehman (eds.) *A Sociological Reader on Complex Organizations*. New York: Holt, Rinehart and Winston.

Lehman, Edward W. 1988. "The Theory of the State vs. The State of Theory." 53 *American Sociological Review*, 6.

Leibenstein, Harvey. 1960. *Economic Theory and Organizational Analysis*. New York: Harper & Row, Publishers.

Lempert, Richard O. 1978. "More Tales of Two Courts: Exploring Changes in the 'Dispute Settlement Function' of Trial Courts." 13 *Law and Society Review*, 91.

———. 1980-81. "Grievances and Legitimacy: The Beginnings and End of Dispute Settlement." 15 *Law and Society Review*, 707.

Levi, Edward H. 1976. "The Business of Courts." 70 *Federal Rules Decisions*, 212.

Levin, A. Leo. 1983. "Court-Annexed Arbitration." 16 *Journal of Law Reform*, 537.

Lieberman, Jethro K. 1978. *Crisis at the Bar*. New York: W. W. Norton & Company.

———. 1981. *The Litigious Society* New York: Basic Books.

Lind, E. Alan, and John Shapard. 1981. *Evaluation of Court-Annexed Arbitration in Three Federal District Courts*. Washington, D. C.: Federal Judicial Center.

Lindblom, Charles. 1965. *The Intelligence of Democracy*. New York: The Free Press.

Litwak, Eugene, and Lydia Hylton. 1962. "Interorganizational Analysis: A Hypothesis on Coordinating Agencies." 6 *Administrative Science Quarterly*, 395.

Lorch, Robert S. 1969. *Democratic Process and Administrative Law*. Detroit: Wayne State University Press.

Lowi, Theodore. 1969. *The End of Liberalism*. New York: W. W. Norton & Company.

Luhman, Niklas. 1972. *Rechtssoziologie, Vol's 1 & 2* Reinbeck: Rowohlt.

Luskin, Mary Lee, and Robert C. Luskin. 1987. "Case Processing Time in Three Courts." 9 *Law and Policy*, 1.

———, and Jo Dixon. 1986. "Court Organization and Processing Time: Does Structure Make a Difference?" Paper presented a the Annual Meeting of the American Society of Criminology, Atlanta, Georgia.

Macaulay, Stewart. 1966. *Law and the Balance of Power*. New York: Russell Sage Foundation.

"MacNeil-Lehrer Report." 9 July 1979.

Magaziner, Ira C., and Robert B. Reich. 1982. *Minding America's Business*. New York: Vintage Books.

Maine, Sir Henry. [1861] 1917. *Ancient Law*. London: J. Murray.

Maniha, John, and Charles Perrow. 1965. "The Reluctant Organization and the Aggressive Environment." 10 *Administrative Science Quarterly*, 238.

Mannheim, Karl. 1936. *Ideology and Utopia: An Introduction to the Sociology of Knowledge.* New York: Harcourt, Brace & World.

_____ . 1940. *Man and Society in an Age of Reconstruction.* London: Routledge and Kegan Paul.

Marglin, Stephen A. 1974-75. "What Do Bosses Do?" 6 *Review of Radical Political Economics,* 20.

Marquant, James W. and Ben R. Crouch. 1985. "Judicial Reform and Prisoner Control: The Impact of *Ruiz v. Estelle* on a Texas Penitentiary." 19 *Law and Society Review,* 557.

Martinson, Robert. 1966. "The Age of Treatment: Some Implications of the Custody—Treatment Dimension." 2 *Issues in Criminology,* 275.

Marx, Karl. 1967. *Writings of the Young Marx on Philosophy and Society.* L. D. Easton and K. H. Guddat, eds. Garden City, N. Y.: Doubleday.

Mashaw, Jerry L. 1983. *Bureaucratic Justice: Managing Social Security Disability Claims.* New Haven: Yale University Press.

Mayers, Lewis. 1964. *The American Legal System: The Administration of Justice in the United States by Judicial, Administrative, Military and Arbitral Tribunes.* New York: Harper & Row, Publishers.

McCabe, Peter. 1979. "The Federal Magistrates Act of 1979." 16 *Harvard Journal on Legislation,* 343.

McConnell, Grant. 1966. *Private Power and American Democracy.* New York: Alfred A. Knopf.

McCree, Wade. 1981. "Bureaucratic Justice: An Early Warning." 129 *University of Pennsylvania Law Review,* 777.

McGowan, Carl. 1969. *The Organization of Judicial Power in the United States.* Evanston: Northwestern University Press.

McIntosh, Wayne. 1983. "Private Use of a Public Forum: A Long Range View of the Dispute Processing Role of Courts." 77 *American Political Science Review,* 991.

McMillan, Richard, and David Siegel. 1985. "Suggestions for a Fast-Track Option Under the Federal Rules of Civil Procedure." 3 *Alternatives,* 7.

Meador, Daniel J. 1982. "The Role of the Justice Department in Maintaining an Effective Judiciary." 462 *The Annals of the American Academy of Political and Social Science,* 136.

Menkel-Meadow, Carrie. 1984. "Legal Aid in the U. S.: The Professionalization and Politicization of Legal Services in the 1980's." 22 *Osgoode Hall Law Journal,* 29.

_____ . 1985. "For or Against Settlement: Uses and Abuses of the Mandatory Settlement Conference." 33 *U. C. L. A. Law Review,* 485.

———. 1985. "Judges and Settlement: What Part Should Judges Play?" *Trial,* (October) 24.

———. 1985. "Portia in a Different Voice: Speculations on a Women's Lawyering Process." 1 *Berkeley Women's Law Journal,* 39.

Meyer, John, and Brian Rowan. 1983. "Institutionalized Organizations: Formal Structure as Myth and Ceremony," in J. W. Meyer and W. R. Scott (eds.) *Organizational Environments.* Beverly Hills: Sage.

Miller, Arthur S. 1968. *The Supreme Court and American Capitalism.* New York: The Free Press.

———. 1976. *The Modern Corporate State: Private Government and the American Constitution.* Westport, Conn.: Greenwood Press.

Milliband, Ralph. 1969. *The State in Capitalist Society.* London: Weidenfeld and Nicolson.

Mills, C. Wright. 1959. *The Sociological Imagination.* New York: Oxford University Press.

Miner, Roger J. 1987. "Research on Judicial Administration: A Judge's Perspective." 12 *Justice System Journal,* 8.

Mintzberg, Henry. 1979. *The Structure of Organizations.* Englewood Cliffs, N. J.: Prentice-Hall.

Mohr, Lawrence B. 1976. "Organizations, Decisions and Courts." 10 *Law and Society Review,* 621.

Montesquieu. [1748] 1978. *The Spirit of Laws.* London: George Bell & Sons.

Moore, Lloyd. 1973. *The Jury: Tool of Kings, Palladium of Liberty.* Cincinnati: Anderson Publ. Co.

Morgan, Edmund. 1966. *The Puritan Family: Religion and Domestic Relations in Seventeenth-Century New England.* New York: Harper & Row, Publishers.

Munger, Frank. 1988. "Law, Change, and Litigation: A Critical Examination of an Empirical Research Tradition." 22 *Law and Society Review,* 57.

Murphy, Walter. 1959. "Lower Court Checks on Supreme Court Power." 53 *American Political Science Review,* 1017.

Murphy, Walter F., and C. Herman Pritchett (eds.). 1974. *Courts, Judges and Politics.* 2d ed. New York: Random House.

Nader, Laura (ed.). 1980. *No Access to Law: Alternatives to the American Judicial System.* New York: Academic Press.

Nader, Ralph, and Mark Green. 1977. *Corporate Power in America.* New York: Penguin Books.

Nardulli, Peter F. 1978. *The Courtroom Elite: An Organizational Perspective on Criminal Justice*. Cambridge, Mass.: Ballinger.

_____. 1979. "Organizational Analyses of Criminal Courts: An Overview and Some Speculations," in Nardulli (ed.) *The Study of Criminal Courts: Political Perspectives*. Cambridge: Ballinger Press.

National Center for State Courts. 1976. *Parajudges: Their Role in Today's Court System*. Denver, Colo.: National Center for State Courts.

Nelson, Robert. 1983. "The Changing Structure of Opportunity: Recruitment and Careers in Large Law Firms." 1983 *ABF Research Journal*, 109.

_____. 1988. *Partners with Power*. Berkeley: University of California Press.

Nelson, William. 1975. *Americanization of the Common Law: The Impact of Legal Change on Massachusetts Society, 1769-1830*. Cambridge: Harvard University Press.

Neubauer, David, and John Paul Ryan. 1982. "Criminal Courts and the Delivery of Speedy Justice." 7 *Justice System Journal*, 213.

Neumann, Franz. 1957. *The Democratic and the Authoritarian State*. New York: The Free Press.

Newman, Donald J. 1966. *Conviction: The Determining of Guilt or Innocence Without Trial*. Boston: Little, Brown and Company.

New York Times, 15 August 1973.

Nimmer, Raymond T. 1978. *The Nature of System Change: Reform Impact on the Criminal Courts*. Chicago: American Bar Foundation.

Niskanen, William A. 1971. *Bureaucracy and Representative Government*. Chicago: Aldine.

Nonet, Philippe. 1969. *Administrative Justice: Advocacy and Change in Government Agencies*. New York: Russell Sage Foundation.

_____. 1976. "For Jurisprudential Sociology." 10 *Law and Society Review*, 525.

_____, and Philip Selznick. 1978. *Law and Society in Transition: Toward Responsive Law*. New York: Harper & Row, Publishers.

Oakley, John B., and Robert S. Thompson. 1980. *Law Clerks and the Judicial Process*. Berkeley: University of California Press.

O'Connor, James. 1973. *The Fiscal Crisis of the State*. New York: St. Martin's Press.

Offe, Claus. 1972. "Political Authority and Class Structures—An Analysis of Late Capitalist Societies." 2 *International Journal of Sociology*, 73.

_____. 1981. "The Attribution of Public Status to Interest Groups: Observations on the West German Case," in S. Berger (ed.) *Organizing Interests in Western*

Europe: Pluralism, Corporatism, and the Transformation of Politics. Cambridge: Cambridge University Press.

———. 1981. "Structural Problems of the Capitalist State," in K. V. Beyme (ed.) *German Political Studies.* Beverly Hills: Sage.

Olson, Susan M. 1984. "Challenges to the Gatekeepers: The Debate over Federal Litigating Authority." 68 *Judicature*, 71.

———. 1984. *Clients and Lawyers: Securing the Rights of Disabled Persons.* Westport, Conn.: Greenwood Press, Inc.

O'Malley, Pat. 1984. "Technocratic Justice in Australia." 2 *Law in Context*, 31.

Oppenheimer, Martin. 1973. "The Proletarianization of the Professional," in P. Halmos (ed.) *Professionalization and Social Change. Sociological Review Monograph*, 20.

———. and J.C. Canning. 1978-79. "The National Security State: Repression Within Capitalism." *Berkeley Journal of Sociology*, 23.

Packer, Herbert L. 1968. *The Limits of the Criminal Sanction.* Stanford: Stanford University Press.

Parness, Jeffrey. 1973. *The Expanding Role of the Parajudge in the United States.* Chicago: American Judicature Society.

Parsons, Talcott. 1971. *The System of Modern Societies.* Englewood Cliffs, N. J.: Prentice-Hall.

Pashukanis, Eugenii B. 1980. *Selected Writings on Marxism and Law.* P. Beirne and P. B. Maggs (eds.) New York: Academic Press.

Peckham, Robert E. 1981. "The Federal Judge as a Case Manager: The New Role in Guiding a Case from Filing to Disposition." 69 *California Law Review*, 770.

Peltason, Jack. 1955. *Federal Courts in the Political Process.* New York: Random House.

———. 1961. *Fifty-Eight Lonely Men: Southern Federal Judges and School Desegregation.* New York: Harcourt, Brace and World.

Peretz, Paul. 1982. "There Was No Tax Revolt." 11 *Politics and Society*, 231.

Perrow, Charles. 1965. "Hospitals: Technology, Structure and Goals," in James G. March (ed.) *Handbook of Organizations.* Chicago: Rand McNally & Company.

———. 1967. "A Framework for the Comparative Analysis of Organizations." 26 *American Sociological Review*, 688.

Persell, Caroline Hodges. 1977. *Education and Inequality.* New York: The Free Press.

Piven, Francis Fox, and Richard Cloward. 1971. *Regulating the Poor.* New York: Pantheon Books.

———. 1977. *Poor People's Movements: Why They Succeed, How They Fail.* New York: Pantheon Books.

Platt, Anthony, and Randy Pollock. 1974. "Channelling Lawyers: The Careers of Public Defenders," in Herbert Jacob (ed.) *The Potential for Reform of Criminal Justice.* Beverly Hills: Sage.

Polanyi, Karl. 1957. *The Great Transformation.* Boston: Beacon Press.

Pole, J. R. 1978. *The Pursuit of Equality in American History.* Berkeley: University of California Press.

Polinsky, A. Mitchell. 1974. "Economic Analysis as a Potentially Defective Product: A Buyer's Guide to Posner's Economic Analysis of Law." 87 *Harvard Law Review,* 1655.

Polsky, Andrew F. 1982. "Political Parties and the New Corporatism." 2 *Democracy,* 42.

Popper, Karl. 1959. *The Logic of Scientific Discovery.* London: Hutchinson.

Posner, Richard. 1972. *Economic Analysis of Law.* Boston: Little, Brown and Company.

_____. 1985. *The Federal Courts: Crisis and Reform.* Cambridge: Harvard University Press.

Pound, Roscoe. 1906. "The Causes of Popular Dissatisfaction with the Administration of Justice." 29 *American Bar Association Report,* 395, Reprinted in 40 *American Law Review,* 729 (1968).

_____. 1940. *Organization of Courts.* Westport, Conn.: Greenwood Press.

President's Commission on Law Enforcement and the Administration of Justice. 1967a. *The Challenge of Crime in a Free Society.* Washington, D.C.: U.S. Government Printing Office.

_____. 1967b. *The Courts.* Washington, D.C.: U.S. Government Printing Office.

Provine, D. Maric. 1986. "Settlement Strategies for Federal District Judges." Washington, D.C.: Federal Judicial Center.

Przeworski, Adam, and Michael Wallerstein. 1982. "Democratic Capitalism at the Crossroads." 2 *Democracy,* 52.

Quinney, Richard. 1974. *Critique of Legal Order: Crime Control in Capitalist Society.* Boston: Little, Brown and Company.

_____. 1977. *Class, State and Crime: On the Theory and Practice of Criminal Justice.* New York: David McKay Co.

Rabin, Robert. 1979. *Perspectives on the Administrative Process.* Boston: Little, Brown and Company.

_____. 1986. "Federal Regulation in Historical Perspective." 38 *Stanford Law Review,* 1189.

Ray, Larry, and Anne L. Clare. 1985. "The Mutli-door Courthouse: Building the Courthouse of the Future . . . Today." 1 *Ohio State Journal on Dispute Resolution*, 7.

Rebell, M. A., and A. R. Block. 1982. *Educational Policymaking and the Courts: An Empirical Study of Judicial Activism*. Chicago: University of Chicago Press.

Rehnquist, William H. 1978. "The Adversary Society: Keynote Address of the Third Annual Baron de Hirsch Meyer Lecture Series." 33 *University of Miami Law Review*, 1.

Reich, Charles. 1964. "The New Property." 73 *Yale Law Journal*, 733.

Reich, Robert B. 1983. *The Next American Frontier*. New York: Times Books.

Renner, Karl. 1949. *The Institutions of Private Law and Their Social Functions*. London: Routledge and Kegan Paul, Ltd.

Resnik, Judith. 1982. "Managerial Judges." 96 *Harvard Law Review*, 376.

———. 1985. "The Mythic Meaning of Article III Courts." 56 *University of Colorado Law Review*, 581.

———. 1985. "Managerial Judging: The Potential Costs." 45 *Public Administration Review*, 686.

———. 1986. "Failing Faith: Adjudicatory Procedure in Decline." 53 *University of Chicago Law Review*, 494.

Rheinstein, Max (ed.). 1966. *Max Weber on Law in Economy and Society*. Cambridge: Harvard University Press.

Richardson, Richard J., and Kenneth Vines. 1970. *The Politics of Federal Courts*. Boston: Little, Brown and Company.

Rogin, Michael. 1970. "Nonpartisanship and the Group Interest," in Green, Philip and Sanford Levinson (eds.) *Power and Community: Dissenting Essays in Political Science*. New York: Vintage Books.

Rohatyn, Felix. 1983. "Time for a Change." *New York Review of Books* (18 August), 46.

Rosenberg, Maurice. 1964. *The Pretrial Conference and Effective Justice: A Controlled Test in Personal Injury Litigation*. New York: Columbia University Press.

Rosett, Arthur, and Donald R. Cressey. 1976. *Justice by Consent: Plea Bargains in the American Courthouse*. Philadelphia: J. B. Lippincott Company.

Ross, H. Lawrence. 1970. *Settled Out of Court: The Social Process of Insurance Claims Adjustment*. Chicago: Aldine Publishing Company.

Rothman, David. 1971. *The Discovery of the Asylum: Social Order and Disorder in the New Republic*. Boston: Little, Brown and Company.

Rothschild-Whitt, Joyce. 1979. "The Collectivist Organization: An Alternative to Rational Bureaucratic Models." 33 *American Sociological Review*, 5.

Rubin, Alvin B. 1980. "Bureaucratization of the Federal Courts: The Tension Between Justice and Efficiency." 55 *Notre Dame Law Review*, 648.

Ryan, John P., et al. 1980. *American Trial Judges: Their Work Styles and Performances.* New York: The Free Press.

Saari, David J. 1970. *Modern Court Management: Trends in the Role of the Court Executive.* Washington, D. C.: U. S. Department of Justice.

_____ . 1976. "Modern Court Management: Trends in Court Organization Concepts— 1976." 2 *The Justice System Journal*, 19.

Saks, Michael J. 1977. *Jury Verdicts.* Lexington, Mass.: D. C. Heath & Company.

Sand, Leonard, and Steven Alan Reiss. 1985. "A Report on Seven Experiments Conducted by District Court Judges in the Second Circuit." 1985 *New York University Law Review*, 423.

Sarat, Austin. 1976. "Alternatives in Dispute Processing: Litigation in a Small Claims Court." 10 *Law and Society Review*, 339.

_____ . 1981. "The Role of the Courts and the Logic of Court Reform." 64 *Judicature*, 300.

_____ . 1982. "Judicial Capacity: Courts, Court Reform and the Limits of the Judicial Process," in Philip Dubois (ed.) *The Analysis of Judicial Reform.* Lexington, Mass.: D. C. Heath and Company.

_____ . 1985. "Legal Effectiveness and Social Studies of Law: On the Unfortunate Persistence of a Research Tradition." 9 *Legal Studies Forum*, 23.

_____ , and Joel Grossman. 1975. "Courts and Conflict Resolution: Problems in the Mobilization of Adjudication." 69 *American Political Science Review*, 1200.

Sarchell, Michael. 1987. "The Toughest Prison in America." 103, *U.S. News and World Report* (27 July), 23.

Schlegel, John Henry. 1984. "Langdell's Legacy or the Case of the Empty Envelope." 36 *Stanford Law Review*, 1517.

_____ . 1985. *"Between the Harvard Founders and the American Legal Realists: The Professionalization of the American Law Professor."* 35 *Journal of Legal Education*, 311.

Schluchter, Wolfgang. 1981. *The Rise of Western Rationalism: Max Weber's Developmental History.* Berkeley: University of California Press.

Schur, Edwin. 1973. *Radical Non-Intervention.* Englewood Cliffs, N. J.: Prentice-Hall, Inc.

Schmitter, Philippe C. 1974. "Still the Century of Corporatism?" 36 *Review of Politics*, 5.

Schrag, Clarence. 1971. *Crime and Justice: American Style.* Rockville, Md.: National Institute of Health.

Schwartz, R. D., and J. C. Miller. 1964. "Legal Evolution and Society Complexity." 70 *American Journal of Sociology*, 159.

Schreiber, Harry. 1980. "Federalism and Legal Process: Historical and Contemporary Analysis of the American System." 14 *Law and Society Review*, 663.

Schumpeter, Joseph. 1954. "The Crisis of the Tax State." 4 *International Economic Papers*, 7.

Scigliano, Robert. 1962. *The Courts*. Boston: Little, Brown and Company.

Scott, William G. 1965. *The Management of Conflict: Appeals Systems in Organizations*. Homewood, Ill.: Irwin Publications.

Scott, W. Richard. 1965. "Reactions to Supervision in a Heteronomous Professional Organization." 10 *Administrative Science Quarterly*, 65.

_____. 1983. "The Organization of Environments: Network, Cultural, and Historical Elements," J. W. Meyer and W. R. Scott (eds.). *Organizational Environments*. Beverly Hills, Calif.: Sage.

_____. 1987. "The Adolescence of Institutional Theory." 32 *Administrative Science Quarterly*, 493.

_____. 1987. *Organizations: Rational, Natural, and Open Systems*. Englewood Cliffs, N. J.: Prentice-Hall, Inc.

Selznick, Philip. 1969. *Law, Society, and Industrial Justice*. New York: Russell Sage Foundation.

Sennett, Richard, and Jonathan Cobb. 1972. *The Hidden Injuries of Class*. New York: Alfred A. Knopf, Inc.

Seron, Carroll. 1978. *Judicial Reorganization: The Politics of Reform in the Federal Bankruptcy Court*. Lexington, Mass.: D. C. Heath & Company.

_____. 1983. *The Roles of Magistrates in the Federal District Courts*. Washington, D.C.: Federal Judicial Center.

_____. 1985. *The Roles of Magistrates: Nine Case Studies*. Washington, D.C.: Federal Judicial Center.

_____. 1986. "Magistrates and the Work of the Federal Courts: A New Division of Labor." 69 *Judicature*, 353.

_____. 1988. "The Professional Project of Parajudges: The Case of U. S. Magistrates." 22 *Law and Society Review*, 557.

Seymour, Whitney North. 1973. *Why Justice Fails*. New York: William Morrow & Co.

Shapiro, Martin. 1980. *Courts: A Comparative Political Analysis*. Chicago: University of Chicago Press.

Shelley, Louise I. 1984. *Lawyers in Soviet Work Life*. New Brunswick, N. J.: Rutgers University Press.

_____ . 1987. "The Structure and Function of Soviet Courts," in *Law in Eastern Europe*. Leiden: University of Leiden.

Sheskin, Arlene. 1981. "Trial Courts on Trial: Examining Dominant Assumptions." in J. A. Cramer (ed.) *Courts and Judges*. Beverly Hills: Sage Publications.

_____ , and Charles Grau. 1981. "Judicial Responses to Technocratic Reform," in J. A. Cramer (ed.) *Courts and Judges*. Beverly Hills: Sage.

Sikes, Melvin P. 1975. *The Administration of Injustice*. New York: Harper & Row, Publishers.

Simon, Rita J. 1968. (ed.) *The Sociology of Law*. San Francisco: Chandler.

Skocpol, Theda. 1980. "Political Response to Capitalist Crisis: Neo-Marxist Theories of the State and the Case of the New Deal." 10 *Politics and Society*, 155.

_____ . 1985. "Bringing the State Back In: Strategies of Analysis in Current Research," in Peter B. Evans, et al. (eds.) *Bringing the State Back In*. Cambridge: Cambridge University Press.

Skoler, David L. 1977. *Organizing the Non-System: Governmental Structuring of Criminal Justice Systems*. Lexington, Mass.: D. C. Heath & Company.

Skolnick, Jerome. 1966. *Justice Without Trial*. New York: John Wiley & Sons.

_____ . 1967. "Social Control in the Adversary System." 1 *Journal of Conflict Resolution*, 52.

Skowronek, Stephen. 1982. *Building a New American State: The Expansion of National Administrative Capacities, 1877-1920*. Cambridge: Cambridge University Press.

Smigel, Erwin O. 1964. *The Wall Street Lawyer: Professional Organization Man?* New York: The Free Press.

Sparer, Ed. 1984. "Fundamental Human Rights, Legal Entitlements and the Social Struggle: A Friendly Critique of the Critical Legal Studies Movement." 36 *Stanford Law Review*, 509.

Spiegel, S. Arthur. 1985. "Summary Jury Trials." 54 *Cincinnati Law Review*, 829.

Spitzer, Steven. 1982. "The Dialectics of Formal and Informal Control," in R. Abel (ed.) *The Politics of Informal Justice*, vol. I. New York: Academic Press.

Stannard, David E. 1977. *The Puritan Way of Death: A Study of Religion, Culture and Social Change*. New York: Oxford University Press.

Steidle, Barbara. 1972. " 'Reasonable' Reform: The Attitude of Bar and Bench Toward Liability Law and Workman's Compensation," in J. Israel (ed.) *Building the Organizational Society*. New York: The Free Press.

Stewart, Charles N. 1979. "Self-Conscious Interest and the Democratic Process." 1 *Law and Policy Quarterly*, 411.

Stewart, Richard. 1975. "Reformation of American Administrative Law." 88 *Harvard Law Review*, 1669.

Stinchcombe, Arthur. 1965. "Social Structure and Organizations," in J. March (ed.) *Handbook of Organizations*. Chicago: Rand McNally & Company.

Stone, Katherine. 1981. "The Post-War Paradigm and American Labor Law." 90 *Yale Law Journal*, 1509.

Stookey, John A. 1982. "Creating an Intermediate Court of Appeals: Work Load and Policy Making Consequences," in Philip Dubois (ed.), *The Analysis of Judicial Reform*. Lexington, Mass.: D. C. Heath & Company.

Strauss, Anselm L. 1963. "The Hospital and its Negotiated Order," in E. Freidson (ed.) *The Hospital in Modern Society*. New York: The Free Press.

Strick, Ann. 1977. *Injustice for All: How our Adversary System of Law Victimizes Us and Subverts Justice*. New York: Penguin Books.

Sudnow, David. 1965. "Normal Crimes: Sociological Features of the Penal Code in a Public Defender's Office." 12 *Social Problems*, 255.

Sykes, Melvin P. 1975. *The Administration of Injustice*. New York: Harper & Row, Publishers.

Taylor, Frederick W. 1911. *Scientific Management*. New York: Harper & Brothers.

Teubner, Gunther. 1983. "Substantive and Reflexive Elements in Modern Law." 17 *Law and Society Review*, 239.

The Third Branch: Bulletin of the Federal Courts. 1974-1985. Washington, D. C.: Federal Judicial Center.

Thurow, Lester. 1980. *New York Times Magazine*, 10 August.

Tigar, Michael E., and Madeleine R. Levy. 1977. *Law and the Rise of Capitalism*. New York: Monthly Review Press.

Thompson, James D. 1967. *Organizations in Action*. New York: McGraw-Hill Book Company.

_____ , and Arthur Tuden. 1959. "Strategies, Structures and Processes of Organizational Decision," in J. D. Thompson, et al. (eds.) *Comparative Studies in Administration*. Pittsburgh: University of Pittsburgh Press.

Tocqueville, Alexis de. 1969. *Democracy in America*. New York: Doubleday, Anchor Books.

Toharia, Jose J. 1976. "Economic Development and Litigation: The Case of Spain." 4 *Jahrbuch für Rechtssoziologie und Rechtstheorie*, 39.

Tolbert, Pamela S., and Lynne G. Zucker. 1983. "Institutional Sources of Change in the Formal Structure of Organizations: The Diffusion of Civil Service Reforms, 1880-1935." 23 *Administrative Science Quarterly*, 27.

Tomasic, Roman, and Malcolm Feeley, (eds.). 1982. *Neighborhood Justice*. New York: Longman.

Trubek, David M. 1972a. "Max Weber on Law and the Rise of Capitalism." 3 *University of Wisconsin Law Review*, 720.

———. 1972b. "Toward a Social Theory of Law: An Essay on the Study of Law and Social Development." 82 *Yale Law Journal*, 1.

———. 1980-81. "Studying Courts in Context." 15 *Law and Society Review*, 485.

Tushnet, Mark. 1978. "A Marxist Analysis of American Law." 1 *Marxist Perspectives*, 96.

Ulmer, Sidney S. 1971. *Courts as Small and Not So Small Groups*. New York: General Learning Press.

Unger, Roberto Magabeira. 1976. *Law in Modern Society: Toward a Criticism of Social Theory*. New York: The Free Press.

U. S. News and World Report, 21 August 1972, p. 41.

Vanderbilt, Arthur. 1949. *Minimum Standards of Judicial Administration*. New York: New York University Law Center.

Veysey, Lawrence R. 1965. *The Emergence of the American University*. Chicago: University of Chicago Press.

Villmoare, Adelaide. 1982. "State and Legal Authority: A Context for the Analysis of Judicial Policy Making." 4 *Law and Policy Quarterly*, 5.

Vining, Joseph. 1981. "Justice, Bureaucracy and Legal Method." 80 *Michigan Law Review*, 248.

Wade, E. C. S. 1950. *American Administrative Law*. London: Sir Isaac Pitman & Sons.

Wald, Patricia. 1983. "The Problem with the Courts: Black-Robed Bureaucracy, or Collegiality Under Challenge?" 42 *Maryland Law Review*, 766.

Walzer, Michael. 1983. *Spheres of Justice*. New York: Basic Books.

Wamsley, Gary, and Mayer N. Zald. 1973. *The Political Economy of Public Organizations*. Lexington, Mass.: D. C. Heath & Company.

Warren, Roland. 1967. "The Interorganizational Field as a Focus for Investigation." 12 *Administrative Science Quarterly*, 396.

Wasby, Stephen L. 1970. *The Impact of the United States Supreme Court*. Homewood, Ill.: The Dorsey Press.

Weber, Max. 1966. *Max Weber on Law in Economy and Society*. M. Rheinstein (ed.) Cambridge: Harvard University Press.

———. 1968. *Economy and Society*, vol. 1. G. Roth and C. Wittich (eds.) New York: Bedminster Press.

Wechsler, Herbert. 1948. "Federal Jurisdiction and the Revision of the Judicial Code." 13 *Law and Contemporary Problems*, 216.

Weinstein, James. 1968. *The Corporate Ideal and the Liberal State*. Boston: Beacon Press.

Wheeler, Russell R., and Howard R. Whitcomb, (eds.). 1977. *Judicial Administration: Text and Readings*. Englewood Cliffs, N. J.: Prentice-Hall.

————, and Charles Nihan. 1982. "Using Technology to Improve the Administration of Justice in the Federal Courts." 1982 *Brigham Young University Law Review*, 656.

White, G. Edward. 1974. "Allocating Power Between Agencies and Courts: The Legacy of Justice Brandeis." 74 *Duke Law Journal*, 195.

White, Welsh S. 1977. "A Proposal for the Reform of the Plea Bargaining Process." 119 *University of Pennsylvania Law Review*, 439.

Wiebe, Robert H. 1967. *The Search for Order, 1877-1920*. New York: Hill & Wang.

Wilensky, Harold L. 1976. *The 'New Corporatism', Centralization and the Welfare State*. Beverly Hills: Sage.

Wilson, James Q. 1975. "The Rise of the Bureaucratic State." 25 *The Public Interest*, 39.

Wolfe, Alan. 1977. *The Limits of Legitimacy: Political Contradictions in Contemporary Capitalism*. New York: The Free Press.

Wolff, Robert Paul. 1968. *The Poverty of Liberalism*. Boston: Beacon Press.

Wolin, Sheldon. 1960. *Politics and Vision: Continuity and Innovation in Western Political Thought*. Boston: Little, Brown and Company.

Wright, Charles Alan. 1970. *Handbook of the Law of Federal Courts*. (2d ed.) St. Paul, Minn.: West Publishing Co.

Wright, Erik Olin. 1978. *Class, Crisis and the State*. London: New Left Books.

————, and Joachim Singlemann. 1982. "Proletarianization in the Changing American Class Structure." 88 *American Journal of Sociology*, 176.

Yankelovich, Skelly, and White, Inc. 1978. *The Public Image of Courts*. Williamsburg, Va.: National Center for State Courts.

Zald, Mayer N. 1970. "Political Economy: A Framework for Comparative Analysis," in M. N. Zald (ed.) *Power in Organizations*. Nashville, Tenn.: Vanderbilt University Press.

Zatz, Marjorie, and Alan J. Lizotte. 1985. "The Timing of Court Processing: Toward Linking Theory and Method." 23 *Criminology*, 313.

Zeisel, Hans, Harry Kalven and Bernard Bucholtz. 1959. *Delay in the Courts: An Analysis of Remedies for Delayed Justice*. Boston: Little Brown.

Zinn, Howard. 1966. *New Deal Thought.* Indianapolis: Bobbs-Merrill Co.

Zion, Sidney. 1979. "A Decade of Constitutional Revision: The First of a Two-part Series." *New York Time Magazine,* 11 November.

Zwerdling, Daniel. 1978a. *Democracy at Work.* Washington, D. C.: Association for Self Management.

_____. 1978b. *Workplace Democracy.* New York: Harper & Row, Publishers.

Index

Note: Tables in this index are denoted by "t" following the page number.